Faith, folk and the far right

Manchester University Press

Faith, folk and the far right

Racist and anti-racist Heathenry and occultism in Britain

Dominic Alessio and Robert J. Wallis

MANCHESTER UNIVERSITY PRESS

Copyright © Dominic Alessio and Robert J. Wallis 2025

The right of Dominic Alessio and Robert J. Wallis to be identified as the authors of this work has been asserted in accordance with the Copyright, Designs and Patents Act 1988.

Published by Manchester University Press

Oxford Road, Manchester, M13 9PL
www.manchesteruniversitypress.co.uk

British Library Cataloguing-in-Publication Data
A catalogue record for this book is available from the British Library

ISBN   978 1 5261 7947 0   hardback

First published 2025

The publisher has no responsibility for the persistence or accuracy of URLs for any external or third-party internet websites referred to in this book, and does not guarantee that any content on such websites is, or will remain, accurate or appropriate.

EU authorised representative for GPSR:
Easy Access System Europe, Mustamäe tee 50, 10621 Tallinn, Estonia
gpsr.requests@easproject.com

Typeset
by Deanta Global Publishing Services, Chennai, India

'The dead are not always quiet, and the past will never be a safe place for contemplation'. (Hutton, 1996: 33)

Contents

List of figures	page ix
Preface	xii
Acknowledgements	xxvi
List of abbreviations	xxvii
Introduction: faith, folk and the far right	1

Part I: Heathenry, ancestors and race

1	Diverse Heathenries: approaching concepts of ancestors, race and indigeneity	23
2	Politicised religion and religious politics: religion, politics and the far right	43
3	Mythic roots: Ariosophy, National Socialism and the emergence of racist Heathenry	60
4	Claims to blood and soil: international racist Heathenry	79

Part II: Racist Heathenry and occultism in the UK

5	British spiritual Aryanism: intersections of racism, Heathenry and occultism	97
6	Three thorns: the Odinic Rite, the Odinist Fellowship and Woden's Folk	115
7	Eclectic 'Esoterrorism': deconstructing the Order of the Nine Angles (O9A/ONA)	138
8	Nazisploitation: racist Heathenry in the far-right cultural scene	159
9	Winterfylleth: from 'National Pride' in 'English Heritage' to '14W' and 'WPWW'	175

Part III: Heathens against hate

10 Declaration 127 and anti-racist Heathen activism	193
11 Visual–virtual Heathen politicking: anti-racist Heathenry on Instagram	210
Conclusion: inferences, implications and future directions	232
References	247
Index	286

Figures

0.1	Cross-in-circle chalk graffiti on a megalith at Wayland's Smithy long barrow, Oxfordshire. The motif is known as the 'sun-wheel' and 'Odin's Cross', often used in modern far-right imagery, but with a precedent in bronze age rock art, its use does not always have a racist meaning	*page* xiii
0.2	James Alex Fields (far left wearing glasses) with other protestors holding Viking-style shields, the one at centre bearing the crossed battle-axe insignia of the Vanguard America group, the one on the left showing an Ariosophist-inspired *Sonnenrad* (Black Sun) image, during the Unite the Right Rally in Charlottesville, 12 August 2017	xv
0.3	Sonnenrad (Black Sun) image used by Himmler to decorate the floor of the north tower of Castle Wewelsburg, a Renaissance castle and cult site for the Schutzstaffel (SS)	xvi
0.4	Sonnenrad (Black Sun) and 'Odin's Cross' (sun-wheel) motifs on equipment used by the Christchurch murderer	xvii
0.5	A logo used by Proud Boys Britannia with crossed Viking-style battle axes	xxii
I.1	Fantoft stave church, Bergen, Norway, after being burned down allegedly by the anti-Christian musician Varg Vikernes of the black metal band Burzum who was convicted of three other church burnings	4
I.2	Fantoft stave church, Bergen, Norway, after restoration	5
I.3	*Kolovrat* (коловрат, 'spinning wheel') sun-wheel image used by Alexey Dobrovolsky, the founder of Russian Rodnoverie, as an equivalent to the Nazi swastika	18
1.1	Members of the Ásatrúarfélagið gather at Thingvellir National Park in Iceland	25
1.2	Heathen neo-shaman 'Runic John' performing *seidr* 'sorcery'. His shamanic drum depicts the world tree Yggdrasill	36
1.3	Votive offerings left behind following a *blot* ceremony at Barbrook II stone circle, Peak District, Derbyshire	37

Figures

2.1	Corneliu Zelea Codreanu, leader of the 'Iron Guard', the Romanian Legion of the Archangel Michael	47
2.2	Aryan Nations Church, Coeur d'Alene, Idaho, 1998	50
3.1	Guido von List	61
3.2	Burg Werfenstein, bought by Lanz for the *Ordo Novi Templi* (ONT) in 1907	69
3.3	Wewelsburg Castle, headquarters of Himmler's SS	75
4.1	Baldrshof, the third temple of the AFA in a former church, Murdock, Minnesota	92
5.1	Flag of the Imperial Fascist League	102
5.2	Sonnenkrieg Division propaganda imagery	108
5.3	Members of the WDL hold a rally	109
5.4	Burning sun-wheel ('Odin's Cross') at the BNP summer camp near Wrotham, Kent, 1961	110
5.5	Colin Jordan and Françoise Dior performing Nazi salutes	112
6.1	Triskel logo of the Odinic Rite	119
6.2	Wolfsangel symbol used by Woden's Folk	127
6.3	Wolf-head logo used by Woden's Folk	128
6.4	Long Man of Wilmington	133
7.1	Logo used by the O9A	154
8.1	DIJ performing with Black Sun and Death's Head imagery	172
9.1	'Runes and their meanings' anti-racist Heathen meme image	189
9.2	Digital release of Runesine's track *Futhorc: New Sonic Rites for the Old English Futhorc* with hashtag #heathensagainsthate and bindrune displayed	189
10.1	Asatru-EU Network statement on inclusivity	197
10.2	Heathens Against Hate logo	199
11.1	Instagram post hashtagged #heathensagainsthate about Heathen symbols	219
11.2	Instagram post hashtagged #heathensagainsthate with a gold hammer of Thor upon the LGBTIQA+ rainbow flag	220
11.3	Instagram post hashtagged #heathensagainstracism with bind runes	221
11.4	Instagram post hashtagged #heathensagainstracism promoting Black Lives Matter	223
11.5	Instagram post hashtagged #declaration127 with the logo of Declaration 127	224
11.6	Instagram post hashtagged #declaration127 using the valknut against racism	225
11.7	Instagram post hashtagged #heathensunitedagainstracism with Thor's hammer smashing Hitler	227

11.8	Instagram post hashtagged #heathensunitedagainstracism stating NO NAZIS IN VALHALLA	228
11.9	Instagram post hashtagged #paganantifa with Thor's hammer against facism	229
11.10	Instagram post hashtagged #paganantifa with a Black Sun cancelled	230
12.1	Witches Against White Supremacy counter-protestors at the Boston Free Speech rally, 19 August 2017	244

Preface

In January 2020, a seventeen-year-old teenager from the city of Durham in north-east England became one of the youngest people to be convicted of planning a terrorist attack in Britain, including targeting a synagogue; he was caught and charged, and then detained for more than six years (BBC News, 2020a). The trial heard that he was an adherent of 'occultist neo-Nazism', and that he had disseminated a terrorist publication entitled 'Storm 88' referencing the Stormfront neo-Nazi website and historically the paramilitary *Sturmabteilung* ('Storm Division'/'Storm Troopers' of the Nazi Party). The cover of his manifesto was adorned with swastikas and the head of Adolf Hitler (BBC News, 2020a). The boy, who was identified as being on the autistic spectrum, 'told jurors his political beliefs were "centre right" and that he had a poster on his bedroom wall signed by Nigel Farage' (the former leader of the UK Independence Party and now Honorary President of Reform UK) (de Simone, 2019: n.p.).

A few months earlier, in August 2019, it was reported that 'Swastikas have been carved onto trees' (Hall, 2019: n.p.) around the site of a Neolithic long barrow in Oxfordshire known as Wayland's Smithy (Figure 0.1). This prehistoric site is situated along the Ridgeway, an ancient footpath popular with walkers. It was alleged that a group named Woden's Folk had 'apparently conducted masked torch-lit rituals there'. The possibility that under cover of night a neo-Nazi Heathen group had co-opted an ancient site which was otherwise a popular family picnic spot during the day, caught the attention of the mainstream press. *The Sun* reported: 'The group are Odinists, meaning they worship the Norse war god Odin, but they also use their religion to forward ideas of an Aryan race. They deny that they are neo-Nazis but make use of far-right tropes and symbols' (Hall, 2019: n.p.).

At a secluded yew grove in Hampshire that same summer, a small group of self-ascribing 'Heathens' met on 21 June to celebrate their annual midsummer festival, Litha, drawing on the Anglo-Saxon calendar year recorded by Bede. Their ritual involved pouring offerings of ale to honour the *wights* (OE for 'land spirits') and 'ancestors' (whom they loosely refer to as 'those

Preface

Figure 0.1 Cross-in-circle chalk graffiti on a megalith at Wayland's Smithy long barrow, Oxfordshire. The motif is known as the 'sun-wheel' and 'Odin's Cross', often used in modern far-right imagery, but with a precedent in bronze age rock art, its use does not always have a racist meaning (Robert J. Wallis).

who came before' or 'predecessors') of the land. They sang *galdr* (OE for 'spells, incantations') for the god Woden and goddess Freyja. They cast runes and interpreted them using the text of the Anglo-Saxon rune poem. Among their number was one of the co-authors of this book (Wallis), who according to the UK government's list of ethnic groups, would be termed 'white British' (Gov.UK, 2022: n.p.). Other individuals performing in the ritual, who might be termed 'inclusivist' Heathens, and therefore anti-racist, felt a connection to Heathenry no matter their 'ethnicity' or 'race'; among them were a person of mixed British and African descent ('mixed white/

black African') and a British-born Indian ('Asian British') (Gov.UK, 2022: n.p.).

We juxtapose these contrasting instances to highlight the one persistent connection between them all, namely the ancient pagan religion(s) of north-western Europe, loosely known by many of today's practitioners reconstructing their faith as 'Heathenry', and the diverse ways in which race and racism can figure within its diverse contemporary manifestations. The Durham teenager was influenced by a neo-Nazi occultist on YouTube affiliated with the Order of the Nine Angles (O9A), an occult organisation with eclectic esoteric interests ranging from Satanism to Heathenry. The case of Woden's Folk, on the other hand, marks an example of how Heathenry specifically has been co-opted by the far right and re-imagined as, according to their founder, 'the authentic folk-religion of the English people...committed to the awakening of the ancestral Saxon Nation' (Woden's Folk, n.d.a). By contrast, the Heathen group in Wiltshire offers an example of what might be termed 'inclusivist', 'progressive' or 'universalist' Heathenry, referring to the vast majority of Heathens in the UK, and indeed globally, who welcome all who are called to the 'Northern path' whatever their ethnic or 'racial' origin. The dynamics and tensions between racist and anti-racist Heathenry are the focus of this investigation.

It is first worth outlining historically how this tension has emerged. Despite the vagaries of the historical and archaeological evidence, a particular concept of ancient 'Germanic' paganism was co-opted by *völkisch* and Romantic movements in the nineteenth century, into a discrete, if highly problematic, sense of German nationhood which crystallised in the first decades of the twentieth century. Drawing upon a historical trajectory of Romantic nationalism, Aryanism, lost world literature, imperialism and anti-Semitism, and against a backdrop of defeat in the First World War, in the 1930s National Socialism made elements of these forms of Germanic paganisms front and centre in its racialised politics. A result of this melding of ideologies, problematic concepts of 'folk' or 'race' (the purity of Aryan blood) and nationhood (the 'holy' German soil) became entangled with a new, modern, albeit *partijnost*, genus of racist Heathenry known as Ariosophy, or the 'wisdom of the Aryans'. This novel and religiously inspired ideology succeeded in influencing directly the creation of the Nazi Party, the rise of anti-Semitism, the evolution of the *Schutzstaffel* (SS) and eventually, the Holocaust itself. Nevertheless, despite the defeat of Nazi Germany in the Second World War, over the course of the following decades, variants of this Ariosophic-inspired thinking have continued to morph into a variety of enduring neo-Nazisms, all united by concepts of 'race'. As Findell (2013: 251) notes, Ariosophy's 'influence on subsequent generations was far-reaching'.

Ariosophy, Nazism, fascism and related far-right ideologies, and the organisations adhering to them are, consequently, by no means only of historical note. Rather, there is an urgency in writing and talking about them; indeed, with the growth of populist and nationalist politics in the first decades of the twenty-first century, elements of Germanic paganism, or as we prefer to term it here, ancient heathenry – including art, language, mythology and society – have provided an important source for a reinvigorated if diversely constituted far-right ideology of significant transnational import. These trappings of ancient heathenry feature in various respects in several of the most recent and violent actions by the far right on the global stage. Reflecting on several recent terrorist murders linked by the broad theme of 'Heathenry', a leading scholar of Pagan Studies, Helen A. Berger, observes: '[t]he killers have all been young men who are linked through the Internet and who in their online manifesto reference earlier terrorists as their heroes and role models. Growingly they are using Nordic Pagan symbols, and in some cases, have self-identified as Asatru or Odinists' (Berger, 2020: viii).

Notable among the latter is James Alex Fields who marched with the 'Unite the Right' rally in Charlottesville in August 2017, and who was arrested for the murder of counter-protester Heather Heyer. During the march, he and other protestors held Viking-style shields bearing a variant of the insignia of the Vanguard America group (Figure 0.2). The imagery draws

Figure 0.2 James Alex Fields (far left wearing glasses) with other protestors holding Viking-style shields, the one at centre bearing the crossed battle-axe insignia of the Vanguard America group, the one on the left showing an Ariosophist-inspired *Sonnenrad* (Black Sun) image, during the Unite the Right Rally in Charlottesville, 12 August 2017 (Stephanie Keith Photography).

upon the repertoire of ancient heraldic symbols favoured by neo-Nazis. In this case it was the hyper-masculine crossed *fasces,* a bundle of rods holding a battle axe, originally used by the Romans but first associated with the far right when it was adopted by Mussolini's Fascist movement. During the rally, Fields marched alongside a man wearing a T-shirt bearing an image of Adolf Hitler. Other protestors brandished shields displaying one of the more widespread of neo-Nazi symbols, the Black Sun, or *Sonnenrad* (SPLC, n.d.a). Derived from Ariosophic imagery, the *Sonnenrad* was specifically created by Heinrich Himmler (1900–1945), one of the leading architects of the Final Solution, to decorate the floor of the north tower of Castle Wewelsburg, a Renaissance castle (Figure 0.3). This fortified site emerged as a major cult site for the Schutzstaffel (Protection Squad or SS), the foremost paramilitary organisation of the Nazi state. The Black Sun is comprised of the rune glyph associated with the sun, named *Sowilō* in the Elder Germanic Futhark rune row, or *Sigel* in the Old English futhorc, and by the Armenan name of *Sig* in Nazi Germany. This rune radiates from the centre and is repeated to form a circle of sun-runes, itself often encircled by a black ring. The image is similar to that found on some bronze and iron age metal artifacts known as *Zierscheibe* especially associated with Alemmannic tribal funerary practices of the fifth to eighth centuries CE. As Pardy (2023a: 7) cautions, 'the Black Sun is not, *in itself,* a Pagan symbol'. Nevertheless,

Figure 0.3 Sonnenrad (Black Sun) image used by Himmler to decorate the floor of the north tower of Castle Wewelsburg, a Renaissance castle and cult site for the Schutzstaffel (SS) (Alamy).

given its history, the symbol has become, consequently, a 'magical invocation of a lost homeland among young neo-Nazis' (Goodrick-Clarke, 2002: 150).

This Black Sun image, as well as a sun-wheel or 'Odin's Cross' (a square cross interlocking with or surrounded by a circle), also appeared on equipment and in 'The Great Replacement' white supremacist and anti-immigrant manifesto published by the Christchurch mass murderer in March 2019 (Figure 0.4). His manifesto ended with the clarion call: 'see you in Valhalla', referring to the 'hall of the slain' of Norse mythology, the eternal resting place of fallen warriors. Additionally, the murderer's gun was covered with text and imagery, including: the names of other mass murderers and their victims; the phrase 'refugees welcome to hell' (written upon the barrel); and, significantly for this study, the rune for 'inherited property' or 'ancestral home/land'. This is *æthel* in the Old English futhorc rune row and *othala*, or *odal*, in the elder Germanic futhark rune row. The *othala* rune tends now to be associated by neo-Nazis with the idea of a whites-only homeland thanks to its use by two SS divisions in Nazi Germany. The Christchurch mosque murders are the deadliest mass shootings in that country; fifty-one people were killed and another forty-nine injured. Berger notes that '[i]t is unclear whether or not the Christchurch killer was a contemporary Pagan. His gun

Figure 0.4 Sonnenrad (Black Sun) and 'Odin's Cross' (sun-wheel) motifs on equipment used by the Christchurch murderer (Wikimedia Commons. Source: Royal Commission of Inquiry into the Attack on Christchurch Mosques).

had Pagan symbols on it and some of the other terrorists he celebrates in his manifesto are Heathens' (Berger, 2020: viii). While neither the Christchurch murderer, nor Fields, explicitly identified as 'Heathen' or even 'Odinist', elements of their discourse clearly interface with the culture of Heathenry, and specifically its racist iterations.

Such trappings of racist Heathenry have been linked to a number of other previous international far-right terrorist incidents. Bologna's train station bombers who murdered eighty-five people in 1980 were inspired by Julius Evola (1898–1974), one of Italy's leading Fascist philosophers associated with the occult and racist Heathenry (Goodrick-Clarke, 2002: 52–3; Evola, 1928, 1934). Evola was not only a confidante of Mussolini and admirer of Himmler but was additionally a staunch advocate 'calling for the harmonisation of Italian and German fascism' (Renton, 2020: 41). In other words, he was hoping for Italy to emulate Germany's anti-Semitic race legislation. In his book *Pagan Imperialism*, Evola (Evola, 1928: n.p.) promotes 'a primordial Nordic tradition' as an ideal Aryan civilisation for Italians to emulate. Most infamously of all perhaps, Anders Breivik, the individual responsible for the bombing and shooting of seventy-seven people in Norway in 2011, also 'openly identifies as an Odinist' (Hall, 2019: n.p.; see also Salomonsen, 2015). Breivik inscribed his pistol with runes spelling Mjöllnir (Thor's hammer), and on his rifle, Gungnir (Odin's spear) (Pardy, 2023a: 34; see also Salomonsen, 2015). Also in Norway, a series of earlier church burnings across that country in the 1990s were associated with Varg Vikernes, a racist Heathen and black metal musician (Goodrick-Clarke, 2002: 204). Furthermore, black metal music and its 'fascination with the occult, evil, Nazism and Hitler' has been cited as a possible motivation behind the 20 April 1999 massacre, the anniversary of Hitler's birthday, of twelve students and a teacher at Columbine High School in Colorado, by two male white youths (Goodrick-Clarke, 2002: 209).

The appeal of racist Heathenry has found an especially receptive audience in North America. Berger cites the work of Patrik Hermannson whose undercover research on white supremacism there discovered that 'members of the alt-right are using Heathen symbols and rituals to celebrate their northern Europe heritage and, most importantly for them, their white identity even if they are not practising Heathens' (Berger, 2020: viii). The US-based Aryan Brotherhood, for instance, is described as having around twenty thousand members and being 'the oldest, largest and deadliest white supremacist prison group in the United States' (Allchorn, 2021a: 27). And in Toronto, Canada, in September 2020, Mohamed-Aslim Zafis, a fifty-eight-year-old Muslim man was attacked and stabbed to death outside a mosque by Guilherme Von Neutegem, a thirty-four-year-old adherent of the same organisation as the Durham teenager terrorist we pointed to in the preface to this book, the Order of Nine Angles (O9A) (Lamoureux, 2020: n.p.).

Most recently, Jake Angeli/Aleri (born Jacob Anthony Chansley and often referred to as the 'QAnon Shaman'), made global headlines during his participation in the attack on the Capitol building in Washington, DC, in January 2021, wearing a Native American-styled outfit and stars-and-stripes facepaint. He also displayed on his unclothed torso prominent tattoos associated with Heathenry, comprising a Mjöllnir (the aforementioned hammer of Thor), a valknut (three interlaced triangles often associated with the god Odin) and a stylised tree motif possibly referencing specifically the Norse tree of life, Yggdrasill. Later analysis of his *Facebook* pages demonstrated posts referring to the UK-based Odinic Rite (The Wild Hunt, 2021: n.p.), although he also claims varied religious influences ranging across Christianity and 'shamanism'. Indeed, during the attack he was also reported as shouting 'Jesus Christ, we invoke your name!' (Spoonley and Morris, 2022: 312). Nevertheless, inclusivist Heathens were quick to condemn Angeli's actions on social media, critiquing his tattoos as an appropriation and citing his eclectic far-right influences well beyond contemporary Heathenry. The Confederation of UK Heathen Kindreds, for instance, stated in a Facebook post (7 January 2021): 'our sacred symbols are not symbols of hate, despite the efforts of unscrupulous individuals to hijack them for political purposes'. Davy (2023: 33–34) makes the point that such images as the valknut are not 'inherently racist, but white supremacists have adopted them as signifiers of their identity. While inclusive Heathens…might hope that racist use of these symbols is spurious rather than the result of religious identity, some Heathens are white supremacists'.

The Odinic Rite, the organisation which the QAnon Shaman followed on Facebook, is one of the three most prominent racist Heathen groups in Britain (with offshoots in the US and elsewhere). Britain, as we discuss in detail in this book, has a significant but overlooked role in the history and perpetuation of Ariosophic-inspired ideas, neo-Nazism and racist Heathenry. Historians have often assumed that Britain was generally unaffected by fascism and have argued that its role in the history of the far right is not consequential. According to Jackson (2018: 1), it is for this very reason 'that it is usually ignored especially by historians'. Macklin (2005: 303) suggests that such disdain by historians and political scientists could have to do with the fact that, as a movement, fascism in Britain is considered merely an 'epilogue' or 'footnote' to more important events elsewhere. Martin Pugh's *Hurray for the Blackshirts* (2006), however, broke new ground by suggesting that fascist sympathies, sometimes with a particular British twist, were far more prevalent in the country, particularly during the inter-war years, than had been generally accepted. In tune with Pugh's thinking, we identify and discuss a pernicious British racist Heathenry which has also largely been neglected by scholarship of the far right and on Paganism today.

The history of racist Heathenry in Britain and its place in British far-right history, culture, politics and religion is, we argue, deserving of closer reevaluation. This is particularly critical now because the threat of lone wolves being influenced by such ideologies and then 'taking on society' (Jackson, 2016: 18), is as pertinent to the case of the UK as it is to the US, New Zealand, Norway and elsewhere. A startling indication of the potential violent nature of this particular form of Heathenry can be found in recent figures for terror-related prison offences in Britain. According to Pardy (pers .com), there are currently seven prisoners in England and Wales who are incarcerated for terror-related offences and who identify as Heathen, five of whom specifically as Odinist. Given that there are, according to the 2021 UK census, currently only about seventy-four thousand UK subjects who identify as Pagan overall, this is a startlingly high percentage. This figure is even more alarming when compared with the seven Christians in prison for terror-related offences but in a national Christian population of over twenty million. What is more, another reason to examine this subject now is that far-right UK-based organisations and individuals have also had a role in helping to spread this gospel of hate overseas, in turn influencing many of the above-mentioned racist incidents.

Key examples of how variations of Ariosophic thinking may have influenced far-right terrorist activity in the UK include David Copeland's (b.1976) nail bombing campaign in London in 1999 and the murder of West Yorkshire MP Jo Cox in 2016 by Thomas Mair (b.1964). Copeland's nail bombs were aimed at London's Black, Asian and LGBTIQA+ communities, killing three and injuring 140, for which he received six life sentences. Copeland was a former member of the British National Party and neo-Nazi National Socialist Movement (NSM). The latter was founded in the 1990s as a break-away organisation from the neo-Nazi terrorist organisation Combat 18. Neo-Nazi literature by the National Socialist Movement's chief leaders, Charlie Sargent and David Myatt, who was also a founder of the O9A, were discovered at Copeland's home in subsequent police searches (Mamlëz et al., 2021a: n.p.). Copeland aimed for his bombing campaigns to start an accelerationist race war, reifying the ideology of Guido von List (1848–1919), the Austrian mystic who termed his Ariosophic-influenced esoteric racism 'Wotansim' or 'Armanism'. List imagined a pan-German Empire of Wotan worshippers stretching across Europe.

Given Copeland's links to the BNP, it is notable that Nick Griffin, that party's former leader and a former Member of the European Parliament (MEP), has also self-identified as a 'pagan' (Macklin, 2020: 472), probably to ingratiate himself with racist Heathens so as to capture their political support. As part of the refurbishment of his father's farmhouse, which he intended to use for political events, Griffin provocatively borrowed from Himmler a sun-wheel design for the flooring (Macklin, 2020: 456). He also had the BNP's youth branch adopt the *othala* (or *odal*) rune for 'ancestral homeland' as their symbol (Pardy, 2023a: 59). Thomas Mair, on the other hand, murdered the Labour MP Jo Cox because of her liberal values and views on immigration, and because he was worried about the future of the 'White race' (Greenwood and Sinmaz, 2016: n.p.). He was sentenced to a whole life term in prison for this assassination (Cobain and Taylor, 2016: n.p.). Like Copeland, Mair had links to a number of far-right groups, including the National Front, English Defence League and National Vanguard. A variety of neo-Nazi literature was found at his home, including 'stones bearing rune symbols' (Cobain 2016: n.p.), as well as press clippings on Anders Breivik and Ariosophic literature, such as von List's *Secret of the Runes*, from which Himmler had chosen his runic SS emblems (Cobain et al., 2016: n.p.).

Tragically, the story of racist Heathenry-inspired terrorist actions on these shores does not end here. We have already pointed to the recent case in 2020 of the neo-Nazi teenager-terrorist from Durham associated with 'occult neo-Nazism' (BBC, 2020a: n.p.). More recently, Danyal Hussein, who was convicted of murdering two sisters in Wembley in 2021, was found to be inspired by O9A materials too (Farley, 2021; Watts, 2021). And also in 2021, Ben John, a student in Leicester, was charged with terror offences on the basis of possessing O9A materials (Gibson, 2021: n.p.). Organisations such as the O9A as well as racist strands of Heathenry more broadly, have strong transatlantic links historically, a connectivity made especially seamless in recent decades thanks to the internet and social media. Proud Boys Britannia, for example, is an emerging chapter of the US-based Proud Boys which has over five thousand members on its Telegram account (an encrypted messaging service popular with far-right individuals and groups). Members of the US-based hate group (e.g. Kitts, 2022), founded in 2016, have been convicted for their role in the January 2021 attack on the Capitol.

The co-option of visual elements of Heathenry by the far right historically and in the present is especially pervasive. The logos and branding of the Proud Boys Britannia, for example, incorporate Viking-style crossed battle axes, symbols of martial strength and military duty, also recalling the aforementioned *fasces* of Mussolini's Fascists and Fields' shield at the Unite the Right rally (Figure 0.5). The text surrounding this symbol, which establishes the organisation's name, can take the form of runes and rune-like glyphs. 'Viking'-style symbols, runic script, Norse mythological imagery and other recognisably 'heathen/Heathen' trappings have, then, been co-opted by the far right without necessarily associating them with Heathen religions.

Figure 0.5 A logo used by Proud Boys Britannia with crossed Viking-style battle axes (Public domain).

Indeed, these motifs of Heathenry can be situated by the far right alongside other apparently very contradictory forms of religious visual culture. The adoptions of a burning or Celtic cross are but two further well-known examples (ADL, n.d.a, n.d.b). The adoption of Christian symbols alongside racist Heathen ones should be seen as part of 'a long tradition among British fascists of using a language of Christian identity to develop racist lines of argument' (Jackson, 2018: 66). At its most bizarre, perhaps, is the example of Augustus Sol Invictus (aka Austin Gillespie), a former leading member of the Proud Boys in the US who also ran for Senate in the 2016 Florida Libertarian Party primary. His professed values include anti-communism, anti-Semitism and violence, advocating that only the strong should rule. He also claimed to be 'a pagan who worships the Goddess' (SPLC, n.d.b), and filmed himself performing an allegedly Satanic 'ritual sacrifice and religious offering' involving killing a goat and drinking its blood. It appears that the trappings of religion are used by far-right extremists whenever it suits their ideological purposes, especially if they have sufficient shock value to garner attention.

Most of the individual extremists we have pointed to here do not identify explicitly as 'Pagan', 'Heathen' or even 'Odinist'. Rather, they have appropriated certain trappings of ancient heathenry and modern Heathenry, particularly visual elements, such as runes, and especially those which have a history of appropriation into far-right ideologies such as the Nazi use of the Black Sun, all in order to promote their extremist ideology in the present. We are interested, in these cases, in how and why such trappings have been co-opted historically and continue to hold currency for these extremists today. This is not to confuse such extremists and their illegal acts of hate with self-identifying Heathen, or usually 'Odinist' organisations and individuals, who are explicitly or implicitly racist but maintain a public front or persona which is in accordance with the law. And crucially, it is important not to confuse either of these strands of racism with the vast majority of Heathens today who are inclusivist, universalist and/or anti-racist. In light of some of the recent extremist events we have pointed out, the latter have become increasingly explicit about their anti-racism. The ways in which elements of ancient heathenry have been used and abused across this spectrum of racist and anti-racist Heathenry historically and into the present, is the focus of this book.

Faith, folk and the far right offers, therefore, the first book-length examination of far-right Heathenry and occultism in Britain and explores how anti-racist Heathens and other Pagans act to counter this discourse. The book is divided into eleven chapters, framed by an introduction and conclusion. The introduction sets out our approach to racist and anti-racist Heathenry, our theoretical and methodological considerations and our own relationship to the research we have conducted. Part I addresses the historical intersections of Heathenry, ancestors and race. Chapter 1 discusses our understanding of the spectrum of contemporary Heathenry, with a focus on how the issues of race, ancestors and indigeneity have impacted on Heathen theology and practice today. This chapter locates the origins of racist thinking in the late nineteenth and early twentieth century and identifies a 'third wave' of racist Heathenry which has emerged with the populist and extreme nationalist politics of the New Right in the twenty-first century. Chapter 2 offers a critical discussion of religion and the far right. Our aim here is to demonstrate that racist Heathenry is not an isolated or novel phenomenon but that the far right, both historically and still today, has had an impact on all religions. Indeed, the first decades of the twenty-first century evidence an increasingly prominent far-right confluence between religion, politics and identity. Chapter 3 then sets out the historical context of how Heathenry has been appropriated by the far right, considering in detail its origins in such thinking as Theosophy, Ariosophy and National Socialism. We propose that there is a direct and continuous link between early twentieth-century *völkisch* thought and early twenty-first-century racist Heathen thinking, including a common foundation myth that 'the folk' are 'descended from an Aryan super-race' (Griffin, 2018: 70), and that to survive they need to carve out for themselves, violently if necessary, racially pure communities. In

Chapter 4, we consider racist Heathenry in Europe and the US as a broader context for the book's specific focus on racist Heathenry in the UK, to which we turn in Part II.

This second part of the book begins with Chapter 5, which considers the historical background to racist Heathenry in the UK, from the British Fascisti (BF) to the English Defence League (EDL), and their co-option of elements of ancient heathen cultures. Chapter 6 introduces and critically discusses the three main racist Heathen organisations in the UK, the three 'thorns in the side' of inclusivist Heathenry: the Odinic Rite (OR), the Odinist Fellowship (OF) and Woden's Folk (WF). All three groups claim to be apolitical, probably because they try to distance themselves from the party politics of the democratic process. The former two have been labelled 'ethnicist' rather than racist by some scholars. But, in their emphasis on the 'folk' and 'blood' ties in the case of the Odinic Rite, and Odinism as 'ethnospecific' for the OF, their implicit racism is, we argue, made explicit. Woden's Folk, meanwhile, are explicitly racist in making use of such neo-Nazi imagery as the Wolfsangel, emphasising 'the blood of our folk' and proclaiming a militarist and nationalist 'English struggle'. Having discussed racist Heathenry in the UK, we then set this within a broader context in Chapter 7, by considering extremist occultism in the UK with the case of the Order of the Nine Angles (O9A). This is an organisation which in its rhetoric intersperses aspects of Heathen religion with eclectic esoteric influences, including Satanism, along with Nazism and Hitlerism. The O9A is notable because, while it is highly fragmented, it has been cited as an influence on a number of far-right terrorist incidents in the UK and overseas. Given the ways in which Heathenry and occultism intersect with politics and wider culture, we also think it important to examine the wider far-right Heathen cultural scene, which we do in Chapters 8 and 9. Music, such as neofolk and black metal (BM), fashion with Nazi-inspired and runic imagery, Nazisploitation films and literature and many internet sites promoting racist propaganda with comparable Heathen trappings, are part of this broader metapolitics which co-opts Heathenry in attempts to influence wider culture. We devote particular attention to British black metal in Chapter 9, with a case study of the band Winterfylleth (OE, 'October'), who promote a specific 'English Pagan' ultranationalist, hyper-masculine identity whilst paradoxically attempting to distance themselves from the far right. We are interested in the complexities of this contradiction, and how this enables Winterfylleth to maintain mainstream BM status and fandom, and so promote their racist Heathen message, despite their more extreme discourse.

Up to this point in the book we have examined a small, albeit vocal, far-right minority in Heathenry today. In order to balance out this treatment, in Part III we examine the tension between racist Heathen groups and the wider majority of anti-racist Heathens who align with the more liberal political values of democratic society. In Chapter 10, we focus on those Heathens who are actively developing anti-racist counter-narratives, including the organisations Heathens Against Hate and Heathens United Against Racism. Our aim is to demonstrate how anti-racist Heathens respond to, and counter, racist Heathenry, a trend which has grown since the pan-Heathen 'Declaration 127'. The latter is a statement initiated in 2016, and since signed by numerous Heathen groups worldwide, in a stand against the racism of the Asatru Folk Assembly, a major white supremacist Heathen association originating in the US but with influence internationally. The need to actively disseminate this anti-racist Heathen counter-narrative is of particular importance for contemporary Heathens concerned to demonstrate that racist Heathenry is a minority, albeit a vocal and concerning one. In Chapter 11 we examine how anti-racist Heathens are using social media platforms in particular to promote their anti-racist messaging and fight back against the racists. At the end of the book, our concluding chapter summarises the inferences arising from our discussion, considers the implications of these findings and points to future directions for research and policymaking. As the first decades of the twenty-first century have witnessed a global rise in populist, nationalist and extremist politics, this book offers a timely consideration of the significant role of Heathen religion(s) in ideologies of the far right in the UK, and how Heathens themselves are kicking back against racism.

Acknowledgements

It is standard in a work of this kind to acknowledge the many colleagues, institutions, friends and loved ones that have assisted the authors during the preparation of their book. Given the sensitive nature of the subject matter, we have decided not to name individuals here. You know who you are, and for your friendship, support and love while we wrote *Faith, folk and the far right*, we are very grateful. This necessary caution aside, we would like to take this opportunity to express our thanks to the excellent team at Manchester University Press and the two anonymous reviewers who offered valuable feedback. We must also thank those members of the former Centre for Analysis of the Far Right (CARR), our two CARR interns, the Searchlight Archives at the University of Northampton, and the intelligence offered by the Police Pagan Association, without whom this book would not have reached fruition. Special thanks to our colleagues at Richmond American University in London and the Open University, as well as Randolph Macon College, Virginia. Valuable feedback was offered at the following conferences and seminars where we presented on various aspects of this research: Century of Radical Right Extremism: New Approaches, Centre for Analysis of the Radical Right and Richmond American University Inaugural Conference (2019); the Rome Fellows Symposium, the former Richmond University Rome Study Centre (2019); virtual panel discussion at the launch of the MA in Terrorism, Security and Radical Right Extremism, Richmond American University (2021); Inform (Information on New Religious Movements) Seminar, 'New Media and New Religiosity: Possibilities and Pitfalls', Kings College, London (2022); and the Work in progress seminar, Department of Art History, The Open University (2022). Generous grants from OpenARC, the Open University Arts Research Centre, the Open University Open Access Book Fund, and the Research Policy Committee at Richmond American University London, assisted with final publication costs for the book. Wit þancie ēow!

Abbreviations

AB	Aryan Brotherhood
AFA	Asatru Folk Assembly
ÁRCHÚ	Anti-Racist Celts and Heathens Unite
AUK	Asatru UK
BF	British Fascisti
BJP	Bharatiya Janata Party
BM	Black metal
BNF	British National Fascists
BNP	British National Party
BUF	British Union of Fascists
CAORANN	Celtics Against Oppression, Racism, and Neo-Nazism
C18	Combat 18
ECER	European Congress of Ethnic Religions
FPO	Freedom Party of Austria
GBM	Greater Britain Movement
GCK	Grimnir's Crossroad Kindred
HAH	Heathens Against Hate
HNH	Hope not Hate
HUAR	Heathens United Against Racism
IAOA	Ásatrú/Odinist Alliance
IFL	Imperial Fascist League
NA	National Action
ND	New Right/Nouvelle Droite
NF	National Front
NMR	Nordic Resistance Movement
NRM	New Religious Movement
NSBM	National Socialist black metal
NSDAP	National Socialist German Workers' Party (Nazi Party)
NSM	National Socialist Movement
NTF	Nordisk Tingsfæling
OE	Old English

OF	Odinist Fellowship
ON	Old Norse
ONT	Ordo Novi Templi
O9A	Order of Nine Angles
OR	Odinic Rite
OVP	People's Party
PF	Pagan Federation
PPA	Police Pagan Association
RSS	Rashtriya Swayamsevak Sangh
TWH	The Wild Hunt (news)
UPG	Unusual/Unverified Personal Gnosis
VAR	Vikings Against Racism
WDL	White Defence League
WF	Woden's Folk
WUNS	World Union of National Socialists
ZOG	Zionist Occupational Government

Introduction: faith, folk and the far right

Approaching Heathenry

Religion has been interwoven with politics throughout history. Despite a tide of growing secularism, this relationship is still in evidence in contemporary Western democracies, including that of the UK. Early medieval people in England and elsewhere in the region would not have ascribed the modern term 'religion' to their beliefs and practices because these were woven into their daily lives rather than separate from politics, economics and wider 'society'. Thus, the archaeological and historical sources pertaining to 'religion' and 'ritual' are fragmented and often enigmatic. For the majority of the early medieval period in England, the 'religious' beliefs and practices of the pagan or heathen 'Anglo-Saxons' prior to, and at the time of the conversion to Christianity, as elsewhere in 'Germanic' northern Europe, were highly diverse, and they were deeply entangled within the politics of feuding warrior-leaders and the kingdoms emerging from the former Roman provinces of Europe (e.g. Yorke, 1990; Scull, 2011). 'Anglo-Saxon' is an historically constructed and contentious term rather than a stable ethnic category of the past, just as can be said for such other 'tribal' groupings of the period, such as 'Frisian', 'Dane' and 'Jute' (and the even broader and more slippery concept of 'Germanic') (e.g. Sayer, 2017). Indeed, in the light of the recent Black Lives Matter movement there has been sustained critical discussion of the term 'Anglo-Saxon' because of its wider historical connotations of colonial imperialism, institutionalised slavery, English nationalism and, in a word, 'racism'. In response, by way of example, in 2019 the former 'International Society of Anglo-Saxonists' voted to change its name to 'The International Society for the Study of Early Medieval England' (ISSEME) (ISSEME, 2019). In terms of early medieval understandings of, and interactions with, other peoples outside of their own communities, the modern concepts of 'race' and 'ethnicity' are outmoded too (e.g. Sayer, 2017). There was communication, exchange and trade just as there was also discrimination, conflict and slavery. The disjointed, diverse and polyvalent nature of the evidence makes it open to interpretation. Nevertheless, some interpretations are certainly more partial than others.

Coming to terms

We recognise, in line with other scholars of the field, that the terms 'fascism', 'populism', 'far right', 'extreme right' and 'radical right' are also, like the term 'Anglo-Saxon' above, subject to interpretation and can be used in different ways and that definitions are consequently 'contentious' (e.g. Feldman, 2021: 186). As Cunningham *et al.* (2022: 12) state: 'There is arguably no consensus on appropriate terminology when it comes to describing the radical right'. Likewise, Pearce (1997: 11) has argued in relation to fascism specifically, that '[t]here are almost as many definitions, or interpretations…as there are historians who have studied the issue'. Added to this, according to Mudde and Kaltwasser (2012: 149), 'populism has been contested for decades'. For Doyle White (2017: 242), 'Radical right' is often used to refer to non-racist nationalists, such as the UK Independence Party, while 'extreme right' frequently refers to racial nationalists, such as the National Front or the British National Party. We generally use the term 'far right' in this work as it encompasses both the 'extreme right' (which includes under its heading ideologies such as fascism), as well as 'radical right' groupings which, whilst normally rejecting pluralism and violence, appear to accept democracy.

Regarding the term 'Heathenry', which we treat more fully in the next chapter, we use this to refer to the modern Pagan religious path which draws inspiration from the pre-Christian religions of north-western Europe, for which we use the lower case, 'heathenry' (ff. Wallis, 2003). Today's Heathens may refer to themselves as such, but many prefer alternatives such as 'Asatru' and Germanic Neo-Paganism. It is important to emphasise that Heathenry is highly diverse. We use 'Heathenry' as a loose, catch-all term for the purpose of analysis (Heathenries would be more accurate but also more cumbersome). 'Racist Heathenry' refers to the varied ways in which race and racism are configured among specific individuals and organisations which claim to be Heathen, but which define their religion in terms of 'race'. 'Inclusivist', 'universalist' or 'progressive' Heathenry, by contrast, is used here to refer to the vast majority of Heathens in the UK and globally who welcome all who are called to the 'Northern path', whatever their ethnic or 'racial' origin, and sexual or gender orientation (Blain and Wallis, 2009a: 422).

Given the frequent blurring of Heathen thinking with esotericism and occultism historically and to the present, our analysis sometimes extends additionally to those individuals and organisations whose far-right thinking takes on motifs and themes of both. By 'occult' we refer to an 'intellectual stream that has its roots in metaphysics, cosmology and religion' and which holds 'that there is a plan to the universe' (Katz, 2007: 1–2). Occult practitioners also tend to believe that they are able to draw on supernatural powers for magical effects. Like Pagans, occultists are highly diverse in their beliefs and practices – as well as political leanings. They can be 'cosmopolitan or particularist, multiracial or racist' (Green, 2015: 386). Heathen occult movements, such as Ariosophy, share too a search for concealed or lost knowledge (Green, 2015: 384), hence they derive their nomenclature from the Latin word *occultus*, or hidden.

Our interest in far-right thinking additionally extends to organisations that include Heathen and occult elements in their discourse, even if they do not explicitly self-identify as 'Heathen'. The former Centre for Analysis for the Radical Right has labelled UK-based extremist groups, such as the Sonnenkrieg (or Sun War) Division and the Order of the Nine Angles (O9A/ONA), as 'Satanic' (Allchorn, 2021ab). We would suggest, however, that Satanism is insufficient to encapsulate the diverse esoteric strands within these groups. We define contemporary Satanism here as an ideology based around a concept of Satan which may be conceived of as atheistic or theistic and broadly encourages the autonomy of the individual acting within an amoral universe, and which is often celebrated through ritual (e.g. Harvey, 1995, 2016; Introvigne, 2016). Whilst Heathenry and Satanism are not directly associated in most cases, there are instances of interconnection. For example, the O9A draws on a range of esoteric and far-right influences, including Satanism and racist Heathenry. What is more, just as in some instances Heathen and neo-Nazi occult thinking permeates into wider popular culture, so we will also treat their extension into this broader cultural milieu, including film and gaming, music and fashion. This is important because these diverse influences, such as listening to black metal music or wearing a band T-shirt, are sometimes tangled up with racism and other far-right thinking. For example, Varg Vikernes, one perpetrator of the Norway church burnings (Figures I.1 and I.2), was a racist Heathen and black metal musician (e.g. International Business Times, 2013: n.p.), and racist Heathen themes in black metal music have in turn been linked to violence, such as the Columbine High School massacre (Goodrick-Clarke, 2002: 209).

Theoretical and methodological considerations

Our theoretical approach to the way in which racist and anti-racist Heathenries are constructed and articulated is informed by thinking on

Figure I.1 Fantoft stave church, Bergen, Norway, after being burned down allegedly by the anti-Christian musician Varg Vikernes of the black metal band Burzum who was convicted of three other church burnings (Bridgeman Images).

critical discourse or textual analysis (e.g. Foucault, 1972; Wodak and Meyer, 2001; Fairclough *et al.*, 2004; Maingueneau, 2006), and in terms of imagery and the relationality between image and text, especially the pictorial turn (Mitchell, 1994, 2005, 2015). Foucault proposed that 'discourse constitutes the real' (Cohen, 2004), by which we understand that discourse facilitates 'the complex interweaving of ideas that shape perception/experience/knowledge and hence possibilities of action' (Blain and Wallis, 2007: 12). This approach considers how words and images are used and woven together into modes of writing ('discourses') which implicitly or explicitly reveal background assumptions and narratives as well as hierarchies of power and are situated within historical and political contexts.

In certain cases, white supremacist discourse is explicit in the writings of racist Heathens, for example those of Woden's Folk who are 'Proud of our Land – Proud of our Folk – Proud of our Blood!' (Hall, 2019: n.p.). By contrast, one of the 'Nine Noble Virtues' set out by the Odinic Rite, is more enigmatic: 'To succour the friendless but to put no faith in the pledged word of a stranger people' (Odinic Rite, n.d.a). The term 'stranger people' requires critical attention because it hints at a racist agenda, exposed more explicitly within their wider discourse on 'Faith, folk and family' and 'things to which we are linked by blood' (Odinic Rite, n.d.b). Discourse and power

Figure I.2 Fantoft stave church, Bergen, Norway, after restoration (Creative Commons 4.0. Photograph: Angeliena).

are thus interwoven. As Maingueneau (2006: 230) proposes: 'to analyse religious or scientific discourse, for example, one must take into account not only their contents but also the institutions that make the production and the management of these texts possible'. Racism offers a key example of how discourse and power relate because racism is intersectional, that is, it cannot be examined in separation from society but must be understood as bound up within systems of inequality which also pertain to gender identity, sexual orientation, class, disability and other elements which are subject to forms of discrimination (Crenshaw, 1989).

The role of digital media offers an example of how this intersectional performance of power inequalities plays out. In the internet age such open-source content management systems (i.e. free website builders) as WordPress, and encrypted social media and messaging platforms, such as WhatsApp and Telegram, enable public and worldwide dissemination of far-right ideologies and other misinformation. Meanwhile, the multi-billion-dollar companies providing these fora sidestep issues of ethics with policies of maintaining 'free speech' and claims that they are online platforms rather than publishers. As Spoonley and Morris (2022: 307) warn in relation to identitarian influences on the internet: '[t]he ideological positions of the alt-right are just as likely to be embedded in video games or music videos'. But the discursive power of internet media can also be claimed for positive action. The use of such platforms as Instagram by anti-racist Heathens in their campaigns to counter racist Heathenry, offers a good example (discussed in Chapter 11). It is in our study of this phenomenon that we draw upon the pictorial turn and the thinking of W. J. T. Mitchell on image and text in particular. Mitchell proposes that new technologies 'are altering the conditions under which human vision articulates itself' (Mitchell, 1994: 24), with the boundary between public/private increasingly permeated in ways which facilitate both the virality of misinformation and opportunities for critical resistance (Mitchell, 1994: 369; 2015: 158–159, 209). We discuss here how new media, and social media, particularly on the dark web, enables covert communication, networking and recruitment among racist Heathen individuals and organisations. Mitchell also proposes (1994, 2005, 2015) that images and texts are never neutral but always political and that they are intrinsically related rather than the one subservient to the other (e.g. Mitchell, 2005: 314–315; 2015: 14). In order to move on from the rupture between 'image/text', marked by a suturing typographical slash, Mitchell (1994: 89) proposes the term 'imagetext' which 'designates composite, synthetic works (or concepts) that combine image and text' and the term 'image-text', with its hyphen which 'designates *relations* of the visual and verbal'. Juxtapositions of imagetext, theorised as having 'multimodal… framing effects' have also been shown to have particular communicative saliency (e.g. Geise and Baden, 2014; Powell *et al.*, 2015: 1000), indicating that analysis of the relationship between images and texts posted on social media are especially relevant. More recently Mitchell has added the term 'imageXtext' to this lexicon, the 'X' citing variously 'the X factor', the 'image of crossing, intersection, and encounter' and 'the phoneme of eXcess, of the eXtra, the unpredictable surplus' (Mitchell, 2015: 39–40), where '[s]omething rushes in to fill the emptiness, some X to suggest the presence of an absence', and crucially, 'the appearance of something neither text nor image' (Mitchell, 2015: 43). As discussed in Chapter 11, Instagram, with its juxtapositions of image and text, fulfils Mitchell's criteria in all these respects. Mitchell proposes that while this media can facilitate expressions of 'soft fascism', it also enables critical engagement with the public domain (Mitchell, 1994: 369). The use of Instagram by anti-racist Heathens similarly offers an opportunity to examine instances of visual-textual critical resistance.

We are also interested in the ways in which racist Heathenry deploys metapolitics; that is, a long-term strategy which attempts to achieve influence outside of mainstream politics and the democratic process by changing the popular discourse on a particular subject (e.g. Badiou, 2005; Maly, 2024). Woodbridge (2015: 41) suggests that post-war, 'a number of far-right ideologues had concluded that, in order to win back or attain legitimacy in politics, they would also have to adopt a cultural approach'. Liyanage (2020: n.p.) argues, furthermore, that metapolitics is all about 'the effort to deconstruct the prevailing ideological and cultural mindset' with the primary intention to undermine 'the foundations of democracy and capitalism'. In other words, the ambition is to realise cultural hegemony by shifting accepted social norms and ideals. Such Gramscian-inspired cultural tactics have, not surprisingly, also been utilised historically by the Left and by minorities 'to spur social change [and] to re-examine race' (Womack, 2013: 124). Indeed, Badiou (sourced above) comes from an avowedly Communist perspective. By contrast, for today's far right, the aim to change the dominant culture is the result of a specific 'post-war political climate inclement towards all "extremisms" which excluded fascism from attracting anywhere in the world a mass following' (Griffin, 2017: 19). As Bale (2020: 25–26) argues in relation to the importance of far-right groups in general: 'such structures can become important incubators of, and transmission belts for, unconventional political ideas that eventually spread beyond their own boundaries'. The strategic benefit of turning to an extremist religious position in particular, as we will discuss below, is that it 'may hold a potentially similar power over people as other religions' (Henderson, 2020: 18). Colin Jordan (1923–2009), one of the UK's leading twentieth-century neo-Nazis and a self-avowed Odinist, was acutely aware that 'party politics would only lead to failure' given the hostile post-war environment, and so he deliberately 'called for the creation for a new faith for the elite' (Jackson, 2018: 9). As such, his racist Heathenry was as much political as it was personal.

In terms of methodology, obtaining details about how racist Heathen individuals and groups operate is difficult. Intelligence sources stipulate that 'much of the alleged behaviour takes place behind closed doors/in private forums, and is not documented' (Pardy, 2019: n.p.). Goodwin (2016: 76–77) similarly observes that extreme-right groups are 'notorious for their intense secrecy, paranoia over infiltration and reluctance to grant outsiders access'. Mudde (2005: 267) adds that the radical right in particular has a 'general suspicion of academics' and so veers towards obfuscation. Conducting such established methods as participant observation, visual ethnography or interviewing are therefore difficult if not impossible in such contexts, and potentially dangerous. Despite being Heathen herself, when researching American Heathens, Snook (2015: 15–16) was refused membership of the Asatru Folk Assembly because of her 'multicultural' leanings and the 'liberal agenda' associated with the so-called 'academic elite'. Whilst researching extreme-right Heathenry in Britain, Doyle White (2017: 246) comments on Snook's experience and the difficulties he too encountered whilst accessing this kind of first-hand information:

> While I am ethnically 'White British' and share the Folkish Heathens' affection for the pre-modern societies of Northern Europe, I do not share their essentialist views about race and culture or their socially conservative attitude toward issues such as women's and LGBT rights. Accordingly, it is highly likely that I – as a non-Heathen, left-leaning academic – would encounter a similar response from these groups to that received by Snook.

As such, while we have had access to intelligence sources, we follow Doyle White by focussing our attention primarily on the 'publicly available material that these Heathen groups have issued, with a particular focus on their online presence' (Doyle White, 2017: 246). There is extensive literature considering the theory and method of such research, including the extent to which the internet presents only a partial view (e.g. Krüger, 2005; O'Leary, 1996; Possamai and Turner, 2012; Rinallo et al., 2016). For example, far-right groups may not make the full content of their views public in such fora and may present a unified view among their membership when such organisations are often highly fractious (Doyle White, 2017: 247). We have supplemented our analysis of online presence with the assistance of journalists and extremist monitoring groups, especially Hope not Hate, Searchlight and the Southern Poverty Law Center, either through their published materials or through personal communications. Increasingly, end-to-end encrypted social media platforms with lax moderation policies and more libertarian viewpoints, such as Telegram, enable far-right individuals and groups to share material. We have monitored some of these and can note that there are, for example, at least eight groups with Heathen-related material and a UK-based focus with Telegram accounts. Whilst not all of these groups are explicitly racist, there is notable cross-posting of extremist content, even on the more moderate groups. During the COVID-19 pandemic, for example, many shared anti-vaccine conspiracy theories. Some of these groups, such The Fyrgen (OE for 'mountain') with more than two thousand subscribers, are highly active.

Although a great deal of racist Heathen material lies behind private and/or encrypted social media platforms, such as Gab, Parler, BitChute, GETTR, rumble, Zello and Telegram, open source and mainstream web platforms, namely Facebook, Twitter, Instagram, YouTube and TikTok, remain the broadest conduits for spreading their extremist messages beyond their own communities. Extremist messaging has increased recently, especially on, for example, Elon Musk's 'X' (formerly Twitter) (e.g. articles in *Private Eye*, *passim*). The more bespoke encrypted channels, with less propagandistic reach, are then used for private messaging. As evidence of the latter, the Survive the Jive YouTube channel, has 160,000 subscribers, whilst its Telegram channel has just under 10,000. Thus, restricting access to certain content and sites, at least until today, has significantly limited their reach (Jackson, 2022: 143). Nonetheless, while some of these channels can be utilised for disseminating extremist propaganda, they can also be utilised for sharing violent accelerationist materials, including bomb-making instructions. Such was the case with a thirteen-year-old boy in Darlington, England, in 2021, the youngest person in the country to be convicted of a terror offence (de Simone, 2022: n.p.).

In addition to web and published materials we have also utilised the assistance of various policing and intelligence sources. Of particular relevance has been the assistance of the UK Police Pagan Association (PPA), an organisation launched in 2009 to initially 'support Pagan police officers and staff'. Since then, whilst working with various Pagan communities, the PPA has become involved with other strands of policing, such as counter-terrorism. It is telling that an organisation which was once concerned with positive liaison between Pagans and the police in order to improve understanding and relationships, is now addressing the issue of how to tackle the threat of the far right within Paganism. Having introduced our theoretical and methodological considerations, we next discuss the previous scholarship on contemporary Heathenry, focussing on the treatment of race, as context for our own study.

Scholarship on the interface between contemporary Heathenry and race

There has been a burgeoning scholarly literature on Heathenry over recent decades, as part of what has now become the discrete field of 'Pagan Studies' (e.g. Harvey and Hardman, 1995; Harvey, 2011; Blain *et al.*, 2004; Strmiska, 2005; Davy, 2006; Lewis and Pizza, 2009; Ezzy, 2014; Williams, 2020; Aitamurto and Downing, 2025). Heathenry tended to be examined as part of wider studies on Paganisms (e.g. Harvey, 1997; Wallis, 2003) rather than in its own right until two pioneering monographs in the late 1990s and early 2000s. Lindquist's (1997) *Shamanic Performances on the Urban Scene* explored the reconstruction of a form of Norse magical practice (*seid* or *seidr*) by neo-shamans in Sweden. The topic of race appears only in a footnote concerning how 'Nordic heritage...has come to be associated with right extremism, extreme nationalism and xenophobia', but Lindquist found that 'the neo-shamanic circles did not have any such political connections whatsoever' (Lindquist, 1997: 130, n.4). This is perhaps due to the influence of core-shamanism as a cross-cultural phenomenon (as promoted by Harner, 1980) and its localised expression in Sweden as *seid* for healing self and community. Blain's (2002) *Nine Worlds of Seid-Magic: Ecstasy and Shamanism in North European Paganism* also examines *seidr* practices, but with a focus on North America and the UK, and with deep attention to identity, gender, discourse and interpretation. *Seidr* is a contested practice, often termed 'women's magic' and associated with *ergi* (ON translating roughly as 'unmanliness' or 'passive homosexuality'), in ancient and some contemporary contexts. In the Poetic Edda, for example, a key source on Norse mythology (as well as Snorri Sturluson's later Prose Edda [e.g. trans. Faulkes, 1998]), the poem Lokasenna (stanza 24) records that the god Odin is regarded by Loki as being *ergi* or a 'pervert' because he practised the *seidr* he had learned from the goddess Freyja (Larrington, 2014 [1996]: 85). The reconstructed practice of 'oracular *seidr*' today has a gendered element, therefore, which is viewed negatively by hypermasculine racist heathens, making it almost exclusively an inclusivist Heathen practice, and hence the discussions of it in these two monographs by Lindquist and Blain respectively do not treat the issue of race in a sustained way.

Given the problematic issue of 'race' in Heathenry, other studies have focussed, perhaps unsurprisingly, on racist Heathenry, and the American context, which has arguably skewed attention away from the inclusivist majority, as well as the varieties of Heathenry in the UK. The landmark works to date are Gardell's *Gods of the Blood: Pagan Revival and White White Separatism* (2003) and Goodrick-Clarke's *The Occult Roots of Nazism: The Ariosophists of Austria and Germany, 1890–1935* (1985) and *Black Sun: Aryan Cults, Esoteric Nazism and the Politics of Identity* (2002). Gardell's theorisation of Heathen ideology in terms of race has been presented above, and Goodrick-Clarke's analysis of pre-war Ariosophy and post-war neo-folkish beliefs are explored in more detail in this study, especially throughout Chapters 3 and 4. Aside from journal articles and book chapters (e.g. Blain and Wallis, 2006, 2009a, 2015), more balanced book-length studies of Heathenry building on the groundwork laid by Lindquist and Blain, and drawing on sustained ethnography, have emerged within the last decade. It is certainly the case that Heathens writing from the inside have tended, again perhaps unsurprisingly, to focus their attention on progressive rather than racist Heathenry, as Wallis would be the first to admit. It is, therefore, important that three recent book-length treatments offer even-handed analyses of Heathenry and do not shirk from considering the issue of racism.

The first of these, Snook's *American Heathens: The Politics of Identity in a Pagan Religious Movement* (2015), offers a Heathen's insider analysis of the religion based on fourteen years of ethnographic research; this has enabled an especially deep and reflexive account of American Heathenry. Snook does not shy away from Heathenry's contentious aspects, pointing to widespread conservative values, including traditional gender roles, and remarks that as such, 'American Heathenry in general is more similar to Christianity than any other Neopagan group' (2015: 45). While this is broadly true, it is important to note a growing number of Heathens who find in the ancient sources evidence of, for example, gender fluidity, which supports their own gender and religious identity. The aforementioned Loki, for instance, the half-giant half-god figure of Norse mythology who in the form of a mare birthed the horse Sleipnir after mating with the stallion Svaðilfari, is drawn upon as an esteemed figure by some LGBTIQA+ Heathens, and there is a growing 'Lokian' identity. Snook usefully identifies how the unique historical, social and political character of the US has influenced Heathenry there. Heathens in the US, distinctively over those in other nations,

> reconstruct their traditions in a historical and cultural context that has been, and still is, quite heavily influenced by the legacy of racial discrimination. These racial meanings and the privilege of whiteness are inescapable; they infect the ongoing construction of heathen ethnicity and make for contentious identity politics and intragroup struggles. (Snook, 2015: 180)

The impact and ongoing legacy of European colonialism and enslavement of Indigenous and African peoples in North America comprises the 'the muck of reality' (Snook, 2015: 183) that Heathens must wrestle with, and Snook devotes an entire chapter to the issue of 'race, ethnicity and whiteness'. She notes that 'Previous scholars, with few exceptions, have approached American Heathenry as a bastion of white supremacy ideology', but argues 'the negotiations involved in navigating whiteness and racial politics in the construction of Heathen religio-ethnic identity are more complex' (Snook, 2015: 180). Furthermore, 'singular portrayals of Heathenry's racist agenda mask the complexity of meanings in ethnic folkways or white ethnoreligious identities and ignore the sizable contingent of outspoken antiracist Heathens' (Snook, 2015: 243). Indeed, Heathenry has increasingly become more integrated into the global Pagan scene (von Schnurbein, 2017: 71), with organisations such as The Troth, for example, working closely with Wiccan and other Pagan organisations (Goodrick-Clarke, 2002: 262). Snook does a good job of teasing out the complexity of contemporary Heathenry in the

US, and yet over the decade since her book was published, the increasing polarisation of racist and anti-racist Heathenry, reflecting wider societal and political concerns, demands further critical analysis.

More recently, Calico's *Being Viking: Heathenism in Contemporary America* (2018), based on five years of ethnographic research, arguably offers the most dense ethnography of American Heathenry to date. The book is important for its meticulous history of US Heathenry and for exploring the variety of the religion, from the well-known inclusivist Troth and exclusivist Asatru Folk Assembly organisations, to smaller, less well-known and localised communities, such as the practitioners of *Der Urglaawe* ('the original faith') based on the history and experience of the Pennsylvania Dutch country and its strong agricultural tradition (Calico, 2018: 201). In doing so, Calico treats such diverse issues as the negotiation of theology, identity, gender and magic, in relation to self, family and community. Calico's main chapter examining Heathenry and race focusses on McNallen's concept of metagenetics in which he offers an even-handed yet critically engaged assessment (for further discussion see Chapter 1). Aside from their consideration of the European sources which have influenced the history of Heathenry in North America, the monographs by Snook and Calico focus on the US, so their discussions of Heathenry, and race in particular, are highly specific to that region. Our own book redresses the imbalanced focus on Heathenry and race in the US by examining the case of the UK, and pays close attention to how anti-racist Heathens are pushing back against the racists.

Looking outside of the specific context of the US, von Schnurbein's *Norse Revival: Transformations of Germanic Neopaganism* (2017), takes an international perspective with a particular emphasis on Germany and Scandinavia, and is based on three decades of study based mainly on historical and textual sources with some contemporary ethnographic material, including reference to the situation in the UK. Concerned about how Heathenry continues to draw upon sources derived from nineteenth-century German romanticism of the era, volkisch nationalism of the first third of the twentieth century (e.g. Guido von List) and neo-volkisch esotericism since the Second World War, she finds that while universalist Heathens might claim to be a-racist or that their approach to Heathen religion is distinct from debates over race, they can nonetheless hold a culturalist understanding of religion (2017: 7). That is, how culture and/or cultural identity have been constructed, in combination with a sacralisation of culture, and how this leads to a deterministic and essentialist approach. A culturalist understanding of religion is by no means exclusive to Heathenry, though, as other religions can be framed in ethnic and racial terms. And not all Heathens are 'culturalist' in asserting a traditional, homogenous past rooted in place, but rather recognise how ancient heathenry was diversely situated, underwent change over time and transformed thanks to travellers, traders and migrants across vast regions. Deeply interested in the original medieval sources, both archaeological and textual, these Heathens use their understanding of the sources to critique the racist position (e.g. Grundy, 2020). Von Schnurbein overlooks the nuanced treatment of these Heathens in reconstructing contemporary Heathenry without recourse to folkish discourse.

In addition to the discussions of the interface between Heathenry and race in these three book-length studies of contemporary Heathenry, there have been two important edited volumes treating race and Paganism more broadly. *Shades of Faith: Minority Voices in Paganism* (Blanton, 2011) and *Bringing Race to the Table: Exploring Racism in the Pagan Community* (Blanton et al., 2015), bring a diverse range of Pagan practitioners together to discuss minority voices and racism within Paganism. As these voices make clear, race and racism are clearly not only issues for Heathens, but in a reflection of wider society, permeate all Pagan paths to varying degrees. The idea of 'Celtic identity', for example, presents an issue for Druidry and others looking to the medieval Welsh, Irish and Scottish sources for spiritual inspiration, with recent far-right nationalist groups in these nations drawing upon 'Celtic' imagery for tattoos and insignia (see e.g. Gallagher, 2009; Pardy, 2023a). These two important works stand as the first written by practitioners themselves addressing 'race' specifically and how racism can be tackled by practitioners. *Shades of Faith* evidences the diversity of minority voices within Paganisms. Paganisms have largely been presented (by practitioners and scholars) as deriving from European traditions and, therefore, implicitly or explicitly, appealing to white audiences. Blanton and colleagues demonstrate this is not the case and that not only have a wide range of Indigenous (e.g. North American), World Religions (e.g. Hinduism and 'shamanism') and other traditions (such as Vodou and Candomblé) long had an influence on Paganisms, but also people from these backgrounds have as legitimate a claim to Paganisms as those of European descent. *Bringing Race to the Table* scrutinises race and racism in Paganisms thoroughly, pointing to 'Racialist Paganism' as 'an overculture that locks out people of colour solely based on race' (Blanton, 2015: 16–17). The authors in the book focus on the case in North America but clearly the case is as relevant for Paganisms in the UK and Europe. The most recent book-length publication to treat the subject of inclusive and exclusive types of Heathenry is the 2025 edited collection by Aitamurto and Downing which examines, through the prism of both practitioners and academics, varieties of Germanic and Slavic-inspired Pagansms. Included in its pages are discussions of 'Pagans on both sides of the Ukrainian conflict such as the former Azov Battalion and the PMC Wagner Group, which have been at the heart of Russian narratives about the war' (Aitamurto and Downing, 2025: 2).

Having pointed to some recent book-length treatments of the subject, we must not overlook the important contribution of, some years earlier, Pagan-scholar Anne-Marie Gallagher (1999: 19) who, for example, raises concerns about the British witch Kevin Carlyon who on 25 March 1997 entered the stones of Stonehenge 'illegally' to raise a Union Jack. She stated this was in reaction to the suggestion by archaeologists that Stonehenge was built by migrating people from what is now France 4,500 years ago, and that 'it is my theory that those living in this country invaded Europe – and not vice versa' (cited in Gallagher, 2009: 577). Gallagher was one of the first researchers to address the nationalistic, sometimes racist and often uncritical use of cultural boundedness by Pagans, with a focus on the UK. She proposes:

> It could be argued that pagans are not responsible for symbols and identities hijacked from our movement. After all, we can't actually stop anybody doing this. But unless we are to be associated with these agendas calling themselves 'pagan', we have to examine what they are finding so attractive and make a positive statement which irrevocably dissociates us from them. (Gallagher, 2009: 587)

She argues for the '[i]mportance of pagans intervening and making positive statements' to counter far-right manipulation of Pagan symbols and identities. She proposes that 'paganism is political' (Gallagher, 2009: 587), and that Pagans must recognise 'proximity of the wider social web' (Gallagher, 2009: 588). Gallagher also promotes 'committed understanding', that is, being 'prepared to accept and find out why' rather than watch from the sidelines assuming a position of social privilege (Gallagher, 2009: 589). Finally, she asks Pagans to consider 'How is my own life-work helping to end these tyrannies, the corrosions of sacred possibility' (Gallagher, 2009: 589). It is clearly important for all Pagans to engage in a process of reflection and dialogue, and as Blanton (2015: 19) has since argued:

> If the mainstream within Paganism is not cognizant of the effects of racism in the overculture, and has not become active in promoting a culture of change that is inclusive of people of colour, then we should be honest that diversity is not our goal. The road forward in an inclusive community would have to start with an honest evaluation of how our actions are causing intentional and often unintentional harm by setting a culture that is not welcoming or embracing of those who do not fall within the walls of our Eurocentric overculture.

Ultimately, the authors in *Bringing Race to the Table*, argue that all Pagans must be 'allies' to peoples of colour: 'becoming an ally is a journey that examines racism as it shows up in the life of the ally and the people around the ally, as well as what the ally will actually do to respond to racism' (Blanton *et al.*, 2015: 9).

A similar proposal is developed in the anthology *Paganism and Its Discontents: Enduring Problems of Racialized Identity* (Emore and Leader, 2020a), the published result of a US-based conference of the same name in March 2018 which the editors cite as 'the first academic conference addressing the specific issue of racialized identity theology in contemporary Heathenry religious traditions that was inclusive of the communities themselves' (Emore and Leader, 2020b: xiv). The book aims to 'assist in broadening the understanding of the narratives in play, with the result being a mitigation of the rising tide of hate and racialized identity' (Emore and Leader, 2020b: xv). Calico (2020), for example, extends his examination of American Heathenry and race in *Being Viking* (2018) in a chapter entitled 'Performing "American Völkisch"'. Rather than seeing folkish Heathenry as an ideology, Calico approaches it as a practice or 'performance' seeking to 'pull together notions of indigeneity, the völkisch folksoul, and American whiteness' (Calico, 2020: 27). He notes how:

> Folkish Heathens maintain that their approach is not racist. They emphasise that a focus on racial specificity and pride in one's ancestry – that Asatru is of and for people of European descent – is not the same as white supremacy, bigotry, or racialised hatred of others. Yet the sort of 'racial pride' expressed by folkish Heathens in America carries a lot of baggage – over 300 years of oppressive, racial history and white supremacy. As such, there are no benign assertions of white racial identity. (Calico, 2020: 22)

The idea of racist Heathenry as more than an ideology, an idea to be subscribed to, but as a lived performance of intersectional identities, is useful. But furthermore and crucially, any attempt to draw on the construct of 'race' to legitimate religious theology is itself a *racist* position. 'Race' is a fallacious and defunct European historical construct (e.g. Memmi, 2000) which has been used to differentiate, subjugate and exterminate, and there is no historical use of it in a positive sense (we deliberately put the term in quote marks, here, to draw attention to this point). To argue that race is a pernicious construct, however, is not to say that racism, resulting from the racist construction of the concept of race, does not exist, with real-world consequences for people of colour and their allies, and we have pointed to how race is intersectional with all aspects of social life above. As argued in the landmark work on anthropology and race, *Decolonizing Anthropology* (Harrison, 1997: 198), 'the just society is never achieved; instead it is a continual process of becoming, and this always involves struggles'. All the more important, then, we argue, to draw attention to the construction of 'race', a concept exclusivist Heathens find so attractive, to call out racism and act positively as allies of anti-racism.

This is a point also raised by the late Stephan Grundy, a scholar of Norse religion and, under the name of Kveldulfr Gundarsson, author of important practitioner books on Heathenry (e.g. Kveldulfr Gundarsson, 1990) and an influential leader in The Troth until his untimely death in 2021. His chapter in *Paganism and Its Discontents* (Grundy, 2020) explores some of the rich evidence for diversity and inclusivity in the ancient heathen past, and concludes that promoting education about these sources and advocacy to counter racist Heathenry, are key ways of making a difference.

In his keynote address to the 2018 *Paganism and Its Discontents* conference, Strmiska, who has written widely on Paganism and Heathenry (e.g. 2000, 2005, 2007), argues that its European origins and sources mean that Paganism 'may not be a religion of racism, but it is often racism adjacent. It may not be racist in essence, but some of its key components may have a massive appeal to racists' (Strmiska, 2020: 14). He (Strmiska, 2020: 14–20) proposes five discrete ways that Pagans and scholars of Paganism can counter racism: 1) actively protesting against racist appropriation; 2) being better scholars by pointing to the biases in nineteenth- and twentieth-century scholarship as well as its qualities; 3) recognising change over time and as a contemporary religion continuing to embrace change; 4) foregrounding how ancient paganism is not part of a homogenous unified systematic, organised past, as evidenced by history and archaeology; and 5) taking a critical approach to the concept of ancestors. In part three of this book, we address how anti-racist Heathens are putting Strmiska's points into anti-racist practice.

As we have discussed, none of these previous publications treats racist and anti-racist Heathenry in Britain in a sustained analysis. This highlights as all the more ground-breaking an essay by Doyle White, 'Northern Gods for Northern Folk: Racial Identity and Right-wing Ideology among Britain's Folkish Heathens' in the *Journal of Religion in Europe* (2017). Doyle White argues (following Snook, 2015: 18–19), that Heathenry, like all religions is inherently political, with politics understood as 'not just something that happens among political parties and elected officials, but rather impacts almost every area of daily life: views on economics, gender relations, and… concepts of racial identity and indigeneity' (2017: 244–245). He too examines the three main Heathen organisations in the UK, the Odinic Rite, the Odinist Fellowship and Woden's Folk, and finds that while all three identify as apolitical they also profess 'strongly political views', and do so in contrasting ways (Doyle White, 2017: 245). Doyle White notes that the Odinist Fellowship does not state publicly any socio-political allegiances. The Odinic Rite, on the other hand, refers to certain political issues (e.g.

anti-multiculturalism, anti-miscegenation), but without a 'fully-rounded critique' or manifesto of how to bring about change. Woden's Folk, meanwhile, more radically has 'a clear, anti-modernist critique of contemporary British society and offers a vision' for the future (Doyle White, 2017: 265). We examine these ideas in more detail in Part II, with particular attention to the agency of these organisations in metapolitics.

It is relevant to mention at this point the wider context beyond the US and UK, because there has been a growth in ethnic and nationalist Paganism, often known as 'Native Faith' movements, particularly in the former Soviet bloc of Europe and the Russian Federation (e.g. Shnirelman, 2002; Ivakhiv, 2005; Shlapentokh, 2012; Aitamurto and Simpson, 2013; Rountree, 2015a; Aitamurto and Downing, 2025). Typically, Native Faith movements emphasise the integrity of the ethnic group and ancestral tradition vis-a-vis foreign influences, especially transnational modernity, but as elsewhere in Europe, these Paganisms are diversely constituted. An early study is Ivakhiv's (2005) exploration of the interface of ethnicity, nationalism and environmentalism in Native Slavic Paganism among Ridnovirs, a Ukrainian expression of Rodnovery, also known as Slavic Native Faith or Slavic Neopaganism, which reconstructs the paganism of the Slavic peoples of Central and Eastern Europe. Two edited volumes, *Modern Pagan and Native Faith Movements in Central and Eastern Europe* (Aitamurto and Simpson, 2013) and *Contemporary Pagan and Native Faith Movements in Europe* (Rountree, 2015a), demonstrate the burgeoning interest in contemporary Pagan movements in this region particularly. Rountree remarks that 'in Central and Eastern Europe, religious authenticity derives from the perceived connection with the indigenous, cultural or ethnic roots of the faith' and that '[t]raditional', 'ancient' or 'indigenous' religions are being used to provide the symbolic capital for new nationalisms' (2015b: 5). Historically, Slavic Paganism has involved nationalist politics and racial violence (e.g. Shnirelan, 2013; Aitamurto, 2015), a case in point being Alexey Aleksandrovich Dobrovolsky (1938–2013) who founded Russian Rodnoverie and was an avowed neo-Nazi (eg. Klein, 2004) (Figure I.3). More recently, Petric and Borenović (2020) consider the case of Slovenian Rodnovery, focussing on the case of the group Veles, which take a more progressive approach than some other iterations.

As with the case of Heathenry more broadly, many of these new religious movements in Europe, such as the maausulised movement in Estonia, Rodzimowierstwo in Poland and Yotengrit in Hungary, all of which draw on the ancient pagan past to reconstruct or reimagine Pagan religions valid for the present, are not explicitly racist; but, they do exhibit tensions between understandings of heritage, Indigeneity (capitalised here as a formal noun recognising sovereignty), nationalism, ethnicity and race. Within this broader context of the reconstruction of Paganism in Europe, racist and anti-racist Heathens

Figure I.3 *Kolovrat* (коловрат, 'spinning wheel') sun-wheel image used by Alexey Dobrovolsky, the founder of Russian Rodnoverie, as an equivalent to the Nazi swastika (Wikimedia Creative Commons CC0).

specifically are marking out their differences. In Norway, for example, Asprem (2008) has examined tensions between racist and anti-racist Heathenry. The organisation Vigrid, founded in 2001 by the neo-Nazi Holocaust revisionist Tore Wilhelm Tvedt, 'blends a racist, anti-Semitic, conspiracy theorist and millenarian neo-Nazi political agenda with an Odinist religious outlook' (Asprem, 2008: 44). In response, members of Bifrost, the largest Heathen organisation in Norway, took 'a very outspoken antiracist position, explicitly distancing themselves from Vigrid's "extreme racist" position' (Asprem, 2008: 62). Regarding claims to indigeneity and ethnicity from privileged 'white' Europeans in north-western Europe, this is clearly highly problematic when a recognised Indigenous community, the Sámi, like other Indigenous peoples worldwide, are continuing to negotiate their own self-determination and survivance (see Vizenor, 2008) following generations of European settler-colonialism, Christian missionisation and cultural disenfranchisement (for fuller discussion of the complexities of Heathenry and neo-shamanism and their intersections with Sámi religion, see Kraft *et al.*, 2015; Fonneland, 2017).

So, while the interface between racist and anti-racist Heathenry has attracted an extensive and sophisticated literature, aside from Doyle White's preliminary article-length treatment of racist Heathenry in Britain, this scholarship

Introduction

has focussed mainly on the US and Europe. One purpose of this book is to correct this imbalance with focussed attention on the case of the UK.

Reflexivity and who we are

At this juncture, before outlining the chapters of the book, we should make clear who we are and why each of us has come to research this topic and write this book. Our approach aligns with the reflexive turn within the humanities and social sciences which requires us to make explicit our attachment to the material and our part in its generation (see e.g. Alvesson and Sköldberg, 2000; Wallis, 2003; Blain and Wallis, 2007). We do this, not to state any particular privileged knowledge nor to claim a greater stake in the subject than anyone else, but to acknowledge our own standpoints and subjectivities. If reflexivity can be recognised as 'a politics of location' (Marcus, 1998: 196; following Myers, 1988), then in a book on racist and anti-racist Heathenries, in which 'ethnicity' and 'race' are highly contentious and contested, it is imperative that we upfront our own locations.

Alessio

I am Canadian, Welsh, Italian and a New Zealander, and am Vice President International and Professor of History at Richmond American University London, a small private liberal arts university offering degrees which are dually accredited in the US and UK. I am a historian interested in theories of empire, the far right, science fiction and lost worlds. My published work on the far right has covered proto-fascism (the role of filibusters giving rise to Mussolini), modern anti-Islamic street movements in Europe (the Welsh origins of the English Defence League), Hindu extremism (the takeover of Bollywood by Hindutva culture), imperialism (ranging from US and Chinese military bases in the Pacific to the Pacific origins of Germany's Second Reich), Polynesian Science Fiction as well as lost world/dystopian literature focussing on Easter Island/Rapanui (e.g. Alessio, 2000, 2008, 2016). As a Roman Catholic saddened by his own faith's sometimes affiliation with the extreme right, whose British family fought the Nazis in the Second World War and whose Italian side were anti-Fascist partisans, my personal history bleeds into my scholarly interests in the far right, the fantastic and religion.

Wallis

I am a Senior Lecturer and Staff Tutor in the Department of Art History at The Open University in the UK. I am interested in the archaeology and anthropology of art and religion, specialising in prehistoric rock art and shamanism (e.g. Wallis, 2021; Wallis and Carroci, 2021/2022), human-raptor relations (e.g. Wallis, 2023a, 2023b, 2024, in press), and the use of archaeology and anthropology by today's Pagans and neo-Shamans. I have published extensively on these topics, including an 'insider'-based 'auto-archaeological' approach to neo-shamanisms (e.g. Wallis, 2003), drawing upon the theory and practice of auto-ethnography and experiential anthropology, and reflexive practice in archaeology. This research focussed on contemporary pagan interfaces with the past, including neo-shamanic interpretations of ancient heathen sources, and engagements with archaeological monuments in Britain and the US as sacred (e.g. Wallis, 2012a, 2015a). I have also collaborated extensively with the anthropologist Jenny Blain, considering today's Heathens' approaches to gender (Blain and Wallis, 2015) and the past (e.g. Wallis and Blain, 2006; Blain and Wallis, 2009a), and wider Pagan interests in 'sacred' archaeological sites (e.g. Blain and Wallis, 2007, 2009b; Wallis and Blain, 2012). In addition to this academic background, I self-identify as a Heathen and have written material outside of academic publishing for Heathen, Pagan and wider audiences (e.g. Blain and Wallis, 2000, 2002; Wallis, 2012b, 2015b; Johnson and Wallis, 2022). As a practising Heathen and scholar, I think that I have an obligation to consider critically how Heathens, and for that matter scholars, have interpreted and indeed misinterpreted the ancient heathen past; and while distasteful and abject to my own liberal worldview this includes elements of the far right. I am also excited by the way in which anti-racist Heathens are fighting back against racism, standing up for the inclusive majority, correcting misinformation and offering complex and nuanced interpretations of the sources in their 'reconstructions' of a pagan religious pathway relevant and vibrant in the twenty-first century.

We think it is important to write ourselves into our research, even if we do not find such identity labels as white, male, heterosexual, cisgender, middle-class, physically able and liberal academic particularly nuanced. In short, we each bring our own 'religious' understanding and socio-political 'baggage' to the research. No doubt other authors would write about the subject differently. Prior to this book, we have together contributed to the discussion in blogs (e.g. Alessio and Wallis, 2020, 2021) and conference papers (e.g. Alessio and Wallis, 2019; Wallis and Alessio, 2022). We hope that this volume will facilitate wider discussion on racist and anti-racist Heathenry, and occultism and Paganism more broadly, as well as point to misunderstandings of these new religious movements, and stimulate further research. We begin, in Part I, by considering the intersections of 'Heathenry, ancestors and race'.

Part I

Heathenry, ancestors and race

Ráðumk þér Loddfáfnir
en þú ráð nemir
njóta mundu ef þú nemr
þér munu góð ef þú getr
gest þú ne geyja
né á grind hrekir
get þú váluðum vel

> *Hávámal*, 135 (thirteenth century; Evans, 1986: 67)

I rede thee Loddfafnir
and hear thou my rede
profit thou hast if thou hearest
great thy gain if thou learnest:
Curse not thy guest, nor show him thy gate
Deal well with a man in want

> trans. Adams Bellows, 1936: 60

1

Diverse Heathenries: approaching concepts of ancestors, race and Indigeneity

Introduction

Our main interest in this study is the appropriation of ancient heathenry and contemporary Heathenry by far-right racists and how anti-racist Heathens are acting to counter this appropriation. The ancient sources themselves indicate that Germanic heathenry valued hospitality and generosity rather than suspicion and hostility when dealing with others whether within or from outside of one's own community. The thirteenth-century *Hávámal*, for instance, an extract from which opens Part I of this book, is ascribed to the god Odin himself, who advises that it is best to 'deal well with a man in want'. By contrast, racist Heathens discriminate against and show enmity for those others they deem foreign or otherwise outside of their own 'race'. Paradoxically and regrettably for many practitioners, then, Heathenry must not be equated with racism, but racism cannot be divorced from Heathenry. As Davy (2023: 31) states, '[h]aving to discuss racism in Heathenry today is somewhat like having to discuss Satanism when talking about Wicca in the 1980s during the "Satanic panic", except some Heathens really are racist. While racism is not part of most Heathen practice, it is so associated with it by outsiders that it has to be addressed'. It is important to state at the outset of this study then, that such extremism is rare and very uncharacteristic of today's diverse Paganisms; the individuals and groups are relatively small and marginal, even if their voices are often loud, dangerous and disproportionately represented in the media.

Paganism is a new religious movement (NRM), and Heathenry is just one of the many paths within it. While some reconstructionist practitioners view Heathenry as distinct from Paganism because the latter can be eclectic in its use of sources, Paganism serves as a useful umbrella term for scholarly purposes within the field of 'Pagan Studies'. It might be argued that to draw attention to racist Heathenry, rather than focus entirely on the much larger movement of anti-racist Heathenry, is to over-represent a minority. Nonetheless, it is necessary to engage critically with, rather than ignore, such racist thinking in order to expose its flaws and call out its proponents. Furthermore, there have been recent book-length studies of Heathenry which focus on its non-racist forms (e.g. Blain, 2002; Snook, 2015; Calico 2018, discussed further below), which do pay some attention to racist Heathenry; but the issue of race, and especially racist Heathenry in Britain, has not been treated in depth. Additionally, the modest size of racist Heathenry does not necessarily indicate a lack of significance. As Bale (2020: 25) points out: 'groupuscules that are nowadays being overlooked may nonetheless turn out to be very important in other ways'. This is all the more crucial considering racist Heathenry's violent and significant history, both past and present. Importantly, by examining racist Heathenry it behooves us, we argue, to also examine anti-racist Heathenry and so shine a light upon the vast majority of Heathens actively countering the racist appropriation of their religion. We begin by defining the terms for that which we seek to discuss.

Defining contemporary Heathenry

Heathenry is a contemporary spiritual path which draws upon medieval northern European pre-Christian (or 'heathen') beliefs and practices. Heathenry can be defined as:

> a polytheist paganism for today, drawing on two main strands: the presentations of cosmology, deity and mythology, and cultural practices within mediaeval writings of northern Europe, together with archaeological interpretations of northern European 'pasts'; and personal experience based in part on these understandings. (Blain and Wallis, 2009a: 414)

Practitioners refer to their path by various terms, including: Ásatrú/Asatru, Germanic Heathenry, Germanic Neopaganism, Norse Paganism, Northern Tradition, Anglo-Saxon Heathenry, Forn Sed, Odinism, Wodenism and Wotanism (e.g. Siegfried, 2013: n.p.). While there are many solo or solitary Heathens, practitioners also organise themselves into small 'hearths' or 'kindreds', and these may coalesce into wider national and international organisations. Heathens show a broad range of political thinking. Ásatrú, for example, translates as 'faith in the gods', or literally 'allegiance to the gods', and typically among practitioners is broadly 'inclusivist', 'universalist' or 'progressive' in its approach, welcoming all who are called to the path, irrespective of gender, sexuality, ethnicity or disability. For instance, the largest Heathen organisation in the US, The Troth, is explicitly inclusivist today, but this and other organisations have historically had to deal with issues of race, or more accurately who is most suited to the religion, often based around concepts of ancestry and ethnicity. The organisation Ásatrúarfélagið (founded by Sveinbjörn Beinteinsson, 1924–1993) was recognised as an official religion in Iceland in 1973 (Gunnell, 2015: 29) and while today is promoted as inclusivist, it was initially formulated as a religion for Icelanders alone (Siegfried, 2021) (Figure 1.1). 'Odinism', on the other hand, is most often linked to extreme nationalism and racism (Kaplan, 1996: 70; 1999) because it can be directly traced back to the German *völkisch* and Ariosophic 'religious upsurge' (Asprem, 2008: 45). Not all those identifying as Odinist are racist, however. For example, Odinshof in the UK, run by Pete Jennings, a former president of the Pagan Federation, is explicitly universalist, inclusivist, progressive and as such, anti-racist. We, therefore, prefer the generic, capitalised term 'Heathenry' to refer to the diversity of *contemporary* belief and practice over such specific terms as those listed above, and the lower-case 'heathenry' (the plural 'heathenries' would be more accurate but cumbersome) to encompass *ancient* beliefs and practices which were variously situated across north-western Europe and in time over at least a millennium. Scholars recognise that it is difficult to detect heathenry in the historic and archaeological records (e.g. Stanley, 1964; Carver *et al.*, 2010). Nonetheless, many Heathens today feel a strong emotional or 'spiritual' connection to the ancient heathen past, as well as

Figure 1.1 Members of the Ásatrúarfélagið gather at Thingvellir National Park in Iceland (Alamy).

showing a deep interest in ancient heathen culture, whether or not they are exclusivist or racist.

Heathenry and Paganism

Heathenry can be situated as a spiritual path within modern Paganism (usually referred to as 'neo-Paganism' in the US), which focuses on engagements with 'nature' as sacred and celebrates and problematises human relationships with a wider-than-human 'natural' world (e.g. Harvey, 2011; Wallis, 2003; Blain and Wallis, 2007). The three most well-known Pagan paths are Wicca (Modern Witchcraft), Druidry (drawing upon Celtic mythology and Iron Age archaeology) and Shamanism (inspired by and reinterpreting Indigenous healing and trance practices). All of these Paganisms are diversely constituted. With the exception of Christian or cultural Druidry, like Heathenry these groups engage with ancient pagan religions for inspiration, focussing on the pre-Christian/conversion period of medieval Europe (Wallis, 2003). They also tend to emphasise the environment and 'nature' as 'sacred' in order to re-enchant modern life (e.g. Harvey, 2011; Aitamurto and Simpson, 2013: 3).

The first surge in Paganism was from the 1960s and 1970s onwards, as the counter-culture sought spiritual direction in the face of an increasingly secular and consumerist modernity, and re-enchantment in defiance of the established monotheistic religions (Gardell, 2003: 613). As one journalist states: 'Ásatrú is a very young religion. And it's less a single codified religion than a loose cluster of religions: it has no central authority or agreed-upon dogma. Although many followers cherish this ideological openness, it may leave the religion vulnerable to misappropriation' (Samuel, 2017: n.p.). Heathenry, specifically, draws upon the historical, literary and archaeological evidence of the pagan polytheistic past in north-western Europe, primarily Norse, Germanic and Anglo-Saxon sources (e.g. Blain, 2002; Wallis and Blain, 2006; Snook, 2015; Calico, 2018), together with personal experience based in part on these understandings, often described as UPG or 'unusual [or "unverified"] personal gnosis' (a term coined by a North American practitioner in the 1990s [Blain and Wallis, 2009a: 414]).

Heathenry differs from other Pagan paths in a number of ways. It is worth noting first, that while the umbrella term Paganism holds value for scholars (e.g. Aitamurto and Simpson, 2013: 3) and some practitioners (it is not solely an academic construct), some Heathens do not see themselves as Pagans or part of a broader religious movement known as Paganism because of Heathens' emphasis on polytheism. Some elements of Paganism are in fact duotheistic (e.g. the God and Goddess of most Wiccan traditions), monotheistic (e.g. some Druid traditions) or even nontheistic. To reiterate, Paganisms today are diversely constituted. The 'Heathenry' page on the the Pagan Federation website, the umbrella organisation for Pagans in the UK, states that '[p]erhaps the primary difference is that Heathens are "hard polytheists": they honour a large number of individual gods, goddesses and other spiritual beings whom they see as existing independently from humans. And in common with many indigenous religions world-wide, they also honour their ancestors' (Pagan Federation, 2023). In contrast to some Pagans then, many Heathens regard themselves as these 'hard polytheists', believing that gods and other beings, such as *wights* (spirits of the land), are not merely archetypes or symbols but instead real beings which can be engaged with, most often through ritual. It is, nonetheless, Heathenry's attention to 'ancestors' which is of particular interest to us here, and which in turn raises serious issues around how concepts of ethnicity, Indigeneity and racism are understood.

In terms of recognising and honouring a pantheon of gods and goddesses and other beings, some groups and individuals focus on a particular deity or group of deities to which they feel they have a particular connection. Vanatru, for example, is the term used by some practitioners who focus on the Vanir deities (e.g. the goddess Freyja and god Freyr) rather than the Aesir deities (such as the goddess Frigg and god Odin). In Norse mythology, the Aesir are primarily associated with war, the Vanir with fertility, and after a war the two pantheons agree treatises, exchange hostages and establish peace. Those who identify most closely with the god Odin may use the term Asatru but may prefer Odinist, although this term does tend to have problematic associations with regard to ethnicity and race. It would certainly be a generalisation to say that those who identify with Odin are more likely to be racist, not least because he is one of the most celebrated and well-known deities and so highly popular among many Heathens. Nevertheless, it is the case that groups and organisations using the label Odinist, Wotanist, Wodenist or similar, are typically racist; for example, as we shall discuss in detail in subsequent chapters, the Odinic Rite and Woden's Folk.

Heathen theologies

There is an extended spectrum of theology within Heathenry, perhaps more so than any of the other Pagan paths. With a wide range of primary textual sources including mythological poetry and prose, sagas and historical documents, as well as a rich archaeological record, many Heathens are widely read on the subject of ancient heathen religion(s) and some are themselves scholars. Some practitioners pay close, critical attention to the sources in their reconstructions of theology and practice. There is a wide literature by these practitioners, addressing a readership extending from beginner to advanced (e.g. Bates, 1983, 1996; Thorsson, 1984, 1987; Howard, 1985; Kveldulfr Gundarsson, 1990; Linsell, 1992; Pennick, 1992; Aswynn, 1990; Runic John, 2004, 2013; Paxson, 2005, 2006, 2017; Gerrard, 2009; Krasskova, 2020; Johnson and Wallis, 2022; Waggoner, 2022). A good example to illustrate the extended spectrum of theology within Heathenry and different approaches to source material, is the way in which Heathens interpret and practise their religious festivals. Many follow the generic eight festivals practised by most Pagans across the respective paths, often known as the 'wheel of the year' and largely based around solar movements such as the solstices. Festivals such as Beltane (May Day or the first day of summer) and Samhain (or Halloween), for instance, celebrate the changing seasons and are based on a variety of ancient sources including from Celtic countries and more recent folklore. Many Heathens, perhaps especially those who turned to or grew up with Paganism in the form of Wicca and Druidry before finding themselves on a Heathen path, are more comfortable with celebrating these eight festivals, associating some of them with heathen celebrations in historical records. For example, the festival of Yule (Old English ġēol), recorded by Bede, has for them become associated with midwinter, the shortest day, or winter solstice. Other Heathens, who are more strictly reconstructionist, argue that such solar festivals as Beltane derive from sources in Celtic countries, are not evidenced in the Germanic sources, and so should not be celebrated. They choose to base their festivals around a lunisolar calendar as evidenced in historical primary sources, in particular the aforementioned Bede. To be sure, the Old English word mōnað, for month, derives from the name mōn or moon. In this case, the festival of Yule began on the full moon after the first new moon after winter solstice, which means it would usually have taken place in January, so was not strictly a winter solstice festival (e.g. Brown, 2022: 32).

Because of these sorts of differences in Heathen theologies some reconstructionists avoid using the term 'Asatru' because they consider it to have become too tainted with a looser, 'Pagan' approach to Heathenry which does not pay close and critical attention to the sources. The group Aldsidu, for example, have the following mission statement on their website:

> This statement is solely intended to help distinguish historical Aldsidu, or Old Saxon Heathenry, from those modern pagan religions, such as Asatru or Wicca, that claim to be 'Old (Historical) Ways' that are clearly not. Asatru and Wicca are fine traditions. However, they do not use the historically attested practices of Germanic Heathen religions and deviate substantially from them in both practice and belief. While we do not mean to insult or discount the

validity of Asatru or Wicca, we absolutely deny any claims of these groups as accurately reflecting historical Heathen Germanic belief and practice, through the surviving historical sources. (Alsidu, n.d.)

As such, it is important to reiterate that Heathen theologies are highly diverse, ranging from strict reconstructionists (many of whom also recognise that while the ancient sources are important, the interpretation of them does involve subjective bias in the present), to those whose approaches are looser, including broader 'Pagan', 'shamanic', 'occult' and other influences. Just as Heathen theologies are highly varied, so the politics of Heathenry are diverse too, particularly where issues of 'race' or 'ethnicity' are concerned, as we next discuss.

Contemporary Heathenry and race

In a global survey of 3,000 participants in 'Germanic/Norse paganism', Cragle (2017: 87) found that while 'discourse on race continues to be a persistent problem within Heathenry', nonetheless 'the data does not support the notion that racism or exclusion represents the perspectives of the majority of Heathens'. Furthermore, 'a substantial number of Heathen organizations have spoken out against racism or extremist politics in public, on organization websites and in multiple groups on social media' (Cragle, 2017: 87). According to Cragle's (2017: 29) data, 'fifty-six percent of respondents believed that racism was at least somewhat of a problem for contemporary Heathenry, suggesting that a majority of Heathens were conscientious of the issue'. Cragle (2017: 113) concludes that many stereotypes of Heathens are 'misleading':

> Contemporary Germanic/Norse Heathens represent an eclectic milieu of individuals from a variety of philosophical and spiritual backgrounds, stretching from Latin America to Eastern Europe. As the survey results have suggested, many of the stereotypes surrounding the Heathen demographic appear to be misleading. Most Heathens appear to reject expressions of bigotry and exclusion. Instead, inclusiveness in relation to gender, ethnicity, sexual orientation, and belief is widespread.

A single survey, even one with respondents 'from Latin America to Eastern Europe' (Cragle 2017: 113), can only be so representative. But as Cragle (2017: 78) points out, his 3000 respondents are a 'substantial percentage' of the world Heathen population of around 16,700 (according to Siegfried's 'World Wide Heathen Census of 2013'; see also Shaffer *et al.*,

2021), amongst a possible three million 'neo-Pagans' worldwide (according to Saunders, 2012: 787). As such, Cragle's findings offer a useful insight into how the issue of race intersects with Heathenry, as well as counter to the perception that Heathenry is a racist religion.

Information provided by the Police Pagan Association (PPA) further corroborates Cragle's conclusions about the level of racism in UK Heathenry, as well as Paganism more broadly. The Chair of the PPA, whilst confirming that there are those who 'join these groups knowing full well what they stand for, and because they share their world view', states that 'those leaving such groups are in a large part those who entered the world of Paganism or Heathenry either unaware that extremism existed in the path, or unaware that the group was extremist' (Pardy, 2019). Indeed, a great deal of the work of the PPA deals with supporting those trying to leave such radical right groups and who 'are often threatened and bullied' (Pardy, 2019) as a result.

Historically, some Heathens have distanced themselves from politics, with the aim of keeping their religion, or at least the way they practise it, neutral and separate from the politics of the past, namely the appropriation of ancient heathenry for racist ends by Nazis and neo-Nazis. Nonetheless, given this historical association between racist ideologies and the interpretation of the heathen past, the issue of race remains an ongoing issue for Heathenry today. The scholarly literature on Heathenry has not shied away from this issue (see especially Kaplan, 1996; von Schnurbein, 2015; Snook, 2015; Calico, 2018), but monographs on Heathenry have tended to focus on religious belief and practice over how these are entangled with politics (e.g. Lindquist, 1997; Blain, 2002; Wallis, 2003; and see especially Horrell, 2013; Krasskova, 2013).

The first to make a distinction between racist and non-racist Heathenry was Kaplan in the mid-1990s, contrasting Odinism as far-right and racist, and Asatru as more liberal and non-racial. This was an important distinction because the perception had been that Heathenry was intrinsically racist. Kaplan made clear that most Heathens are not racist, but that there is a persistent and concerning racist minority. Writing in the early 2000s, Gardell (2009: 611; see also 2003: 153) elaborated to identify three main ideological trends in Heathenry, along a 'non-racist' to 'racist' spectrum:

1) 'racist' Heathenry (Odinism): 'an expression of the Aryan racial soul and hence an exclusive creed open to whites only' and which dismisses non-racist Asatru as 'an effeminate new age corruption';
2) 'ethnic' Heathenry: 'an ethnic religion, native to northern Europe and therefore "natural" to Americans of northern European ancestry', with a genetic inheritance somehow determining spiritual disposition, therefore sharing certain presumptions with racist Paganism; and

3) 'non-racist' Heathenry, which is polytheistic and welcomes any genuinely interested person irrespective of race or ethnicity.

Gardell identifies two main waves of racist Heathenry since Ariosophy and National Socialism, from the 1960s to 1970s and then the 1980s to 1990s. The first of these was less pronounced because Heathens in the 1960s and 1970s were, as Gardell puts it, mainly 'left-leaning hippies' (Gardell, 2009: 613), while the right-wing politics of the Reagan and Bush eras provided the backdrop to racist Heathenry during the second wave. Over two decades later, we will set out how Gardell's position now requires revision to account for a prominent anti-racist wing of contemporary Heathenry.

More recently, von Schnurbein (2015: 6–7) has added some nuance to Gardell's three strands of ideology in light of her more recent research:

1) 'racial religious': defining religion on a biological basis of race and promoting racial and religious purity;
2) 'folkish' or 'ethnicist': stressing that religion is based on a traditional, homogenous heritage rooted in place, nature and culture, that is to be preserved or restored; and
3) 'universalist', 'anti-racist' or 'a-racist': which rejects race as a construct, avoids conflating biological heritage and tradition, and is inclusive of individuals of all backgrounds.

Von Schnurbein (2015: 7) argues that 'the racial-religious groups have been increasingly marginalised throughout the 1990s and 2000s, while the mainstream, most widely accepted and visible part of Asatru today, moves in the field between ethnicist and a-racist'. However, this grouping of universalist, anti-racist and a-racist Heathens into one category brushes over the activity and prominence of the anti-racist position in recent years, as we will discuss in Part III of this book.

In the years since the work of Gardell and von Schnurbein, we identify additionally a shift that has occurred in the three ideological stands of racial, folkish/ethnic and universalist/anti-racist/a-racist Heathenry, and how they intersect with the issue of 'race'. We identify a new, more dynamic and dangerous third wave of racist Heathenry, one which has found its feet in the populist, nationalist politics of the New Right in the first two decades of the twenty-first century. In her examination of right-wing Paganism, Hale also proposes that 'the changing political and cultural climate of the twenty-first century in the United States and Europe has created new markets for right-wing and "third positionist" material', particularly among 'Radical Traditionalists' who 'critique modern society as deeply degraded, chaotic, and corrupt, and argue that only through a return to traditional social structures, values, and belief systems can the world be redeemed and returned to the state of divine order' (Hale, 2011: 78–79; see also Hale, 2015). 'The New Right ideal', she explains, 'is one of radical regionalism where homogeneous cultural groupings reflect elitist "natural" Indo European social stratification and order' (Hale, 2011: 79). As such, 'we are seeing more consolidated efforts to promote New Right positions and political action within Pagan and other esoteric subcultures' (Hale, 2011: 96). Folkish Heathens have, then, found renewed vigour in Radical Traditionalism, and racists have found in Heathenry suitable religious and cultural ground in which to root their extremist thinking.

The term 'culture war', as used in the mainstream media, is not useful or sufficiently nuanced to address the increasing politicisation and polarisation of Heathenry and Paganism, and indeed wider society more broadly. But there are clear examples in the cultural milieu from recent years which evidence how a polarisation of politics has impacted upon society more broadly. In the US, the populist politics leading up to the first Presidency of Donald Trump (2017–2021) exacerbated historical tensions surrounding race, sexual freedom and gender identity. The Unite the Right rally in 2017 (and in more diminished form in 2018), the disputed election result which ended Trump's Presidency in 2020 and the subsequent storming of the Capitol building by Trump supporters on 6 January 2021, inflamed these tensions further. In the UK, too, increasing polarisation culminated in the Brexit referendum in 2016 and subsequent departure of the UK from the European Union in 2021; but Brexit was more than just about the single issue of whether the UK should leave the EU, exacerbating ongoing tensions over migration and immigration (which arguably intersect with race), sexual and gender identity and Trans rights. The toppling of the statue of slave-trader Edward Coulson in the city of Bristol in 2020, following global protests in reaction to the murder by a white policeman of the Black man George Floyd in the US, highlighted tensions over Britain's own history of slavery. Months later, the National Trust's decision in its Colonialism and Historical Slavery Report to adopt a decolonizing approach resulted in the charity being labelled 'woke' and the head of the charity receiving death threats.

These few examples (among others in Europe, North America and more broadly worldwide, that it would be digressive to list), illustrate how society has become increasingly polarised along left-right political lines in the 2010s and 2020s. In Heathenry today, too, the lines are drawn around the polar opposites of racist/anti-racist. While once Gardell could distinguish 'racist' from 'ethnic' Heathenry, and von Schnurbein could separate 'racial' from 'folkish', these categories are now, we argue, fluid. Among many progressive Heathens, folkish now equals racist, and while some inclusive Heathens have historically aimed to use the term 'folkish' in more positive ways (such as a focus on local community and issues) and to mean something different from 'racist', this is arguably frequently no longer the case. Furthermore, while Gardell originally used the term 'non-racist' to refer to inclusive Heathenry, just a decade or so later von Schnurbein deemed it necessary to nuance the category. She utilised the aforementioned descriptors 'universalist', 'anti-racist' or 'a-racist', since non-racist was too broad and it was clear that at this time Heathens were themselves presenting a richer understanding of how they might position themselves on the subject of 'race'.

In the years since von Schnurbein's book, however, due to the increasing polarisation of politics in society and in response to the recent events we have highlighted above (for example, the Trump administration in the US and Brexit in the UK), our research indicates that it is no longer feasible to identify Heathens as 'a-racist'. Those attempting a position of neutrality on whether race should be an issue in Heathenry, and therefore merely watching from the sideline, are themselves permitting racism and facilitating its perpetuation. The main factor prompting Heathens to take an explicitly anti-racist stance was the Asatru Folk Assembly's increasingly whites-only 'folkish' agenda during the early 2010s. As Snook (2015: 149) puts it, 'as the United States' political landscape has become increasingly tumultuous, the tenuous divide between Heathen religion and political ideology has further eroded'. Emboldened by the increasingly populist, nationalist and right-wing political milieu of the time, racist Heathen organisations became more public, more vocal and visibly emboldened.

The response from progressive Heathens making their anti-racist stance explicit (although many groups had already been doing this for some years) began around this time with the Icelandic Ásatrúarfélagið releasing in 2014 a statement denouncing the use of Heathenry for racist purposes. This was followed in 2016 by the organisation Huginn's Heathen Hof publicly denouncing the racial and sexually discriminatory ideology of the AFA in their 'Declaration 127', which has since been signed by many organisations and individuals worldwide. This all culminated in the Frith Forge conference in 2017 'to discuss inclusion in religion and to promote cultural, religious, and educational exchange' (The Troth, 2017), an event which has now become a regular fixture in the international Heathen calendar, with the 2024 conference held in Costa Rica.

Calico is correct to write that '[a] particular Heathen group or individual is likely to manifest ideas from *many* tributaries in different patterns and formulations. Heathens draw on a bounded but contested set of ideas into which specific intellectual tributaries flow in order to curate their own specific topography of Heathen identity' (2018: 132). Here we too recognise the many ways in which Heathens, and indeed people across society, construct their identities, drawing upon diverse strands of thought and practice.

Callison and Slobodian (2021: n.p.) identify how today's cultural and political milieu in which conventional authority and democratic processes have been challenged, can lead to 'diagonal thinking'. Diagonalists,

> tend to contest conventional monikers of left and right (while generally arcing toward far-right beliefs), to express ambivalence if not cynicism toward parliamentary politics, and to blend convictions about holism and even spirituality with a dogged discourse of individual liberties. At the extreme end, diagonal movements share a conviction that all power is conspiracy. (Callison and Slobodian, 2021: n.p.)

It is not difficult to see how in a religion in which such issues as tradition, ancestors, family, individuality, sacrality of place and nature are valued and contested, within a contemporary moment in which issue of migration, cosmopolitanism, globalisation and the climate emergency are also hotly debated, diagonalism can emerge, drawing people towards right-wing thinking and conspiracy theories.

Heathenry, like the rest of society, is intersectional (as we first set out in our Introduction). Intersectionality denotes the multiple factors, impossible to separate from one another, that shape identity and how they create different forms of privilege and discrimination (Crenshaw, 1989). Race, then, has now become a central issue in Heathenry whether practitioners want to recognise it or not, just as it has been recognised as intersectional in wider society, in particular since the growth of the Black Lives Matter movement. To be Heathen today is, we propose, to be either racist or anti-racist. As John T. Mainer, Redesman of The Troth, has stated, 'It is not enough to be inclusive: Heathenry must be anti-racist' (Mainer, 2017: n.p.). While the polarisation of society has negative consequences for eroding a possible middle ground and centrist politics have been significantly diminished at least for the foreseeable future, it has permitted racists to come into plain sight, in turn paradoxically enabling anti-racists to point them out and fight against their hate. While the atomisation of society elides nuance, then, in the case of racist and anti-racist Heathenry it has been a force for positive change. There are growing calls for Heathens and other Pagans to take anti-racist action (e.g. Blanton, 2011) and become 'allies to people of colour': 'becoming an ally is a journey that examines racism as it shows up in the life of the ally and the people around the ally, as well as what the ally will actually do to respond to racism' (Blanton *et al.*, 2015: 9). For Willowe (2015: 76) 'the individual Pagan and Pagan communities need to ask themselves what they can give back in return to communities of colour. The obvious offering that White Pagans can give is using their power and privilege to challenge racism and support people of colour in and outside of the pagan world'. We explore how anti-racist Heathens are taking a stand and becoming 'allies to people of colour' in Part III of this book, and hope that this book in itself will stand as part of the anti-racist kickback against racist Heathenry and occultism.

Ritual and ancestors

Having identified a spectrum of Heathen theology from universalist to strict reconstructionist, and the polarisation of Heathen ideology comprising racist vis-a-vis anti-racist, it is important to consider next how this thinking impacts upon what Heathens actually *do*, that is, their ritual practice. This also gives us the opportunity to elaborate on how the concept of 'ancestors' is brought into the mix across racist or inclusivist Heathen ideologies. In short, how Heathens treat 'ancestors' in their ritual practice offers a means by which to determine whether they are racist or anti-racist, exclusivist or inclusivist. Heathens have various ancient sources available from which to reconstruct or take inspiration for their rituals. The latter range from charms (*galdr*) for healing and a shamanistic-type form of 'sorcery' termed *seidr* (Figure 1.2), to detailed descriptions of the *blot*, a ritual sacrifice to the gods, and *symbel*, a ceremonial sharing of food and drink. The hindmost two are the principle forms of ritual which most, though not all, Heathens across the spectrum recognise in the ancient sources and choose to practise.

The *blot* (OE *blōt*, ON *blót*), literally a 'sacrifice', with connotations of a 'gift', in ancient heathenry involved the ritual killing of animals (and in some recorded cases, humans) with their blood being used to honour *wights*, deities and/or ancestors (e.g. Price, 2020: 216). In certain cases, as is recorded in the Old Norse saga of Hákon the Good, during a *blót* at a Yule feast, special twigs were dipped into bowls of blood and then shaken to spray droplets onto the participants, statues of deities and the walls of the temple, after which toasts were made to the god Odin for victory, to Njorth and Frey for the harvest and for peace and to 'departed kinsfolk' (Snorri Sturluson, trans. Hollander, 1999: 107). Archaeological evidence suggests that in some instances the manner of the sacrifice resulted in the spectacle of an arterial spray of blood (Price, 2020: 216). Blood sacrifice has mainly been replaced in contemporary Heathen *blots* with the sacrifice of a beverage, such as beer or mead, and/or a share of one's portion of food (although slaughtered food-animals are used, albeit controversially, in some Heathens' rituals; see Strmiska, 2007). This offering may be poured from a drinking horn onto the ground to honour *wights*, at a prehistoric burial mound to honour ancestors or onto deity-statues; and it may be sprayed over participants in the ceremony using twigs, all in a reconstruction of how it was done in the ancient past according to the available sources (Figure 1.3).

Figure 1.2 Heathen neo-shaman 'Runic John' performing *seidr* 'sorcery'. His shamanic drum depicts the world tree Yggdrasill (Photograph: Runic John Spedding).

The *symbel* (OE) or *sumbl* (ON), a special 'feast' or 'banquet' in ancient heathenry, involved the sharing of a meal at which drinking ale or mead from a horn vessel, speech-making and gift-giving were important aspects. A famous example is in the Old English heroic poem *Beowulf*; when a feast is held for the hero hallowed ale is served by female ale-bearers, boasts are made, oaths sworn and arm-rings given. The ale that is drunk, the way in which it is served, those by whom it is served and the extent to which it is drunk, indeed every aspect of the socio-political ritual, is clearly more than simply drunken feasting. *Symbel* is not only a mechanism for social and political cohesion but is itself a means to do honour to the gods. For

Figure 1.3 Votive offerings left behind following a *blot* ceremony at Barbrook II stone circle, Peak District, Derbyshire (Creative Commons 4.0. Photograph: Ingwina).

Heathens today *symbel* is read as a drinking ritual in which a communal horn of mead or ale is passed around a circle of participants, with each making a toast, boast or oath, whether to the deities, *wights*, ancestors, one another or all of these. While other forms of contemporary Heathen ritual exist, based more or less on the ancient sources, perhaps the majority of those today are conducted in private by solo practitioners, or perhaps increasingly since the COVID-19 pandemic, in closed groups online. *Blot* and *symbel* are particularly relevant here because they are the most communal and sometimes most public (e.g. performed in a local park or at a campsite during a festival date), and therefore offer a reflection of communally shared, deeply held beliefs. And they are also particularly relevant because they often involve attention paid to 'ancestors'.

Ancestors and race

Among progressive Heathens, the term 'ancestors' encompasses a wide range of agencies. This would include those close family members who have died during one's lifetime, as well as people in previous generations whose names may be remembered or recorded. It would often also include all those within one's family line and extended family, even if those individuals and their names are forgotten or were never known (Blain and Wallis, 2009a: 418), in other words, 'amorphous ancestors who lacked precise individual identities' (Doyle White, 2016: 355). The point is to honour them in any case, because they are ancestors. For many inclusive heathens, the concept of ancestors extends to all those who have trodden foot and died in the land one lives, the 'imagined ancestors' (Davy, 2023: 40). This is an important point because a distinction is not made based on ethnicity, race or blood connection. Progressive Heathens do not limit ancient ancestors to Anglo-Saxons or other members of Germanic tribes. In this view, to honour all those people who have lived and died in the particular landscape where one lives is sufficient to form an 'ancestral' connection. This relatively loose concept of ancestors as one's predecessors within a particular living landscape is particularly prevalent in the original homelands of the ancient sources, including England, Scotland, Iceland, Norway and Sweden. As Runic John (2023), a Heathen shaman living in Lancashire, England, states: 'if the gods call yer, the gods call yer, no matter what colour yer are!' The living landscape and the location where the sources were laid down are held to be sacred. For inclusive Heathens it does not matter what an individual practitioner's 'ethnic' or 'racial' heritage is, only that they are interested in Heathenry, feel a connection to the land (European or otherwise) and its sacred beings, and live there. As Davy (2023: 45) concludes in relation to the progressive Heathen group of Raven's Knoll in Canada, for these Heathens:

> ancestor veneration is about honoring ancestors of various sorts, not only biological ancestors. It is not about celebrating one's lineage as a means of elevating oneself, but rather honoring the worthy dead who have passed on. Ancestor veneration is an important part of their religious practice, but not all biological ancestors are venerated, and the dead who are venerated include those who are not blood ancestors. It is not about racial pride.

With the benefit of a modern scientific understanding of genetics and human evolution, the ancestors honoured by universalist Heathens may also be understood to stretch back to the earliest humans in Africa. In this case the element of inclusivity extends from land into the common human inheritance and continues to elide constructions of ethnicity or 'race'. Finally, the concept of 'ancestors' for many progressive Heathens, especially those working within an animist and/or totemist understanding, can reach out to include certain animals, plant and other-than-human beings with whom one makes a connection via the interpretation of such Old Norse terms as *hamingja* ('personification of a person's luck' [Price, 2020: 61]), *fylgja* ('follower', 'fetch' [Price, 2020: 62]) and *landvaettir* ('land-spirits'). The key point within the context of this book is that among progressive Heathens the 'ancestors' can extend beyond the human (Davy, 2023: 41), once more reiterating how the concept has little or nothing to do with ethnicity, 'race' or 'blood'.

By contrast, a racist Heathen interpretation of *blot* and *symbel* involves a very different concept of 'ancestors', crystallising around 'pride' in a perceived ethnic heritage, which in some cases may comprise a central focus for the ritual over other deities and beings, so making 'ancestry about self-aggrandizement, rather than appreciation for what ancestors have given and a sense of obligation to ancestors and future generations' (Davy, 2023: 36). For racist Heathens living in one of the 'homelands', land is important because this is where the sources were formed and where the people who formed them originate. But only those born in that land and with 'Aryan'/'white' heritage are seen, according to this essentialist worldview, as being eligible to participate in Heathen rituals. The 'ancestors' in turn are defined by a perceived ancestral bloodline and essentialised cultural heritage which extends back to the Norse, Anglo-Saxon and/or other Germanic 'cultures' of Northern Europe. The land and ancestors of England, for example, are thus seen to be bonded in ways which only a white English person can appreciate. This is the basis from which 'blood and soil' (*Blut und Boden* in National Socialism) racist ideologies emerge and gain power, both historically in the form of National Socialism and in the present among 'folkish' Heathens.

Issues of cultural heritage can take special importance for Heathens living outside of the ancestral homelands of Northern Europe, such as in North America. In a land which was and is sacred to Indigenous peoples, but which has been colonised by Europeans with devastating consequences for those Indigenous communities, making a spiritual connection to the landscape is not as seemingly straightforward as it might be for a Heathen in England or Sweden (notwithstanding the fact that there is no cultural continuity in Europe). In parts of the North American continent where historically immigrants from Germanic Europe resettled, Heathens there may form groups based around a shared relatively recent historic heritage of, say, Swedish or Danish extraction. A tension may then emerge as to whether people with an interest in the religion can authentically partake in it if they are not of this North European heritage. For inclusivist Heathens, this does not present a problem because anyone who feels called to the path has a legitimate interest and should be welcomed. But for racist Heathens, it is important that these seekers can demonstrate their Scandinavian heritage or, a broader racial concept is applied, that they are of European extraction, that is, 'white'. It is 'race' or 'ethnicity', consequently, which is perceived to enable these exclusivist Heathens to make a spiritual connection with their ancestors despite being far from the original homelands. In this case, ties of 'culture' and blood are more significant than ones to a New World landscape. As Davy (2023: 32) states:

When I asked the Heathens of Raven's Knoll about the potential of ancestor veneration to promote racism their answers revealed an important difference between inclusive Heathens' practices of ancestor veneration, and what they see as a misplaced pride in ancestry and ethnic heritage among 'folkish' Heathens.

'Race', Indigeneity and 'neo-tribes'

Over the last quarter century or so, the concept of being Indigenous, or Indigeneity, has gained prominence, as Indigenous peoples (the proper noun attempting to recognise Native peoples' sovereignty) negotiate their identity, sovereignty and 'survivance' (a term articulating Indigenous dynamism and resilience; see Vizenor, 2008). Heathens and other Pagans (e.g. Owen, 2019) have also begun to draw upon concepts of 'indigeneity' (the lowercase indicating a distinction between European peoples appealing to indigeneity in ways that are not equivalent to the sovereignty of Indigenous peoples themselves) in their discourse, for example feeling that their 'revival' of the ancient polytheistic religious traditions of the North is in some way itself 'indigenous' and/or 'tribal' (see discussion in Snook *et al.*, 2017), and representing themselves as 'new-indigenes' and 'neo-tribes' (e.g. Blain and Wallis, 2007: 9–10). This trend is of particular relevance here because of how the terms 'Indigenous/indigenous' and 'tribes' can be diversely understood within Heathenry across a spectrum of inclusivity and exclusivity. In their book, *Becoming Indigenous*, Chandler and Reid (2019: 1) note that 'indigeneity is increasingly becoming a crucial marker for imagining new modes of living and governing in our contemporary condition of climate crisis and economic uncertainty'. In terms of religion specifically, 'indigenising movements', such as Paganism and 'native faith' groups in Europe, evidence a tension between ethnicity/human-oneness and localising/universalising (see also papers in Harvey, 2020).

For many progressive Heathens, claiming to be 'indigenous' is not to draw a direct equivalence between modern Pagan paths and Indigenous peoples but to look to the Pagan religions of ancient Europe as the once-Indigenous religions of these lands, and to which anyone living in these lands may feel 'called' (whatever their 'ethnicity' or 'race'). This turn to indigeneity emerged in the 1990s when many Pagans, having developed an interest in the resonances between the ancient pagan sources and academic literature on shamanism and other Indigenous practices, and aiming to avoid the appropriation seen in previous decades (see Wallis, 2003: Chapter 2), engaged in dialogue with Indigenous practitioners regarding their animist approaches to knowing the world. The British Druid Philip 'Greywolf' Shallcrass, for instance, states:

> There are many Native Americans who dislike white folks ripping off their traditional spirituality or being wannabe Indians. When I explain that what I do is teach and practice Native European spirituality we get on fine…There is a common understanding that we are working in the same areas, just expressing what we do through localised language. (Wallis, 2003: 89)

California-based Heathen, Diana Paxson, meanwhile, told Wallis that:

> she was fascinated by Native Americans traditions, but her main concern is with a 'European tribal heritage' and connecting with that to be on a level footing with Native Americans. In a meeting with Native Americans not long before our interview in 1998, Paxson was introduced by them as 'practising what we do but in European terms', and, she said, this is exactly the kind of response she aimed for. (Wallis, 2003: 100)

The 'Native European spirituality' and 'European tribal heritage' these inclusivist practitioners refer to, are not without political implications, however, as the same sort of language surrounding indigeneity and tribalism is used by exclusivist Heathens, and increasingly so. The racist Heathen group Woden's Folk, for instance, proclaim their opposition to immigration and multiculturalism because of its perceived erosion of localism and tribalism. For the Odinic Rite, blood is likewise envisioned as the binding element to preserving social and cultural survival; one blogger even uses the analogy of a native forest and trees to make his point about the dangers of immigration: 'Would you cut down an ancient forest and replace it with non-native saplings?' (Asbrandir, n.d.: n.p.). But as Snook *et al.* (2017: 59) argue,

> So long as the identities [these Heathens] seek to reconstruct are unproblematically (and invisibly) synonymous with whiteness, they are perpetuating the categories, structures, and logics of imperialism. So long as they seek a 'white indigeneity', their claims to indigeneity, or their efforts to achieve it, are undermined and contradicted. Whiteness, as an artefact and tool of colonial control and imperial status, is inherently and definitively contrary to the category of indigenous. Until heathens begin to actively emphasise that their reconstructed identities are pre-white, in the same way that they are emphasised as pre-Christian, any Heathen claims to be indigenous will continue to be ironic and troubling at best.

Many inclusive Heathens are very aware of these tensions and attempt to address them in their public output. Rune Hjarnø Rasmussen, author of *The Nordic Animist Year* (2021), posted on his Instagram account (@nordic.animism, 7 March 2024):

> The animist perspective is inspired by the way that contemporary indigenous populations apply 'indigenous knowledge' to contemporary topics like environmental activism, the broad struggle against colonialism, extraction capitalism and coping with climate change. In this respect, however, it is important to note that we do not claim indigeneity for ourselves…We want to avoid compromising actual indigenous empowerment initiatives. We unambiguously distance ourselves from white nationalism, whether the so-called alt right or otherwise.

While race is a starkly pernicious issue in Heathenry, the less obvious concept of 'tribalism' also requires problematisation. Snook *et al.* (2017: 49) discuss how an emphasis on the simplicity and freedom of a perceived tribal Heathen past,

> allows Heathens to construct their own indigeneity through the structures and language of tribalism while idealizing the 'pure', pristine past of their ancestors. Heathens frequently refer to their 'native traditions' and their 'tribal' social structures, appealing to a sense of indigeneity and likening themselves to Native peoples who have 'tribes', a term evoking images of authentic, primal, geographically situated groups whose connection to land and ancestry is taken for granted.

The appeal to tribalism sits within a wider project of traditionalism as a solution to the problems of modernity. By emphasising anti-capitalism, anti-urbanism and self-sufficiency, the racist Heathen group Woden's Folk for instance, constructs a vision of a rural idyll which, emerging out of early modern romanticism, has also become a persistent theme in post-war British fascism (Dack, 2015: 9) and persists in the radical traditionalism of the New Right (e.g. Sedgwick, 2023). At its most extreme, radical traditionalism has a militarist incentive also: Woden's Folk, for example, promotes 'Guerilla Survivalism' as a way to prepare for a future race war (for full discussion, see Chapter 6). As Ahmed and his fellow anthropologists (Ahmed *et al.*, 2023: 8) comment in their analysis of 're-tribalisation in the 21st century', especially for those who feel disenfranchised by the current system, 'individuals and communities may resort to reinforcing or rediscovering their primordial identity and the security of the group, which in some case could lead to extremism and even violence'. Concepts of the indigenous, native, tribal and traditional have, therefore, also become embroiled in the politics of Heathenry in the UK and internationally, and we explore these themes further in the following chapters. In the next chapter, we consider the broader context for how racism intersects with Heathenry by examining the history of religion and the far right.

2

Politicised religion and religious politics: religion, politics and the far right

Introduction

Given the recent cases of far-right acts of hate and terrorism linked to racist Heathenry that we have highlighted, it is remarkable that Mudde (2016: 11) has identified religion and the far right as one of a number of contemporary '*important yet understudied* [our italics] political issues'. Lo Mascolo and Stoeckl (2023: 27) make the same claim about the study of the Christian Right in contemporary Europe, stating that the subject is 'underestimated by the general public, politics, and academia, as well as within religious groups themselves'. Disconcertingly, this very same gap in academic and intelligence circles with regard to religion was identified as the central reason as to why security and policing services had failed to identify the terrorist threat that in turn led to the 2019 Christchurch mosque attacks:

> The secular bias of intelligence and security agencies, alongside the orthodoxy of secular scholars and commentators, has led not only to the abject failure to recognize the nature and extent of the threat of white nationalists but also to prioritise the Islamic terrorist threat. They have assumed that religiosity and religious identification are essentially non-Western. (Spoonley and Morris, 2022: 313–314)

It is, therefore, timely to examine the interface between the far right and racist Heathenry specifically and to situate this within the broader scholarship on religion and the far right overall (see also Blee and Creasap, 2010: 280; Mudde, 2019). As Berger argues:

> The alt-right is not only a Heathen or contemporary Pagan problem but as Heathen symbols become integrated into terrorists' attacks and as more young white supremacists embrace the religion as an extension of their radical views or become radicalised through online Heathen websites that are 'folkish', the religion has come under the spotlight. (Berger, 2020: ix)

Given its violent proclivities, in early 2020, *Hope not Hate* (HnH, 2020a), a UK-based anti-fascist and anti-racist advocacy group, called for a ban to proscribe one of the most extreme of these far-right religious groups, the aforementioned Order of the Nine Angles (O9A/ONA; also HNH, 2019a, 2020b). *Hope not Hate* argued that the O9A represented an imminent danger to the public. The former Centre for Analysis of the Radical Right had similarly warned that the greatest threats from the far right no longer came necessarily just from the political sphere, but instead now presented themselves from other quarters:

> Radical right extremism in the United Kingdom has undergone a significant transition in the past ten years. With the decline of the neo-fascist British National Party and also (latterly) the Eurosceptic United Kingdom Independence Party (UKIP), radical right extremist actors have increasingly exchanged candidates at the ballot box for boots on the street. (Allchorn, 2021b: 5)

A study of racist Heathenry in the UK is all the more pressing, then, given that, as demonstrated above, there is a substantial gap in knowledge in this area. As one British policing specialist in the anti-terrorism Prevent unit points out, there is 'no specific information…given to educational institutions concerning these groups' (Layton-Scott, 2019: n.p.). With regard to the relationship between neo-Nazism and the occult in particular, other scholars have also pointed out that '[m]uch more needs to be done' (Katz, 2007: 176). Copsey and Richardson (2015: 1) similarly have warned more broadly in relation to aspects of UK society and the far-right scene, that 'the cultural landscapes of post-war British fascism have yet to be examined in any detail'.

One reason for a dearth of scholarship in this area, at least in the UK, is a long-standing intellectual neglect of extreme-right ideology, and particularly of British fascism (see e.g. Renton, 2020), primarily on the basis that, as mentioned above by Macklin (2005: 303), it was thought to be relatively insignificant. Pugh argued similarly that '[s]uch assumptions reflect a comforting and widely held British view that fascism is simply not part of our national story' (Pugh, 2006: 1). Jackson (2018: 1), too, has argued that 'British neo-Nazism has been, and remains, a quite marginalized political milieu, and…is one that is usually ignored especially by historians'. More recently, Macklin (2020: 4) has added that the historiography on the far right in the UK, 'remains disproportionally weighted towards' the political, especially the British Union of Fascists (BUF). The BUF, formed by Oswald Mosley in 1932, was 'undoubtedly', says Jackson (2022: 24), the 'most impactful of the fascist organisations in Britain' – hence most eyes have tended to be concentrated on it. The history of the far right in the first half of the twentieth century more broadly has, consequently, either been understudied or limited by its focus primarily on political parties and their leadership; analysis of the influence of the far right since, the role of religion in this dynamic and the role of racist Heathenry specifically, is less well-examined. Given that by 2019 'Britain had some of the most watched vloggers and influencers within the international far right' (Jackson, 2022: 143) – including Kati Hopkins, Stephen Yaxley-Lennon (aka Tommy Robinson), Milo Yiannopoulos, Carl Benjamin (aka Argon of Akad), Paul Watson and Colin Robertson (aka Millennial Woes) – it is timely to extend the breadth of the analysis now. In particular, it is important consider racist Heathenry in Britain today, focussing on its history, main proponents and counter-actions against it.

Whilst many of the Heathen and occult-related aspects of far-right thinking examined here first emerged in a particular cultural milieu in late nineteenth- and early twentieth-century Germany and Austria, it is also clear that as these subcultures were transported elsewhere they developed their own unique, national and localised interpretations. This is also true of fascism and Nazism as a whole. A case in point is John Bean (b.1927), the former founder and leader of the UK's National Front and someone who explored 'the more esoteric aspects of extreme right-wing völkisch ideology' (Macklin, 2020: 362). When describing his associate, the far-right activitist John Tyndall (1934–2005), a former chairman of both the National Front and later the British National Party, Bean stated: 'although he was an admirer of Hitler, he had little time for Germany as such – or any other "foreigners", come to that. Such was his patriotism that I had the impression that secretly he wished Hitler had been British!' (quoted in Liddell, 2012). But it is also important to consider such thinking beyond the politicians, in wider culture; for example, a similar far-right outlook specific to Britain is evident with the contemporary British black metal band Winterfylleth who describe themselves as uniquely 'English Heritage' themed. When asked what this identity meant in an interview, Chris Naughton, the band's lead vocalist, stated that instead of copying Norwegian, Scandinavian or US-based black metal, the band wanted to 'put a uniquely, hopefully, English twist [on their music] and talk about, well, stories of England and the British Isles and stuff that matters to us' (Rich Reviewz, 2013: n.p.). Simon Lucas, Winterfylleth's drummer, similarly stated that the band was founded 'with the intention of honoring England's proud ancestral heritage and rich national culture' (Richard, 2010: n.p.). A photograph of Lucas performing a Nazi salute brings the meaning of this 'proud ancestral heritage' into sharp focus (for full discussion see Chapter 9). The focus on the UK in this book, then, additionally offers the opportunity to discuss how specific, localised concepts of nationhood in terms of 'Englishness' and 'Britishness' have been developed by individuals and groups drawing on the trappings of Heathenry.

Considered as a contemporary religious path, Heathenry is itself by no means a topic of overlooked scholarly attention. Since the late 1990s and early 2000s to the present, there has been a burgeoning academic literature on the subject (e.g. Lindquist, 1997; Blain, 2002; Snook, 2015; von Schnurbein, 2015, 2017; Calico, 2018; discussed in greater detail in Chapter 1) following a substantial practitioner output during primarily the 1980s and 1990s, both in the UK (Bates, 1983; Howard, 1985; Linsell, 1992; Pennick, 1992; Fries, 1993; Runic John, 2004; Gerrard, 2009; Johnson and Wallis, 2022), and in the US (e.g. Thorsson, 1984, 1987; Kveldulfr Gundarsson, 1990; Aswynn, 1990; Paxson, 2005, 2017). Book-length studies treating racist Heathenry and occultism have tended to focus on the historical background in Europe and especially the US (especially, Gardell, 2003; Goodrick-Clarke, 1985, 2002; Aitamurto and Downing, 2025), over the UK. Academic studies of Heathenry more broadly have tended to focus on its non-racist forms (e.g. Lindquist, 1997; Blain, 2002; Snook, 2015; Calico, 2018), especially with the case of the UK (but see Doyle White, 2017). This also includes one of the present authors: in Wallis' (2003) book on neo-shamanism, with two chapters treating Heathen neo-shamanisms in the UK and the US, he states that research on racist Heathenry is 'much needed, not only to address issues of the far-right which undoubtedly exist in some sections of Heathenry, but also to respond to the misleading view that Heathenry itself can be characterised as far-right in outlook' (Wallis, 2003: 135). With a dearth of literature over the two decades since treating the 'much needed' topic of racist Heathenry in the UK, this book attempts to redress the imbalance. Intriguingly, however, despite this gap in UK-related literature dealing with contemporary Heathenry and the far right, the same issues, a least at the historical level and vis-a-vis other faiths and extremist politics, have not always gone unnoticed. The latter now forms the basis of the next section of this chapter.

Religion and the far right

Although Hitler's and Mussolini's regimes seem to have been generally anti-religious overall, extreme-right ideologies, such as fascism, are not necessarily irreligious. Indeed, certain fascist leaders even claimed to be directly inspired by a religious wellspring. Corneliu Zelea Codreanu (1899–1938), the leader of the infamous Romanian Legion of the Archangel Michael, also known as the Iron Guard, explicitly emphasised a Christian Orthodox outlook to help his party emerge as one of the most successful inter-war fascist parties in Eastern Europe. Codreanu 'claimed to have been visited by the Archangel Michael while in prison' (Renton, 2020: 20), whilst some of his followers, many of whom wore large triple crosses, were reputed to have 'ritually drank each other's blood' (Passmore, 2002: 84) (Figure 2.1). This extreme, almost cultish religious viewpoint, when combined with a unique ethnic origin myth that Romanians were descended from a warrior tribe of Aryan Geto-Dacians, resulted in one of the most successful fascist parties in Eastern Europe (Kallis, 2003: 195; Griffin, 2018: 73). So influenced by religious faith were some of these followers, that in the 1937 election in Romania 33 of the party's 103 candidates were in fact Orthodox priests, and the party as a whole secured third place in the country's elections that year (Renton, 2020: 8). When speaking about the Iron Guard and Codreanu, and whilst comparing it with its Italian and German counterparts, critics point out that it was, thus, very different from other western European variants, specifically on account of its 'overt religiosity', especially its degree of Christian 'political evangelism' (Fischer-Galati, 2006: 245).

Figure 2.1 Corneliu Zelea Codreanu, leader of the 'Iron Guard', the Romanian Legion of the Archangel Michael (Public domain).

Given this context, it is clear that associations between religion and the far right are neither new nor exclusive to Heathenry alone. In fact, elsewhere in the historical and political academic ether, the subject has 'attracted considerable attention' (Eatwell, 2003: 145). Indeed, in 2007 a whole issue of the *Journal of Contemporary History* (volume 42, issue 1) was devoted to the role of Christianity in Germany either supporting or working against the Nazi regime. A great deal of this literature, however, seems focussed on the interwar and Second World War period. During a discussion of this topic in relation to the role of Catholicism in war-time Croatia, Feldman (2021: 180) consciously utilises religious metaphors to describe fascism's character there as a:

> specifically modern form of secular 'millenarianism' constructed culturally and politically, not religiously, as a revolutionary movement centring upon the 'renaissance' of a given people (whether perceived nationally, ethnically, culturally, or religiously) through the total reordering of all collective energies towards a utopia.

Contemplating this relationship in Germany, Griffin (2005: 22) states that 'scholars are still divided about fundamental issues relating to the religious content of Nazism and how best to conceptualize it'. Some, for example, 'identify rightist movements as fundamentalist to underscore how they mirror religious fundamentalism in their…millennialism' (Blee and Creasap, 2010: 270). Parallels between fascism and millenarianism, occultic and/or fundamentalist political approaches aside, much has been written on actual interwar clerical fascism, especially 'the links between the churches and fascism' (Eatwell, 2003: 145). Such a relationship is not surprising given the fact that religious beliefs were 'historically intrinsic' to many of the modern societies in which historical fascism emerged; thus, religious elements in these locales had already often been 'partially nationalised' (Davies and Lynch, 2002: 130). As a result, religious elements and beliefs could provide a suitable and convenient ideological, unifying and symbolic inspiration for some parties of an ultranationalist persuasion.

Nevertheless, there remain still gaps in understanding the religious-political nexus, even in this more widely studied interwar period. Feldman (2021a: 175), for instance, argues in relation to Catholic Croatia and the history of its wartime Ustaša-run government, that 'too little has been said about the religious dimension of this genocidal hybrid between crucifix and dagger'. Such an extremist interplay in Croatia between religion and politics can be ascertained in the statement on 22 October 1941 from the Roman Catholic priest Dionizije Juričev who was also the Head of State Direction for Renewal for that regime: 'In this country only Croats may live…I will eradicate everyone who is against the Ustaša state and its rule – right down to babies!' (quoted in Feldman, 2021a: 179). Nor was the UK free of clerical-fascist ideas either, with accusations that in the 1930s British fascism 'found a level of support from the lower Anglican clergy' (Jackson, 2014: 9). The first fascist party in the UK, the British Fascisti, shortly after renamed the 'British Fascists' in 1924, was in fact 'deeply Christian' and its members were directed to 'promote faith in God' (Jackson, 2022: 19).

In terms of this entangled relationship between the far right and religion in the modern period, scholars have suggested that in the US, Christian nationalism, is 'a particularist (almost ethnic) form of Christianity' (Baker et al., 2020: 275) that longs to go back to a 'mythic' archetype of America as a Christian country, and which has been a significant influence on contemporary anti-immigrant, anti-Muslim and xenophobic attitudes (Baker et al., 2020: 273). Today it is perhaps the racist millenarian creed associated with Christian Identity (aka Real Christian Identity), however, and which views Aryans as the true descendants of the lost tribes of Israel and as a white 'chosen people', that appears as the most blatant manifestation of this ostensibly 'Christian' association with the extreme right (e.g. CTEC, 2021).

According to the FBI (1989: n.p.), Christian Identity comprises an ideology 'that combined religious concepts with elements of racism', and whose 'proponents…often quote and provide explanations for Biblical passages' that support their more extreme interpretations of scripture. The movement emerged in the US in the early twentieth century out of British Israelism, a much more pro-Semitic ideology which envisioned the British as the descendants of the Lost Tribes of Israel who had escaped ancient Assyrian persecution and eventually made their way to Europe. However, Christian Identity members today, who possibly number a few thousand, turned this worldview on its head; instead, they now see themselves as the rightful 'chosen people', and in turn describe Jews as 'mud bloods' and as the offspring of Eve and the Serpent in the Garden in Eden. Their followers thus perceive Jews as 'the enemies of God' and the 'children of Satan' who are working, in tandem with Black and Latino people, to undermine Christian civilisation (FBI, 1989: n.p.).

In order to fight this so-called Jewish conspiracy, labelled the Zionist Occupational Government (or ZOG), many followers of this extreme interpretation of Christianity, an interpretation which all mainstream Christian churches adamantly reject, advocate for local armed pushback against non-white and Semitic groups in the form of county militias (known as the *posse comitatus*) and for the creation of isolated and enclosed armed compounds in order to prepare for an inevitable race war. Whilst half a dozen or so groups are loosely affiliated with this movement, as there is no organised 'church' per se, the most infamous of their compounds was perhaps that

50 Heathenry, ancestors and race

Figure 2.2 Aryan Nations Church, Coeur d'Alene, Idaho, 1998 (Alamy).

belonging to the so-called Aryan Nations in Idaho (Figure 2.2). In the mid-1980s, several supporters of this ideology had also founded a particularly violent group known as The Order which was responsible for a series of armed robberies and murders. Whilst their numbers are small, their influence, like that of extremist Heathens, has been significant. According to the Anti-Defamation League (ADL): 'Christian Identity penetrated most of the major extreme-right movements', including the KKK, various militia groups, neo-Nazi communities and racist skinhead organisations (ADL, 2017: n.p.).

Nevertheless, it is not only Christian or Heathen religious views which have been accused of far-right sympathies. Supporters of India's extremist Hindutva politics have been similarly criticised for their anti-Islamic and anti-Christian violence, in particular the waging of a religious 'war of position' designed by the Hindu nationalist organisation, the Rashtriya Swayamsevak Sangh (RSS), to 'engineer fundamental cultural change' (Ahmad, 2000: 287). To critics of India's current Bharatiya Janata Party (BJP), the political wing of the RSS, the apotheosis of this radical right political-cultural project, was the election in 2014 of Narendra Modi as the country's new Prime Minister. According to Leidig (2020), this Hindutva ideology, replete with violent paramilitaries and supporters (it was a former RSS member who had assassinated Mahatma Gandhi in 1948), and with its focus on religion and race (which 'emerged through sustained interaction with ideologues in Fascist Italy and Nazi Germany'), has been overlooked as a form of far-right extremism by scholars on the extreme right (Leidig, 2020: 215). This is despite the fact that Hindutva's early leaders in the 1930s suggested that the Nazi treatment of Jews should be 'a model for India's Muslim "problem"' (Leidig, 2020: 222–223).

What is particularly interesting with regard to comparisons between Hindutva and racist Heathenry, in addition to a dearth of scholarly attention focussing on their respective manifestations of religion interfacing with the extreme right, is their unlikely synergies, including the fact that both: emerged in the late nineteenth century; emphasise the centrality of race; that some individuals within Nazi Germany in particular held 'a belief in the ethno-religious connections between the lost Ario-Germanic civilisation of Thule (Atlantis) and an Indo-Aryan civilisation centred in northern India' (Kurlander, 2017: 184; see also Leidig, 2020: 224); and that their ideologies are 'centred on religion' (Leidig, 2020: 220). There is also a strong link between the RSS and racist Heathenry of the post-war period too, namely in the form of Maximiani Julia Portas (1905–1982), who later adopted the Hindi name of Savitri Devi (meaning 'Sun-rays Goddess'). Devi was a European writer and Axis spy in the Second World War whose sympathies for a Hindutva ideology led her to help foster a popular European Aryan origin myth in post-war neo-Nazi circles, especially in the UK (Kaplan, 1999; Goodrick-Clarke, 2000). She was in fact a friend of both Colin Jordan and his wife Françoise Dior (discussed in Chapter 5), both of whom were in the vanguard of keeping racist Heathen ideas alive in Britain. Devi was present, alongside Colin Jordan, at the founding of the National Socialist Movement, the co-founder of which was also David Myatt, a leading protagonist of the far-right occult organisation the Order of the Nine Angles (O9A) (see Chapter 7). One of Devi's most famous publications cultivating such a notion was *The Lightning and the Sun* (1953), a book 'which claimed that Hitler was a reincarnation of the god Vishnu' (Leidig, 2020, 226). It is not surprising to read, therefore, that the racist Heathen Anders Breivik's infamous manifesto *2083: A European Declaration of Independence* (2011), referred to the common goals between the RSS and far-right European groups (Leidig, 2020: 216).

It is, moreover, not only Heathen, Christian and Hindu elements which have been appropriated by far-right extremists. Recently, given the rise of ISIS, the neologism Islamofascism has become a topic of interest. Mudde

(2016: n.p.) argued that 'rhetorically the struggle against "Global Islam" has made populist radical right partiers emphasize in turn the "Christian" or "Judeo-Christian" values of Europe'. In the past few years, academics have also identified a 'rise of extreme nationalism in mainstream Israeli politics', including a 'xenophobic nationalism' that views asylum seekers as a 'demographic threat'; according to such sources, this scenario is encouraged by Jewish myths about 'exceptionalism', the maintenance of a supposed 'supreme culture' and a belief in a 'special moral mission' (Feinstein and Bonikowski, 2019: 742–744). In sum, then, not only is it impossible to separate politics from religion but also no religion seems immune to far-right influence.

Political religion versus religious politics

In addition to approaching the far right as either driven by, or closely intertwined with, religious conviction, it is important to consider fascism not necessarily as a genuine religion but rather as strategically appropriating religious iconography and discourse for its own advantage (Kurlander, 2012, 544). In other words, seeing religion as an instrumentalist means of social control (Griffin, 2005: 13). Consequently, the language and symbols of religion, rather than its ideology, are envisioned as being utilised by rightist groups in a deliberately calculated manner for 'tying the populace to the state' (Eatwell, 2003, 155). For instance, to the horror of the Vatican, Mussolini in Italy referred to Fascist laws as his 'Ten Commandments' (Delzell, 1971: 146), with Commandment Ten, 'Mussolini is always right', mirroring Papal infallibility. In wartime Ustaša-dominated Croatia, too, the regime was sometimes using Catholicism primarily for 'its own needs' and not out of a genuinely faith-based inspiration (Henderson, 2021: 13). Jackson (2018: 35), while not denying the sincerity of his beliefs, similarly suggests that Colin Jordan, one of the UK's most prominent post-war neo-Nazis, deliberately turned away from the political due to circumstance: 'after 1945 all fascists have radically recalibrated their organizational styles, in order to meet the challenges posed by the much more hostile environments they have faced'. Sincerity and survivalism are not, it seems, mutually exclusive. The appropriation of religion in this manner continues today in the UK. Britain First, a far-right counter-Jihad organisation, was similarly 'denounced by every major Christian denomination in the UK' (Edwards, K., 2017: n.p.) for their usurping of Christian symbols in their anti-Muslim and anti-immigrant drives. This conscious appropriation of faith for a deliberate political agenda has been referred to by scholars as the 'high jacking of religion' (see Lo Mascolo and Stoeckl, 2023: 16).

But it was the pre-Second World War Nazis in Germany who were especially successful at this religious appropriation: rallies frequently replicated revival meetings; swastikas were transformed into holy symbols; flags were consecrated; those who died for the cause were awarded martyr status; leaders were venerated as messiahs; parade grounds became open-air cathedrals; and the language of political discourse became peppered with terminology evoking notions of 'sacrifice', 'cause', 'crusade', and 'mission'. According to Evans (2007: 5), a number of scholars 'saw in the entire practice of Nazism a kind of political religion, where banners, rituals, ceremonies, the adoration of the Leader, the cult of sacrifice…inspired the unthinking and fanatical devotion of millions'. Pardy (2023a: 37), in his critique of the appropriation of Paganism by the far right, is equally critical of the motivations of their membership:

> the right-wing movement is not necessarily aligned with, loyal to, or motivated by religiosity pertaining to the symbols they use or even with the historic cultural identity of their country, but more with the effect such imagery and symbolism can have in unifying people behind a contemporary nationalist ideology that seeks to promote a war against the perceived 'other' as historically motivated and legitimate.

Given the importance of the interface between religion and the far right, this discussion topic has subsequently become a 'growing scholarly preoccupation' (Griffin, 2005: 32). Bar-on (2014: 15), for example, mentions it in correlation with the French New Right/Nouvelle Droite (ND), with its focus on *jus sanguinis* (citizenship based on a right of blood) as opposed to *jus soli* (citizenship acquired through birth on the soil of a territory). The New Right emerged in the late 1960s under the leadership of the French philosopher and writer Alan de Benoist (b.1943) as a more 'sophisticated' and 'academic' form of fascist intellectual revisionism which, intent on building a revived and powerful European civilisation, intentionally focussed upon that continent's 'pre-Christian [read Pagan] mythic roots' (Griffin, 2017: 20–21).

Much of the current intellectual debate surrounding religion and far-right politics, however, surrounds the writings of the Italian scholar Emilio Gentile and his concept of fascism as a 'political religion', one that is deliberately employed by totalitarian governments 'with the chief objective of conquering society' and the ultimate ambition of creating a palingenetic 'new man' (Gentile, 2005: 33–34). For Gentile (2005: 35), the notion of political religion is not to be confused with a genuine 'system of beliefs'. Rather, Gentile's concept of a political religion remains rooted in a desire by a fascist individual or party to fashion a full-scale and 'new supranational civilisation'; thus, his notion of political religion is a means to a totalitarian end, namely absolute control in this earthly life. It is about being saved in this world rather than the next. According to Gentile (2005: 35), a political religion is, therefore:

> a type of religion which sacralises an ideology, a movement or a political regime through the deification of a secular entity transfigured into myth, considering it the primary and indisputable source of the meaning and the ultimate aim of human existence.

In other words, culture, in the form of religion, has been weaponised as a political tool to forge national unity and direction. The aim, according to Jackson (2018: 28), is 'the total subordination of the individual to a new form of collective identity'. Gentile's use of the term political religion is, however, not a suggestion that fascism is a religion per se, or that it merely utilises a religious ritual and style simply for its own political agenda; rather, he argues that it is much more, namely that fascist totalitarian governments require a sincere *revolutionary* act of *political faith* that can inspire the masses, one wherein the state becomes the subject of worship rather than 'any suprahistorical holy entity' (Griffin, 2005, 18). God, in other words, becomes the state.

In our study of racist Heathenry in this book, we do not disagree with Gentile's definition of 'political religion', nor its use. Indeed, we envision the concept as an extremely helpful heuristic device to interrogate fascism. What we recognise in Gentile's approach, however, is that the term 'political' is seen to 'prevail in historiographical and theoretical analysis' (Griffin 2005: 66). By contrast, the *crux* of our research is focussed instead on *actual religious praxis*, namely genuine faith-based versions of Ariosophy – both old and new – as well as Germanic and British, and how such praxis becomes thoroughly enmeshed with politics. Thus, perhaps a better theoretical approach for this particular study on far-right Heathenry might be to consider these beliefs first and foremost as a type of *religious politics* as opposed to Gentile's *political religion*. In other words, with our particular case studies, the religious dimension is entirely entangled with the political. Instead of God being the state, believers in religious politics aim to create their God's/Gods' kingdom on Earth through their political ideology. Supporters of these extreme faiths are, therefore, perfectly genuine in their beliefs. According to Fischer-Galati (2006: 247), Codreanu was envisioned by all accounts as being entirely sincere in his convictions. Findell's description of Ariosophists viewing runes as 'sacred hieroglyphs [with] the status of Scripture' (2013: 271) and who view the poetic Eddas, the well-spring of their ideas, as a 'Nordic Bible' (2013: 255), would support such an analysis. Jackson (2018: 18), when addressing the very question of sincerity in his biography of Colin Jordan, concludes that such fascists 'really do believe their claims'. Feldman (2021a: 185) makes the same point, albeit differentiating Islamism from fascism; he argues that the former's core belief is sacred or supernatural rather than primarily political and ideological.

If, since the long eighteenth century ('Enlightenment'), religion across the Euro-American centre has been gradually eroded from the political and wider social sphere, and indeed analysis of this sphere, in a process of 'disenchantment' (to use Weber's [1946] terminology [but see e.g. Jenkins, 2000]), the reactionary turn in racist Heathenry can be seen, consequently, as sincere and anti-modern. As Nagl (1974: 185) argued in a discussion on the influence of Hollow Earth theory (the idea that a superior lost human race inhabited, and may continue to thrive, at the centre of the earth), Ariosophy and Atlantean Studies on the rise of Nazism in the immediate aftermath of the destruction and defeat of Germany in the First World War: 'myths and magic moved out of the drawing rooms and coffee houses to fight against reason'. Thus, this turn to the anti-modern and the world of mythology and pseudo-mythology could, in addition to demonstrating a genuine religious zeal, also help to mark this ideology out as fascist. Gentile (2005: 356), paraphrasing Griffin's definition of fascism which emphasises a palingenetic myth of national rebirth, suggests that his own definition of religious politics is regenerative too, and thus also falls under the rubric of fascist.

This focus on the spiritual does not disavow, however, the fact that racist Heathenry is also a practical realpolitik response to an environment wherein there is widespread hostility to outright fascism or Nazism. When writing about Colin Jordan, Jackson (2018: 9) suggests that this leading post-war British Nazi was acutely aware that 'party politics would only lead to failure', so he intentionally 'called for the creation for a new faith for the elite'. Jackson does not expound further in his biography, however, on the nature of Jordan's belief system, again revealing a gap in the historical material. Nevertheless, the important consideration in this discussion of religious politics and political religion, is the fact that they are not mutually exclusive. When it comes to the far right, racist Heathenry still works as an exemplar of radical political ideology in that it is 'extremist and exclusive...does not accept coexistence with other political ideologies and movements...[and] sanctifies violence as a legitimate weapon in the struggle against those it considers internal and external enemies' (Gentile 2005: 329). The difference is simply upon the emphasis.

Nazism and Ariosophy

We recognise that we are far from the first to identify occult-Heathen and Nazi linkages (see especially Goodrick-Clarke, 1985, 2002). Davies and

Lynch (2002: 134), for instance, have suggested that there is evidence that the Nazis 'were influenced by...occultist value systems'. Eatwell (2003: 157) identified Nazi occultism as 'a major concern', arguing that Himmler, one of the most powerful leaders of the Reich, the architect of the Holocaust and the infamous commander of the SS, was so 'fascinated by the occult' that he 'sought to turn the SS into the basis of an official state cult (2003: 157). Kurlander (2012: 531) states that Nazism from its very inception seemed especially prone to a pagan-inspired 'supernatural imaginary', and according to Koehne (2014: 789), 'the Nazi Party included those who advocated paganism'. Indeed, the Palestinian communist Muhammad Najati Sidqi (1905–1975) went so far as to refer to NSDAP ideology as 'Nazi paganism' (Gershoni, 2012: 487). Numerous others, by contrast, are far more reticent about lending much credibility to the influence of occultism on the Nazi far right. Evans (quoted in Griffin, 2005: 19), states that 'Hitler was at great pains to insist that Nazism was not a religion'. Steigmann-Gall (2005: 91) also rejects this political-religious theory and the idea that Hitler was a follower of occult mysticism. Indeed, he argued the very opposite, 'that the paganists were less important in the end than the proponents of a...nazified Christianity' (quoted in Evans, 2007: 6).

Our approach to far-right Heathenry tempers the excesses of some scholars on historical Nazism who are 'inclined to re-centre the Nazi "neo-pagans" as the locus of Nazi ideology', or emphasise the importance of a Nazi attempt at creating 'a new *Religionsersatz* to replace Christianity' (Steigmann-Gall, 2005: 83). In this study we thus try to take the middle road and argue that given the existence of occult Paganism and its influence in certain Nazi circles, perhaps a more nuanced position is needed. We recognise that Hitler was probably not an occult Heathen believer himself and that there is no direct evidence to sustain this position either. We are also aware that the NSDAP later banned many occult practices and groups, which does indicate that they recognised its significance and influence. As Nagl (1974: 188) states, Ariosophy was 'of considerable significance in the early development of the Nazi Party, its ideology, and its later cadre organization'. While there is no denying the influence that Ariosophy had on the beginnings of the Nazi Party, especially upon some of its leading disciples if not directly on Hitler himself, it is important to recognise how such thinking may have indirectly influenced Nazi culture.

Like Goodrick-Clarke (2000: vii), we suggest, therefore, that it was this niche Pagan-occult ideology which *partially* helps to 'explain the success' of the Nazis, especially their emphasis on racial dominance, evil Jews and palingenetic visions of Germanic greatness. Kurlander (2012: 53) likewise agrees, stating that 'there is little question that the party had its organizational roots in the Wilhelmine occult milieu'. What we try to do here, therefore, with the sections discussing Nazism, is to bring the Pagan-occult into the frame and to demonstrate how elements of racist Heathenry led directly to the creation of Nazism and to trace the influence which some of these ideas had on some leading Nazi apparatchiks. We look, consequently, at the origins of racist Heathenry and the impact that this ideology is continuing to have today. As such, whilst not centring Paganism as the be-all and end-all to understanding Nazism, we do not discard it entirely either. Instead, we suggest that racist Heathenry was but one of the many significant proto-fascist elements, alongside romanticism, anti-Semitism, colonialism, the First World War, racism, nationalism, folkism and Vitalism, amongst others, that led to the toxic brew which we now recognise as Nazism. The origins and influence of Ariosophy on early Nazism are, therefore, not the prime subject of this work, a topic that has been treated elsewhere in detail; rather, we examine instead how occult racist Heathenry emerged in order to then demonstrate how it survived and expanded its influence; and so we subsequently argue that, given its ongoing violent impact and reach, the phenomenon demands further study today.

In discussing racist Heathenry, it is also important to note that it was not only in inter-war Germany that such ideas could be found. In Italy, home of both Fascism and the centre of Roman Catholicism, Paganism existed too, albeit as a relatively minor force and primarily in the writings and thought of the aforementioned Evola: 'a profound student of magic, the occult, alchemy and…ancient pagan tradition' (Goodrick-Clarke, 2002: 53–55). Evola too gave credence to the existence of an advanced Hyperborean race ruled by 'a warrior priesthood' (Eatwell, 2003: 157). In a 1934 article entitled 'The Mystery of the Prehistorical Arctic – Thule', he stated that 'the Arctic, the North Pole, the fabulous Hyperborea was evidently the primordial fatherland of a highly civilized prehistoric white race – so civilized indeed that it was considered "divine" by the ancients'. He went on to argue that an elite vanguard with superior leadership qualities was needed to head a Western spiritual rebirth following racial inter-mixing with inferior peoples. For Evola, Germans had maintained their racial purity by resisting, with Odin's inspiration, what would become a Christian-dominated and effete Roman Empire (Goodrick-Clarke, 2002: 62). According to Macklin (2005: 304), many of Evola's ideas eventually made their way to the UK in the late twentieth century as a result of the arrival in London of Italian fascist members of Terza Posizione and Nuclei Armati Rivoluzionari (two extremist terror organisations) who were fleeing Italy after the Bologna railway station bombing in 1980. We identify how the reification of this racist Heathen idea of a 'weak' Judeo-Christian aeon has been a primary pseudo-myth for the Order of the Nine Angles and its esoterrorist mission towards a new aeon of a superhuman Aryan race, in Chapter 7.

Having noted briefly the significance of Evola, it is worth pointing out how such Pagan-fascist links are evident elsewhere. In the Southern Mediterranean, for example, albeit later, it is evident with Greece's Golden Dawn Party, which advocates for the prevention of further Muslim immigration and calls for the Hellenization of the Balkans. The organisation had originally started out in the 1980s as an allegedly Pagan organisation (Trilling, 2013: n.p.). These ideas are apparent too in Catholic-dominated Poland, namely in a small cadre of supporters of Zadruga, a Warsaw-based Nazi-Pagan group that developed in the mid-1930s. In Latin America, the former Chilean diplomat and poet Miguel Serrano (1917–2009) stands out as one of the most important voices on the occult right, giving credence to a 'polar myth of Aryan origin' and an alleged hidden sanctuary to which Hitler escaped after the war (Gardell, 2003: 185). In New Zealand, Kerry Bolton (b.1953), who founded the Church of Odin, has been described as a prominent 'neo-Nazi' by Goodrick-Clarke (2002: 227). Finally, in the US it was the National Resistance Party and the writings of James H. Madole (1927–1979) which helped to make that country the leading proponent of extreme-right occult notions of Atlantean racial decline (Goodrick-Clarke, 2002: 81–85).

Conclusion

The relationship between the far right and religion is complex, and it is important to stress, as we do in Part III when considering the contributions of anti-racist Heathens, that typically religion is not the handmaiden to extremist politics. Many religious leaders have in fact been critical of fascism. In Germany during the Second World War, Count Clemens August Graf von Galen (1878–1946), the Roman Catholic Bishop of Münster, amongst other Catholic and Protestant religious leaders, publicly denounced the Nazi Party's euthanasia policy. Likewise, 'Figures like the Protestant pastor Martin Niemöler and the theologian Dietrich Bonhoeffer had protested loudly and clearly against Nazism's inhumanity' (Evans, 2007: 5). The staunchly conservative Cardinal Pedro Segura of Spain similarly 'actively protested Franco's flirtation with the Nazis and the violence of the Falangists' (Davies and Lynch, 2002: 130). And even some leading rightwing Spaniards, such as Ernesto Gimenez Caballero (1899–1988), also known as the 'Spanish D'Annunzio', had contemplated a Latin Catholic alliance of fascists against the growing power of what he perceived to be an extreme Nazi variant (Payne, 1995: 258). Meanwhile, Feldman points out that across the Adriatic in Italy Pope Pius XII 'was deeply admired' by Holocaust survivors and Jewish leaders for his role in ensuring that 80 per cent of the country's Jews survived the Holocaust, 'compared by the sobering figure of 80% of European Jews who did not' (Feldman, 2021a: 177). The same story of anti-racist opposition is repeated in the contemporary US. Whilst Christianity 'has played...a central role in the groups that make up these new far-right coalitions...The mainstream American churches are currently openly combating this support in their ranks' (Spoonley and Morris, 2022: 312–313). According to Lo Mascolo and Stoeckl (2023: 25), it is the Vatican under the leadership of Pope Francis that has taken a leading role in denouncing the Christian Right in Europe by labelling their transnational networks as an 'ecumenism of hate'. The same fightback can be seen in the work of Savera, a group of South Asian Indian organisations committed to fighting Hindu extremists. It should not be surprising, then, that anti-racist Heathen groups are also in the vanguard of the struggle against the appropriation of their faith by a minority of extremist elements.

Complicating even further any simple statements about the nature of fascism vis-a-vis religion is the fact that, in addition to the extreme right allying itself with religious groups or critiquing others, there were also fascists who were demonstrably anti-religious. Filippo Marinetti (1876–1944), the leader of the Futurists and an early ally of Mussolini's, called for the Pope to be expelled from Italy. Hitler himself was also 'overtly hostile to organised religion' (Davies and Lynch, 2002: 133). Overall, it can be said that there is 'a wide range of beliefs and views' (Koehne, 2014) with regard to far-right attitudes towards religious faith and that any single attempt to generalise does not do justice to the messy reality. Such a conclusion is not surprising given the aforementioned discussion about contested definitions of fascism and/or the far right. Indeed, as if to confuse matters further, as McLean and McMillan (2003: 460) somewhat unhelpfully point out: '[t]here can be no precise and agreed definition of religion' either. Therefore, having now set out some of the dynamics between religion and the extreme right, and importantly having underlined how faiths of all persuasions, not just Heathenry, have become tragically and shamefully entangled and befouled by racism and ultranationalism, we next chart the origins of racist Heathen thinking in the Ariosophic movement.

3

Mythic roots: Ariosophy, National Socialism and the emergence of racist Heathenry

Introduction

Ariosophy, or the 'wisdom of the Aryans', was a term coined by Jörg Lanz von Liebenfels (1874–1954) (the pseudonym of Adolf Josef Lanz) in 1915, and it has since come to be associated with an esoteric racist form of Heathenry developed by the Austrian mystic Guido von List (1848–1919) (Figure 3.1), with his pupil von Liebenfels, in the first quarter of the twentieth century. Before discussing Ariosophy and its racist appropriation of the ancient heathen past in detail, it is worth reinforcing the point that in contrast to Ariosophy, ancient heathens across north-western Europe did not conceive of themselves as Aryans, nor as part of an especially wise race, and were in many respects highly cosmopolitan rather than exclusivist. Archaeological research in particular, examining ancient DNA and artefactual evidence, 'shows that the people of fifth and sixth century England had a mixed heritage and did not base their identity on a biological legacy. The very idea of the Anglo-Saxon ancestor is a more recent invention linked closely with the English establishment' (Sayer, 2023: n.p.). And it is not only those most widely travelled northern Europeans of the migration age, the 'Vikings', who were so internationally minded (e.g. Williams et al., 2014). As Grundy (2020: 141) wryly states: 'Rather than showing any indication of racial awareness, let alone exclusivity, it is more accurate to say, that all branches of the Germanic peoples would happily marry, raise children with, and otherwise breed with anyone who couldn't run away fast enough'.

In terms of religion, the archaeological and historical evidence indicates that pre-Christian communities in Northern Europe did not have a specific name for their 'religion', with day-to-day life and what we might term 'religious' and 'ritual' practices being very much fluid, and varying greatly across the region amongst different communities (as outlined in our Introduction). In Iceland, around the year 1000, the term 'heathen' was used by newly converted Christians to refer to followers of the traditional pagan religion. While Iceland was officially Christian by this date it was

Figure 3.1 Guido von List (Creative Commons: By Bundesarchiv, Bild 183-2007-0705-500 / Conrad H. Schiffer / CC-BY-SA 3.0, CC BY-SA 3.0 de).

permissible for pagan practices to continue in private, and *heiðni*, 'heathen', was not envisioned as a pejorative term (e.g. Zoëga, 2004: 190). By contrast, in Anglo-Saxon England after the arrival in the late sixth century of the missionary St Augustine and the gradual conversion of the country to a Romanised form of Christianity over the course of the following century, the introduction of various laws against 'heathen' or 'superstitious' practices, and even other competing Celtic Christian ones, suggests that the blurring of folkloric traditions and traditional religious thinking presented a particular problem for the Church at this time (e.g. Pollington, 2000: 21). Nevertheless, the terms 'heathen' and 'pagan' (from the Latin term *paganus* for 'country dweller') only became pejorative, implying backwardness, in the Late Modern period (Gardell, 2003: 31). Ironically, it was the native Christian British Church, rather than Germanic pagans, which faced the initial wraith of Augustine and his missionaries: 'if St Augustine was less than charitable towards the British Christians, he proceeded with considerable care and restraint in relation to the Germanic pagans. And he did so on the explicit orders of Pope Gregory' (Davies, 1999: 200).

It was, eventually then, the secularism of the Enlightenment which ended up becoming the key driver to the negative descriptions of pagan England. In a lecture he gave in 1918, the German sociologist Max Weber proposed that the growth of rationalism and decline of religion since the Enlightenment had resulted in the 'disenchantment of the world' (Weber, 1946: 155). Contemporary Heathens draw upon the archaeological, historical and literary evidence, such as miniature Thor's hammers worn as pendants, the pantheon of gods presented in rich detail in the Eddas, as well as records of heathen deeds and rituals in the Norse and Icelandic sagas, in order to reconstruct and reinvent a religion seen to be relevant in today's world. Whilst the majority of today's Heathens are non-racist or anti-racist, it is impossible to separate elements of their thinking from the context in which this reconstruction was being framed, namely in an earlier, nineteenth-century Romantic interest in pre-Christian heathenry, paganism, nationalism and new ideas surrounding Aryanism and cultural evolution which took shape in the early twentieth century. The focus of this chapter is on this early 'Paleozoic' origin period in the ascendancy of racist Heathenry.

The historical origins of Ariosophy

The term 'Aryan' emerged in the late nineteenth and early twentieth century as a neutral ethnolinguistic term to refer to people originally from around Persia. They spoke a proto-language form of Sanskrit, which became known as Indo-European, and from which many modern European languages are derived. 'Aryan' was also a self-designation among Indo-Iranian peoples, used for example by the Indic people of Vedic Period India. It was utilised as well by Iranian people in the Avesta Scriptures (the sacred books of Zoroastrianism), hence the title of the nation of Iran derives from 'Aryan'. But following the publication of Darwin's new work theorising the evolutionary hierarchy of species, his concept of evolution soon metastasised and developed a pronounced racial focus. This Social Darwinism proposed the idea that cultures, like species, themselves evolve, with 'rational', 'enlightened', 'modern' Europeans at the apex. This can be seen, for example, in the writings of Arthur de Gobineau (1816–1882), the French aristocrat who helped to popularise so-called 'scientific racism', and Houston Stewart

Chamberlain (1855–1927), the Anglo-German writer who so influenced the German *völkisch* movement that he has been envisioned as a kind of John the Baptist figure to Hitler (Brackman, 2020). The *völkisch* movement itself grew out of German romantic nationalism, specifically Johann Gottfried Herder's (1744–1803) 'holistic concept of a nation or Volk' (von Schnurbein, 2017: 22; see also diZerega, 2020). Against this background, a romanticised and racist form of Aryanism came to have a central place in the writing and thinking of the early twentieth-century Ariosophists, such as List, who 'believed that contemporary humanity was engaged in an apocalyptic struggle between the superior Aryans and the degenerate offspring of earlier, less evolved, races of humanity' (Findell, 2013: 252).

Aryan origin myths were particularly influential in Germany, where it was widely believed that the 'Vedic Aryans' were ethnically identical to the Goths, Vandals and other ancient Germanic peoples of the *Völkerwanderung* (migration period). This thinking fed directly into Nazi ideology, with the Aryan race being seen by some intellectuals as the most racially pure version of an ancient master race. Such ideas are exemplified by the Nazi racial theorist Hans F. K. Günther (1891–1968) who distinguished between racial types according to physical and psychological elements, including a 'racial soul', and who cautioned against mixing blood, especially with Jews. His 1922 work *Rassenkunde des deutschen Volkes* (*Racial Science of the German People*) also influenced directly Hitler's racial policy, and with Nazi backing Günther attained a position in the anthropology department at the University of Jena in 1932 where Hitler attended Günther's inaugural lecture. Another prominent Nazi ascribing to Ariosophic-inspired Aryan ideas was Rudolph Hess, the future Deputy Führer who has been described as a 'lifelong devotee of the occult' (Kurlander, 2012: 542). Hess, who was apparently a member of the Thule Society (Kershaw, 1998: 138), although this fact is disputed, especially favoured astrology and clairvoyance (Wolffram, 2010: 143). The name of the Thule Society itself derives from a mythical land believed by Greek and Roman geographers to be in the Arctic. Similarly, Alfred Rosenberg (1893–1946), the future Minister of Culture, editor of the *Völkischer Beobachter* and one of the leading Nazi opponents of Christianity, was also a great believer in an Aryan origin myth and, according to Kershaw (1998: 138), a fellow Thule member too. His 1930 publication, *The Myth of the Twentieth Century*, and which was reputed to have sold over one million copies, maintained that Aryans were descended from Atlanteans (Gardell, 2003: 26).

Of particular import to the rise of Ariosophy, and another movement which was also heavily influenced by Aryanism, was Theosophy, a popular late nineteenth-century New Religious Movement (NRM). It too advocated that waves of Indian migrants had made their way westwards and that Indians were thus one and the same peoples as Europeans. Such a development is perhaps not surprising given the historical context, namely that Theosophy emerged during the so-called 'high age' of European, American and Japanese imperialism. Thus, Aryanism, at least in western thinking, gradually became linked additionally to a racial hierarchy with white Europeans at the apex. Such Social Darwinist thinking is exemplified by the remarks made by the Vice President of the Royal Society of Tasmania who declared in 1890, in relation to the decline in numbers of Tasmanian Aboriginal peoples, that 'It has become an axiom that following the law of evolution and survival of the fittest, the inferior races of mankind must give place to the highest type of man' (quoted in McGregor, 1997: 48). Social Darwinism also became entangled with emerging ideas of nationhood and the nation-state. Ivakhiv (2009: 214) consequently makes the point that 'blood' and 'tradition' – and ultimately nationality and nation-state – became rooted in a specific territory, an idea with precursors in European and Soviet thought (Rountree, 2015b: 5). For Ivakhiv (2009: 221), religion and ethnic politics could not now be separated: 'identity is based on a primordialist and territorialized notion of ethnicity'. Such thinking is in evidence especially with the writings of the aforementioned Anglo-German writer Houston Stewart Chamberlain who wanted a Teutonic-specific 'true religion' devoid of what he perceived of as Semitic and Latin influences (Thomas, 1971: 697).

As a result, Theosophy helped to spread such new racist-infused ideas about Aryanism as well as a number of other viewpoints which would go on to influence racist Heathenry, and especially its earliest manifestation in the form of Ariosophy. Theosophy draws upon a combination of Eastern religions, including Hinduism and Buddhism as well as Western esoteric traditions such as Neo-Platonism, Manicheanism, Gnosticism, Free Masonry, Aryanism and esoteric magic. Theosophical thinking was first set out in the late nineteenth century by Helena Petrovna Blavatsky (1831–1891), who co-founded the Theosophical Society in New York in 1875. Blavatsky stated that an ancient and secret order of highly powerful and evolved spiritual 'Masters' (or 'Mahatmas') with supernatural abilities had shared with her their esoteric knowledge with a view to reviving these lost powers. At the centre of this esoteric knowledge is the idea of a single, divine being, of which the universe is the outward expression. Also central to Theosophical thinking is the belief that the aim of human existence is spiritual transcendence. Blavatsky proposed that humanity had evolved through a series of seven 'root races': the first being a realm of spirit; the second originating in the Arctic (Hyperborea); the third in Lemuria (a fictional continent supposedly stretching from what is now Australia to Rapa Nui/Easter Island); the fourth Atlantis (where humans became physical); the fifth, where the 'Aryan' race predominated and which encapsulated her own historical time period; the sixth, a near-future time period which was to be inaugurated through a prophet figure; and the last, when humanity leaves the Earth.

Blavatsky claimed that she had been shown this knowledge by these adepts in sacred secret texts at a monastery hidden deep in the Himalayan mountains in Tibet, where the majority of the Masters/Mahatmas were said to reside. She then translated and published this gnostic knowledge as *The Secret Doctrine* (1888) with a view to sharing it with the world. Blavatsky asserted that these texts revealed the universe working in cycles of birth, death and rebirth which were shaped by a divine force known as 'Fohat', a concept possibly borrowed from Bulwer-Lytton's Victorian notion of 'vril' (Goodrick-Clarke, 2002: 113), and one which became highly popularised in his best-selling lost world novel, *The Coming Race* (1871). Blavatsky thus argued that the Aryan race had descended from a long line of the other noble/semi-divine races that had once populated Hyperborea, Lumeria and Atlantis. In theory, Theosophy was 'to form a nucleus of the Brotherhood of Humanity without distinction of race' (Theosophical Society of England, 2024: n.p.). Nonetheless, in tune with then current thinking about 'vanishing races theory' and 'salvage ethnography' in the emerging discipline of anthropology, other races deemed 'inferior', especially Indigenous African, American, Australasian and Oceanic peoples, were all assumed by followers of this movement to be dying out (Blavatsky, 1888 [II]: 162). Consequently, given that Theosophy had a propensity to promote 'the biological interests of the Aryans' (Flowers, 1997: 135), it is no surprise that it has been accused by its critics of overlapping 'with the nationalistic and racist' (Katz, 2007: 173).

Scholars today are increasingly recognising that Theosophy was a significant nineteenth-century intellectual movement with a global reach, as witnessed by the growing academic interest in the subject (e.g. Bayly, 2010; Scheer *et al.*, 2019), and one with some interesting political outcomes. Annie Besant (1847–1933), for example, president of the Theosophical Society which was head-quartered in India, went on to become president of the Indian National Congress (Oates, 2021: n.p.). Not only did Theosophy play a part, therefore, in helping to establish Home Rule in India, but it has also been suggested that it may have even influenced the rise of that nation's Hindutva ideology (Garrity, 2014). More importantly for this work, the movement also had an influence in Europe and the Americas as it was significant in helping to popularise Hinduism and Buddhism in the West as it drew upon a number of South Asian religious beliefs and practices, including concepts such as karma. Consequently, Theosophy inadvertently helped to popularise Aryanism (Garrity, 2014). Ironically, despite its racist subtext, Theosophy had an impact too upon Black activists who appropriated in turn some of its ideas; the 'pioneer of electronic music' Herman

Poole Blunt (1914–1993), better known as Sun Ra, the Afrofuturist musician who named himself after the Egyptian sun god Ra, had, for example, developed an elaborate cosmology which called for a free and independent Black colony in space (Womack, 2013: 59). However, Blavatsky's metanarrative of Hyperborean-Atlantean-Lemurian-Aryan civilisational rise and fall, when combined with its secret orders and esoteric knowledge, also had an especially significant influence on the occult far right. Blavatsky's writings went on to directly inspire Evola's occultism (Goodrick-Clarke, 2002: 59) as well as, as mentioned, Guido von List's Ariosophy (Gardell, 2003: 23). According to Findell (2013: 252), many of List's 'inner circle' were also members of Theosophical societies. Theosophy's popularity could also help to explain, therefore, the aforementioned Savitri Devi's interest in India and her Indian pro-independence leanings.

In the light of new archaeological discoveries in the nineteenth and early twentieth centuries, such as Ninevah in the 1840s, Troy in the 1860s, Hattusis at the cusp of the nineteenth and twentieth centuries and Macchu Pichu in 1911, there appeared to a be an element of scientific validity to the possibility of these lost worlds having existed as well as to Blavatsky's root races theory. This partly explains the growing interest in the lost world narrative genre to be found in works such as Jules Verne's *Journey to the Centre of the Earth* (1864), Edward Bulwer-Lytton's aforementioned *The Coming Race* (1871), H. Rider Haggard's *King Solomon's Mines* (1885), Arthur Conan Doyle's *The Lost World* (1912), James Hilton's *Lost Horizon* (1933) and even to an extent, the monster movie *King Kong* (dir. Merian C. Cooper and Ernest B. Schoedsack, 1933). It was in this intellectual and cultural milieu that American writer Ignatius Donnelly published *Atlantis: The Antediluvian World* (1882), an immensely popular work suggesting that Egypt and Central America had a common Atlantis-based origin. Shortly after, in 1896, Augustus Le Plongeon published his *Queen Móo and the Egyptian Sphinx*. In this work Le Plongeon argued that Atlantis's real name was 'The Land of Mu' and that this lost world was the location from which the Mayans colonised Asia and Europe.

This Mu thesis led also to the best-selling Anglo-American author James Churchward (1851–1936) eventually publishing five works relating to the existence of a supposed lost continent which, according to him, had existed in the South Pacific but which had supposedly sunk beneath the waves around 12,000 BCE. (e.g. Churchward, 1974 [1931]). Churchward, who like Blavatsy was also supposedly given special insight into early prehistory on a visit to India and by a secretive Hindu priest sharing his lost knowledge, argued that Mu was the real homeland of Atlantis. Thus, by the 1880s the genre of what became known as 'Atlantean Studies' had taken off (Alessio, 2016: 55–56). It was Blavatsky, consequently, who had first helped to popularise the idea that the Aryan race had originated from an apocryphal lost continent of Atlantis, albeit via the North Pole. It was Blavatsky too, as a result of her familiarity with India, who first associated Aryanism with the swastika, a Hindu symbol for the sun (Matthews, 2009: 112), and also an image expressed in north European cultures from the Bronze Age through to the medieval period. As Gardell (2003: 22) states, these 'Theosophical themes of racial redemption, secret knowledge, subterranean cities, hidden masters, lost worlds, and exalted Aryan origins in the hyperborean motherland fit perfectly with *völkisch* imagination'.

Ariosophy, the 'wisdom of the Aryans'

Given the above, it is not surprising to learn that Aryanism, Theosophy and lost world literature were hugely influential in the evolution of Ariosophy (also known as 'Armanism', after the runes it was reputedly based upon), and as designed by the Germanic revivalist Guido von List. One other possible influence on Ariosophy that in turn went onto impact too the Church of Satan founder Anton La Vey as well as Katja Lane (who ran the 14 Word Press, a US-based far-right publisher dedicated to 'Wotanist' writing), was Ragnar Redbeard's widely disseminated *The Philosophy of Power*, also known as *Might is Right* (1896). Redbeard, a pseudonym for the New Zealand farmworker and writer Arthur Desmond, ending up fashioning an anti-Christian 'urtext for elements of the extreme right, especially within neo-pagan/Aryan groups'; in this work he also argued that 'egalitarianism cannot exist and that the white race is innately biologically superior to other races' (Derby, 2022: 99, also 105, 107–109).

List went on to mix Blavatsky's ideas with nationalist, anti-Semitic, anti-Christian and proto-fascist ones. He proposed that Teutonic or Germanic peoples were superior to all others because they were the most recent 'race' to have evolved from ancient Aryans. He invented the Armanen runes (or *Armanen Futharkh*), a series of eighteen runes, based on existing Scandinavian ones (the Younger Futhark), and he published his findings in 1906 as *Das Geheimnis der Runen* (*The Secret of the Runes*). The occult and true meaning of these archaic Nordic runes were apparently only 'revealed' to List's 'inner eye' whilst he remained in an eleven-month state of temporary blindness after a cataract operation on both eyes in 1902. List stated that his Armanen Futharkh were encrypted in the poem, 'Sayings of the High One' (*Hávamál*) in the Icelandic Poetic Edda, with stanzas 147 through 165 setting out the eighteen wisdoms of Odin, interpreted as being the 'song of the 18 runes'. According to Pardy (2023a: 6), List's interpretation of these runes was confused, replete with inversions, falsehoods and facetious additions, all of which render it 'pseudo-runic'. Yet List and many of his followers believed that these runes represented the 'primal runes' upon which all historical rune rows were based. While List's work lacks scholarly rigour and while his anti-Semitism is contrary to inclusive Heathenry today, it is impossible to ignore his influence on how the runes are used in contemporary Heathenry (Findell, 2012: 251–252). His work is cited in some of the key texts of modern runecraft, including Edred Thorsson's *Futhark* (1984) and Kveldulfr Gundarsson's *Teutonic Magic* (1990), and List's associations with the Nazi regime are downplayed in the latter (1990: 22).

List and his fellow Austrian Ariosophic co-founder, Lanz von Liebenfels, by exploring the evidence for Germanic paganism and interpreting the meaning of the Armanen Futharkh, thereby 'prophesied the resurgence of the ancient Indo-European Aryan race, now supposedly embodied by the Germanic people, through adherence to a series of arcane pagan religious practices and strict racial purity' (Kurlander, 2012: 529). As such, Ariosophy, whose origins lie in Theosophy, Aryanism and lost world/Atlantean Studies, went on to directly influence Nazism and then racist Heathenry today. In many ways, therefore, Ariosophy was the apex of the anti-scientific, anti-Semitic, anti-internationalist and anti-Catholic Aryan-German religion for which Houston Chamberlain had been advocating, one completely stripped of any vestiges of Christian association (e.g. Thomas, 1971).

Ariosophy is, then, like Theosophy, a convoluted combination of pre-existing ideologies made up of many strands. Another of these strands is Nietzchean in inspiration, given that the German philosopher 'did not think equality was a desirable way upon which to base good government', and who had divided the history of the world into two moralities, master (Classical Pagan) and slave (Jew), both of whom since ancient times had been contending for supremacy (Molas, 2021: n.p.). A persistent German *völkisch* nationalism also offers an important context for Ariosophy, consisting of a *fin-de-siècle* revulsion against the perceived evils of modernity and which called for the reunification of all German-speaking peoples to rebuild a Greater Germany. Part and parcel of this pan-Germanism was a version of the aforementioned explicit Aryan racism which, anxious about Slavic, Jewish and Catholic-Latin influence, called for a pure German blood line (e.g. Gardell, 2003: 2–4, 20).

Ariosophists subsequently claimed that there had once been a halcyon Golden Age and homeland wherein an enlightened priesthood comprised of an elite warrior class ruled over an advanced and racially pure Aryan society. The Ariosophists sometimes called this mythic North Pole homeland 'Arktogää' (Gardell, 2003: 23). They believed this mythological fatherland to have been a utopia brought down by a series of catastrophic seismic events whose descendants eventually had been forced to migrate to a series of new

Mythic roots

homelands, the last one being in present-day Austria around 8,000 years BCE – just after Atlantis was supposed to have sunk beneath the waves. However, non-Aryans bent on ensuring this Teutonic pagan civilisation and its aristocratic elite never rose again, allegedly began proselytising egalitarianism (Christianity) and introducing racial intermixing (with e.g. Jews). So, in order to rebuild a new, pure Aryan empire led by a race of semi-divine superheroes, Ariosophists sought to put an end to Judeo-Christian spiritual dominance; thus, they began to found a number of secret religious orders dedicated to the revival of lost knowledge, with esoteric links to other secret organisations such as the Knights Templars, Rosicrucians and Freemasons. This knowledge was to be furthered by way of a re-awakening of ancient blood memories through a programme of eugenics and by a deep reading of the Norse myths and runes. The name given by List to the priesthood adepts in this secret esoteric knowledge was the 'Armanenschaft', with List believing himself to be one of their last pure-blooded priest kings (Gardell, 2003: 25).

To achieve this Aryan utopia Lanz, a former Cistercian monk evicted from his order on account of sexual impropriety and with an interest in Arthurian Grail literature, purchased in 1907 Burg Werfenstein, a ruined medieval castle on the River Danube (Figure 3.2). From this castle he flew a

Figure 3.2 Burg Werfenstein, bought by Lanz for the *Ordo Novi Templi* (ONT) in 1907 (Von Tiefkuehlfan – Eigenes Werk, CC BY-SA 4.0).

swastika flag (claiming it as an ancient Aryan symbol), established a periodical known as *Ostara* and founded his own secret order of knights: the *Ordo Novi Templi* (ONT). These knights were to be comprised of persons of 'pure blood...namely...blond-haired, blue-eyed and possessed of an "ario-heroic" figure' (Goodrick-Clarke, 1985: 110). According to Lanz, the ONT were like Medieval Templars who had kept non-Western/daemonic forces at bay to prevent racial interbreeding. Lanz thus called for a racial war wherein races deemed inferior were to be either sterilised, deported to Madagascar, enslaved or incinerated as divine sacrifices (Goodrick-Clarke, 1985: 97). He also thought that Aryan women should be sent to elite stud farms to mate with his pure-blood warriors (Gardell, 2003: 22), foreshadowing the later Nazi *Lebensborn* (Fountain of Life) eugenics programme which, organised by Himmler, 'encouraged German women to bear the children of SS officers' who were deemed to be racially pure and fit (Collier and Pedley, 2000: 118). Lanz also called for the creation of 'strict marital racial laws' (Goodrick-Clarke, 1985: 64) to preserve Aryan wholesomeness, and for a ruling male elite to govern all – again very similar to Himmler's future SS (Goodrick-Clarke, 1985: 65). According to Lanz: 'all higher scientific wisdom...is to remain the secret knowledge of a numerically small, pure-bred, heroic – Aryan ruling elite' (quoted in Nagl, 1974: 193). Thus, Ariosophy was a programme 'with striking similarities to the National Socialist policies that were to come' (Gardell, 2003: 22). Indeed, List's prophesy of a 'strong one from above' coming down to earth to introduce a divine Aryan dictatorship uncannily resembles the opening scenes in Leni Riefenstahl's *Triumph of the Will* (1935); for as Hitler descends in a plane from the clouds amidst beams of sunlight shining onto Germany he appears in an 'unmistakably messianic' form (Bach, 2007: 36)

A further secret order to emerge out of this Ariosophic-charged atmosphere was the Germanenorden (Germanic Order). Created in 1912 by the journalist and publisher Theodor Fritsch (1852–1933), then one of Germany's most prominent anti-Semites, its primarily upper-class membership, many of whom were disciples of Ariosophy, used the swastika as their symbol, regarded medieval Icelandic literature as their inspiration, were avowedly anti-Semitic and celebrated pagan festivals. One of their most conspicuous members was Adam Alfred Rudolf Glauer (1875–1945?), who took the name Rudolf von Sebottendorff 'after being adopted by an Austrian of that name (Katz, 2007: 174). Von Sebottendorff ran a Munich-based variant of the Germanenorden that 'adopted many of von List's views', including the use of a dagger with a swastika symbol as their emblem (Katz, 2007: 174). Given its anti-Semitism, anti-communism, violent disposition and extreme nationalist politics, and in order to hide its revolutionary intentions from the short-lived Communist government that controlled Munich in 1919, the branch was given a cover name: the Thule Society. The reference to the mythical Greco-Roman land is, of course, akin to Blavatsky's Hyperborea or the Ariosophist's homeland Arktogäa.

There is no doubting that Sebottendorff was under 'an unmistakable Listian influence' with a pronounced 'penchant for Ariosophy' (Goodrick-Clarke, 1985: 145, 149). In 1918 the Thule society bought a local newspaper, *The Munich Observer*, to propagate their ideas. When, in 1919, the German Workers' Party (DAP) was formed, it is probable too that Thule-inspired ideas, as well as members and associates, directly influenced its creation and party membership, including the aforementioned Rosenberg and Hess as well as Dietrich Eckart. As Goodrick-Clarke (1985: 133) maintains: the Germanenorden was 'an important *volkisch* organization which witnessed the birth of the Nationalist Socialist Party'. Indeed, one year later in 1920 the DAP morphed into the Hitler-led National Socialist German Workers' Party (NSADP), and the Thule newspaper, eventually under the aforementioned editorship of Alfred Rosenberg, became the Nazi's main voice of propaganda: the *Völkischer Beobachter* (*The People's Observer*). Although the exact relationship between the Thule and the DAP is 'indeterminate' (Goodrick-Clarke, 1985: 150), the similarities between the ideology, origins, history, membership and symbols of both organisations suggest significant cross-over. As Goodrick-Clarke (1985: 151) attests with regard to their use of symbols: 'It is possible to trace the origin of the Nazi [swastika] symbol back through the emblems of the Germanenorden and ultimately to Guido von List'.

Ariosophy and Hitler

Although Lanz's ONT had less than three hundred 'knights' and the Nazis eventually turned hostile to all occult and secret groups as part of their quest for full totalitarian control, Ariosophic ideas continued to permeate elements of Nazi ideology nonetheless. Special editions of the now Nazi-controlled *Völkischer Beobachter* included the writings of List and Lanz and reported Christmas as 'an entirely pagan event' (Koehne, 2014: 777). In terms of a 'probable' direct link between Hitler and Lanz (Goodrick-Clarke, 1985: 194), Lanz proclaimed that 'Hitler is one of our pupils' (Goodrick-Clarke, 1985: 192). He also stated that Hitler had visited him in 1919 (Katz, 2007: 174). Without naming sources Dave Flitton, the writer and director of the television documentary entitled *The Occult History of the Third Reich* (1991), a documentary co-production by Lamancha (which had at one time been Scotland's largest documentary film company) and one with a reputable series editor (John Erickson, a professor of history who had taught at Oxford and then Edinburgh University, and a Second World War expert), stated that Lanz was visited in 1909 by Hitler who was in search of back copies of the *Ostara* collection.

Nevertheless, following Goodrick-Clarke (1985), we have found no factual evidence anywhere of this encounter between Lanz and Hitler, or any other direct connection. But as Kurlander (2015: 498; see also papers in Black and Kurlander, 2015) argues, 'virtually all Nazi leaders appeared to recognize the widespread popularity of occult practices and "border-scientific" thinking across the German population and within the Nazi Party itself'; and furthermore, 'most Nazi officials worked to differentiate between popular or commercial occultism, which they deemed ideologically "sectarian", and acceptable "scientific" occultism, which was generally tolerated and intermittently sponsored by the regime'. For example, the ONT's *Ostara* publication was circulated widely in Vienna while Hitler resided there, and 'given the ubiquity of occultism in Central Europe during Hitler's childhood and youth, it would have been difficult for him to avoid acquaintance with the occult milieu in some form or other' (Wolffram, 2010: 141). It is worth noting here, for example, that the German Faith Community (founded in 1951 and banned in 2023) and another organisation named the Germanic Community of Faith, were two later esoteric and neopagan organisations that grew following the rise of National Socialism, their beliefs revolving 'around the claim to be the chosen people and a willingness to act and make sacrifices for the "Germanic race" as a "blood and religious community"' (Hoppadietz and Reichenbach, 2019: 218).

There are also some striking ideological similarities between Nazism and Ariosophy, such as Hitler's conception of an Aryan *Herrenvolk* (Aryan master race) that aimed for a pure Germany by introducing the Nuremberg race laws of 1935 and which classified as racially acceptable only those of German blood. In addition, the swastika, used by Theosophy and the ONT and then also adopted as an emblem of the Thule society, was additionally utilised as the official symbol of the NSDAP. This symbol, which had been introduced by List as an actual rune, was especially important for Ariosophists as it appeared in numerous 'different places and cultures', and this was 'taken as proof of the existence of a high Aryan civilisation which had once dominated the whole globe' (Findell, 2012: 257). In addition to magical runic symbols, other supernatural features also permeated Hitler's vocabulary, namely his comparisons of Jews to vampires and monsters (Kurlander, 2012: 538), not to mention the 'Werewolf' allied resistance plan of 1944 with its Wolfsangel rune.

Yet, as stated above, there is no direct evidence of the leader of the Nazi Party attending ONT or Thule events or giving credence to Ariosophy. Hitler was in fact openly critical of Himmler's neo-paganism: 'What nonsense!

Here we have at last reached an age that has left all mysticism behind, and now he wants to start that all over again' (quoted in Steigmann, 2005: 93). Himmler actually had to make a concerted effort to keep his occultic activities 'under wraps', as he was in no doubt that Hitler regarded these ventures with suspicion' (Longerich, 2012: 515). Instead, it seems that Hitler was not interested in occultism *per se* and possibly even looked with disdain upon the Thule's upper-class elitism, preferring to attract working-class and indeed all Germans', support to his cause. When he met the Australian Odinist Alexander Rud Mills, the latter lamented that 'He would not discuss my theme' (quoted in Macklin, 2020: 41). According to Trigger (2006: 46), Hitler quite possibly even 'viewed Nazi officials aggressively seeking to replace Christianity with their own versions of German neo-paganism as another source of unwanted conflict'.

This concern about image and popular support is a theme also touched upon by Piper (2007: 50), who argued that while Hitler did genuinely see Christianity as the enemy and as a threat to a belief in the fatherland, he was not yet in a position to move against the religion. Indeed, some 95 per cent of Germans were still members of either the Roman Catholic or Protestant faiths: they were, it seems, 'too strong for him to risk a final confrontation'. According to Evans (2005: 234), there were at least twenty million Catholics alone residing in Germany at that time, roughly a third of the population. However, Hitler is also on record as saying that 'Once the war is over, that's the end of the Concordat' (quoted in Piper, 2007: 51), and that 'Christianity was ripe for destruction' (quoted in Kershaw, 2001: 40). A forestate of his destructive ambition against Christianity can be seen in the number of leading Catholics killed by Nazism as early as the 1934 Night of the Long Knives (Evans 2005: 237). On that hit list was included the former Reich Chancellor Heinrich Brüning himself, who only fortuitously escaped his fate on account of the fact he was overseas at the time. The fact that such a high standing Christian figure could be openly targeted for death demonstrates unequivocally the level of Nazi anti-Christian animosity.

If Hitler was not sympathetic to Ariosophy and the occult, he was arguably influenced by its more mundane elements rather than its esoteric or otherworldly ones, namely its anti-Semitism, extreme nationalism, symbolism and its belief in Aryan race superiority (Goodrick-Clarke, 1985: 202; Kurlander, 2012: 544). To be sure, Hitler, although not a practising Christian, seemed also to admire the historical Jesus on the basis of a distorted anti-Semitism; that is, the idea that Jesus 'took up his position against Jewry' (Steigmann, 2005: 97). Hitler may also have cultivated *völkisch* nationalism as a political tactic to draw workers away from communism and other political outlets: 'The fact is the god of Hitler was *not* Satan or Wotan…He tolerated and used – the widespread neo-heathenism in

Germany...to his own ends' (Flowers, 1997: 120). Nor was Hitler opposed to using Heathenry sometimes as a useful 'political religion', in particular for its powerful symbolic political uses; as Findell (2013: 251) points out, Ariosophy is 'the ultimate source of the National Socialist *Seig Heil!* greeting', an acclamation which immediately and publicly made one's loyalty to Hitler and the Nazi state apparent. It had, therefore, a useful propaganda and political purpose.

As a result of this dearth of specific evidence pertaining to a Hitlerian support for occultism, Wolffram (2010: 144) argues that 'there is little proof that this fascination with the occult' affected his decisions beyond the practical political. Nonetheless, Hitler did elect to have his body burned, akin to a Viking funeral, after his suicide in the last days of the war. In her discussion of the complicated relationship between Hitler and occultism, Wolffram draws attention to the need for a more nuanced approach to the topic and warns not to assume that Hitler was a believer or even supporter of the movement. As Phelps argued too in relation to Ariosophic tenets, '[i]t is hard to decide the extent of their influence' on Hitler and his Nazi colleagues (1963: 247). What is indisputable, nonetheless, is that elements of Ariosophy with its tales of lost Aryan worlds and secret societies when combined with its extreme anti-Semitism, ultranationalism and Aryanism, were to have a direct and palpable impact on other prominent Nazis in the Führer's circle, and most notably of all, Himmler.

Ariosophy and Himmler

Of all the leading Nazi *apparatchiks* intrigued by racist occultism and Heathenry, it was Heinrich Himmler, the Reichsführer (Commander) of the SS, who was especially fascinated by pan-Aryan racialism and its esoteric context. Not only did he proactively recruit astrologers and mystics to the SS, but he even promoted Karl Maria Wiligut (1866–1946), a self-proclaimed Ariosophic magus, to SS-Brigadeführer (Brigadier). Wiligut, like List, declared himself to be a direct blood descendant of a line of ancient Aryan god kings and went on to become 'the most powerful of the Nazi occultists', taking the pseudonym 'Weisthor' (Katz, 2007: 176). Wiligut was a former highly decorated officer in the Austrian army and had 'frequented... esoteric circles in Vienna before the first World War' (Longerich, 2012: 283). Like Blavatsky, Wiligut believed in seven historical epochs, with his lifetime occupying the fifth one (Longerich, 2012: 284). It was also Wiligut who advised Himmler to create a magical 'SS Vatican' at Wewelsburg Castle in Westphalia in order to study Ariosophy (Goodrick-Clarke, 1985: 188) (Figure 3.3). As a result, a ceremonial centre was established there, its centre

Figure 3.3 Wewelsburg Castle, headquarters of Himmler's SS (Creative Commons CC BY-SA 4.0. Photograph: Carsten Steger).

piece being the aforementioned Black Sun/Sonnenrad symbol on its floor. There were also plans for a planetarium, a dragon-inspired 'hoard of gold and silver' and even a 'Gobelin tapestry' (Longerich, 2012: 295). Wiligut was additionally responsible for designing the infamous silver Totenkopfring (Death's Head/Skull ring), decorated with runes and Nazi pseudo-runes, a personal award given by Himmler to SS officers.

Wewelsburg soon became a base from which Himmler and Wiligut devoted considerable SS resources to investigating the archaeological evidence for Germanic Aryanism through the *Ahnenerbe* (Research Institute of Indo-German Prehistory and Archaeology) which was established on 1 July 1935. It financed expeditions all over the world in search of powerful religious relics intended to 'enhance the power and prestige of the Third Reich' (Kurlander, 2012: 542). Designed to deliberately encourage German pride and a belief in a mythic Aryan past, the 'most ambitious of the Ahnenerbe's expeditions was intended to prove that the site of Tiwanaku, in Bolivia, was an Aryan colony that had come from Atlantis over a million years ago' (Trigger, 2006: 45). The various research branches of the Ahnenerbe also took up other esoteric interests, ranging from a study of dowsing to Cosmic Ice World Theory (a belief that the planets were formed by collisions of huge ice blocks).

At Wewelsburg, Himmler also oversaw 'pagan wedding ceremonies... for SS officers and their brides' (Goodrick-Clarke, 2002: 125), and set out approved holidays based on pagan Germanic festivals, making Yuletide the climax of the year at which SS staff and their families had feasts and bonfires. It was Wiligut's interest in runes which also led the Schutzstaffel to adopt the *Sowilō*, 'S', rune into their emblem. This rune, referencing the sun, was taken from ancient heathen source material but was then 'corrupted by Guido von List' and came to mean 'victory' or *sieg* (Pardy, 2023a: 51). To be sure, the SS itself appears to be a ONT '2.0', as it was also intended as an elite unit of warrior knights utilising Pagan-occult ritual for ceremonies and symbols with its end result the creation of a utopian Nordic race (Longerich, 2012: 139). Himmler, like the earlier Ariosophists, also believed in a lost race provenance and an Atlantis origin story (Longerich, 2012: 281). For Himmler, however, it was from Tibet that Aryan Germans had originally emerged, an idea intersecting with Blavatsky's mythic origins for the teachings of Theosophy. How or why Himmler, a former Roman Catholic, became a supporter of Ariosophy is open to debate. He had been an early member of the post-war Freikorps Oberland (Longerich, 2012: 28), a Bavarian-based paramilitary group which had been founded by none other than von Sebottendorff who had also been President of the aforementioned Thule Society. Himmler was also much influenced by Houston Chamberlain's writings (Longerich, 2012: 59), in particular his anti-Semitism, anti-Catholicism, his calls for a German religion and his belief in Aryan racial superiority. Himmler's growing anti-Catholicism and sympathy for Paganism might have also led to his interest in his 'Special Witch Project', an attempt to catalogue a history of the church's persecution of witches with a view to undermining its moral authority (Longerich, 2012: 225). Longerich, Himmler's biographer, suggests that one reason for Himmler's anti-Christianity, and thus adherence to Ariosophy, was also the church's focus on sexual morality. Himmler might have seen the latter as standing in his way of planning a 'biological revolution' which would rebuild a pure Aryan race (Longerich, 2012: 265).

A further contextual reason for Himmler's interest in Ariosophy was the fact that 'occult phenomena' were all the 'vogue' during the early 1920s (Longerich, 2012: 77), not only in Germany but across Europe and the US. Indeed, a belief in the occult in Germany during the interwar period was not limited only to a few thousand Nazi disciples. Occult ideas had in fact 'several million' followers in Germany who could be found 'permeating every level of society, high and low, rich and poor' (Wolffram, 2009: 193). Whilst this 'occult epidemic' was partly a modern reaction to Enlightenment rationalism, it was also the result of 'civil unrest and political uncertainty' as Germans struggled for direction and meaning in a traumatic, post-First World War environment (Wolffram, 2009: 192–193). Given this context it is not surprising to understand the attractiveness of Ariosophy for a particular cohort of Austrians and Germans frustrated by the purported 'slave treaty' imposed upon Germany by Versailles.

Conclusion

Just as there are many paths within Heathenry today, it is important to note that Ariosophy was not the only branch of Germanic Paganism and occultism to emerge in this *fin-de-siècle* German milieu, with astrology, fortune telling, faith healing and spiritualism all attracting popular interest. What is more, some offshoots of occultism, parapsychology in particular with its promise of real-world applications and growing interest in the efficacies of hypnotism, seemed to also enjoy some initial scientific and official support. Alongside vegetarianism, an interest in organic food production and temperance, these alternative worldviews were seen by many 'as a way of reversing the negative effects of rapid urbanisation and industrialisation on social cohesion and health' (Wolffram, 2010: 143). Just as most Heathens today are not racists but inclusivist, most of these different inter-war esoteric and alternative interests groups did not share the racist, elitist, masculinist and violent inclinations of the Ariosophists. Spiritualism was, for example, frequently envisioned as a *liberal* movement with a propensity for female participation and leadership (Alessio, 2000: 67). Indeed, according to Green (2015: 389), sometimes 'the occult provided religious avenues of social mobility that were otherwise closed by the racial, gendered, and class-based hierarchies of established religions worldwide'.

This diversity of occult opinion with its majority liberal inclinations also helps to explain in part why, after the Nazis came to power, Hitler began to distance himself from the occult. Thus, the '1930s witnessed the introduction of increasingly restrictive legislation against occultists', with the state forcibly dissolving 'occult, theosophical and psychical research groups' (Wolffram, 2009: 219–220). As part of this policy of an anti-occult *Gleichschaltung* it is not surprising to learn that prominent individuals, such as Hans Driesch, 'one of the leaders of German parapsychology', was dismissed from his university position as early as 1933 on account of his pacifism and opposition to racism (Wolffram, 2009: 192, 207). On taking power Hitler might have also wanted to curry favour amongst more conservative elements of the German population who viewed practising occultists as fraudsters or threats to law and order. Indeed, in addition to not wanting to upset the majority Christian population of Germany at this time, Hitler's concern about law and order might have been a factor as to why Himmler was always careful not 'to profess belief in public in Wotan or other Germanic deities' (Longerich, 2012: 266).

Part of this Nazi move against occultists could have been for personal reasons as well as political ones, in particular professional or personal jealousy. When the first wave of persecution occurred, in 1933, Wiligut joined the SS. He had, however, begun promoting his own particular brand of Ariosophy, which he termed 'Irminism' after a supposed German deity. Wiligut then went on to denounce other Ariosophists as false prophets and heretics, all in order to secure his position within the Nazi hierarchy. This Irminist-Ariosophist schism could also help to explain the necessity for a later Nazi decree that was signed by Himmler himself 'outlawing occultism' (Wolffram, 2010: 145). Anti-occult actions in Nazi Germany, then, do not indicate that Nazism was turning hostile to all occult groups, but rather only those that were not towing the SS party line. However, the fact that Wiligut was eventually dismissed by Himmler in 1939 might be viewed as a sign of later Nazi discomfort with Ariosophy. Yet Himmler did not turn his back on his racist Heathen beliefs; rather, he simply retired his former colleague to avoid embarrassment after Wiligut was outed as a former inmate of an institution for the mentally ill.

In the early 1940s these levels of occult persecution increased further in Germany, with the Gestapo arresting and imprisoning, in June 1941, '[l]arge numbers of occultists...as part of a campaign known as "Aktion Hess"' (Wolffram, 2010: 220). This second wave of anti-occultism is likely to have been motivated by a particular political context, namely the deliberate scapegoating of Rudolf Hess, Hitler's Deputy Führer. Hess was an avowed occultist who had flown to Scotland the month before, apparently as a result of a dream and on his own volition (although this is open to dispute), to try to negotiate a separate peace with the British Empire before Germany's invasion of Russia (Wolffram, 2010: 140). Once more it appears that this move against racist Heathenry and occultism was more about saving face than turning face. The historical trajectory of Ariosophy and Nazism in pre-Second World War Germany whilst the Nazis were in power, discussed in this chapter, is important background and context for approaching the origins and unfolding of racist Heathenry in the second half of the twentieth century. In the next chapter, we begin this analysis with an overview of racist Heathenry in an international context, before focussing in detail on the UK.

4

Claims to blood and soil: international racist Heathenry

Introduction

On 10 January 2016, Stephen McNallen, the leader of the Asatru Folk Assembly (AFA), the most prominent racist Heathen organisation in the US, posted the following statement on the AFA's Facebook page: 'Germany – that is the German people, not sellout traitors like Merkel – deserve our full support…Where are the Freikorps when we need them?' (see e.g. The Wild Hunt, 2016a: n.p; Calico, 2020: 34). The *Freikorps* ('Free Corps') were German far-right paramilitaries who morphed into the *Sturmabteilung* (SA), 'Storm Division' and *Schutzstaffel* (SS), 'Protection Squadron', during the rise of the Nazi Party. McNallen was responding to media reports of sexual assaults on thousands of women by 'Arab' and 'north African' immigrants during New Year's Eve celebrations across towns and cities in Germany (Connolly, 2016: n.p.). Following similar reports of assaults in Helsinki, a recently formed group calling themselves the 'Soldiers of Odin' announced they would patrol the streets to protect native Finns from immigrants (Rosendahl, 2016: n.p.) and 'keep our women safe' (Faiola, 2016: n.p.). Groups claiming an affiliation with The Soldiers of Odin have since emerged elsewhere in Europe, including the UK.

We take these two linked recent examples, from the US and Europe, to highlight how a narrative which perceived ancient heathen religion through the lens of eighteenth- and nineteenth-century Germanic romanticism and nationhood, late nineteenth-century concepts of race, cultural evolution and ethnic exceptionalism and early twentieth-century constructs of Aryanism and Ariosophy, combined with far-right political movements, has proven to have such currency; it has endured despite the horrors of the Second World War and well into the twenty-first century. The persistence and transformation of racist Heathenry in the second half of the twentieth century has been critically addressed by Stephanie von Schnurbein (2017) in her book, *Norse Revival: Transformations of Germanic Neopaganism*. Similar trends in the US in particular have been explored by Mattias Gardell (2003) in *Gods of the Blood: Pagan Revival and White Separatism* (2003), with more recent, nuanced attention in Jennifer Snook's (2015) *American Heathens: The Politics of Identity in a Pagan Religious Movement* and Jefferson Calico's (2018) *Being Viking: Heathenism in Contemporary America*.

The purpose of this chapter is not to rehearse the findings of these important studies but to consider racist Heathenry internationally since the second half of the twentieth century as a broader context for this book's specific focus on racist Heathenry in the UK, to which we will turn in Part II. This chapter also offers us the opportunity to consider recent developments in international racist Heathenry in the years since these previous books have been published. Here we focus in particular on how concepts of 'blood and soil' have been transformed internationally and regionally, comparing and contrasting the cases of North America and the UK. This is especially important given that, as we have identified and argued, Heathenry has become more polarised in recent years with racist Heathenry increasingly prominent and emboldened, as the examples of the AFA in the US and Soldiers of Odin in Europe, both demonstrate. A concomitantly more visible anti-racist Heathen contingent developing strategies to campaign against these racist Heathens is the focus for Part III.

An overview of international Heathenry and its discontents

The 1970s and 1980s were key decades for the transformation of Heathenry on the international stage. Building on late nineteenth- and early to mid-twentieth-century interests in occultism and Eastern religions, the counter-culture emerging from the 1960s also sought alternative forms of religiosity outside of the mainstream Abrahamic religions of the book; it looked not only to world religions such as Hinduism and Buddhism, and such indigenous religions as 'shamanism', but increasingly to the pre-Christian pagan/heathen traditions of Northern Europe. This 'upsurge of new religious Paganism' (Asprem, 2008: 47) led to the crystallisation of modern Paganism in subsequent decades even if forms of 'Wicca', 'Druidy' and 'Heathenry' already had their emerging interwoven histories (see Hutton, 1991, 2013). On the other hand, established folkish organisations, such as German Faith and ideologies including Ariosophy, 're-grouped and once again recruited a younger membership' (von Schnurbein, 2017: 54), and found new vigour in areas outside of Europe, especially North America.

Of particular note in this development of post-war racist Heathenry internationally was Alexander Rud Mills (1885–1964), an Australian lawyer, anti-Semite, anti-communist and Nazi sympathiser who was heavily influenced by Guido von List. Mills spent considerable time in the UK where he met Arnold Leese and supported his work, and in turn created 'his own unique blend of ariosophy [sic]' (Asbjørn Jøn, 1999: 77). Mills wrote *The Odinist Religion: Overcoming Jewish Christianity* (1930) and founded in 1936 the 'Anglecyn Church of Odin' which he intended to replace the established Anglican church as the official religion of the empire (Goodrick-Clarke, 2002: 259). Whilst Mill's influence in the UK might have been limited he remains, nevertheless, an 'important' (Asbjørn Jøn, 1999: 77) figure in the history of Odinism as he did have a significant impact on Else Christensen (1913–2005), 'the Grand-Mother of racial paganism' (Gardell, 2003: 165–166). Christensen was a Danish white nationalist inspired by Nazi ideology who believed that Odinism was a spiritual cure for the diseases harming the Aryan race – primarily Christianity, capitalism and communism (Goodrick-Clarke, 2002: 261). She founded the Odinist Fellowship in Florida, an explicitly 'racial-religious' (von Schnurbein, 2017: 58) organisation, in 1969. Her journal, *The Odinist* (founded 1971), promoted white supremacism, conspiratorial history, a perceived warrior ethos of the Vikings, 'tribal socialism' or 'decentralized folkish communalism' (Gardell, 2009: 616), as well as the Jungian idea of the 'racial soul' and the Norse gods as 'archetypes…genetically engraved in the Nordic peoples' (Asprem, 2008: 46). The organisation focussed their efforts on recruiting among vulnerable groups, particularly in prisons (Gardell, 2009: 614).

Around the same time that Christensen's Odinist Fellowship was emerging, a second key figure in US racist Heathenry, the above-mentioned Stephen McNallen (b.1948), founded the Viking Brotherhood, officially registered in 1972. McNallen claimed his own search for Germanic spirituality was not racial-religious in impetus but rather primarily anti-Christian, with 'the perception that the God of the Bible was a tyrant and that his followers were willing slaves, and an admiration for the heroism and vitality of the Norsemen as depicted in popular literature' (quoted in Kaplan, 1997: 18; see also Goodrick-Clarke, 2002: 257; von Schnurbein, 2017: 58). But it did not take long for McNallen to take an increasingly ethnicist (i.e. racist) approach. Internal ructions in the Viking Brotherhood led to McNallen founding the Asatru Free Assembly in 1974, but this organisation fragmented in the late 1980s (von Schnurbein, 2017: 59). While the politics concerning this fragmentation were not solely about race, it was certainly a factor, and it led to the formation in the late 1980s to mid-1990s of the main racist and anti-racist Heathen organisations in the US today, the Asatru Folk Assembly (AFA) and The Troth, respectively.

While McNallen founded the explicitly ethnicist Asatru Folk Assembly, Michael 'Valguard' Murray, a former AFA member and former vice-president of Else Christensen's Odinist Fellowship, as well as a former associate of the American Nazi Party, founded the 'ethnicist' (von Schnurbein, 2017:

128) Asatru Alliance. Separately, and more explicitly seeking 'a white revolution', 'Wotansvolk' was formed around 1995 by David and Katja Lane with Ron McVan, as 'an Aryan call to arms with an esoteric teaching, based in part on Jungian psychology, völkisch philosophy and occult national socialism' (Gardell, 2009: 618). David Lane had been a member of the Klu Klux Klan and Knights of the Klu Klux Klan in the 1970s and in 1981 joined the Aryan Nations, a white supremacist militant group, becoming its State Organiser in Colorado (Hoppadietz and Reichenbach, 2019: 219). Lane was already incarcerated at the time of Wotansvolk's founding, for crimes related to the racially motivated murder of Alan Berg, a Jewish radio host. Lane, amongst other members of the racist terrorist group The Order (or Brüder Schweigen), had murdered Berg in his driveway in 1984. From prison, Lane published the 'Fourteen Word Press' to promote Wotanism and spread his white supremacist beliefs (Goodrick-Clarke, 2002: 269–271). He is also credited for the notorious 'Fourteen Words' or '14W' motto: 'we must secure the existence of our people and a future for white children', which remains a favourite slogan of white supremacists. David Lane died in prison in 2007.

Lane's 'Wotanism' nomenclature functions both as a reference to the Germanic god Wotan and as the acronym W.O.T.A.N., 'Will of the Aryan Nation' (e.g. Azani *et al.*, 2020: 32). Influenced directly by List's Armanism and Lanz's ONT, Wotansvolk believe that Wotanism is the inherited religion of the Aryan people and that their race should abandon globalisation in order to preserve their collective cultural identity and rediscover their lost 'folk consciousness' (Gardell, 2009: 620). Wotanism attributes the current weakness of humanity in particular to Christianity, which is viewed by members as a foreign faith 'diametrically opposed to the natural order'. They also claim that '[c]ompassion between species is against the law of nature', whereas Wotanism is 'a natural religion' which 'preaches war, plunder and sex' (Gardell, 2009: 619). According to Lane, the 'White race cannot share Gods, religion, technology, food, women, territory or anything of value with another race' (SPLC, n.d.c). In 1996, Lane's ideas were exported to Europe and a London-based Wotansvolk group was established, although the organisation dissipated. Nonetheless, Gardell (2009: 625) notes that by the turn of the millennium in the US, 'nearly every prison, both state and federal, has a kindred, and in nearly every case…Odinism or Wotanism, are now officially recognised by the prison authorities'.

By way of a further example in the US, the Aryan Brotherhood (AB) is deserving of some note given its size and violence. Formed in 1964 by incarcerated Irish bikers supposedly for protection from Black inmates during the Civil Rights era desegregation of prisons, their members can be identified primarily by their tattoos, including 'a shamrock inscribed with the number 666, swastikas, the abbreviation A.B., and double lightning bolts, which stand for Hitler's SS' (SPLC, n.d.d). However, it appears that religious or racist convictions are of secondary importance for this group compared to their focus on criminal activity, in particular narcotics trafficking.

Arising from the disagreements over ethnicity and race in the AFA, The Ring of Troth (now, The Troth) was formed in 1987 by AFA members Stephen Flowers, also known as Edred Thorsson, and James Chisholm, the former also founding the Rune-Gild, an initiatory order which went on to inaugurate a European branch (see e.g. Granholm, 2010). Perhaps, unsurprisingly, The Troth has also experienced some controversy, with Flowers and Chisholm criticised for their ongoing involvement with the Temple of Set, an offshoot of Anton LaVey's Church of Satan. Flowers' extensive publication list (as Edred Thorsson) includes such influential titles as *Futhark: A Handbook of Rune Magic* (1984) and *Runelore: A Handbook of Esoteric Runology* (Thorsson, 1987). But he has a persistent interest in Nazism and occultism, with such books (as Stephen Flowers) as *Fire and Ice: Magical Teachings of Germany's Greatest Secret Occult Order* (Flowers, 1990), *Lords of the Left-Hand Path. A History of Spiritual Dissent* (Flowers, 1997) and *The Occult in National Socialism: The Symbolic, Scientific, and Magical Influences on the Third Reich* (Flowers, 2022), which has attracted criticism from inclusivist Heathens. His translation of List's *Secret of the Runes*, for example, has been accused of 'white-washing List's obvious racism and ideas of German superiority' (Khan, 2019: n.p.). It is also notable that since leaving The Troth in the mid-1990s, Flowers continued to maintain a relationship with McNallen, with the latter involved with his Rune-Gild (Granholm, 2010: 98). Indeed, more recently, Flowers signed the rights of some of his books over to McNallen's publishing wing. One blogger opines:

> He talks about Indo-European traditions being blood-quantity locked and compares them to living Indigenous Cultures. Indo-European cultures don't exist anymore and therefore aren't members of oppressed nations or cultures such as Indigenous people from the Americas or the Sami. Norse Paganism is not a closed tradition and *metagenetics* is racist NeoNazi bullshit.
>
> TL;DR Edred Thorsson/Stephen Flowers == Nazi. Anyone can be Heathen regardless of bloodline. (North of Annwn, 2019: n.p.)

Despite historical controversies, The Troth today is the leading inclusivist Heathen organisation in the US with significant influence on Heathenry worldwide. The Troth now maintains an anti-racist alignment made explicit by their mission statement:

> The Troth is *open to all who seek to know and to worship the Gods*, honor the ancestors, and live by values of the Germanic Heathen traditions, regardless

of tradition, race, ethnicity, sexual orientation, ability, gender, or family structure. The Troth stands against any use of Germanic religion or religious symbols to advance causes of racism, sexism, transphobia, homophobia, ableism or white supremacy. (The Troth, 2024c: n.p., original emphasis)

But the Troth remains today more complex and controversial in its treatment of ethnicity and race than this public inclusivity statement might suggest. Siegfried (2021: 48) observes that Diana Paxson, a leading figure in the organisation and editor of its journal, *Idunna*, discusses the history of the racist Heathen Asatru Folk Assembly in her book *Essential Asatru* (Paxson, 2006: 48–52), 'yet makes no mention of racial politics involved or connections to the American Nazi Party'. Her book also addresses the racist Heathen Asatru Alliance as 'essentially conservative and libertarian in attitude, but nonpolitical', 'without', as Siegfried (2021: 48–49) highlights, 'providing further information on the group's by then well-documented extremist connections'. When 'recommending' (Siegfried, 2022: 48) the AFA as a Heathen organisation, she describes this 'religion that belongs to people of European stock' as like 'the traditional tribal religions belong[ing] specifically to Native Americans' (Paxson, 2006: 176). And more recently (Paxson *et al.*, 2015: 28) she has described Heathenry as 'an indigenous as well as an ethnic religion' (cited in Siegfried, 2022: 49). As we have noted (see Chapter 1), appeals to indigeneity and ethnicity from Heathens of white European descent are not without political consequence. As Siegfried (2022: 49) likewise argues, '[b]y asserting Asatru's indigeneity and ethnicity, she repeats a claim central to McNallen's folkish theory'. Paxson is not the only leading member of the 'inclusive' Troth to be caught up problematically in the discourse on Heathenry and ethnicity. Kveldulfr Gundarsson (2020: n.p.) states 'that those folk whose clans do not include any Germanic ancestors, however distant, should be encouraged at least to learn about and appreciate the beauty of their own personal heritage before seeking out a stranger's faith', a view in accord, as Siegfried notes (2022: 49), with the 'folkish trope regularly appearing in AFA materials'. The Troth today, then, 'publicly declares that all who wish to participate in the religion are welcome while maintaining a complicated relationship with their folkish counterparts' (Siegfried, 2022: 51). Ultimately, Sigfried identifies how The Troth's concept of 'inclusivity' seems, problematically, to include racist Heathens.

A European branch of The Troth was established by Freya Aswynn (born Elizabeth Hooijschuur, 1949) in 1993, after a falling out with Edred Thorsson and his UK branch of the Rune-Gild, since headed by Ian Read (von Schnurbein, 2017: 71). Born in Holland, Aswynn has lived mainly in London and been a significant figure in Heathenry, particularly in Britain, with such influential books as *Leaves of Yggdrasil: A Synthesis of Runes,*

Gods, Magic, Feminine Mysteries and Folklore (1990) and recent rune cards with her original artwork *Runes of Yggdrasil* (2016). A controversial figure with associations across the political spectrum of Heathenry, Aswynn has been involved with Flowers' Rune-Gild, was active in the 1980s neofolk scene (she was associated with controversial UK bands such as Death in June and Sol Invictus), and was a friend of Hilmar Örn Hilmarsson, the current chief priest of Iceland's inclusivist Ásatrúarfélagið. Following allegations of 'Islamophobic rhetoric' in 2018, The Troth removed Aswynn, 'a longtime member and elder' from the organisation citing a 'violation of its inclusiveness policies' including 'remarks on social media which belie the spirit of inclusiveness The Troth strives to foster' (The Wild Hunt, 2018: n.p.). Aswynn said she was 'pleased with the board's decision. Freedom of mind' (The Wild Hunt, 2018: n.p.).

Ultimately, wranglings over blood and soil issues are, therefore, enduring issues for Heathens in Europe, just as they are for Heathens in the US. In Sweden, for example, Gregorius (2015: 79) found that 'Heathens rarely have a negative view on immigration and multiculturalism', and that 'there is a positive correlation between the emergence of a multicultural society in Sweden and Heathens' employment of rhetoric regarding the need for tolerance towards alternative faiths' (2015: 80). But in Denmark, Amster (2015: 49) quotes one informant who proposed that whilst Danish people have a 'predisposition for Asatro' and 'some of the collective memory is in the genes', s/he also thought 'that is not racism in my world; that is almost logical'. Another of Amster's informants was more extreme, believing that: 'Asatro was a religion exclusively for Danes, something that he saw as clearly having a genetic foundation in his blood' (Amster, 2015: 50). This particular Heathen held 'extreme views on immigration and the primordial aspects of Asatro' (Amster, 2015: 51), and yet he was 'explicitly opposed to fascism' (Amster, 2015: 51). By contrast, the Nordisk Tingsfæling (NTF) organisation was formed in 2010 with the precise intention of 'practicing religion in an environment free of politics' (Amster, 2015: 43); they:

> want to create rituals that link them to the local landscape, but which do not do so in a fashion that does not support an ethnic agenda or imply the exclusion of others. In this sense, their project is consistent with mainstream Danish values, which embrace freedom of expression and multiculturalism. (Amster, 2015: 59–60)

Amster concludes that politics have 'a tenuous place' in Danish Asatro, and that 'quite diverse views can co-exist in this movement' (Amster, 2015: 53). Indeed, as Amster's informants show, diagonalism enables ongoing contradictory thinking. Issues of blood and soil are, then, complex and diversely understood for Heathens in Europe, as they are elsewhere.

The increasing polarisation between racists and anti-racists in Heathenry that we have identified above, responding to the rise of populist and nationalist politics, is, however, being played out in Paganism more broadly too. The European Congress of Ethnic Religions (ECER), for instance, to which a number of racist Heathens have sought membership, is an organisation of ethnic European pre-Christian/Pagan religions. Their 2023 congress news statement specifically rejects 'modern occult or ariosophic theories/ideologies' (ECER, 2023) and in a 1998 Declaration state that their member organisations, including the Heathen groups Ásatrúarfélagið (Iceland) and Forn Siðr (Denmark), are 'categorically opposed to discrimination, suppression or persecution based on race, colour, social class, religion or national origin' (ECER, 1998). But the ongoing wrestling of an ethnic-oriented organisation with issues of 'race' and 'colour' since its foundation is evidenced by the fact that one of its former members, the Germanische Glaubens-Gemeinschaft (i.e. German Faith), was banned as a hate organisation by Germany's Federal Ministry of the Interior in 2023.

Issues of blood and soil

This overview of the development of Heathenry internationally underscores how race and ethnicity are enduring themes across the spectrum of Heathenry into the present, as well as how a much more polarised racist/anti-racist discourse and positioning has emerged in recent years, even if individuals and individual organisations offer ambivalent messaging. There are important regional and thematic variations, however. Racist Heathenry in Europe has historically largely been defined by 'blood and soil' issues, that is, claims to ethnicity/race in terms of an Aryan and/or Germanic (and in the case of the UK, Anglo-Saxon) ancestry, usually in tandem with nationalist claims to territory. So, for racist Heathens in England, as we discuss in the next chapter, it is one's (perceived) Anglo-Saxon heritage, in other words white English identity, alongside the fact that one was born in an island in which the territory of 'England' was set out around a thousand years ago, which enables an alleged coherent 'blood and soil' connection to Heathen religion, usually conceived as Odinism. Framing this in terms of recent politics, Pardy (2023a: 44) states:

> Paganism is seen by the far-right as the indigenous religion of the Anglo-Saxon British people, reintroduced into Britain by the Germanic tribes perceived by the British far-right as the progenitors of Aryan racial supremacy,

and existing before a time of mass immigration and miscegenation – for which both Christianity and Islam are often blamed.

For anti-racist Heathens in Europe, the 'blood' element of the 'blood and soil' equation, whether presented as ethnicity, race or Germanic heritage, is irrelevant (which is not to say that they do not debate the intersectional issues of racism and immigration). Members of the Moon-Women groups in Berlin studied by Hegner (2015), for example, reconfigure ethnicity within the contemporary cosmopolitan context of this modern city by being 'creative, eclectic and inclusive' (Rountree, 2015b: 15). Rountree usefully identifies that,

> While a strong connection exists between indigeneity, ethnicity, attachment to place and nationalism in many Central and Eastern European Paganisms, in other groups in Central and Eastern Europe and elsewhere the first three of these are less likely to be yoked with nationalism – at least, a politicized form of nationalism. Moreover, even where indigeneity and ethnicity are strongly connected with local nationalism, a form of transnationalism may also be identified involving these groups and individuals. (Rountree, 2015b: 9)

In essence, for Heathens looking beyond 'blood' (ethnicity and race), the issue is how 'to link spirituality with the land in ways that avoid the clichés of nationalist discourse' (Blain, 2002: 206). An attachment to local landscapes can be expressed without recourse to nationalism because inclusive Heathens hold interests in the ancient heathen religions of the place in which they live, and often how this relates directly to the land in terms of history, archaeology, place names, folklore and a 'feeling' one has for the landscape, typically conceived in terms of animacy and relationship (e.g. Blain and Wallis, 2007). In this sense, anyone living in, for example the landscape known as England, has a legitimate reason to want to engage with Heathenry today. This sort of approach to land does without concepts of race and ethnicity in favour of a felt connection, attunement and celebration of local landscapes to which any person may be called whatever their biological past. What is more, the vast length of time between ancient 'indigenous' (variously conceived) heathen past(s) and the Heathen present, must certainly elide an ethnicist/racist myopia concerning 'indigenous' people in England, when those ancient ones can in any case be accommodated under the concept of 'ancestors' or 'predecessors' without recourse to the pernicious concepts of ethnicity and race.

In the case of Heathens in North America, however, living outside of the original European homeland of ancient Heathenry, blood and soil present different issues and challenges. With respect to the issue of land, it is not straightforward to claim a connection to a landscape which already has Indigenous peoples and 'pagan' religions in it, especially when American Indians have been subject to five centuries of disenfranchisement at the hands of white European peoples' settler-colonialism, and over which time many generations of people of African descent have also made their lives, including a rich tapestry of polytheist religions, among them Voodoo, despite an ongoing history of oppression. Typically, both racist and anti-racist Heathens voice a respect for American Indian and other animist and polytheist religions, whether framed as fellow 'indigenes' and 'polytheists' or similarly 'ethnically' closed to others. Of course, people of European descent living in North America can and do make respectful connections with their landscape, but those doing so by drawing upon American Indian traditions attract criticism for being 'white shamans' and 'plastic medicine men' (Wallis, 2003). It is one thing to make rightful claims to Indigeneity when one continues to fight for sovereignty for one's own people after centuries of colonial-disenfranchisement, but quite another to claim equivalent indigeneity when one is a privileged white person of European descent. American Heathens, as Snook (2015: 171) puts it:

> reconstruct their traditions in a historical and cultural context that has been, and still is, quite heavily influenced by the legacy of racial discrimination. These racial meanings and the privilege of whiteness are inescapable; they infect the ongoing construction of Heathen ethnicity and make for contentious identity politics and intragroup struggles.

Practitioners taking an inclusive approach, then, face,

> a daunting task: the reinvention of Germanic (i.e. white) ethnic and spiritual identities, as a subset of the larger category of whiteness, that would be clearly distinguished, if not totally divorced from, the legacy of white supremacy in a country in which racial politics and exclusion are woven into the culture's political and economic foundation. (Snook, 2015: 144)

Those Heathens attempting to make respectful connections with the land in North America via Heathen religion must do so with results which are different from Heathens in Europe because, quite simply, the land is different and 'speaks' in different ways. The principal way in which inclusivist Heathens have succeeded in doing so in the US is by celebrating an interest in the ancient heathen past, and respect for the place in which they live while welcoming all people that share that interest irrespective of ancestry, ethnicity or race. But arguably, the colonial legacy in North America does mean that a recourse to an ethnic European heritage of heathenry over a felt connection to the land can be attractive, for example so as to avoid charges of neocolonialism, and hence a demonstrable European ancestry is the key factor for authentication among racist Heathens.

Metagenetics

Addressing this very issue, McNallen himself actually aimed to sidestep the loaded terms of 'race' and 'whiteness' (Kaplan, 1997: 80–84), and proposed a theory of 'metagenetics' in his earlier writing (McNallen, 2006; originating in an article of 1980, as discussed by Waggoner, 2020: 50). This is the idea that not only physical characteristics but also culture and religion are encoded in the DNA of a group of people over time, to result in 'a specific group of people sharing a common descent…bound by blood to a particular set of Gods and Goddesses' (McNallen, 2006: 2). In part, this theory draws on the concept of metagenetics proposed by the Swiss psychiatrist and psychoanalyst Carl Jung (1875–1961). Jung's early works on metagenetics and cultural transmission, as well as his 1936 essay 'Wotan', have often been used subsequently to support racialism (e.g. McNallen, 2006). For McNallen, deities are mental attributes shaping the consciousness of an individual and their cultural group, the 'cultural soul' (Goodrick-Clarke, 2002: 260). McNallen's metagenetics also derives from nineteenth-century German romanticism and early twentieth-century Ariosophy in identifying ancient 'Aryan' or heathen religion as one of which modern 'Germanic' peoples are the true inheritors. Genetics are consequently seen as the means of transmission for religious and ethnic identity; so descendants of the Germanic/Norse heathens are presumed to have a blood essence of Aryan spirituality in them; *ergo*, in order to preserve this transmission of cultural soul, genetic purity must be maintained (Kaplan, 1996: 81). The idea also appropriates from Indigenous ethnic identity thinking, including the American Indian Movement (Calico, 2020: 29). Combining this spiritual and genetic approach, as McNallen puts it himself, Heathenry is 'an expression of the soul of our [Nordic] race' (Kaplan, 1997: 83).

McNallen's approach to metagenetics is highly problematic in several respects. First, his belief that people and deities are 'bound by blood' does not sidestep the issue of race and whiteness but reifies them. McNallen may not see himself as a racist (Gardell, 2003: 271; Calico, 2018: 189–190) because he does not promote racial superiority, but he does hold to a concept of race and does believe in racial separatism and protectionism (whether 'Norse', Native American or Tibetan). Metagenetics is also problematic for insisting on a cultural essentialism, neglecting the historical dynamism of cultures, cultural change and exchange over time, as well as the ethnic complexity of many white Europeans and Americans (Calico, 2018: 188). Indeed, research suggests that modern Icelanders, for instance, share more or equal amounts of Celtic genes than they do Scandinavian ones (Minority Rights Group International, 2007: n.p.). Despite McNallen's insistence on the boundedness of 'Germanic' culture, it is an archaeological fact that peoples of Viking age northern Europe engaged with diverse cultures resulting in cultural hybridisation and genetic intermixing (e.g. Price, 2020: 24). While it is framed in terms of culture and genetics and was originally an attempt to move folkish Heathenry beyond issues of race (for nuanced analysis see Calico, 2018: 181–189), McNallen's thinking ultimately boils down to a theory of religious inheritance based on race and whiteness, and these are terms which he has since used openly on YouTube and other fora. As Gardell put it, the liberal wing of Heathenry viewed McNallen as a racist, while racist Heathens thought he was not racist enough (Gardell, 2003: 280).

'Roots in the soil'

While the 'blood' in 'blood and soil' has had particular saliency in racist Heathenry in North America, 'soil' can also be an important part of their racist narrative. The AFA has used the terms 'native' and 'indigenous' by 'claiming similar protections afforded indigenous nations under the Native American Graves Protection and Repatriation Act (1990) as well as by asserting the '"organic" nature of the faith in the Americas' (Saunders, 2012: 799). The AFA points to the evidence of the (short-lived) Viking settlement at L'Anse aux Meadows in Newfoundland, Canada, dating to around a millennium ago, and the account of Leif Erikson, 'the founder of Vinland' (Saunders, 2012: 799), in the Saga of Erik the Red, as an authentic 'Odinic' and ancestral claim to North American soil. The AFA also made a controversial claim over 'Kennewick Man' in the US (e.g. Wallis, 2003: 190). When prehistoric human remains were discovered in 1996 on the banks of the Columbia River in Kennewick, Washington, and dated to around 7000 BCE, they were initially interpreted by physical anthropologists as having more 'Caucasian' than 'Mongoloid' features. While local American Indian tribes argued that the remains should be reburied in accordance with the 1990 Native American Graves Protection and Repatriation Act, McNallen claimed the remains indicated the first known European in the US and that they should be able to decide how the remains should be treated. Rituals with the remains of Kennewick Man were facilitated for both interest groups. Only in 2015 was Kennewick Man proven by DNA testing to be of Palaeo-Indian origin, and in 2017 duly returned to the local American Indian communities for reburial. The AFA's 'Odinic' claim to the soil, in a neocolonial approach to the land of North America itself, is part of a bigger picture of contemporary far-right politics in the US.

McNallen has drawn upon the colonial history of North America and western expansionism to proclaim, 'we must sink down roots in the soil, and insist on our right to be here…Our forebears fought and died to carve out this place in the world, and we will not give it up' (McNallen, 1998: n.p.). As Calico (2020: 32) puts it, '[h]ere, völkisch themes flow into the iconic narrative of the Wild West to stage a new American völkisch performance… To sink down roots is literally to become indigenous, an American völkisch reversal of ethnogenesis that expands the geographical space of American whiteness'. This neocolonial approach to the land of North America and claim to indigeneity can be contextualised within wider far-right politics and how being born white in the US makes one not only 'indigenous' but also obliged, as a neo-tribe, to fight for that land against other 'races', in particular against 'the Great Replacement' (see also Snook, 2015: 149–150), especially as conceived in terms of Hispanic immigration. McNallen's (1998: 6) essay entitled 'Wotan v. Tezcatlipoca: The Spiritual War for California and the Southwest', concludes that:

> The spiritual descendants of the Aztecs are looking northward, coveting land which, they have convinced themselves, should be theirs – and, perhaps quite unconsciously, they are moving to concrete by mass immigration, by language, by cultural influence. A dangerous few want to conquer by force of arms. But then, they haven't reckoned with Odin and Thor, and Frey and Freya, or the other mighty powers of Asgard and Vanaheim! Nor have they figured, in their calculus of conflict, on the spiritual will of those who follow them.

For McNallen, this is, as Calico (2020: 32) puts it, 'a supernatural race war for cultural supremacy'. But the double paradox of US racist Heathens' assertions to indigeneity is, that their claim 'decouples the concept of land and indigeneity altogether, emphasising instead a biological and "metagenetic" determination of belonging (i.e., racial)'; and yet, simultaneously, 'this heathen approach to ethnicity is precisely a claim to the land elsewhere in an effort to be indigenous *here*, in the United States' (Snook *et al.*, 2017: 58). The AFA's claims to US soil recently bore fruit with the purchase in the years since 2020 of several disused churches which have been converted into Heathen 'hofs' (temple) to provide for their 'whites only' AFA groups, including in: Murdoch, Minnesota; Brownsville, California; Linden, North Carolina; and Jackson, Tennessee (Davy, 2023: 34) (Figure 4.1).

Figure 4.1 Baldrshof, the third temple of the AFA in a former church, Murdock, Minnesota (Myotus – Own work, CC BY-SA 4.0).

Conclusion

McNallen's incendiary statement in the US and the 'Odinist' vigilantism in Europe, with which we opened this chapter, were met with widespread criticism, including from inclusive Heathens. The 'Soldiers of Odin' had limited international prominence and as is typical with membership of far-right vigilante groups, 'members have transferred to other far-right groups with more local preoccupations' (Archambault and Veilleux-Lepage, 2019: 272; see also Reid Ross and Burley, 2016). By contrast, as one of the largest and longest running racist Heathen organisations in the world, the AFA became energised by the media coverage despite the ensuing controversy. McNallen refused to apologise and later stated that he 'stands with Germany' (The Wild Hunt, 2016a: n.p.), a position which is arguably among several factors leading to his 'retirement' as AFA leader (announced 1 May 2016) after forty-five years as one of the most prominent voices in US Heathenry. Since standing down as leader, McNallen has been more involved in white nationalist politics, with his 'Wotan Network' using social media channels to expand his audience and to 'overtly pursue a politically oriented white nationalist agenda' (Calico, 2020: 34). In a YouTube video in March 2017, McNallen stated his 'allegiance to the white race and racially oriented politics, as well as his identification with the 14 words, confirming what many progressive Heathens had suspected all along' (Calico, 2018: 211). On social media a few months later, he expressed his support for the Unite the Right march in Charlottesville, stating 'where there is light, there is hope...#wotannetwork' (Smith and Burley, 2017: n.p.). The following day, Unite the Right protestor James Alex Fields drove his car into counter-protestor Heather Heyer, killing her, and nineteen other people were injured (see Preface).

McNallen was succeeded as Alsherjargothi (leader) by Matthew Flavel and Patricia Hall. As Calico (2018: 210) states: '[t]he new leadership faced two alternatives: either open and liberalise, moving away from the stances of the past; or double down on a hard-line folkish position, adopting an increasingly entrenched stance against progressive Heathenry. The new leadership chose the latter'. Flavel stated on the organisation's Facebook page:

> Today we are bombarded with confusion and messages contrary to the values of our ancestors and our folk. The AFA would like to make it clear that we believe gender is not a social construct, it is a beautiful gift from the holy powers and from our ancestors. The AFA celebrates our feminine ladies, our masculine gentlemen and, above all, our beautiful white children. The children of the folk are our shining future and the legacy of all those men and women of our people back to the beginning. (quote in: *The Wild Hunt*, 2016b: n.p.)

The increasingly explicit and public white supremacist and homophobic agenda of the AFA caused an outcry among inclusive Heathens. One Facebook user replied to Flavel, 'Am I misunderstanding the message here or does this mean that if someone wasn't white or if they were queer they wouldn't be welcome in the AFA?' Flavel responded, 'You are not misunderstanding' (quote in The Wild Hunt, 2016b: n.p.). In 2018, the Southern Poverty Law Center designated the AFA a 'Neo-völkisch hate organisation' (SPLC, n.d.e). Since 2020, the second point of the AFA's Declaration of Purpose, 'The preservation of the Ethnic European Folk and their continued evolution', reads:

> If the Ethnic European Folk cease to exist Asatru would likewise no longer exist. Let us be clear: by Ethnic European Folk we mean white people. It is our collective will that we not only survive, but thrive, and continue our evolution in the direction of the Infinite. (AFA, 2024)

As the AFA has developed into the 2020s, its racist Heathen agenda has crystallised, and it is now expanding into the teaching of children. The

Asatru Academy homeschool curriculum was launched in September 2022, beginning with kindergarten/primary-age children (SPLC, n.d.e). We return to the implications of an increasingly emboldened and explicitly racist, political and nationalist AFA in Part III, when considering the development of anti-racist Heathen activism in the late 2010s and early 2020s. Before doing so, and having given a sense in Part I of this study of the historical and international context for racist Heathenry, now in Part II we move on to focus upon the intersections of racism and Heathenry in the UK, historically and to the present.

Part II

Racist Heathenry and occultism in the UK

Soþ hit sylf acyþeð
Durham Proverbs 21 (Arngart, 1981)

Truth will make itself known
trans. Evans, 1986: 65

5

British spiritual Aryanism: intersections of racism, Heathenry and occultism

Introduction

Although there has been considerable research on racist Heathenry in North America, the situation in the UK is less well known. The two latest monographs on Heathenry, Snook's (2015) *American Heathens: The Politics of Identity in a Pagan Religious Movement*, and Calico's (2018) *Being Viking: Heathenism in Contemporary America*, focus almost entirely on the US, as their titles indicate. Yet, 'a close examination of neo-Nazi literature in Britain makes it quite clear that Paganism is being pressed to the cause of Spiritual Aryanism' in these islands as well (Gallagher, 1999: 25; see also Gallagher, 2009). What is more, the UK appears to be an important and long-standing epicentre of racist Heathenry, both in the past and into the present, and in forms which are manifestly very different from those elsewhere such as in North America. Indeed, one of the reasons why the preceding chapter on international racist Heathenry was necessary and important was partly in order to demonstrate how British radical-right Heathenry was both influenced by, and influencing, events elsewhere, particularly in North America.

The impact of the Odinic Rite on the QAnon Shaman (mentioned above), or the infiltration by the O9A of the Atomwaffen Division (AWD), a neo-Nazi terrorist organisation linked to a swathe of attacks and murders across the US (to be discussed below), are but two examples. Alexander Rud Mills' influence on Else Christensen, as mentioned in the last chapter, is another case in point; although Australian, Mills spent considerable time in the UK where he was influenced by Arnold Leese (1878–1956), a pivotal figure in the history of racist Heathenry in the UK during the inter-war and early post-war period. Arnold Leese in turn later became, 'celebrated by American neo-Nazi cultures' (Jackson, 2022: 23). One of Leese's staunchest disciples, Colin Jordan (1923–2009), would also have 'a significant impact' and emerge at 'the centre of the establishment of the World Union of National Socialists, a global neo-Nazi network that was run by both Jordan and his friend, George Lincoln Rockwell, the leader of the American Nazi Party' (Jackson, 2018: 107). Inspired by racist Heathenry and Ariosophy in particular, Jordan too believed that Christianity was a 'faith created by Jews' that 'threatened racial revival' (Jackson, 2018: 132, 191). This chapter, therefore, intends in the spirit of the Durham Proverbs, with which we have opened Part II of this book, to 'make known' the early history of Aryan, blood and soil, fascist, anti-Semitic and racist Heathen themes in the UK, and to demonstrate how these ideas were kept alive, and by whom, during the interwar and early post-war periods. Although these organisations and figures remained entirely fringe, they laid the foundation for a third generation of racist Heathen offshoots. It is this latest third iteration which is the focus of Part II of this book.

The interwar period

Even before the advent of the Nazi Party, British racists had advocated for the Aryan greatness of the Germanic race and its distinctive ties to the islands of Britain. Such 'blood and soil' themes also frequently, but not always, appropriate Norse mythology and other elements of ancient Heathen religions into their political ideologies; they tend to be concepts suggesting in particular 'indivisible, historical bonds between a race and their nation – or a people and their countryside – and the legitimacy of spilling blood on behalf of territory, the state and aggressive territorial claims' (Pepper, 1996: 229). The Asatru Folk Assembly and Wotansvolk in the US, for example, are two such organisations that have received substantial scholarly attention for expressing blood-and-soil ideologies (e.g. Gardell, 2003; von Schnurbein, 2015; Snook, 2015). These ideas have a long history, however. The British-born philosopher Houston Stewart Chamberlain (1855–1927) was one of the most prominent and influential of these early believers. Fascinated by Hinduism and an outspoken anti-Semite, Chamberlain argued that Teutonic peoples were descended from Aryans. His best-selling history book, *The Foundations of the Nineteenth Century* (1899) influenced Hitler directly, with Chamberlain becoming both mentor and friend to the future German leader. Publications such as this, as well as others by the likes of Arnold White (a well-connected but anti-Semitic journalist advocating the restriction of Jewish immigration from Russia and promoting instead the idea of a Jewish colony in Argentina) and Anthony Ludovici (a philosopher and eugenicist as well as a former member of the intelligence services who critiqued egalitarianism and racial mixing), suggest 'that Britain played her part in laying the foundations for inter-war racist and fascist thinking' (Pugh, 2006: 13). Many of these individuals, who were also of a conservative and aristocratic disposition, were particularly anti-Semitic as they associated Judaism with a fear of a Bolshevik take-over. The foundation of a Communist Party in Great Britain in 1920 only added fuel to this anti-Semitic fire.

Other early instances of such far-right thought in the UK were apparent too just after Mussolini came to power in Italy, including the anti-immigrant and anti-Semitic organisation 'The Britons'. The latter was formed in 1919 and was founded by Henry Hamilton Beamish (1873–1948), a well-connected 'scion of a distinguished family' who, contrary to many of his countrymen in the post-First World War period, placed ethnicity above nationhood and favoured co-operation amongst Aryan peoples (Macklin, 2020: 28). Membership of The Britons 'was restricted to those who could prove that their parents and grandparents were of British blood' (Pugh, 2006: 28). Beamish's Aryanism and anti-Semitism resulted in a visit to Germany in 1923 during which time he was invited to address the newly formed Nazi Party. He also developed a strong acquaintance with Dietrich Eckart, a leading figure in the Thule Society (Macklin, 2020: 28). Furthermore, Beamish advocated that Jews should be deported to Madagascar. Although The Britons had ceased to exist by 1925 and Beamish was forced to reside outside of the UK during the inter-war years to avoid a court fine for slander, the publishing arm of his organisation continued to operate until the early 1930s. In fact, The Britons Publishing Society kept the *The Protocols of the Elders of Zion* (1903), an infamous anti-Semitic forged text purporting to outline a Jewish plan for world domination, in circulation. According to Pugh (2006: 29), it 'created the seedbed from which many of the British fascist organisations sprang', Arnold Spencer Leese's the Imperial Fascist League, to be discussed shortly, being one of them.

The creation of The Britons was followed in 1923 by the appearance, just after Mussolini's March on Rome, of the first UK fascist political party, the British Fascisti (BF). Named in emulation of their Italian counterparts, this heavily aristocratic, conservative and anti-communist party changed its name to the 'British Fascists' the next year in 1924 to avoid being seen as too much under the influence of their Italian counterparts. Its most infamous member was William Joyce (1906–1946), also known by the nickname Lord Haw-Haw, who went on to broadcast Nazi propaganda to the UK for most of the Second World War. The party was founded initially by a woman, Rotha Lintorn-Orman (1895–1935), who drove ambulances in the First World War and who had worked for the Red Cross. The movement gained attention following Mussolini's arrival onto the political scene and attracted considerable 'admiring attention', both for its anti-Communism and its aggressive moves to prevent a perceived national decline, in 'leading Conservative journals, including the *English Review*, the *National Review*, the *Saturday Review* and *The Patriot*' (Pugh, 2006: 38). Following the largely unsuccessful 1926 strike it declined in relevance but 'its impact was lasting' as many of its former members joined other later far-right groups (Jackson, 2022: 18).

One of a number of these other British-based far-right organisations with prominent blood-and-soil themes which emerged in the inter-war period was English Mistery. Founded in 1930 by William Sanderson (1883–1941), the aim of the group was 'to regenerate the English nation' by restoring the monarchy, ruling through the aristocracy, reviving the countryside and developing a 'homogenous' British race that was devoid of the supposed taint of alien and Jewish blood (Stone, 2003: 339–346). Comprised of a cohort of influential and well-connected members, including the overt 'Nazi sympathiser' (Pepper, 1996: 228) Lord Lymington (1898–1984), the Conservative member of Parliament for Basingstoke from 1929 to 1934 who would in 1936 lead a break-away group called the 'Array', some of its members were at times willing to work with other British fascists. Both English Mistery and the Array, however, disappeared by the start of the Second World War. Whilst not explicitly Heathen, both of these movements were racist, ultranationalist and advocated a traditionalist return to the land. Although neither English Mistery nor the Array became big political players on the far-right scene, they are mentioned here as a number of their members 'had links, both personal and ideological, with much wider strands of thought in interwar Britain, from the ecological and rural revivalist to the National Socialist' (Stone, 2003: 337). Indeed, one member of both groups was Rolf Gardiner (1902–1971), an advocate of Morris dancing and organic farming who in 1945 became a founding member of the Soil Association. A racialist concerned about the decline of English stock, Gardiner has been described as a 'pro-German ecologist, supporter of Nazi rural policies and of paganism' (Pepper, 1996: 227). Gardiner also contributed pieces for *New Pioneer*, the Array's journal, which was financially supported by the aforementioned Lymington and carried 'anti-Semitic propaganda' (Pugh, 2006: 280). Another contributor to *New Pioneer* was the influential British journalist and writer A. K. Chesterton (1899–1973). Although Macklin (2020: 189) states that Chesterton 'did not plunge headlong into "magic and mysticism"' like some other influential far-right racists of the period, he certainly skated close to thin ice; not only was he anti-Semitic, anti-immigrant and anti-race mixing, but he also expressed 'an unshakeable belief in the racial predestination of the British' (Macklin 2020: 207).

Arnold Leese

Many of the above-mentioned groups and individuals, despite sharing anti-Semitism, concepts of 'blood and soil', ultranationalistic racism, anti-Communism, Pagan sympathies or beliefs and a rejection of democracy, do not appear to have had much of a direct impact on the current far-right scene. Indirectly, however, they kept many of these flames alive, helping to acculturate and influence later racist Heathens. They are also significant because they demonstrate a unique strain of fascism in the UK. As Pugh (2006: 72–73) states regarding English Mistery: 'it sought to recapture the original spirit of the British race'. However, one organisation, the Imperial Fascist League (IFL), which was set up in 1929 by the virulent anti-Semite Arnold Leese (1878–1956), is certainly deserving of further comment vis-a-vis racist Heathenry. This movement, whose motto was 'Keep Troth' (Fascism is a Renovated State of Mind, n.d.), was especially significant with regard to its later ability to socialise post-war generations with these ideologies. At its height in 1941 the League's membership probably numbered around one thousand followers (Macklin, 2020: 29), although the League itself claimed over double that membership (Pugh, 2006: 71).

Leese, who in his autobiography describes his ancestors as 'tall, fair, blue-eyed, with heads broader than the typical Nordic average…good intelligence with a strong sporting trend' (Leese, 1951?: 1), was a veterinarian by training who had lived in India for six years whilst employed by the Indian Civil Service. He was an early member of the aforementioned BF and became one of the first democratically elected fascist councillors in Britain. Nevertheless, he left the BF partly on account of the fact it was not anti-Semitic enough since it welcomed into its fold Jewish members. Consequently, in 1926, he and a handful of other defectors from the BF formed a new, albeit short-lived, splinter party: the British National Fascists (BNF). Their members, inspired by events in Italy, wore black shirts, celebrated militarism and praised fascism as 'a religion' (Macklin, 2020: 26). Leese's admiration for Mussolini was gradually supplanted, however, by that for Hitler, whom Leese saw as more genuinely committed to the cause of anti-Semitism. After the BNF disintegrated and following his retirement from veterinary work, Leese moved to the town Guildford in Surrey, where he formed the aforementioned Imperial Fascist League; he instructed his followers at this time to wear the swastika (Macklin, 2020: 30) and the flag of the organisation incorporated this at the centre of the Union Jack (Figure 5.1). Followers also wore a blackshirt uniform, black boots and adopted the Roman salute (Pugh, 2006: 70). Leese's detestation of the Jews was so strong that he advocated, years before the Nazis implemented their own 'Final Solution', 'their extermination using a "lethal chamber"' (Macklin, 2020: 23). According to Pugh (2006: 215) Leese was the first to do so; nevertheless, as we have seen above (Chapter 3), the Ariosophists had beaten him to that dubious distinction, with Lanz calling for their incineration. Leese also went on to

Figure 5.1 Flag of the Imperial Fascist League (Public domain).

develop a relationship with Julius Streicher in Germany, editor of the Nazi mouthpiece *Der Stürmer*.

Despite his arrest as a possible German sympathiser in 1940, during the post-war period Leese continued to espouse extreme-right ideas. In a pamphlet 'Our Jewish Aristocracy: A Revelation' (1949), Leese listed all the members of the British aristocracy who had married Jews or who had Jewish blood. To all intents and purposes, this was an early version of the 'Great Replacement Theory', a white nationalist conspiracy theory later popularised by the French author Renaud Camus in his 2010 work *Le Grand Remplacement*. Whilst Camus's modern work suggested that European culture and civilisation were being replaced by Islamic immigration, for Leese it was a Jewish elite who were behind a movement to take over the nation; as a consequence, he subsequently warned Britons 'that their race is being displaced and replaced' (Leese, 1949: 3). Whilst Camus suggested that a major influence on his writing was Enoch Powell's infamous 1968 'rivers of blood' speech, Leese's use of the specific term 'replaced' suggests that such ideas were already in public circulation in the UK at least a decade earlier.

Leese was additionally on close terms with John Hooper Harvey, a member of the IFL who in 1933 had founded the Nordics, 'a small völkisch sect… of racial nationalists' (Macklin, 2020: 37–38), who were inspired partly also by home-grown variants of British Aryanism. The latter was directly influenced by the writings of Lieutenant-Colonel Lawrence Augustine Waddell, who later became Professor of Tibetan at University College, London. Waddell's readings of various sources, including the *Eddas*, appear very similar to those of the early Ariosophists; however, Waddell argued that it was in Britain where the descendants of the truest Aryans, meaning

Indo-European Sumerians, could be found (Macklin, 2020: 38). According to Pardy (2023a: 12), Waddell argued that '"Aryan" blood was in fact concentrated in Britain'. Not content with just describing his own personal ancestors as intellectually and athletically superior, Leese additionally went on to praise all Nordics as 'practical...far-sighted...energetic...adventurous [and] brave', as well as rational, science-led and law-abiding (Leese, 1947: 6). Thus, a unique native strain of British racist Aryanism seems to have co-existed alongside its Austrian-born Germanic parent. Notions of a home-grown British variant of Aryanism were not, however, unique solely to Leese or Waddell. Intriguingly, William Sanderson was equally at pains to demonstrate that English Mistery's blood and soil dogma was no foreign ideology (Stone, 2003: 347), but rather a British-based variant.

It was not only Leese's belief in the racial superiority of Aryans that mirrored Ariosophy. He was also virulently anti-Semitic, believing that Jews had infiltrated everywhere and that a Semitic Christianity which preached racial equality required Nordic peoples to re-populate and rebuild Aryan civilisation (Leese, 1947: 7). The anti-Semitic tone of his thinking can be seen vividly in the official anthem of the IFL:

Men of the Nordic strain,
Take up your load again,
Leading the grand campaign,
For troth world-wide.

Heed not the subtle lie,
Cant of equality,
Let instinct pass it by,
In rightful pride.
Judah! Thy course is run!

'St. George our Guide', *c.* 1930s; lyrics by Leese for music by Henry Hedges

Another important influence on Leese's growing interest in 'racialised paganism' (Macklin, 2020: 41), was the aforementioned Alexander Rud Mills' 'Anglecyn Church of Odin', which adopted 'racial mysticism fused with Rosicrucian, Masonic, and conspiracy-theorist elements' (Asprem, 2008: 45). It was openly anti-Semitic and anti-Christian and intended to replace the established Anglican church as the official religion of the empire (Goodrick-Clarke, 2002: 259). Mills too gave credence to the Ariosophic notion that there once had been an advanced Nordic civilisation brought down as a result of miscegenation (Asbjørn Jøn, 1999: 77). The 'pagan' elements of his religion were, therefore, cleverly imposed upon a Christian template, with the main aim being a 'political racialist programme' (Asprem, 2008: 45).

Although Mills also had little immediate impact in the UK beyond Leese, his writings did eventually go on to influence directly the aforementioned Christensen's US-based Odinist Fellowship (Goodrick-Clarke, 2002: 259). Thus, racist Heathenry in the UK can be seen as having helped to kick-start phase two of modern radical right Heathenry in the US. But it was not only Mills, however, who was to keep the beacon of racial Heathen Aryanism alive in the UK. As demonstrated, both Waddell and Leese had their own British variants of Pagan Aryanism too, and both in turn were to influence a second-generation British Pagan and a major player in the British fascist scene: Colin Jordan (1923–2009) (Macklin, 2020: 42). Indeed, Leese's post-war publication of a series of anti-Jewish pamphlets under the title *Gothic Ripples* – with Gothic, according to a particular reading of Lieutenant-Colonel Lawrence Augustine Waddell, being synonymous with Aryanism (Macklin, 2020: 54) – became a wellspring for future Holocaust deniers.

Consequently, although many of these early to mid-twentieth-century figures and ideologies appear to have been extremely marginal in the history of the far right within the UK, some were to have 'an outsized influence upon post-war generations' (Macklin, 2020: 1). According to Jackson (2022: 23), 'Leese's importance lies in his influence, as he rather than Mosley inspired a new generation of neo-Nazi activities'. Stone (2003: 337) makes a similar conclusion regarding blood-and-soil rural movements generally in inter-war Britain, such as English Mistery:

> [P]eripheral movements are not always as irrelevant as they seem; even if it was never remotely likely to storm the bastions of Westminster…Its interest lies not in whether it presented a challenge to the established political authorities – it did not – but in the fact that it had links, both personal and ideological, with much wider strands of thought in interwar Britain, from the ecological and rural revivalist to the National Socialist and all the movements, interest groups, and political groupings on the intervening spectrum. Most important, the English Mistery proves that a movement that is recognizably fascist could develop in Britain, thus scotching the comforting myth that fascism was foreign to the British political tradition.

Britain's most infamous early far-right party was undoubtedly the British Union of Fascists (BUF). Founded in 1932 by Oswald Mosley (1896–1980), a former Labour Party minister, with the initial support of *The Daily Mail* newspaper, the party was an amalgam of pre-existing far-right groups, including the former British Fascists. However, it is perceived as having 'largely lacked the obsessive anti-Semitism' found in the other aforementioned British variants, at least in the early years (Pugh, 2006: 131). It also turned to Italy, rather than Nazi Germany, for its inspiration. At its height, BUF membership may have reached a figure of some fifty thousand (Jackson, 2022: 28), which suggests that it was a UK extreme-right variant that was moving beyond the fringe. Despite Mosley's apparent lack of interest in 'blood-and-soil' themes, the BUF was not entirely immune to racist Heathen ideas or symbols, with Mosley adopting the *Sowilō* pseudo-rune (flash and circle), as well as the actual *Sowilō* (S) rune in imagery for the party. According to Pugh (2006: 219–220), Mosley's later turn to a more anti-Semitic position was not religiously inspired either; rather, it was motivated primarily for 'opportunistic' rather than spiritual reasons, and was aimed primarily at stopping the late 'decline of the movement'. What is more, with the outbreak of war, Mosley, alongside around 1,500 other British fascists, was imprisoned, and by 1940 the BUF had collapsed. It seems that the social, economic and political conditions in Britain, unlike those in Italy or Germany, were not conducive for the BUF's success (Macklin, 2020: 96). Consequently, despite his anti-Semitism, Mosley was not enough of an extreme racial nationalist, and for this reason was spurned by the more radical racists such as Leese and Jordan. On account of Mosley's more internationalist tone and apparent moderation, Leese emphasised in his own publications, and in big letters, that the Imperial Fascist League had 'No Connection with Sir Oswald Mosley' (*The Plan of the Jews c.* mid-1930s: 2). Indeed, after the war Mosley tried instead to proselytise a vision of a united fascist Europe based on a shared concept of a white civilisational cultural achievement which specifically rejected Aryan and *völkisch* theories (Macklin, 2020: 126–127).

The post-war years

The Imperial Fascist League and The Britons were not the only organisations focussed on overt blood and soil issues to emerge in the UK. The Nordic League (NL), which was formed in 1937, was another secret society aimed at curtailing Jewish influence and advocating Germanic racial links. It ceased to operate once war had been declared. Post-war, however, many of these older fascist father-figures 'rekindled the movement' (Jackson, 2022: 30), and more overt support for the far right began to return to the UK in the 1960s and 1970s. This was spurred on following a process of increasing immigration from Commonwealth countries, exemplified by the emergence of John Tyndall's National Front (NF). Tyndall (1934–2005) was one of the UK's most well-known extreme-right figures of the second half of the twentieth century, having chaired the National Front, 'the largest extreme right-wing street movement in Europe, from 1972 to 1974 and again between 1976 and 1979', and whose membership reached as high as

17,500 (Macklin, 2020: 347). Although Tyndall's racist nationalism was not of the religious esoteric type, he certainly networked in those circles and was heavily influenced by figures such as Leese and Jordan (Macklin, 2020: 359). Indeed, there are those such as Michael Billig in *Fascists: A Social Psychological View of the National Front* (1978), who argue that the NF 'had an esoteric ideology at its inner core' (Jackson, 2022: 47). In 1964 when Tyndall founded the Greater Britain Movement (GBM), a short-lived extreme-right political group created after a split with Jordan, its symbol interestingly enough became a sun-wheel under a lion to demonstrate the UK's 'Nordic folkish heritage' (Macklin, 2020: 357). Other friends and colleagues with whom Tyndall collaborated and who also held racist Heathen beliefs, included: Savitri Devi (1905–1982), the previously discussed and hugely influential Franco-Greek Nazi sympathiser and occultist; Matt Koehl (1935–2014), the US leader of the New Order (formerly the American Nazi Party) and an esoteric occultist himself; and Joshua Buckley, co-editor of the journal *Tyr*. This journal was named after the Norse god Týr, primarily a god of war whose Anglo-Saxon iteration, Tiw, is also the origin of the name Tuesday. Amongst the contributors to *Tyr* were other leading international racist Heathens, including Stephen McNallen of the Asatru Folk Assembly and Alain de Benoist of the Nouvelle Droite.

Having failed to achieve any real effect electorally, the NF was eventually replaced in 1982 by the British National Party (BNP), the fifth such iteration of this name; it attempted to gain a modicum of respectability that saw some limited political success, including two seats in the European parliament and some fifty local councillors. One of these MEP positions was represented by Nick Griffin (b.1959) who seized control of the party from John Tyndall in 1999 and remained in control of it until 2014, and the other by Andrew Brons (b.1947). Both Griffin and Brons were influenced by a particular 'indigenous lineage' of 'British *völkisch* nationalism [apparently] distinct from Nazism' (Macklin, 2020: 442). It appears that theirs was primarily a traditionalist, Arcadian worldview, one shaped by the writings of William Morris and Robert Owen and which stood in opposition to the perceived evils of urbanism and industrialisation. It was possibly for these reasons that Griffin would eventually move to rural Wales and develop a smallholding there. This might also explain his friendship with the Italian neo-fascist politician Roberto Fiore (b.1959) of Terza Posizione (TP), and their sympathy for Pope Leo XIII's Encyclical *Rerum Novarum* (1891) which, while calling for improved working conditions, advocated a rejection of both socialism and unrestricted capitalism.

Racist-Heathen thinking was influential on all of these individuals. Fiore, for example, was heavily influenced by the writings of Julius Evola (Macklin, 2020: 447–8). And Griffin, who would end up eventually critiquing Fiore and TP as too Catholic, went on in the mid-1990s to edit *The Rune*, a small pro-Nazi and UK-based publication which celebrated Odinism and whose name and masthead was the Odal rune, often appropriated by the far right because of its associations with 'native land' or 'homeland'. Furthermore, an investigation by the anti-fascist organisation *Searchlight* into Griffin also maintains that he was another central figure on the British extreme right who was inspired by racist Heathenry (Breenan, 2019: 24). The aforementioned sun-wheel motif decorating his refurbished farmhouse is suggestive of such sympathies, but the extent to which Griffin's Heathen faith is genuine is opaque. As one commentator quipped: 'Griffin is happy to agree with the theology of the last person he speaks to, especially if a profession of faith can earn him a few quid' (Williams, 2021: 10). In other words, politicians on the far right are often happy to draw on the trappings of religion, Heathen or otherwise, if it adds grist to their mill. In another case, Stephen Sargent, the younger brother of Charlie Sargent who was the head of Combat 18, a stewarding group created in 1992 to protect members of the BNP from anti-fascist activities, published *Thor-Would*, 'a pagan C18 magazine, from his home in Barnet [in London]' (Goodrick-Clarke, 2002: 45), drawing on the hammer-wielding god of Norse mythology. The readership, number of copies and extent of this magazine's influence remains unknown but was likely minimal.

Following Griffin's expulsion from the BNP in 2014 and the demise of the party, it was then left to the English Defence League (EDL) to emerge in 2009 as the leading far-right force in contemporary Britain; yet its anti-Islamic focus eventually splintered. Given the continuing failures of the above organisations and movements over the course of the second half of the twentieth century, a number of more secretive and violent far-right groups had begun to emerge, albeit in parallel with the NF and BNP, including, but not limited to: Blood and Honour (1987), the White Wolves (1994), Aryan Strikeforce (*c.* 2009) and National Action (NA) (2013), the latter becoming the first extreme-right organisation to be proscribed (in 2016) since the British Union of Fascists in the Second World War (e.g. Macklin, 2018). Following the Home Office's proscription of National Action in 2016 the organisation fragmented into a series of new movements, including Scottish Dawn, System Resistance Network and then in 2018, the Sonnenkrieg (German for Sun War) Division, all of which were also then proscribed (see e.g. Nicolson, 2017). Whilst many of these more radical and violent movements demonstrated an interest primarily with nationalist politics and racism, racist Heathen elements remained a constant presence on their fringes. Members of Woden's Folk (see Chapter 6), for example, have been photographed wearing face coverings used by National Action. And David Myatt, a leading figure in the Order of the Nine Angles (see Chapter 7) is named

Figure 5.2 Sonnenkrieg Division propaganda imagery (Public domain).

as a member of the White Wolves, whose manifesto included Norse poetry (Stott, 2019: 57). Similarly, the Sonnenkrieg Division frequently combine images of Nazism with runes (Figure 5.2), whilst their sun-wheel logo visibly links it to Himmler's esotericism.

Colin Jordan

In addition to Leese and Mills, the aforementioned Colin Jordan (1923–2009), stands out as perhaps the leading later twentieth-century English-speaking

Nazi who emphasised the importance of a blood kinship with Nordic peoples and who expressed an overt interest in racist Heathenry. According to Jackson (2018: 41), Jordan studied history at Cambridge during the war and this is where his interest in politics began; however, upon leaving university in the 1950s, he became even more overtly a neo-Nazi. Jackson (2018: 73) says that this was a result of falling more under the influence of Leese and his accomplices. Despite only meeting Leese once but corresponding with him frequently, Leese was to become a mentor to Jordan; indeed, Jordan later proclaimed himself as 'an Arnold Leese disciple for life' (quoted in Macklin, 2020: 259). It was with the financial aid of Leese's widow, who had inherited Leese's estate upon his death in 1956, that Jordan was able to carry on much of his own far-right political activities, including the creation in 1958 of the White Defence League (WDL). The WDL was intended as a violent paramilitary organisation; it was avowedly pro-Nazi, anti-Semitic and anti-immigrant, and its members had to be of 'northern European ancestry' (Macklin, 2020: 267); their members also wore armbands decorated with a sun-wheel (Figure 5.3).

Figure 5.3 Members of the WDL hold a rally (Getty Images).

In 1960 Jordan would merge the WDL with the National Labour Party, a small neo-Nazi political party, to form the race-fixated British National Party (BNP), whose 300 or so membership was restricted to Northern Europeans and who utilised again the sun-wheel as their logo (Macklin, 2020: 271). John Bean became its Deputy National Organiser whilst a wealthy Norfolk farmer named Andrew Fontaine was appointed as its President. Contemporary descriptions of the BNP summer camp near Wrotham, Kent, held on Fontaine's estate that first year, include a celebration of the rural (as opposed to 'the cosmopolitanism of the cities'), pilgrimages to an iron-age tomb and 'a giant sunwheel – constructed by campers from branches bound with foliage, and mounted on a tall pole' (Macklin, 2020: 272–273) (Figure 5.4). Numbers remained quite small initially, with just under forty campers taking part in this first event. At another camp in Norfolk the following year, a giant wooden sun-wheel was ceremonially burned to commemorate the victory of the German tribes under the command of Arminus over the Roman legions in 9 CE (Macklin, 2020: 275). According to Pardy (2023a: 55), the sun-wheel has now emerged to become one of the most ubiquitous symbols of the British far right. One of the speakers at the above Norfolk event was Savitri Devi, with whom Jordan subsequently developed 'a lifelong friendship' (Macklin, 2020: 276).

Figure 5.4 Burning sun-wheel ('Odin's Cross') at the BNP summer camp near Wrotham, Kent, 1961 (Searchlight Archive, University of Northampton).

Devi, as mentioned earlier, has been described as a 'missionary of Aryan paganism' (Goodrick-Clarke, 2000: 217).

In 1961 Jordan, alongside John Tyndall, founded 'The Spearhead', a paramilitary formation of more active BNP members who wore grey shirts and sun-wheel armbands. However, Jordan's increasingly pro-Nazi position resulted in his eviction from the BNP and the cessation of the sun-wheel as their political symbol with its replacement by the Celtic cross. Jordan in turn went on to found in 1962 the National Socialist Movement (NSM) with a view of 'pan-Aryan Nazism underpinned by a cosmological religion of race' (Macklin, 2020: 278). Not too surprisingly, Jordan's writings called for a rebuilding of Britain as 'an Aryan racial community', but one purged of foreign 'Negro, Asiatic and Jewish influx' (Jordan, n.d.: n.p.). Estimates of its membership vary, ranging between 187 and 680 (Macklin, 2020: 279). In August of 1962 Jordan also arranged an international conference for some forty people in Gloucestershire, including the American Nazi Party leader George Lincoln Rockwell, and which saw the launch of the World Union of National Socialists (WUNS). At this gathering Jordan was proclaimed 'world Führer'.

Jordan's predilection for Nazi esoteric sympathies is demonstrated during the events surrounding his marriage to French Nazi Marie Françoise Suzanne Dior (1932–1993), the niece of the French fashion designer Christian Dior (Figure 5.5). Instead of a traditional Christian wedding the couple bound themselves to one another in a Nazi-inspired ceremony with racist Heathen trappings:

> A suitably Nordic wedding ceremony – 'plighting the troth' – took place at NSM headquarters...Standing behind a candlelight table, bedecked with a swastika flag, Jordan and Dior declared they were 'of Aryan descent and racial fitness' over an SS dagger before each making a small incision in their ring fingers which were held together to symbolise the mingling of blood. A drop of this mingled blood was then allowed to fall on the blank forepage of *Mein Kampf*. Each in turn then placed a swastika engraved ring on the finger of the other, after which they declared the marriage enacted. The attendees then gave the fascist salute...and toasted each other with Mead, 'the ancient drink of the Nordic peoples'. (Macklin, 2020: 288)

Newspaper reports at the time estimate that about thirty people attended this event at what was then the headquarters of the British National Socialist Party at 74 Princedale Road, Notting Hill, London. They also reported that, in addition to serving mead, other suitably traditional British liquors were consumed, including 'gin, whisky, sherry and port', whilst Dior was ironically allowed a foreign Beaujolais given her French origins and preferences (*Yorkshire Post*, 1963: n.p.).

Figure 5.5 Colin Jordan and Françoise Dior performing Nazi salutes (Alamy).

Kaplan argues that much of Jordan's writings contained 'religious themes of a decidedly Odinist flavour' (2001: 44). Jordan himself remarked that he was 'not a Christian' but that he was 'religious' (Macklin, 2020: 278), while Goodrick-Clarke (2002: 42) states that Jordan's views were 'quite incompatible with Christianity'. In a 1965 interview with Françoise Dior the *News of the World* reporter Ron Mount (1965: n.p.) also recorded that Dior said she was not only 'against Christianity' but was 'a true pagan'. Whilst Jackson's 2018 biography of Jordan does not expand on his religious views, further indications about his Ariosophic and racist Heathen leanings can be gleaned elsewhere. He named his property in Pateley Bridge, Yorkshire, 'Thorgarth' (Jackson, 2018: 186), and his cottage in Diabaig, Scotland, 'Thor Nook' (Jackson, 2018: 225). Jackson states that Jordan also described Christianity as a 'spiritual cancer' that 'threatened racial revival' (Jackson, 2018: 191).

Following the break-up of his marriage to Dior in 1966, a spell in prison for contravening the new Race Relations Act (1965) and the rise of the National Front as a result of a merging in 1967 of Chesterton's League of Empire Loyalists and the British National Party, Jordan closed down the National Socialist Movement. He then created two small parallel organisations. The first was the British Movement, an apparently more moderate attempt at creating a political party designed to win votes. The second was the more extreme National Socialist Group (NSG) which kept close links with other leading neo-Nazis (Jackson, 2018: 153). Both failed to gain traction, however. Jordan subsequently focussed his attention on writing. Not only did he take up the creation of a new newsletter in 1979, the aforementioned *Gothic Ripples*, in homage to Leese, but he additionally penned a series of novellas. Jordan's third stab at literature, *The Uprising* (2004), is the story of an elite vanguard of ultranationalists seizing power in the UK through violent revolutionary means; the plotline is not far removed from Ariosophic notions of an underground order of martial knights working to reconstitute a new Aryan epoch. The plot appears somewhat similar as well to the infamous *The Turner Diaries* (1978), by William Pierce, which directly influenced Timothy McVeigh's bombing of the Federal building in Oklahoma in 1995 which killed 168 people. *The Turner Diaries* also directly inspired the formation of the Order. Jordan's *The Uprising* also references directly the members of the Order, including David Lane, the co-founder of Wotansvolk in the US. Furthermore, the novella's central protagonist, Cedric, is described by Jordan as going to Valhalla when he dies, a theme picked up by the Christchurch murderer.

Conclusion

At first glance, Mills, Leese and Jordan are minor figures in the history of the far right in the UK. They were eclipsed by bigger far-right movements and parties, such as the BUF, the NF and then the BNP. In the history of racist Heathenry in the UK, however, they remain important nevertheless for keeping these ideas alive from one generation to the next. In particular, their thoughts and actions led to the emergence in 1997 of a second National Socialist Movement (NSM) from a group of C18 activists, the leader of which became David Myatt (see Chapter 7). These newer third generation far-right groups with racist Heathen elements will be the central focus of the subsequent chapters, including, in chronological order to formation: the Order of the Nine Angles, or 'O9A' (founded in the late 1960s to early 1970s); the Odinic Rite (established 1973); the Odinist Fellowship (established in the 1990s following divisions in the OR), a UK-based chapter of the German

Heathen Front (late 1990s to early 2000s); the previously mentioned but short-lived branch of Wotansvolk; the Order of the Jarls of Baelder in 1990; Woden's Folk (founded 1998); the meta-political discussion group the New Right (founded 2005); and most recently, the Sonnenkrieg Division (SKD), founded in 2018 as a NA offshoot and associated with Myatt's Order of the Nine Angles (O9A). The latter has been affiliated with the now-proscribed National Action and has been described as a 'violent occultist Nazi group' with a 'disturbing' interest in Satanism, paedophilia and rape' (*Hope not Hate*, 2019b: 49). Two members of the SKD, Michał Szewczuk and Oskar Dunn-Koczorowski, were named in the British press for suggesting that Prince Harry be shot for marrying someone who was not white (Sandford and De Simone, 2018: n.p.); the pair have since received prison sentences (BBC News, 2019). In 2020 the SKD was also banned. Other less significant radical-right organisations include Aryan Hyperborean Heritage (existing primarily online) and the now 'greatly depleted' Wulfeshéafda þéodscipe (Pardy, 2019). Having now outlined the significance of pre- and post-war historical examples of racist Heathenry operating in the UK, we next turn to critically examining the leading racist Heathen and occult groups in the UK today.

6

Three thorns: the Odinic Rite, the Odinist Fellowship and Woden's Folk

Introduction

The Old English rune poem was written down by an anonymous author in the tenth century but has themes which reflect an earlier oral tradition, with some 'heathen' themes among them. For example, the seventeenth rune, with the glyph and letter 'ᛏ', and the name Tiw, refers to the Anglo-Saxon iteration of the deity known as *Týr* in Old Norse. Each stanza of the poem is a riddle, the answer to which is a specific rune (OE rūn, 'mystery', 'secret', 'counsel') of the 'futhorc' (named after the first six runes) rune row. The text for the third rune, 'Þ', 'thorn', whether referring to blackthorn, hawthorn, briar rose or some other plant with thorns, is emphatic that thorns are sharp and 'grim' to encounter:

Þorn byþ ðearle scearp; ðegna gehwylcum,
anfeng ys yfyl, ungemetum reþe,
manna gehwelcum, ðe him mid resteð.

Old English rune poem, stanza 3, the thorn rune,
Hickes' *Thesaurus* (1703), British Library (Halsall, 1981: 86)

Thorn is very sharp for all warriors
Extremely grim and evil to grasp
For all those who settle in its midst.

Old English rune poem, stanza 3, the thorn rune, our translation

But the poem, as a 'store of common sense' (Larrington, 1993), also alludes metaphorically to other 'thorns' one may experience in life, perhaps 'evil' people among them. In the Scandinavian tradition *Þorn* becomes *Þurs*, 'giant', the chief enemies of the gods in Norse mythology. And for many Heathens today, to cast this rune during a divination, is a possible sign that the querent has a 'giant' of some sort to deal with. Having set out the historical context for racist Heathenry in the UK in the previous chapter, here we take the thorn rune as a cue to examine the three main 'thorns in the side' of progressive Heathenry in the UK, namely the organisations, the Odinic Rite, the Odinist Fellowship and Woden's Folk. For the first time in its State of Hate report, for 2024, Hope not Hate devoted a whole section (106–107) to 'far-right Heathens', focussing on these three organisations. Sustained critical examination of each of them in turn, as we offer here, before then considering the implications of our findings, seems especially timely.

The Odinic Rite: faith, folk and family

The Odinic Rite, which uses the acronym OR, was originally The London Odinist Committee for the Restoration of the Odinic Rite, founded in 1973 by John Gibbs-Bailey, also known as 'Hoskuld', and John Yeowell (1918–2010), or 'Stubba' (after an Anglo-Saxon chief he believed had ruled the Kingdom of Essex). Doyle White (2017: 251) hints that the former may have also been influenced by Alexander Rud Mills, whilst Yeowell, who had probably been raised a Catholic, 'had been a member of the French Foreign Legion and a bodyguard for the British Fascist leader Oswald Mosley' (von Schnurbein, 2017: 57). Yeowell had also possibly served in the pro-Francoist Irish Brigade in the Spanish Civil War and according to Doyle White (2017: 251), may have been a card-carrying member of the British Union of Fascists too. Yeowell produced the OR's *Raven's Banner* magazine and authored a number of books, including *This is Odinism* (1974), *Hidden Gods: The Period of Dual Faith* (1982), *The Book of Blots* (1991), *The Odinist Hearth* (1992) and *Odinism, Christianity and the Third Reich* (1993). Renamed as the OR in 1980, the organisation achieved recognised charity status in 1988, prior to which British law had only permitted monotheistic beliefs charitable status (Jones and Pennick, 1995: 219). This charitable status was lost during a schism in the organisation after Yeowell stood down as leader in 1989, and while the splinter group initially called itself the 'Odinic Rite', it was later renamed the 'Odinist Fellowship' (OF), discussed below in more detail as the second 'thorn' of racist Heathenry in Britain. After his death in 2010, Yeowell was cremated in a Christian ceremony, but his ashes were scattered in a ritual led by OR member 'Asrad' at the White Horse Stone in Kent (Doyle White, 2017: 253). The OR had previously claimed this 'sacred' site as 'the birthplace of England' because of folkloric associations with the legendary fifth-century warriors Hengest and Horsa and the Anglo-Saxon migration to Britain. They have since been involved in several successful campaigns to protect the area from development (Doyle White, 2016).

The OR today claims to be 'the world's longest running, continually active Odinist movement' (OR, n.d.b). Von Schnurbein (2017: 57) describes it as 'one of the earliest and most internationally influential post-war Heathen foundations'. Branches of the organisation have been founded in Australia, Germany and throughout North America, the latter partly due to Yeowell's extensive contact with Else Christensen (Doyle White, 2017: 252). Indeed, there is a special application for those members residing in 'Vinland' with European ancestry, including membership discounts for incarcerated persons. In the group's official website, forums and blogs, there are numerous posts by members from Washington, Texas, Georgia, New York, California, Wisconsin and Sweden, although the exact size of the organisation cannot be reliably ascertained. In 1997 the OR joined with the Asatru Alliance and Asatru Folk Assembly to form an International Ásatrú/Odinist Alliance (IAOA), an alliance of folkish Heathen organisations 'at a time of strong sectarian conflicts with those they labelled "universalists"' (WikiPagan, n.d.; also von Schnurbein, 2017: 78). The union was unsuccessful due to internal and interpersonal disputes (Doyle White, 2017: 253) and disbanded in 2002, although the OR stated 'it makes no difference to the Odinic Rite as an organisation, for it will continue to promote and defend our holy religion as it has done in the past' (WikiPagan, n.d.).

On their website, the Odinic Rite claims to be apolitical: 'The Odinic Rite is not a political movement – a member's political outlook, if any, is up to them as free people', and 'Under no circumstances are members permitted to use Odinism as a tool for the promotion of their political views and they should never present their own views as those of the Odinic Rite' (Odinic Rite, n.d.c). But this stance is immediately qualified: 'This does not mean members cannot comment on matters which affect us all. Indeed, individual members would be abrogating their civic duty if they neglected or ignored the ethical matters that are constantly being discussed in the wider community' (Odinic Rite, n.d.c). These 'ethical' issues of concern to the OR are made clear in their alliterated maxim: 'Faith, Folk, Family'. The subheading to the 'Welcome to the Odinic Rite' page is 'Folkish Odinism in the Modern World', and they introduce themselves as: 'an international organisation dedicated to the advancement of Odinism, a modern-day expression of the ancient indigenous beliefs of our Northern Indo-European ancestors. Drawing on ancestral wisdom from the dawn of our folk, The Odinic Rite is a unique denomination of Odinism' (Odinic Rite, n.d.d). The explicit use of the terms 'folk', 'indigenous' and 'ancestors' alongside a self-identification as 'Odinist' is far from benevolent or apolitical, and Harvey (1995: 54–55) proposes that their focus is 'racially essentialist'. In other words, they are a racist Heathen organisation (according to Gardell's [2003, 153: 611], von Schnurbein's [2017: 6–7], and our own definitions [see Chapter 1]). In support of this, a 'corpus analysis' of the discourse used on the OR website (Thomas, 2007), finds that certain key words are used to positively denote the in-group (i.e. the OR), including 'Odinic', 'folk', 'Aryan/s', 'nation' and 'race', and negatively the 'out-group', including 'Christian', 'alien', 'foreign', 'stranger/s', 'Jews', 'Hebrews' and 'Africa/n/s' (Thomas, 2007: 14); in other words, the implicit ideological lexicon of the OR can be identified as racist.

Doyle White (2017: 259) makes the point that by claiming to be apolitical, organisations such as the OR can gloss over the 'divergent political positions' within their membership; he goes on to argue that professing an explicit political position would not only compromise the requirements for UK charitable status but also invite unwelcome investigations from the authorities. Doyle White (2017: 259) highlights the possibility that the OR holds a narrow view of what is political: 'viewing "politics" as something that only happens among elected officials, and that they instead wish to bring about socio-political change through cultural and religious means'. Their strategy, then, whether implicit or explicit, can be identified as a metapolitical one (see our Introduction).

The Odinic Rite promotes a code of conduct known as 'the Nine Charges', or 'Nine Noble Virtues', which members aim to adhere to. They are:

- To maintain candour and fidelity in love and devotion to the tried friend: though he strike me I will do him no scathe.
- Never to make wrongsome oath: for great and grim is the reward for the breaking of plighted troth.
- To deal not hardly with the humble and the lowly.
- To remember the respect that is due to great age.
- To suffer no evil to go unremedied and to fight against the enemies of Faith, Folk and Family: my foes I will fight in the field, nor will I stay to be burnt in my house.
- To succour the friendless but to put no faith in the pledged word of a stranger people.
- If I hear the fool's word of a drunken man I will strive not: for many a grief and the very death growth from out such things.
- To give kind heed to dead men: straw dead, sea dead or sword dead.
- To abide by the enactments of lawful authority and to bear with courage the decrees of the Norns (Odinic Rite, n.d.a).

Despite the use of pseudo-arcane language, there is no ancient heathen text outlining these 'virtues' in such clear and coherent terms. It is, then, a modern interpretation and one which not only cannot evade 'politics' but also has come to be associated with several folkish Odinist organisations concerned to arrive at an ethical code; notably, it is not generally used by inclusivist Heathens. The sixth clause, 'To succour the friendless but to put no faith in the pledged word of a stranger people', is especially problematic and can be cited as a clear example of their folkish, racist and exclusivist metapolitical agenda. This wording can be interpreted as implying that Odinists should not trust those who are not their 'people', that is, of their own white racial stock (see e.g. Blain and Wallis, 2009a: 423), and in general terms, immigrants and foreigners.

On the OR website the racist leanings of the organisation are further evidenced by their triskel logo and their understanding of its meaning (Figure 6.1). The symbol consists of a simplified triple spiral motif in white on a red background encircled by the black upper-case text 'ODINIC RITE FAITH FOLK FAMILY'. In addition to the use of black, red and white, the often-favoured colours of the far right, there is a broad resemblance of the design to a sun-wheel or swastika. The OR themselves describe the meaning thus: 'The triskel is a very ancient symbol…The design of the black OR triskel on a red background creates 3 blood drops which is wonderfully symbolic of Faith, Folk and Family, things to which we are linked by blood' (Odinic Rite, n.d.b). Claims to the 'ancient' past and 'blood' linkages to legitimate current doctrine are typical of right-wing thinking, and racist Heathenry in particular, as we have discussed in relation to historic Ariosophy and contemporary folkish organisations, such as the AFA. The 'triskel' might be 'ancient' (for example a triple spiral is engraved in the

Figure 6.1 Triskel logo of the Odinic Rite (Public domain).

Neolithic passage tomb of Newgrange in Ireland), but just like the swastika, it is not specific to the Anglo-Saxons, either archaeologically or historically. It is particularly prominent in early medieval Insular art in Britain, which, ironically, shows international influence, including from Celtic parts of Britain as well as from the continent (e.g. Webster, 2012; Marzinzik, 2013). The motto of 'Faith, Folk, Family' also foregrounds an exclusivist orientation for the organisation, in spite of their claims to be apolitical, serving to metapolitically demarcate 'our' folk (i.e. white British) from everyone else, especially it can be surmised, from immigrants. The motto's emphasis on faith and family as well as its catchy, alliterative three-word form, is reminiscent too of the Nazi-era motto: *Kinder, Küche, Kirche* (children, kitchen, church).

Like other far-right organisations, the OR emphasise the importance of traditional heterosexual family values. They claim to be 'proudly working to restore the true and holy nature of the male/female polarities in proper relationship to each other, so our folk will be restored to their rightful strength' (Eowyn, 2008: n.p.). It is quite clear that there is no room for expressions of gender and sexuality outside of this biologically essentialist 'polarity'. The homepage of the OR shows a photograph of a young family holding hands with their backs to us, their arms raised to honour the setting sun which frame their silhouettes; a man, woman, two boys and a girl, all of them white. For the OR:

> A vital part of [our] future involves reawakening the folk soul in women so that they join with the Rite, knowing it is a safe and nurturing haven where trust and respect are paramount – where they can truly heal and thus mediate the power of the Disir to the folk in positive ways. Hence, they must be able to see the Rite values [sic] all their womanly gifts and choices, not just those of childbearing (as crucial as that is of course); for otherwise, infertile or child-free women may falsely perceive they have no place in the Rite. (Eowyn, 2010: n.p.)

The OR acknowledges that women who are not child-bearers still hold social value, but the role of sexual reproduction remains the benchmark and the 'Rite values' for women are generally restricted to those traditionally valued by heterosexual men, coalescing around the ideal housewife. The latest iteration of this persistent sexist trope is the 'tradwife'; by choosing a homemaking role in their marriage 'tradwives' argue that they are not sacrificing equality with men or women's rights. But as Pardy states: 'By providing a façade of respect for the role of motherhood and housekeeper, the far-right perpetuate an ideology in which the woman is expected to remain at home, care for her hard-working husband and prevent the great replacement by birthing many children' (Pardy, 2023a: 27). The OR's discourse on women and the family, then, intersects with their discourse on race, and is arguably in tune with the far right and white supremacism more broadly, in promoting heterosexist values.

Although the Odinic Rite claims to be apolitical and non-racist some of its members have made explicit racist comments on the OR website. Asbrandir (n.d.), described on the OR website as a 'young Odinist', in explaining in an article 'What it means to be folkish', states that Odinism is: 'A belief and subsequent action in racial preservation and promotion…This Ancestral Memory is what Odinism seeks to protect and promote, and by protecting we mean keeping to our racial integrity, holding the line that connects us with our ancestors and thus their memory and wisdom'. He goes on to state that to be in the OR entails 'A belief and subsequent action in race preservation and promotion'. A similar emphasis upon the significance of preserving blood purity is made by another OR member, Sam Coles (2011), in 'The Importance of Preserving Heritage, Tradition and Race': 'If people do not care about their heritage and the traditions…by physically destroying them via miscegenation…they [have] betrayed their ancient ancestors… [T]he Folk Spirit…of an Englishman is very different to that of a Black African…The two races are just not compatible'. Analogously, a Texas-based OR supporter writes: 'I joined the OR after already being Odinist for 11 years…The OR is a shield wall for our faith…I loved the pan-Aryan focus of the rite along with the pan-Germanic tradition…We need a shield wall! Hail the Rite!' (Vidarolf AOR, Texas, USA; OR, n.d.e). 'Vidarolf' cites the 'pan-Aryan focus' in the teachings of the organisation, highlighting their general concern with race and its blood connection to their perceived indigenous, ancestral religion. It is not made explicit in the blog either why Vidarolf thinks 'we need a shield wall'; but, given the reference to 'a stranger people' in charge six of the organisation's 'nine charges', it is arguable that this is to protect 'our folk' from 'immigrants'. This thinking can be situated within the broader context of the anti-immigration metapolitics of the far right, the 'Great Replacement' conspiracy theory in particular. For Vidarolf and presumably for other members of the OR in western nations, a 'shield wall' might comprise a metaphorical wall to stop miscegenation, as well as a physical wall, as in the case of Trump's controversial wall to stop Latino immigrants entering the US and proposals for gun boats in the English Channel to stop illegal small boat crossings to the UK.

The view of the OR is that the 'Great Replacement' is indeed a reality in the UK which must be assertively countered. This concern is made explicit in one of the more recent articles on the OR website, entitled the 'Grey squirrel folk allegory' (Railbeart, 2020: n.p.). The author uses the example of the success of the non-native grey squirrel (introduced to the UK from

North America) and the decline of the native red squirrel, as a metaphor for the importance of a 'shield wall' against immigration to avoid catastrophic results. Pointing to those who 'promote the greys', Railbeart proposes that their 'naivety will result in the total destruction of the indigenous species. Only then, will their actions and recklessness become clear'. Of course the issues of migration and immigration are legitimate topics for critical discussion in contemporary Britain, but the racist anti-immigration stance taken by Railbert is thinly veiled by an analogy which reductively conflates environmental competition between two entirely different species (which cannot sexually reproduce), with a fabricated cultural conflict between groups of humans (incorrectly referred to as 'races', itself a term invented by racists), who can actually sexually reproduce as they are members of the same species.

The Odinist Fellowship: 'The original, indigenous faith of the English people'

Emerging from a rift in the Odinic Rite in 1989, the Odinist Fellowship (OF) was officially formed in 1996 by Ralph Harrison, known as 'Ingvar', who took the OR's charitable status with him (Doyle White, 2017: 253). The OF shares many characteristics with the OR, including the Nine Noble Virtues, which they summarise as 'Courage, Truth, Honour, Fidelity, Discipline, Hospitality, Industriousness, Self-reliance and Perseverance (OF, n.d.). They too claim to be apolitical, probably because they limit their understanding of politics to 'party politics', and perhaps also in order to retain charitable status (Doyle White, 2017: 258–259). Nonetheless, they continue also to represent Heathenry in ethnic (i.e. racial) terms as 'the original, indigenous faith of the English people' (OF, n.d.). The entry text on the organisation's website states in more detail that 'Odinism' is:

> the name we give to the original, indigenous form of heathen religion practised by our forefathers, the Angles, Saxons and Jutes, and by the related Teutonic peoples of the Continent. It is, accordingly, the ancestral, native religion of the English people, and, as such, our very own spiritual heritage. (OF, n.d.)

The core of the OF's understanding of Heathenry, as with the OR and other folkish organisations, is that this 'spiritual heritage' belongs only to the descendants of the Anglo-Saxons, in other words, people born in England who according to the UK government's list of ethnic groups would be termed 'white British' (census data does not differentiate between the British nations; see Gov.UK, 2022: n.p.). Given the OF's self-representation in these terms, Gardell (2003: 153, 611) would categorise the organisation as a branch of 'ethnic' rather than 'racist' Heathenry, while von Schnurbein (2017: 6–7) would use the terms 'folkish' or 'ethnicist'. As we have set out in Chapter 1, however, the distinctions between racial, folkish and ethnicist are far from discrete, and there is strong evidence from which to argue that the organisation can be identified as racist. Indeed, the OF themselves refer to their religion as 'ethnospecific':

> Odinists do not desire to convert the whole world to Odinism, because, whereas paganism is universal, the Odinist form of paganism is ethnospecific. Indeed, were we to receive a request to administer the Odinist Pledge of Faith to, say, a Japanese or a Nigerian, we would encourage that person to embrace his indigenous form of heathenism, because heathens of all nations believe in being true to oneself and to one's ancestors. (OF, n.d.)

This claim to ethnospecificity is very much in tune with the folkish tropes of other Odinist organisations such as the Asatru Folk Assembly (discussed in Chapter 4). So while the OF is not explicitly racist, to approach Heathen religion based on ethnicity in this way is reductive both biologically and culturally. It elides critical attention to the diversity of 'white' people in England today as demonstrated by DNA data (e.g. Gretzinger *et al.*, 2022). It also lacks critical attention to the contentious nature of 'Anglo-Saxon' as a stable ethnic category of the past (e.g. Sayer, 2017). And, it neglects to recognise the way in which 'Anglo-Saxon' culture has been (re)constructed historically from the medieval period to the present (e.g. Stanley, 1964). The OF, as Doyle White puts it, 'biologizes' spirituality (Doyle White, 2017: 261); in other words, ethnicity or ethnospecificity is a euphemism for race. Encouraging people to embrace their own 'indigenous' form of 'heathenism', then, presents a simplified and naive view. As Doyle White (2017: 261–222) further argues:

> No attempt is made to critique the vast academic literature arguing that 'race' is a cultural construct, nor any sign made that these practitioners are even aware of such literature. Even if they were, it is perhaps likely that they would dismiss it as part of the socio-political establishment's nefarious plan to erode 'the folk', alongside other tactics like multiculturalism and miscegenation. Fundamentally, the belief in the objective reality of distinct racial groups remains an act of faith for Folkish Heathens.

The OF's defence of ethnicity does not address how someone of mixed heritage should take direction. Historically, similar dilemmas faced Nazi and South African apartheid authorities regarding persons of mixed Jewish or

Black parentage. Indeed, the faith-based justification of the OF appears to have much in common with the Calvinistically inspired religiosity of 'Christian Nationalism' in apartheid-era South Africa. It too 'sought, for the most part, to distance itself from biological theories of inherent difference. In part, this can be ascribed to a deep reluctance of the part of Afrikaner theologians to rely on biological and evolutionist models of human difference' (Dubow, 1998: 76) Nevertheless, like the Homelands or Bantustan policies of the apartheid-era South African government, justifications for discrimination based on ethnicity or culture remain racialised (Payne, 1995: 340).

The ascription of the term 'racist' to the OF is lent further support from an interview given by Ralph Harrison (Avsnitt, n.d.). The leader of the OF emphasises that there is no relationship between the OF in the UK and its namesake in the US, but he does concede that the origins of the OF derive from the writings and beliefs of racist Heathens. He cites the aforementioned anti-Semitic and anti-Christian Alexander Rud Mills who attempted to establish the Anglecyn Church of Odin (and who had influenced Arnold Leese [Imperial Fascist League] and Colin Jordan [White Defence League, British National Party, British Movement, National Socialist Movement; also associated with David Myatt of the O9A, on which see Chapter 7]). Harrison cites Else Christensen too, who was also influenced by Mills and founded the OF in the US (Avsnitt, n.d.). The fact that Harrison's interview was conducted for a 'Survive the Jive' podcast (discussed further in Chapter 8), a YouTube channel with substantial far-right as well as racist Heathen and esoteric content, is also revealing of the far-right politics of the leader of the OF in the UK.

Since its foundation, the OF has aimed to 'institute a network of temples in every county, and in every major town and city up and down the land. However ambitious this long-term project may seem, it remains an indispensable precondition for the revitalisation of the faith' (OF, n.d.). This ambition began to take shape with the purchase of a Grade II-listed sixteenth-century former church building in Newark-on-Trent, Nottinghamshire. The building was consecrated by OF leader Ralph Harrison on Midsummer's Day, 2014, 'as the first Heathen Temple in England for well over a thousand years – and we hope and pray that it will be the first of many to come!' (Newark Odinist Temple, n.d.a). In November 2015, the temple was 'registered by the General Register Office as a place of worship under The Places of Worship Registration Act 1855'; and in October 2016 it 'was registered as a religious charity by the Charity Commission of England & Wales' (Newark Odinist Temple, n.d.b). Building on this success, in 2017 the OF wrote a letter to the Archbishop of Canterbury demanding the return of two churches in reparation for 'crimes against the Odinists' during the early medieval Christianisation of England (Rudgard, 2017: n.p.). The OF sees its first temple as 'a great stride forward for Odinism. We now believe that it will serve as a showcase for the religion and help to stir up among our people a greater interest in the ancient spiritual heritage of this land' (Newark Odinist Temple, n.d.a). The OF presents itself and its first temple as public-facing, with 'open' services (at the harvest ceremony on 24 September 2023, for instance, there were twenty-three in attendance 'including three children') (Newark Odinist Temple, n.d.b), and free open days on Wednesday afternoons. However, the reference to 'our people' again restricts their form of Odinism to white English people whom they presume to be of Anglo-Saxon descent. Furthermore, the OF 'utilise ministry and chaplaincy to access the prison and probation services and the armed forces', and a key purpose of their temple is to 'actively recruit and radicalise those who attend' (Pardy, 2023a: 75).

The OF have additionally hosted a number of school visits in recent years, and according to their website have developed a good relationship with a local Church of England primary school. On the one hand, this can be viewed as educating children about 'Odinism', now recognised as a religion by the 'General Register Office, an official government agency' and just as they might learn about other religions in diverse contemporary Britain. On the other hand, based on Pardy's interpretation of the temple as a forum for radicalisation and our argument that the OF is a racist Heathen organisation, the report from the OF following this school visit, stating that 'I think we have planted some seeds in their little minds and – who knows? – in years to come some of them may well become Odinists' (Newark Odinist Temple, n.d.b), is a source of some concern. For the OF, Odinism is important and necessary as a 'native and national faith' because currently 'our nation is at risk of being cast spiritually adrift' (Newark Odinist Temple, n.d.a). Odinism, for the OF, offers a way to address this perceived concern, by bringing other white English people together as Odinists in the face of increasing cultural, religious and 'ethnic' diversity in Britain. But for the next organisation we scrutinise, Woden's Folk, this concern over the Great Replacement requires even more extreme measures in terms of an English 'Spiritual Revolution'.

Woden's Folk: an English 'Spiritual Revolution'

Woden's Folk (WF) was, according to its leader, Wulf Ingessunu (also 'Ingesunnu'; born Geoffrey Dunn in 1947), founded on St George's Day, 23 April 1998, following his own mystical experience, a dream prophecy foretelling the rise of a '"Folk-Führer" who will lead a rebirth of England' (Henry, 2022: n.p.). Even from these few terms and phrases used to explain the mythology of its founding, then, Woden's Folk can be identified as an explicitly racist far-right Heathen organisation and stands out distinctly from the two previous 'thorns' of racist Heathenry in the UK in two main respects. First, there is focus on a particular charismatic individual, whose pseudonym draws on the Old English term for 'wolf', and the power of his spiritual experiences foretelling a new era. And second, for marrying English nationalist ideology, such as St George's Day as a key date, with far-right folkish and National Socialist ideals, with Wulf as a 'Folk-Führer'. As with other far-right Odinist groups, however, WF deny any political allegiances: 'Woden's Folk is a *Religious Order* and has nothing to do with politics' (quoted in Doyle White, 2017: 258). As with the OR and OF, this can be read as myopically delimiting politics to the activities of political parties rather than recognising the wider body politic and other forms of power relations in society. But, it is no mere aside to state that Wulf (we use the most common and consistent name in his published output) was a member of the National Front in the Leicester area in the 1970s and early 1980s (Henry, 2022: n.p.). WF's leader even says that he started Woden's Folk not because of his religious convictions but because he was disillusioned by the lack of progress on the political front made by nationalist parties (Wulf, 2014: n.p.). Despite claiming personal mystical inspiration for his new political direction, Wulf has historically been associated with other racist Odinist groups, including the OR in the 1980s (Doyle White, 2017: 255), and the Wotansvolk organisation in the US (Doyle White, 2017: 256). These organisations were clearly insufficiently radical for the leader of WF, however. As Hope not Hate's *State of Hate 2024* report highlights (HnH, 2024: 106), '[a]ctivists to have passed through Woden's Folk include former members of the National Front, the British National Party and also National Action, a nazi [sic] group banned since 2016 under anti-terror legislation. It also includes current and former members of Patriotic Alternative'.

In choosing the Old English 'Woden' in preference for the group's title, unlike the OR and OF which prefer the more generic 'Odin', Wulf's 'Wodenism' has a 'clear English identity' (Doyle White, 2017: 254) as 'the authentic folk-religion of the English people…committed to the awakening of the ancestral Saxon Nation' (Woden's Folk, n.d.a). As with the other two racist Heathen organisations in the UK, though, such key terms as 'authentic', 'folk', 'ancestral' and 'nation', and an appeal to the tribal origins of Anglo-Saxon England, are commonly used in WF's discourse. But in contrast to the OR and OF, Wulf is explicit that this religion looks to build a new race- and 'warrior'-based Heathen faith, and in so doing does not rely particularly on the historic and archaeological evidence but draws upon an eclectic range of other sources, including from popular culture, as we shall discuss.

One of the challenges presented by the public output of WF is that it has proven to be highly ephemeral. Their original Facebook page, for example, had as its brand image an anonymous individual wearing the skull mask face covering 'commonly used by neofascist militant accelerationist groups' that emerged from the Iron March far-right web forum (CTEC Staff, 2023), and particularly in the UK members of National Action during their far-right demonstrations, whilst waving a flag with the Woden's Folk logo. National Action has been designated a terrorist organisation by the UK government since 2016 and this Facebook page for Woden's Folk is no longer active, although the image does now appear on their blogspot.com website (Inglinga, 2015a). In some cases, such inactive sources can still be located in online archives (e.g. archive.today, n.d.), but even when held only in historical data files collections they remain valid material for analysis. Their ephemerality can also be highlighted as an indicator of their contentiousness. In the following discussion, wherever possible we cite current links and the citations make clear if a link is no longer active.

WF espouse a far-right and especially martial rhetoric which, when contrasted with the other two 'thorns' of racist Heathenry in the UK, is quite particular to this group. The homepage of the WF website makes striking use of a bold white Wolfsangel symbol on a dark background with silhouetted trees (Figure 6.2). Pardy (2023a: 7) describes the Wolfsangel originating as 'a medieval crampon used to capture wolves and protect livestock', but later featuring in 'Hermann Löns' novel *Der Wehrwolf* (1910), which was popular with Hitler'. The symbol was then used by the National Socialist German Workers' Party before the NSDAP adopted the better-known swastika, and

Figure 6.2 Wolfsangel symbol used by Woden's Folk (Public domain).

by several SS battalions during the Second World War. Brighton Antifascists note that 'Displaying this symbol is illegal in Germany', yet in Britain and elsewhere it has 'been adopted by many Neo-Nazi [sic] groups as a more acceptable version of the swastika' (Brighton Antifascists, n.d.). The use of the colour white for the WF Wolfsangel can as such be read as a reference to the white skin of 'the English Folk' (Guerilla Survivalism, 2023: n.p.), presumed to be the true inheritors of 'Wodenic' religion. In their self-representation on the WF website homepage, then, WF use established far-right symbolism such as the Wolfsangel to make their racist politics abundantly clear.

Further far-right imagery on the WF website homepage comprises their logo, at the centre of which is a wolf's head, its jaws open, sharp teeth bared, wearing a studded collar (Figure 6.3). The wolf motif, particularly in attack mode, is often used by the far right, particularly those with militaristic tendencies, drawing upon this apex predator as a totemic animal of sorts. In addition to being used in the insignia of the Nazi *Werewolf* division, the wolf was a favourite animal of Adolf Hitler who referred to one of his military headquarters as *Wolfsschanze*, 'Wolf's Lair'. The predominating white colour of the motif used by WF, like the white Wolfsangel, again arguably refers to the white skin of 'the English Folk' (Guerilla Survivalism, 2023: n.p.). The studded collar is a somewhat anachronistic, rather kitsch addition, which is in tune with the other eclectic influences on WF, as we discuss further below. The wolf-head in the WF logo is surrounded by a white oak-leaf wreath, similar to that used in insignia to distinguish generals

Figure 6.3 Wolf-head logo used by Woden's Folk (illustration by Megan Durkin, after Woden's Folk website, https://wodensfolk.blogspot.com).

in the Luftwaffe during the Second World War. The oak leaf is, however, common to other Pagan groups too, especially Druidry, where its associations with strength and longevity usually have nothing to do with racism (although there are, of course, racist 'Celtic' Pagan groups). However, below the wolf-head, upon the wreath, is a white Wolfsangel symbol, reinforcing WF's far-right agenda as iterated in the main Wolfsangel on the homepage. This imagery in the logo is surrounded by a white circle and the upper-case text 'WODEN'S FOLK' above and 'FOLKISH HEATHENISM' below, each phrase interrupted by an odal rune on either side. This rune, translating as 'inherited property' or 'ancestral home/land', *æthel* in the Old English futhorc rune row, *othala* or *odal* in the elder Germanic futhark rune row, as we have discussed, has been appropriated by the far right since it was first used by two SS divisions in Nazi Germany. It has since been associated by neo-Nazis with a whites-only homeland and appeared on the guns of both Anders Breivik and the Christchurch mass murderer. It is, then, abundantly clear from the homepage of the WF website that their metapolitical agenda is firmly on the far right.

In previous online output, WF's militaristic agenda is evidenced by their promotion of an 'English struggle' out of which a new, purer society, will be born:

> The English struggle begins here – it is our struggle. The English Folk will arise from the ashes of the destruction of the British State. A new religious movement is arising and the struggle for England is under way…The Spirits of our Ancestors call out to us to take back this Holy Land from the forces of decay and destruction. Proud of our Land – Proud of our Folk – Proud of our Blood!…This is our sacred struggle, to find the secret contained in the Blood of our Folk, and to awaken the latent powers that reside in the Blood of the English Folk. This relates to the Ancestral Spirits and to the Ancestral God – Woden. The struggle for England must first take place on a spiritual level…. Only through the creation of a new and virile English Religion will the English Struggle be taken up in earnest. (Woden's Folk, n.d.b)

This attention to hyper-nationalism, 'our folk', 'ancestors', and in particular several references to 'blood', explicitly identifies WF as an overtly racist Heathen organisation. In a previous iteration of the website, they have used the slogan 'Blood and Soil' which Doyle White (2017: 261) identifies as 'reflecting their belief in an ancestral connection between an ethnic group and a particular geographical territory'. But more emphatically, any use by a contemporary Heathen group of the term 'blood and soil', with its antecedent in the National Socialist *Blut und Boden*, can be interpreted as unequivocally racist.

In tune with far-right thinking more broadly, Woden's Folk is also against establishment capitalism, globalisation, consumerism, urbanism and multi-culturalism:

> We oppose the economic consumer society based upon gross materialism and mass production with a spirituality-based order of self-reliance, self-sufficiency and a return to ruralism and craftsmanship. Urbanism is for the inert masses and economic consumerism [sic]; it is also multi-racial in essence and form, which makes [sic] essential to the Old Order. (Woden's Folk, n.d.c)

To counter the ills of modern society, WF advocates autarchy and suggests self-sufficiency in small-family units, or 'Guerilla Survivalism', as a way to prepare for a future conflict leading to the ideal society. As one WF statement puts it, 'there is no reason why any individual cannot plant fruit in the countryside, away from the "madding crowd"' (Woden's Folk, n.d.c). By emphasising anti-capitalism, anti-urbanism and self-sufficiency, WF consequently embraces a number of long-standing rural themes apparent in post-war British fascism (Dack, 2015: 9) and the radical traditionalism of the New Right (e.g. Sedgwick, 2023). Doyle White (2017: 263) suggests a connection specifically between WF and the Nouvelle Droite which similarly 'critiques the egalitarian ethos of Christianity and liberal democracy, claims to be "beyond left and right", promotes cultural change as a prerequisite for political change, and envisions a federalised Europe consisting of small-scale regional communities'.

This reactionary conservatism extends to WF's thinking on sex and gender, emphasising the role of women as child-bearers, just as we have seen with other far-right racist Heathen groups, such as the Asatru Folk Assembly in the US and, in the UK, the Odinic Rite:

> The feminine within our movement is encouraged...Our Anglo-Saxon women-folk were honoured for their role as seeresses, healers and for defending the tribe when their men-folk were out 'A-Viking', raiding and pillaging lands in order to gain new territory and new wealth through plunder. The future of our people depends upon our women-folk producing strong and healthy children for the future. Our women-folk are as much Warriors of Woden as their men-folk who stand beside them in the English Struggle. (Inglinga, 2018a: n.p.)

This understanding, in common with other Odinist groups, 'entrenches the asymmetry of power and agency between men and women. Fetishised images of hypermasculinity and nurturing femininity reinforce misogyny and rigid gender roles within Folkish spheres. This objectification is conflated with notions of cherishing women as keepers of the home and bearers of life' (SPLC, n.d.c). And as Weber (2019: n.p.) puts it:

The misogyny within the movement makes sense for a culture that goes hand in hand with the hypermasculinity and rejection of femininity that's common in the groups' literature (and its social media, as Wolves of Vinland and other Odinists often add '#brosatru' to their posts, a play on the words 'bros' and 'Ásatrú'). It's also in their disparagement of Christianity as a feminine, weak religion.

WF's approach to sex and gender, then, is in tune with other racist Heathen groups and the far right in general.

In contrast to the Odinic Rite and the Odinist Fellowship, which have straightforward membership processes, Woden's Folk is 'not a membership organisation and we have no "members"; to become active it is necessary to become a WF Activist"' (Woden's Folk, n.d.b). This requires subscribing to the organisation's magazines and newsletter in order to 'get details of our local national activities' (Woden's Folk, n.d.d). Given the militaristic elements of WF we have identified thus far, this can be read as facilitating anonymous individual and small-group far-right activism. While it is difficult to ascertain its size, WF have claimed to have fourteen kindreds in the UK as well as many 'lone wolves' and Doyle White (2017: 256) proposed there may be one to two hundred members. A more recent report suggested it might have circa fifty associates (Hall, 2019), although *Hope not Hate* that same year (HnH, 2019b: 49) gave membership numbers of between twenty and thirty. *Hope not Hate* also report that Garron Helm, a former National Action member with links to both the Order of the Nine Angles (O9A) (see Chapter Seven) and the Sonnenkrieg Division (SD), is an active member of WF. It describes Helm and his sister Ebony, who uses the name Thorum, as holding solstice ceremonies in the North-West of England (HNH, 2019b: 49). Pagan Police Association information states, moreover, that 'several members of Woden's Folk were also National Action members beforehand' (Pardy, 2019). According to the Centre for Radical Right Analysis, since the banning of National Action in 2016, many of its members as well as former members of Combat 18 have now migrated to WF (Allchorn, 2021b: 28). Of the three thorns in the side of inclusivist Heathenry in the UK, Woden's Folk is, then, of particular concern as a network for far-right recruitment and radicalisation.

The activities of WF include rituals, moots and camps at ancient sites around England. Like the Odinic Rite, which identifies the White Horse Stone in Kent as an especially sacred location, Woden's Folk sees a number of ancient sites as spiritually significant. These include Wayland's Smithy long barrow where, as cited in the preface to this book, the national press reported on WF's 'masked torch-lit rituals there' with the 'use of far-right tropes and symbols' (Hall, 2019: n.p.). WF themselves state that:

> When we started the *English Resistance* through a Torchlight Rite at Avebury and Wayland's Smithy we started the long struggle to take back our Ancient

Sites of Albion – the *White Island* – from the so-called 'pagans', 'wiccans' and 'new-agers' who seemed to consider these sites belonged to them, and them alone. This was not a one-off and we shall resume this during 2016 – indeed, we shall reclaim these English Sites for Folkish Wodenism. (Inglinga, 2015a: n.p.)

As such, WF is highly critical of progressive Heathenry and related Pagan paths who also hold ancient sites as sacred and perform rituals there, on the basis that they are multicultural, 'left-leaning', 'mainstream' and advocate 'peace' (Inglinga, 2018a). For Woden's Folk, inclusivist Paganism is specifically rejected and membership of their organisation is restricted for these reasons to 'Anglo-Saxon', that is white English, people only. Their justification is that Folkish Wodenism 'is a religion arising from our roots, a religion suited to our Folk...our own Ur-Religion can only be suited to our own Folk' (Inglinga, 2018a). They go on to state that:

We do not follow the more 'universalist' forms that are not Race-Conscious but suggest that anyone can take up this religion. Wodenism is Race-Conscious because we believe that race has importance in this world especially in view of the destruction of our Folk...It is the most natural thing in the world to fight for the survival of one's own kind. (Woden's Folk, n.d.a)

As such, the racialist view of WF is very much in sync with that of other Odinist groups, worldwide.

Of all the 'sacred' ancient sites in England, the Long Man of Wilmington, an ancient chalk hill figure in East Sussex (Figure 6.4), has been a particular focus of attention for WF. This chalk outline of a human figure (the gender is not clearly specified, unlike the prominent depiction of genitals in the Cerne Abbas giant in Dorset) holding a staff-like object in each hand, is identified by WF as a male warrior and the 'Spiritual Centre of the Woden Folk-Religion'. Wulf, described as the 'Folk-Warder' of the group, is said to have had a 'mystical experience' at the site. The hill figure is understood as:

The helmeted Wændel who once sported a Horned Helmet and Twin Spears. This shape can be found in bracteates from Scandinavia (particularly Sweden) and on the Finglesham Buckle found in Kent. The figure is that of Woden as the Great Initiator of the Männerbünde and the Cultic-Warrior. He is seen as a dancing warrior performing the War-Dance or Fire-Dance associated with the Cultic-Warrior bands of Teutonic Legend. As the Wændel he is the god responsible for awakening the Kan-Force (Kundalini) within the Cultic-Warrior. Another name of this Kan-Force is the Vril-Force, a name associated with the Virile Male Warrior Ethos. This makes the figure of the Long Man of Wilmington extremely important in regard to the archetype of the Virile Warrior, as well as the appearance of the Last Avatara. (Woden's Folk, n.d.e)

Figure 6.4 Long Man of Wilmington (Photograph by Cupcakekid at English Wikipedia, CC BY 2.5).

Little is known archaeologically or historically about the chalk hill figure, so this over-blown interpretation, ascription of male gender and warrior status, assembles a wide range of often unrelated sources from archaeology (e.g. Scandinavian bracteates, the Finglesham buckle), history (i.e. literary sources on the god Woden), Ariosophy (e.g. Teutonic legend), yoga (Kundalini, Avatara), Theosophy (Vril) and popular culture on the Vikings (Virile Male Warrior Ethos), which is typical of WF's eclectic and unsystematically constructed philosophy, into an idealised, hyper-masculine Heathen warrior. There is nothing in the archaeology or history of the site to support this representation (e.g. Castleden, 2012; Butler and Bell, 2022).

Wulf elaborates further on the thinking and practice of WF in his books, of which there are now at least a dozen (see Woden's Folk, n.d.f), including:

Collected Writings of an English Wodenist, Ar-Kan Rune-Lag: The Secret Aryan Way, Along the Wodenist Path: The Memoirs of Wulf Ingessunu, The Spear of Woden, Sword of Wayland, At-Al Land: Aryan Mysteries of the Northern Seas, Inglinga: The Resurrection of Woden, England's Hidden Lore: Mysteries, Runes and Initiations, The Kingdom of Light: A Practical Guide to the Sajaha Prophecies and the Mysteries of the Black Sun, Of Gods and Runes: Further Insights into the Mysteries of Woden's Folk (three volumes), *The Wodenist Handbook,* and most recently, *The Woden Cult: Initiations into the Secrets of Folkish Esotericism.* All of the books are undated, print-on-demand and primarily available via the WF website and the Black Front Press on Facebook. Two are listed on Amazon but as being out of print. Considered together, the terms 'English', 'Aryan' and 'Black Sun' in these book titles mark out the rhetoric as being on the far right. The references to 'spear' and 'sword', additionally, as we saw in the interpretation of the Long Man of Wilmington, reify WF's militarist approach. Likewise, the terms 'secret', 'mysteries', 'hidden', 'prophecies' and 'esotericism' draw attention to the importance of mysticism and alleged esoteric truths set out in Wulf's teachings. The language used in the titles of Wulf's books, then, is yet further revealing of how WF can be identified as a far-right, racist Heathen organisation whose emphasis on ancient heathen mysteries and militant nationalism are intended to inspire revolution.

Wulf's personal connections to far-right political activists are made clear by his association with Troy Southgate (b.1965), the editor and publisher (as the far-right Black Front Press) of all but one of his books (*Sword of Wayland* is subtitled *Collected Articles from the Legendary Woden's Folk Magazine*). Southgate is a former member of the National Front and Society of St Pius X, was initially raised an Anglican, became a Catholic (after becoming interested in the extreme-right ideas of Terza Posizione and Nuclei Armati Rivoluzionari following their visit to London), and then converted to an Evola-inspired Odinism because he perceived Christianity as being 'weak' (Macklin, 2005: 306). Having taken a degree in theology and religious studies from Canterbury University and having, like former BNP leader Nick Griffin, been influenced by the Victorian socialism of William Morris, Robert Blatchford and Robert Owen, Southgate became convinced of the need to recreate 'an English pastoral idyll' modelled on an anti-capitalist and anarchic (i.e. decentralised) tribal regionalism based upon racial communities (Macklin, 2005: 305). Southgate now runs the London New Right, a 'meta-political lecture and discussion group…to discuss a range of "esoteric" ideas…that are traditionally…associated with extreme right-wing politics' (Macklin, 2015: 177). The organisation uses a Black Sun-inspired design as its logo and favours elitism, antidemocracy and polytheism, and rejects egalitarianism (Macklin, 2015). This organisation does not appear to be particularly active and perhaps unsurprisingly, Southgate found a spiritual alliance with Wulf, the Woden's Folk community and their Heathen 'radical traditionalism' (Hale, 2015: 113).

Wulf's publications consider such topics as lost races, lost continents and other conspiracy theories which have typified the more fantastical extremes of far-right folkish thinking since early twentieth-century Ariosophy. Wulf also directly references, and then uses, the Armanen runes of Guido von List (the rune row fabricated by the far-right co-founder of Ariosophy) as a magical means by which 'to awaken the Folk to their divine destiny and, thus, help them evolve towards a higher state of consciousness' (Woden's Folk, n.d.e). Another overt link between Ariosophy and Woden's Folk is a belief in the lost world of Hyperborea. In his book *At-Al-Land: Aryan Mysteries of the Northern Seas* (n.d.), Wulf 'looks at the myths surrounding the lost continent of At-al-Land' which he claims existed in the North Sea and was also known as Atlantis (Inglinga, 2015b). Elsewhere in a piece written on the history of lost races he argues that 'a series of catastrophes…sank the ancient Ur-Lands and with each catastrophe waves of Folk-wanderings occurred'. Apparently borrowing from Theosophy and Ariosophy, Wulf argues that an 'ancient Solar Race' settled in the Far North in what became known known as Hyperborea. But following a major event he states that their descendants went to At-al-land in the North Sea, and after yet another catastrophe one group made their way to the Himalayas where they hid their mysteries in 'secret caverns' (Inglinga, 2015b: n.p.). This recalls Blavatsky's alleged discovery of esoteric Aryan secrets in the Himalayas and Churchward's Mu history of multiple colonisations. Other Aryan descendants, according to this Woden's Folk pseudo-history, then seem to have found refuge in South and Central America, Rapa Nui/Easter Island, Egypt and Northern Europe.

A final, equally fantastical and bizarre source of inspiration for Wulf seems to have been folklore surrounding Herne the Hunter, the horned ghost recorded in Shakespeare and an inspiration for the popular HTV television series *Robin of Sherwood* (1984–1986). Wulf's 'The Hooded Man Prophecy' draw upon these strands of literary and popular culture influences in prophesying the arrival of a messianic Heathen leader, the Hooded Man, who presumably is meant to be Wulf himself:

> In the days of the Lion, spawned of the Evil Brood, The Hooded Man shall come to the forest. There he will meet with Herne the Hunter – Lord of the Trees – to be his Son and do his bidding. The Power of Light and the Power of Darkness shall be strong within him. And the guilty shall tremble! (Inglinga, 2014: n.p.)

As one critic put it, Wulf's 'prophecy' is, however, 'a statement so vague as to be meaningless, written for a television series and later adopted by a bigot who sees himself as a holy man and visionary' (Benn, 2014a: n.p.; see also 2014b). Wulf's prophecy does offer an interesting example, though, of how elements of popular culture, from literature and television to heritage sites, can be successfully co-opted by far-right thinking in the promotion of a racist agenda.

Conclusion

The three racist Heathen organisations in the UK discussed in this chapter share several elements but also have their differences. They are united by an interest in an exclusivist Heathenry and by their construction of a singular Odinism or Wodenism in particular as an authentic, indigenous and ancestral religion for English people today (in contrast to ancient Heathenry which was diverse in theology and ethnicity). In the case of the OF, the religion is held to be 'ethnospecific' to the Anglo-Saxon and other Germanic peoples, thereby 'biologising' their spirituality (Doyle White, 2017: 261), a racist approach without recourse to that term, but eliding critical attention to 'Anglo-Saxon' or indeed 'English' as a stable ethnic, racial or historic category. The OR and WF use the terms 'blood', 'our blood' and, in the case of the WF only, 'the blood of our folk', to make an explicit racialised and folkish connection between their Odinism, or in the case of the WF, 'Wodenism', and those who can legitimately practise it. All three groups can, therefore, clearly be described as racist.

The interest in ancestors for all three groups enables them also to make claims to the land, the nation of England, and specific ancient sites in particular, as authentic locales for performing their rituals and materialising their racist ideology in place. For the OR, this includes the White Horse Stone, for WF Wayland's Smithy long barrow and in the case of OF the consecrating of an ancient church building in the name of Odin. These groups view themselves as white English Odinists/Wodenists and consequently as the only legitimate practitioners of Odinism/Wodenism, at these sacred sites, reclaiming their 'ancestral' monuments whether from Christians or other Pagans. A feature marking WF out from the other two groups, however, is their martial aesthetic and militarist approach, combined with an eclectic mix of influences, including fantastical and more overt esoteric far-right conspiracy theories, all coalescing around one charismatic individual. Given its overt racism, militarism, dynamic web presence, numerous publications/blogs, not to mention its links with other far-/extreme-right individuals and groups, it would be a mistake to underestimate the potential of WF and its eccentric cultish leader, as situated within racist Heathenry more broadly, in far-right recruitment and radicalisation. Similar militarism, eclecticism, occultism and conspiratorial theorising are shared with the final 'racist Heathen' group we consider, in the next chapter, the Order of the Nine Angles (O9A). The O9A, does not define itself as 'Heathen'; but, as we shall show, it includes racist Heathenry among its range of key far-right influences.

7

Eclectic 'Esoterrorism': deconstructing the Order of the Nine Angles (O9A/ONA)

Introduction

We opened this book by highlighting the case of a teen 'occultist neo-Nazi' who in January 2020 became one of the youngest people to be convicted of planning a terrorist attack in the UK (BBC News, 2020a: n.p.). Among other extremist material, he was in possession of literature by the Order of the Nine Angles (O9A or ONA), a secretive far-right religious organisation that emerged in the UK in the 1960s and 1970s and has been described as 'an institution with a literature and mythology to rival Scientology' (Miller, 2018). The O9A has also been associated with several other terror incidents in the UK, from the nail bomber David Copeland in 1999 and the murder of two sisters in Wembley in 2021 (Watts, 2021), to the charging of a student in Leicester with terror offences (Gibson, 2021). One Yorkshire-based cell of the O9A, Drakon Covenant, was reportedly run by Ryan Fleming (aka A. A. Morain), a former member of the now-banned UK terrorist group National Action and with links to the O9A-affiliated Tempel ov Blood group in the US. Ryan was imprisoned in 2012 for falsely imprisoning, torturing and sexually abusing a young boy, and then again in 2017 for having sex with a fourteen-year-old girl whom he had groomed online (HnH, 2019b: 83). He then went on to use an anonymised account to message children and 'joined a chat group containing young participants in which thousands of messages were exchanged', violating the sexual harm prevention order imposed on him in 2017 for which he was jailed for six months in 2021 (de Simone, 2021a: n.p.). In between his stints in prison, it is claimed that Fleming 'returned to O9A activity' (HnH, 2021: 93). Another O9A-linked individual convicted of terrorism was Harry Vaughan, who had previously been an activist with the also banned Sonnenkrieg Division (SKD); he pleaded guilty to fourteen terror offences and two of possessing indecent images of children (HnH, 2021: 13).

Following the proscription of the Atomwaffen Division (e.g. Hatewatch Staff, 2018) as a 'neo-Nazi terror group' by the UK government in April 2021,

Hope not Hate (HnH) criticised the government's counter-terrorism strategy for failing to proscribe the O9A, an 'incubator of terrorism', at the same time (Lowles, 2021: n.p.). HnH's CEO Nick Lowles (HnH, 2021: n.p.) described the O9A as 'dangerous', 'a key influence on the AWD and several other nazi-terror groups', and proposed the UK should follow the lead of the US and Canada and ban the organisation. Labour's Shadow Secretary for State, Yvette Cooper MP, said the Home Secretary 'should immediately' refer the O9A to the government's proscription review group (de Simone, 2020: n.p.). Hope not Hate's *State of Hate* report (2021) sets out how the O9A 'seeks the overthrow of modern society and the formation of a new National Socialist order', and states that '[m]any of Britain's Nazi terrorists have been directly or indirectly influenced by' the O9A'. The O9A is of specific interest to our study because of the way in which it draws upon ancient heathen, neo-Nazi and racist Heathen sources. The O9A is deserving of particular scrutiny in a book on racist and anti-racist Heathenry in the UK because, disturbingly, 'people have died of it' (Mamlëz *et al.*, 2021b: n.p.). We are therefore mindful of the advice, attributed to Odin himself, in *Hávamál* ('Sayings of the High One'), that people should never be made glad by wickedness but pleased with good things:

Ráðumk þér, Loddfáfnir,
en þú ráð nemir.
njóta mundu ef þú nemur,
þér munu góð ef þú getr:
illu feginn
verþú aldregi,
en lát þér at góðu getit.

Hávamál 128; Evans, 1986: 65

I rede thee, Loddfafnir!
and hear thou my rede,
Profit thou hast if thou hearest,
Great thy gain if thou learnest:
In evil never
joy shalt thou know,
But glad the good shall make thee.

trans. Adams Bellows, 1936: 57–58

The purpose of this chapter is to identify the main aim of the O9A, to explore the eclectic esoteric strands within its thinking and practice, ranging from Satanism to racist Heathenry, and to consider the implications of how racist Heathenry permeates into the wider far-right counter-culture beyond Heathenry itself.

The O9A's 'ultimate concern'

In an important analysis of the O9A, Shah *et al.* (2023: 10–11) draw upon Wessinger's (2000) research on religiously motivated violence 'to evaluate the ONA's characteristics that may cause concern for wider society, including its propensity for violence', by identifying the O9A's 'ultimate concern'. This can be summarised as being to transcend the current 'failed' world system by building a superhuman civilisation (see e.g. Lawrence *et al.*, 2020; Shah *et al.*, 2023). The various primary sources (mainly online, authored or allegedly so by O9A adherents) indicate that the O9A views modern society, especially Western democratic liberalism but also all political models, as well as the main religious movements and especially Judeo-Christianity (also referred to as 'Magian' and 'Nazarene'), as 'weak'. The only way to escape this failed system, it is claimed, is through the accelerationist use of 'sinister' ritual magic and violent revolutionary tactics to create a new world order. The superhuman beings it is proposed that this new world order will be populated by are envisioned by O9A adherents as 'a higher species' known as 'homo galactica', led by a prophet named 'Vindex' (Myatt, 1997: 5), which will then 'explore and settle other planets and star systems' (Sauvage, 2013: n.p.) (see e.g. ISD, n.d.). As Shah *et al.* (2023: 12) put it, 'the movement displays progressive (practically social Darwinist) and catastrophic millennialism', and in this way its purpose is in tune with other accelerationist far-right organisations such as Woden's Folk, discussed in the previous chapter.

The world and cosmic change the O9A seek can be brought about, it is alleged, through both individual and group esoterrorist action. Individuals attempt to transcend modern society and its constraints (as they perceive it) through radical personal transformation; this is described as requiring many years of mental and physical fitness training and the mastery of occult ritual, also known as the 'Seven Fold Way', the praxis for which 'is a decades-long esoteric and exoteric personal quest for Lapis Philosophicus, for Wisdom' (TWS Nexion, 2018: n.p.). O9A adherents are not necessarily initiated by more advanced individuals within their order, as would be the case in other esoteric organisations, but by a process of self-evaluation. This highly individualistic and self-selecting strategy avoids the need for hierarchy and leadership and offers the flexibility for anyone to become a self-identifying O9A adherent.

Individual practitioners can strive to bring about social, religious and cosmic change by almost any form of criminality or violence which disrupts and transgresses normal society and simultaneously unsettles the cosmic order. One key O9A publication, *The Dreccian Way* (the root word 'drec' apparently meaning 'to vex' or 'cause trouble', but DREKK also referring to an O9A skinhead faction), encourages O9A adherents to commit crime, 'spread it, encourage it, incite it, support it' (Audun, 2009). According to Shah *et al.* (2023: 11–12), at the esoteric level these individual and group actions 'open the channel between this "causal" world and the unseen "acausal" world (where the Dark Gods reside)' and so 'create "chaos from which a New Aeon will emerge"'. Specific violent acts, 'genuine modern heresies' or 'Sinister Standards' that are recommended, include group sex, animal sacrifice, 'ritualised rape, random attacks on innocent victims and "human culling"' (HnH, 2019b: 81). Such activity is, according to the O9A's Social Darwinist 'natural justice' ethical position, that 'the strong survive, and the weak perish. Good riddance to the weak' (quoted in Shah *et al.*, 2023: 18, n.29).

The 'weak', also known as 'mundanes' and 'opfers', named after a Nazi pseudo-rune, comprise anyone identified by the O9A as counter to their project, especially Christians and Jews. A post by Brett Stevens (4 March 2022) on one O9A blog finishes 'Hail the strong, kill the weak'. *The Dreccian Way* actually promotes the 'culling' of opfers as central to the O9A's mission: 'Culling is natural and necessary. To cull humans is to be ONA. To cull – according to our guidelines and tests – is what makes us ONA' (Audun, 2009). Culling is held to be a key role and indeed initiatory requirement for O9A adherents enabling 'status elevation', and is also a rhetorical strategy 'for the ONA to "out-dark" other Satanists, and to present itself as the darkest and therefore most genuine expression of Satanism' (Shah *et al.*, 2023: 7; also Sauvage, 2013: 77–79). This 'black aesthetics' (Matthews, 2009: 139–158) or 'aura of elitism, cool and danger-seeking' (Shah *et al.*, 2023: 1) makes the O9A particularly 'enticing to certain individuals precisely because it frightens, and holds status as the "edgiest" set of beliefs available' (HnH, 2020a: 32).

While such disparate terms as Satanism, occult neo-Nazism, Paganism and Heathenry have been used by and applied to the O9A as key defining elements of its thought and practice, none of these are sufficient on their own and together they lack coherence. This is in tune with Shah *et al.*'s (2023: 1) proposal that it is important to consider the esoteric dimensions of the O9A 'as a new religious movement (NRM)' alongside, rather than separate, from their far-right politics; together these elements add up to a powerful ideology which has led to specific criminal, violent and/or terrorist acts. Taking the blend of esoteric thinking and practice together with far-right politics and violent criminality into account, we agree with Partridge (2013) that the O9A can most be usefully approached not as 'Satanic', 'occult neo-Nazi' or 'Heathen' but as an 'esoterrorist' organisation.

O9A key protagonists

One origin narrative of the O9A is that the organisation began with an unnamed woman in the 1960s in Shropshire, England, and the subsequent merging of three small Pagan groups: Camlad, the Noctulians and the Temple of Sun. These groups claimed to be part of a long-standing pre-Christian pagan tradition, and 'shared a synthesis of hermetic, pagan and Satanic elements…to appeal to a broad range of potential followers' (Shah *et al.*, 2023: 2–3). In the early 1970s, the story goes, this female founder left for Australia and one of the organisation's main protagonists, David Myatt (b.1950), took over (HnH 2021: 84). Myatt was additionally a member of Combat 18, a banned neo-Nazi terrorist organisation in several countries but not at that time the UK, where members were just not permitted to join the military, police or prison service. With members of Combat 18, Myatt went on to found the British neo-Nazi National Socialist Movement (NSM), as well as its faction, Reichsfolk (Miller, 2018). He was also a 'former mercenary and bodyguard to fascist British Movement leader Colin Jordan' (Miller, 2018). Jordan (as examined in Chapter 5), was one of the leading figures in the history of twentieth-century British fascism. Consequently, a direct three-generational intellectual lineage can be traced from Leese through to Jordan and then to Myatt. On these grounds, Myatt's influence on the O9A can be identified as having a particular far-right and specifically fascistic component.

Under Myatt's leadership the O9A took a unique direction combining politics and religion, neo-Nazism and Satanism. Under his own name and various apparent pseudonyms, including Anton Long, Stephen Brow, Godric Redbeard and Darklogos, Myatt has written an extensive O9A literature, including handbooks, grimoires, blog posts and messages on far-right social media platforms. As such, Myatt has been described as the O9A's 'movement spokesperson' (Hammer, 2004: 36), a 'trickster figure' (Campion, 2018: n.p.), a prophet-cum-messiah (Shah *et al.*, 2023: 13) and 'arguably England's principal proponent of contemporary neo-Nazi ideology and theoretician of revolution' (Michael, 2023: 59). According to an interview with 'Anton Long' in 2011, Myatt/Long 'spent his teenage years (pre-1960s) in the "Far East"', explaining:

> My practical experience and study of Taoism, a Taoist based Martial Art, and the diversity of religions I encountered in the Far East, which all inspired me to ask questions, [led] me to read [Carl] Jung and thence led me to Western Alchemy and Western Occultism. (Inform ONA files, cited by Shah *et al.*, 2023: 3)

O9A sources suggest that Myatt/Long spent some years developing the O9A's esoteric philosophy and initiation system, especially from the mid-1980s to the 2000s. During the early 2000s the organisation grew internationally with the foundation of supposedly other O9A offshoots, such as the Tempel ov Blood in the US and the Temple of THEM in Australia (Sieg, 2013: 253; Monette, 2015: 94–95; Shah et al., 2023: 2–3).

One O9A source claims that HnH's Nick Lowles conducted an interview with Myatt in a pub in Shropshire in which he denied that he was Anton Long (whom he described merely as an established academic) but that he did have an association with O9A members in the 1980s in order to promote National Socialism and a 'politically revolutionary situation' (quoted in Shah et al., 2023: 3). Myatt elsewhere denies that he is Long (HnH, 2021: 35; Harvey, 2016: 34), stating that he has no connection to the O9A (Kapiris, 2019), refuting that he is a Satanist (Stirling, 2021), and claiming to have rejected violent extremism altogether. Myatt says that he converted to Islam in 1988 and adopted the name Abdulaziz ibn Myatt al-Qari (or Abdul-Aziz bin Myatt); nevertheless, he later claims to have renounced Islam in 2010 (see e.g. Miller, 2018). While a Muslim it has been alleged that Myatt 'became a strong supporter of Hamas and al-Qaeda, writing long diatribes in support of terrorism and suicide attacks' (HnH, 2020a). As such, he has 'enshrouded himself in self-contradictory disinformation – something he has mythologised as the Order's "Labyrinthos Mythologicus"' (Miller, 2018). If Myatt has distanced himself from the O9A, Satanism and violent extremism, he has, however, consistently promoted neo-Nazism, stating: 'my occult involvement, such as it was in the 1970's [sic] and later, was for the singular purpose of subversion and infiltration in the cause of National-Socialism' (quoted in Miller, 2018: n.p.).

A more recent leadership figure within the O9A, according to Miller (2018: n.p.), is the artist and musician Richard Moult who uses the pseudonyms Christos Beest, Beesty Boy and Audun. He may have inherited leadership of the group from Myatt and has been heralded as its spokesperson or 'Outer Representative', involving 'training and initiating new members, editing its journal, *Fenrir*, and "giving a direction to [its] strategies"' (Miller, 2018: n.p.). Moult's strategies have included various musical and artistic projects, such as performing and recording with the experimental folk/improv Irish band United Bible Studies (Miller, 2018). Writing as Christos Beest, Moult states that 'Musick creates itself...[T]he composer, if naturally gifted, is a living NEXION. Thus, like any numinous form, Musick has the capability to presence forces and so alter the causal' (quoted in Miller, 2018: n.p.). Used as a proper noun and spelt with a 'k' (drawing on the occultist Aleister Crowley's spelling to differentiate ritual 'magick' from stage-based conjuring tricks), 'Musick' here is granted a supernatural agency, especially in relation to the O9A concept of a Nexion, a sort of combined material/physical and psychic/abstract outpost of activity. Moult has also been associated with the musical work of Tony Wakeford from Sol Invictus, as well as Death in June (Miller, 2018: n.p.), both neofolk bands controversially associated with the far right (see Chapter 8). But he has also used his musical connections to the O9A's advantage, 'to gain a wider audience for the Order of Nine Angles' (Miller, 2018: n.p.).

Indeed, some of Moult's musical output, along with other O9A-affiliated musicians, is relatively popular, if measured by YouTube views. 'River Redlake', for example, which was possibly composed by Christos Beest, had nearly 44,000 views as of summer 2023, many of them positive about the music and many of them also clearly familiar with the O9A's messaging. Some of the most viewed items in the O9A's musical repertoire also appear to be Satanic chants, such as 'Meseanas – Sanctus Satanas'. The latter has over 33,000 views on YouTube as of summer 2023. After various images of the devil which accompany this particular musical video, a portrait of an individual in camouflage appears about halfway through, his back turned to the viewer, when he then takes aim from a window with what appears to be a sniper's rifle. The association between music, Satanism and violence, is overt in this video.

Like Myatt, Moult has spread self-contradictory disinformation about his involvement with the O9A. He claims to have left the organisation in 2001, 'regretted involvement' (IPSO, 2020), and stated 'I utterly condemn, reject and denounce any individual or organisation – INCLUDING THE ONA/O9A – which glorifies and/or encourages acts of suffering and destruction' (quoted in Miller, 2018: n.p.). In tune with Myatt's own tacking between different political ideologies and religious systems, he then apparently converted to Catholicism and went on to live a quiet life with his wife and children in the Hebrides (Miller, 2018: n.p.). In his privately published autobiography, *Myndsquilver* (2011), Moult alleges that attempts to link him to Satanism are part of an MI5 plot to discredit him. But he was still writing O9A material under the pseudonym Audun by the late 2000s, including involvement with the O9A handbook, *The Dreccian Way* (Audun, 2009), which states: 'At this time of writing the ONA is concerned with several major undertakings in preparedness for the return of the Dark Gods, three of which are…to create new forms, in image, word and musick, which depict and presence the manifesting acausal dark – the essence of the Dark Gods'. Moult's conversion to Catholicism, then, as with Myatt's to Islam, can be read as an O9A 'Insight Role', with the aim to 'infiltrate, explore and subvert other organisations and religions' (HnH, 2019b: 82). In another similar instance of this infiltration strategy, Garron Helm, also associated with Woden's Folk and the Sonnenkrieg Division, enrolled in the government's anti-terrorism Prevent strategy. Extreme-right sympathisers are now also alleged to be secretly infiltrating UK police forces (Dodd, 2020). O9A 'insight roles' are, then, a form of entryism so as to propagate their esoterrorist mission. As Miller (2018: n.p.) states:

> Far right groups have long attempted to make headway into other outsider or underground scenes – particularly punk, noise, black metal and neo-folk music or heathen strands of paganism – it's now almost impossible to differentiate a white nationalist's use of runic symbols from those of a peace-loving heathen. The next stage of development following such an infiltration is the normalisation of extreme ideas and memes within the targeted subculture followed by, as we are now seeing all around the world, the normalisation and acceptance of once unacceptable ideas within mainstream political discourse.

As such, the O9A, like Woden's Folk and the neofolk and black metal musicians we will discuss (in Chapters 8 and 9) engage in metapolitical strategies, attempting to bring about change in popular discourse rather than via mainstream politics using such channels as outsider and underground religion and music.

In 2011 Moult produced a limited-edition tarot deck, *The Emanations Tarot*, also known as the Sinister Tarot, using his own paintings. Imagery on the cards includes a portrait of Myatt and the decapitated head of Claus von Stauffenberg, the German officer who led the plot to assassinate Hitler in 1944 (Miller, 2018: n.p.). An accompanying booklet, still available online, states that the deck is not for divination but for 'visualisation, and attracting cosmos energies, called Dark Gods, according to the Tree of Wyrd' (Christos Beest, 2008: n.p.). This offers a good example of how the O9A output co-opts heathen material. Using the term *wyrd*, Old English for 'fate', as well as the modern use of the term weird to mean something strange, Moult conjures an aura of mystery and strangeness around the tarot deck which is very much in tune with an O9A aesthetic. The particular format of the tarot deck, the most popular of oracular systems in the West, is by no means a casual choice, but, as Miller (2018: n.p.) puts it: '[e]very aesthetic expression of the Order of the Nine Angles – every text, every image, and every piece of music – is propaganda for the Order and its associates, and with it comes the potential for recruiting new members'. Furthermore, according to Miller (2018: n.p.), 'Moult's own memoir, *Myndsquilver*, published the same year as the tarot deck, makes clear that he had never fully abandoned the O9A, and continued to author texts and advise initiates long after his alleged exile'.

The use of the Old English term 'wyrd' has been co-opted by another individual associated with the O9A, Craig Fraser, also using the name 'Rafe

Grimes', who is the main figure behind the 'Wyrd Isle Collective'. Fraser is listed among 'other leading activists' in the O9A in Hope not Hate's 2021 State of Hate report (HnH, 2021). The Wyrd Isle Collective website sells 'hand-picked and dried mugwort', a wayside herb celebrated by Heathens because it is referred to in the Old English 'Nine Herbs Charm' (in the *Lacnunga* manuscript, a type of 'leechbook' or healer's manual; see e.g. Storms, 1948; Griffiths, 1996; Wallis, 2010). This might seem innocuous enough, but alongside this is a cassette of an 'alternative soundtrack' to the controversial sado-masochistic film set in Fascist Italy, *Salò, or The 120 Days of Sodom*. The picture becomes more concerning within the context of Fraser's past: he provided physical training for National Action before its proscription in 2016 under the guise of 'Sigurd Legion' and wrote a physical fitness manual for 'Operation Werewolf', a far-right Heathen group headed by white supremacist Paul Waggener (CTEC Staff, 2023). In recent years he has published O9A-related material as Lux Alba Novus Press, which on its Instagram account posted images of Nazi-tattooed power-lifters, artwork by Richard Moult, imagery of O9A 'Drexx' graffiti, literature by the O9A and Black Order (the neo-Nazi Satanist group headed by Kerry Bolton in New Zealand), alongside such hashtags as #occultpublisher, #hyperborean, #ubermensch and #esotericwarfaredivision. The banned Telegram account of Wyrd Isle Collective included 'mentions' of 'Kato's Aryan Outlaw Hangout', 'Aryan Fitness', 'Embrace Eco-Fascism' and the 'Survive the Jive' podcast (the latter a far-right YouTube channel fronted by self-identifying Heathen/Pagan Thomas Rowsell, discussed further in Chapter 8). As one intelligence source states, 'Many of the fascist dog-whistles used [here] are familiar to fascists, but are not understood by those whose circles [they are] seeking support from'. Just as Moult has used underground music as a means by which to promote O9A esoterrorism, Fraser's output attempts to co-opt the current popular interest in British folklore, folk horror, witchcraft and Paganism/Heathenry, in order to garner metapolitical influence in this scene.

A notable and recently active O9A adherent, also associated with The Black Order, is the West Country musician Michael Morthwork, who runs the label MMP Temple and collaborated on a musical project with Moult in 2017, *The Man Whom The Trees Loved* (Miller, 2018: n.p.). Morthwork has released black metal and O9A chants under the monikers Hammemit and Deverills Nexion (the reference to a group of villages known as 'the Deverills', probably locating Moult and his O9A cell in the county of Wiltshire). Facebook posts from MMP Temple display a range of Nazi/neo-Nazi imagery (e.g. swastikas, sigel runes, Wolfsangel) as well as Morthwork wearing a Nazi-style uniform sporting a swastika, and the remains of ritual activity at West Country locations which include swastikas made from tree branches and, possibly, human remains (Miller 2018). In an interview with Miller, Morthwork described the 'so-called alt-right' as 'meaningless abstraction' and stated 'call us neo-Nazis if you will, but do not make assumptions otherwise about our motives or alignments...All hail darkness and evil!' So, while Myatt has historically attempted to emphasise the neo-Nazi politics of the O9A over its occult-religious element, Moult and Morthwork have promoted the Satanic component over the political ideology. This may reflect the different audiences these O9A protagonists have found receptive to their ideas over time. As 'Nameless Therein' (2022), states recently on one O9A website: 'I am against National Socialism and Nazism in any form and want to see them removed from the tradition, I really mean it'. The resurgence of Pagan and Heathen spirituality and their affiliates in the British folklore and folk horror revival scene has been co-opted into populist and far-right politics during the 2010s and 2020s, because their interest in past traditions and their value in the present speaks to the increasing normalisation of far-right thinking (e.g. Hale, 2015).

Networks of nexions

While their individual contributions have moulded and expanded the O9A, and garnered particular media and scholarly scrutiny, to focus only on these main protagonists of the organisation risks overlooking the power of its decentralised organisation and fragmentary membership more broadly. One O9A source, for instance, denies Moult's leadership role, describing the O9A as leaderless and 'anarchist', with members 'free to interpret and to manifest Occult philosophy in whatever way they choose' (Kapiris, 2019). Unlike other new religious movements or cults, the O9A has no agreed leader(s), doctrine, foundational or central text or theology. As such, facts about the O9A are difficult to pin down, exacerbated by the extent of intentionally distributed contradictory information across varied media channels including since-removed social media activity. One source states, for example, that 'the O9A does/does-not exist, never has existed, and is/is-not defunct' (The Order of Nine Angles, 2012). Another source states, 'nowhere in the corpus of O9A texts...does the O9A advocate random attacks on innocent persons' (RDM Crew, 2019). Alongside the way in which such O9A protagonists as Myatt and Moult have released contradictory information about themselves, this sort of obfuscation by other O9A sources might be read as an attempt to avoid government intervention or further scrutiny, particularly since the calls from HnH and others for the Home Office to ban the group. More likely, such disavowals can be interpreted as being part of a deliberate strategy to spread disinformation and so enable the O9A to continue in its esoterrorist mission.

'Membership' of the O9A, if the term is used rather loosely, is focussed around so-called 'Nexions', although this term has several meanings. Moult states that an individual O9A adherent can be their own nexion, citing the example of how an adept occultist musician can perform as 'a living NEXION' who can 'presence forces and so alter the causal' (quoted in Miller, 2018: n.p.). Put differently, 'a nexion is a gateway that connects the world we experience with our senses and a realm beyond this one – what it refers to as the "causal" and "acausal" world' (Shah et al., 2023: 17, n.3). In this sense, a nexion refers to not only to an O9A individual but also to an occult gateway between worlds and the embodiment of this gateway in the form of the adept O9A occultist. This is in tune with other esoteric thinking, encapsulated by such aphorisms as 'as above, so below' and 'man is a miniature macrocosm', and ritual magical practices aiming to bridge human and supernatural worlds. But where right-hand path occultists might use such concepts and practices to connect people and cosmos for personal growth, empowerment and transcendence, the concept of the nexion in O9A terms is all about furthering their accelerationist esoterrorist mission. The O9A 'Mass of Heresy', after all, states 'We believe in the inequality of races' (quoted in Kaplan, 2000: 237).

In addition to referring to an occult gateway manifested by an O9A adherent, the O9A use the term nexion to refer to local cells or sub-groups, 'operating with apparent autonomy' and consisting of a small number of individuals who hold O9A values but mainly act as individuals. Hope not Hate states that there are 'at least five Nexions in the UK', with areas of activity centred around Oxford, Wiltshire, Shropshire and Yorkshire (HnH, 2021: 92–93), while Miller (2018) reckons there were around 2,000 adherents globally by the end of the 2010s. It is important to state that there have been no recorded Nexion/group terrorist actions by the O9A; all have been by individuals acting autonomously. Most recently, on 12 September 2023, after a man in Queens, New York, was arrested on gun possession charges, the FBI issued a public warning about a hitherto unknown 'Satanic cult' called 764 which uses encrypted social media channels and other online platforms to promote, *inter alia*, animal cruelty, paedophilia, self-harm and suicide, as well as the live-streaming of these acts in 'gore' videos, which they aim to disseminate particularly among young people (Winston, 2023: n.p.). 764 has now been identified as a nexion or cell of the O9A in the US (Winston, 2023: n.p.), possibly using an alternative moniker to evade detection and continue their spread of O9A-themed esoterrorism. But as the example of the man arrested in New York shows, the real power of the O9A as with other terrorist groups lies with the individuals who claim affiliation to it and act on its credo. This is particularly the case since the late 2000s when beyond small, private print runs of obscure texts, O9A adherents have been able to exploit the growth of the internet and social media, and especially the dark web and encrypted messaging services, to disseminate information/disinformation and encourage acts of esoterrorism. HnH (2020b: 40) report that:

> [t]here are several small dedicated O9A channels and groups on Telegram, spaces where PDF files of O9A/ToB texts and music are shared, and occult propaganda, sometimes featuring Myatt's face, is posted. The relatively large channel 'RapeWaffen', which claims to have splintered from AWD, states that its 'official beliefs are o9a Satanism and Esoteric Rapistism', encouraging followers to 'JOIN YOUR LOCAL NEXION'.

The dark web and encrypted media have, then, made the O9A a transnational movement (Koch, 2022). Shah *et al.* (2023: 1) think that the O9A's 'aura of elitism, cool and danger-seeking' (Shah *et al.*, 2023: 1) 'influences the selective appropriation of the ONA's symbols and publications amongst violent neo-Nazis who may then go on to perform lone wolf acts of terror in the name of the O9A'. But this problematically marks a distinction between the O9A as an organisation from individuals who have been convicted of terrorist acts in the name of the O9A, as if the two can be so dissociated. Yet, as the O9A encourages violent criminality, to 'spread it, encourage it, incite it, support it' (HnH, 2019b: 81), these lone wolves are actually model O9A adherents; the esoterrorist actions of individuals is at the core of their praxis. Having discussed the ultimate concern of the O9A, explored the contributions of its main protagonists, and considered the significance of its nexions, we next examine the strengths and weaknesses of characterising the association as Satanic.

Satanism, eclecticism and post-Satanism

The O9A has been labelled 'Satanic' (Allchorn, 2021b: 26), the 'largest Satanist organization on the world' (Introvigne, 2016: 359), the 'most sinister' of all Satanic organisations today (Harvey 2016: 27), and even 'the most extreme Satanist group in the world' (HnH, 2019b: n.p.). Satanism has been described as 'occult practices that include the worship of Satan and rejection of Judeo-Christian religions' (Allchorn, 2021b: 13), but the term Satanism, its use by and application to the O9A, is far from straightforward, with diverse meanings, practices and practitioners. In a more nuanced definition, Satanism can be defined as an ideology based around a concept of Satan which may be conceived of as atheistic or theistic and broadly encourages the autonomy of the individual acting within an amoral universe, and which is often celebrated through rituals which may parody Christianity and also draw on wider occult literature (e.g. Harvey, 1995, 2016; Introvigne, 2016; Granholm, 2016; Lewis, 2016). Occultists believe in the existence of supernatural forces or beings which can be manipulated via ritual magic, with the 'right-hand path' aim to advance the individual or group towards spiritual transcendence, whilst adhering to a moral code of one kind or another; this can be evidenced for example, in the work of the early twentieth-century occultist and Theosophy-influenced Dion Fortune (e.g. Fortune, 1962). Left-hand path occultists, on the other hand, tend to utilise a differing approach to magic, one that frequently employs a taboo-busting perspective. This usually involves the use of sex, drugs, pain and other transgressive techniques, combined with the control of 'sinister' supernatural forces, in order to effect a more direct and potentially dangerous route towards spiritual advancement; this can be evidenced, for example, in the work of Kenneth Grant (e.g. Grant, 1975; and in a different example, Granholm, 2004). These definitions of 'left- and right-hand paths' to magic are subject to debate within esoteric circles, but given our previous attention to the role of Theosophy, it is interesting to note that they were first conceived of by Blavatsky when she founded the Theosophical Society.

The main aim of the O9A adherent, deriving from the western ritual magic tradition and innovating upon this in terms of cosmic evolution, is to understand and master one's own being, the 'meaning and purpose of our lives' (O9A, n.d.), through a rigorous mental, physical and spiritual programme, so as to transcend the existing individual/social circumstances. As one O9A source puts it,

> A Satanist seeks and makes real his/her fantasies and then masters the real-life situations and all those desires/feelings which give birth to those fantasies – they live them and then transcend them, creating from those experiences something beyond them: a new individual. (Sauvage, 2013: 117–21)

But the O9A does tend to take Satanism in an especially extreme direction. Another O9A publication states:

> Let us not be mis-understood: genuine Satanists are evil…They cause, and strive to cause, Chaos, disruption, revolution…they bring joy, ecstasy and laughter, but perhaps most of all they bring death…death to those who have shown by their actions that they have a weak character or are a nuisance, or a hindrance to the spread of darkness. (O9A, 2008)

Satanism recognises a binary of good and evil and draws an emphatic line between them, but in the peculiar case of the O9A, the specific aim of Satanists is to promote evil especially by committing murder (of those that are weak), or 'culling' (ONA, 1986). This approach would be out of step with other Satanic organisations, however. The Satanic Temple, for instance, is 'an international nontheistic religious organization advocating for secularism and scientific rationalism' and which opposes racism and bigotry (e.g. Greaves, 2017). For O9A adherents, this sort of Satanism is not extreme enough. As Moult writes in *Myndsquilver*, 'the Temple of Set and the Church of Satan...were contrived gothic circuses...they held for me nothing of the arcane darkness I was searching for' (quoted in Miller, 2018: n.p.). The O9A's approach is therefore extremist, even among Satanists.

One particularly significant reason why an appeal to Satanism and left-hand path 'sinister' occultism suits the O9A it that it has shock value. This can be ascertained in headlines that serve the O9A's interests, such as: 'U.S. soldier's alleged connection to satanic Nazi extremist group renews calls to ban it' (Givetash, 2020: n.p.); 'A 23-year-old was arrested for gun possession. It led the FBI to a global Satanic cult' (Winston, 2023); and 'Hunt for "Satanists" after bizarre ritual discovered in New Forest' (Somerville, 2023). This kind of media attention attracts readers and so increases the profile of the O9A. In this sense, the O9A's aim is not only to recruit adherents but is also metapolitical. Such metapolitics can also be understood, by O9A members at least, to operate at a supernatural level, the magical meme perpetuated via media and public interest, and so the 'magic' is perceived to 'work', contravening and disrupting Judeo-Christian religion and Western social norms so as to achieve their Imperium. As one O9A source puts it, 'What if we could use...magic to create a new world 300 years from now?' (Darkness Converges, n.d.: n.p.). Satanism, then, is just one element of left-hand path occultism re-presented by the O9A as being particularly relevant to their 'sinister' ambitions, and with particular saliency because of the way it attracts sensationalist media headlines.

According to a source credited as Myatt/Long, the O9A does not have 'a traditional hierarchy nor any dogma/theology which has to be rigidly believed in or adhered to' (Inform ONA files, cited by Shah *et al.*, 2023: 4). O9A adherents draw on any 'sinister' forces they perceive or construe in other cultures – paganism/Paganism and heathenry/Heathenry among them (see e.g. Audun, 2009). The O9A's sinister left-hand-path esoterrorism is therefore more than Satanic, being highly 'eclectic' (Peterson, 2009: 2, 4), which is why scholars have used so many labels for it; for example, Kaplan (2001: 53) uses 'hermetic', 'neo-Nazi', 'Pagan' and 'Satanist', while for Gardell (2003: 292) the O9A is a 'heathen satanic path'. As such, the key thinking and practice of the O9A has usefully been theorised as an example of religious bricolage, that is, drawing on a diverse range of religious material and creatively innovating upon it in ways meaningful to the contemporary period (Hammer, 2004: 15; Shah *et al.*, 2023: 4). Satanism alone is insufficient but provides one of the 'causal forms' (T.W.S. Nexion, 2018: 9) by which O9A esoterrorist revolutionary change can realised – it is a means but not the end (O9A, 2012). One O9A source even attempts to move away from the confines of the Satanism label by describing the movement as 'post-satanist' (HnH, 2021: 93). So as we have shown, over time, the O9A has foregrounded certain elements of its thinking over others so as to target the most receptive and new audiences for its ideas and aims. Therefore, while the label of Satanist, among others, holds value, to emphasise this particular aspect risks overlooking other elements within eclectic O9A thought and practice which enable the group to attract interest and so propagate their esoterrorist mission. Taking this into account, in the next section we discuss the way in which the O9A has been associated with paganism/Paganism, heathenry/Heathenry and, in turn, neo-Nazism.

O9A, paganism/Paganism and heathenry/Heathenry

While the O9A has largely been approached as a Satanic organisation, it is important not to neglect its appeals to a generic 'paganism'. The O9A's main protagonist, Myatt, has often referred to the relevance of 'pagan' religion to O9A thinking. He proposed, for example, that 'for those of us who are of North European descent, the old pagan religions of our ancestors expressed some – but not all – of our nature…[including]…the religion of the Vikings…[T]hese old religions were the religion of warriors, and reflected the nature and beliefs of ancient warrior societies, and thus that part of our Aryan nature which is warrior-like' (Myatt, 2016: n.p.). Also, that such deities as Odin can be invoked for destroying 'contemporary ethical norms', especially Judeo-Christian cultural dominance (Matthews, 2009: 113). One O9A source, 'Rachael Stirling' (possibly a pseudonym), states that the organisation's 'ethos is essentially pagan' (2018: n.p.). In their analysis, Gartenstein-Ross and Chace-Donahue (2023: 1) propose that a key tenet of O9A thinking is that 'Western civilization is pagan but has been corrupted by Judeo-Christian values'.

But the O9A's interest in paganism can be read in several respects. First, it can be interpreted as a genuine interest in paganism as being a pre-Judeo-Christian religion, prior to the aeon in which the perceived corruption of Western society begins. Secondly, paganism is seen as being in ideological opposition to Judeo-Christianity and its 'weak' values. These characterisations of paganism, however, elide the diversity and historicity of ancient paganisms; as we have stated at various points thus far, pagan religions varied in their expression across north-western Europe and in some instances people absorbed the figure of Christ into their pagan pantheon. But a simplistic if unrealistic concept of a singular paganism, for the O9A, enables them to promote the idea of a primordial pre-Christian religion, in opposition to Judeo-Christianity, and one which was also 'tribal' as opposed to being, allegedly, cosmopolitan, multicultural and urban. Such a simplistic stereotype of pagans also elides the fact that paganism in the migration age shows international connections, hybridisation with other religions, urban growth focussed around international ports, or the fact that one of the largest and longest-lasting of all ancient empires, the Roman one, was in fact pagan for a good deal of its early, highly cosmopolitan, history.

The O9A's appeal to paganism can also be read, in another sense, as interfacing with contemporary Paganism as a potential recruitment ground or forum within which to propagate their esoterrorism. While the majority of today's Pagans are liberal and inclusivist, as we have shown in previous chapters and develop in Part III, racism and far-right values can filter into any religion. And there are several specific racist Heathen groups in the UK, such as Woden's Folk, whose extremist elements interface with O9A thinking and practice. Furthermore, certain elements of contemporary Pagan thinking can be identified as conservative, with the potential for being hijacked by the far right. These can include: an interest in the balance of nature as a guiding moral principle; an interest in ancient traditions as holding essential truths, especially the pagan traditions of tribal early medieval England; and the idea of a polarity of male and female principles which manifest in divinity/divinities. This latter point among today's Heathens in particular can lead to a misogynistic stereotyping of women into traditional, stereotypical terms, as mothers, wives and home-keepers (e.g. Pardy, 2023a: 25–29).

There are several specific instances where among its eclectic influences the O9A draws upon ancient heathen sources and contemporary Heathen thinking. We noted above that Moult's Sinister Tarot is used to attract 'Dark Gods' on 'the Tree of Wyrd' (Christos Beest, 2008), drawing on the Old English for 'fate' as well as referencing the Norse tree of life Yggdrasill, which translates to 'Odin's-horse' but also to 'terrible-steed' and can therefore be co-opted into a suitably dark O9A aesthetic. In another instance, the 'Nine Angles' (Figure 7.1) of the association's moniker have associations with 'the three fundamental alchemical substances, Salt, Sulphur, Mercury, whose nine transformations form the "nine angles" of the O9A', and which are further represented in their 'Star Game', a magical rite associated with initiation (O9A, 2019). The nine angles may therefore also refer to astronomical/astrological objects and the connections made between them in esoteric symbolism (Introvigne, 2016: 360). Alternatively, they may derive from the nineteenth-century French occult and radical socialist thinking of

Figure 7.1 Logo used by the O9A (Haisollokopas, CC BY-SA 4.0).

Éliphas Lévi, an associate of Edward Bulwer-Lytton who went on to influence Theosophy, who developed a chart of the nine orders of angels (angles and angels being theorised as interchangeable in this esoteric thinking) (Mackley, 2020). Given the O9A's references to heathen sources, furthermore, the nine angles may also relate to the nine worlds situated on the Yggdrasill world tree of Norse cosmology, with nine being an especially auspicious number in Northern traditions, for example, the nine nights Odin hangs on Yggdrasill in seek of wisdom, Odin's arm ring Draupnir produces eight new rings every ninth night, and the nine steps of Thor before his death at Ragnarok. Rather than having an emphatic or singular meaning, the possibility of multiple interpretations for the title of the order magnifies the aura of 'sinister' mystery with which the O9A seeks to surround itself. These various readings also reiterate the fact that the O9A cannot be typified as a Satanic organisation, but rather, as an eclectic esoterrorist phenomenon. Paganism/paganism and heathenry/Heathenry are prominent among the diverse sources used by the O9A and one key reason for this is, as we have shown in previous chapters, their historic and ongoing association with far-right thinking and neo-Nazism in particular, to which we now turn.

The O9A, occult neo-Nazism and racist Heathenry

While the O9A has been typified as a Satanic neo-Nazi group, it can be argued that the association between Nazism/neo-Nazism and racist

Heathenry proves a more robust historical lineage. Myatt was associated with Savitri Devi (1905–1982), the Nazi occult sympathiser who viewed Hitler as a Hindu avatar and was present, alongside Colin Jordan, at the founding of the National Socialist Movement, with Myatt as a co-founder. Myatt proposes that 'the purpose, of the old religions…is that they have… prepared the way for the divine revelation made manifest in the new religion of National-Socialism' (Myatt, 2016: n.p.). Also, he has proposed that O9A rituals should be conducted at '"pagan" sites (such as on hilltops, in forests and glades)', as well as, notably, 'in places connected with Adolph Hitler' (Myatt, 2003: 146). This clear connection made between 'paganism' and Hitlerism is also evidenced in other elements of O9A thinking. Myatt and other O9A authors frequently use the dating system 'yF' in place of AD or CE. This concept derives in part from the National Socialist Movement's calendar. The movement was founded in 1962 on 20 April, Hitler's birthday, and their calendar consequently starts in 1889, the year of Hitler's birth, with the abbreviation 'yF' denoting 'year of the Führer' (e.g. Myatt, 2003). The invention of fascist dating systems to distinguish a new far-right age has a pedigree; Mussolini had introduced the terminology of 'Era Fascista' into the Italian calendar, beginning in the year of the march on Rome in 1922 (or Anno 1 in the Fascist system). The O9A's use of 'yF' may also derive from the infamous occultist Aleister Crowley's concept of 'e.v.', 'era vulgaris'; while Crowley's work is rarely cited by the O9A, it does make use of 'e.v.' as well as 'Yf', and Crowley's influence continues to reverberate in the twenty-first-century occult scene.

The O9A's calendar shows further links with National Socialism and indeed extends into Social Darwinism. It consists of five aeons, or discrete periods of time, from Primal, Hyperborean and Sumerian to Hellenic and Western, each of which marks the progression of humanity towards the forthcoming sixth aeon of the galactic Imperium; this era will emerge supposedly once humanity has relinquished the perceived shackles of 'Judeo-Christian tradition' (Senholt, 2013; 2017). Senholt (2017) suggests that this idea of aeons or 'civilizational cycles' probably originates with the writings of the German historian and former Nazi sympathiser Oswald Spengler. But the notion of aeonic periods of evolutionary civilisation is also important in Theosophy and Ariosophy. Blavatsky promoted the notion of a Hermeticist secret knowledge passed down through aeons of time from prehistory to the present, and Aryanism comprised the fifth period in her system, which also resonates with the O9A's fifth aeon. Both Theosophy and the O9A also share the same term for their second time period, the Hyperborean. In terms of parallels with Ariosophy, List too formed his secret Thule society to bring about a new Aryan civilisation purged of Jewish and Christian influence.

Elsewhere in O9A thought and practice, Hitlerism and National Socialism are combined with references to paganism and Satanism. This can be seen in the O9A 'Mass of Heresy', which plays on Christianity's 'Lord's Prayer':

> Adolf Hitler was sent by our gods
> To guide us to greatness
> We believe in the inequality of races
> And in the right of the Aryan to live
> According to the laws of the folk.
> We acknowledge that the story of the Jewish "holocaust"
> Is a lie to keep our race in chains
> And express our desire to see the truth revealed.
> We believe in justice for our oppressed comrades
> And seek an end to the world-wide
> Persecution of National-Socialists.
>
> quoted in Kaplan, 2000: 237

The text of the Mass of Heresy valorises Hitler and National Socialism, incites racial division, promotes Aryanism and denies the Holocaust. Presenting Hitler as a divine messenger 'sent by our gods', blends messianic Hitlerism with paganism/Paganism, these 'gods' probably referring to not only a generic pagan pantheon but the Norse deities specifically, because of the pedigree offered by their historic co-option by occult Nazism. The use of the terms 'mass' and 'heresy' in the title suggests this text should be recited as part of a blasphemous (i.e. Satanic) ceremony parodying Christian ritual, thereby bringing Satanism into the mix. The Mass of Heresy, therefore, offers a good example of how the O9A blends several extremist strands together, comprising Hitlerism, National Socialism, anti-Semitism, racist Heathenry and Satanism, into a powerful formula, a type of anti-prayer in fact, or, perhaps more accurately, a magical esoterrorist invocation. It also mimics and plays on Mussolini's parodying of the Ten Commandments, with commandment ten being 'Mussolini is always right'.

Conclusion

The O9A's peculiar strand of 'esoterrorism' (Partridge, 2013), which combines 'sinister' occultism – drawing on an eclectic mix of, *inter alia*, Theosophy, Ariosophy, Social Darwinism, racist Heathenry, Satanism and fascism – together with the promotion of criminality, violence and social disorder, that is, revolution, stands out from the racist Heathen groups discussed in the previous chapters of this book in several key respects. First, it cannot be pinned down as a discrete 'racist Heathen' religious group because it is not inspired primarily by the ancient heathen past. Neither, however, is it purely Satanic; rather, it draws upon a diverse range of esoteric and far-right influences, racist Heathenry being one of the primary ones – hence its inclusion in this study. However, any ideology and practice which can be manipulated to further the O9A's ambitions, or any organisation that can be infiltrated so as to disrupt society, are viewed as fair game by the O9A. Second, the O9A does not favour a genetic heritage traced to ancient Germanic peoples and their traditions (as with OR and OF) or 'Anglo-Saxons' in particular (in the case of WF); instead, it promotes white supremacism based around a broader Aryanism with the aim to facilitate the evolution of a superior white civilisation. Third, it does not take a nationalist approach to the land/landscape of England/Britain/Northern Europe, but rather is transnational and indeed interstellar in its far-right ambitions, aiming for its superior civilisation to colonise space.

As with other examples of racist Heathen organisations and individual proponents we have examined, such as Woden's Folk's bizarre appropriation of the 1980s *Robin of Sherwood* TV mythos, the aims and claims of the O9A are fantastical. To be sure, if it were not for the demonstrable links between the O9A and specific terrorist incidents they might be dismissed as simply a 'fringe' group. As Evans has argued, 'one of the more frustrating elements about covering the fascist right is that much of what they say sounds ridiculous and makes them appear less than serious. This is why it is important to remember that these groups have a body count and represent a real threat. Their absurdity does not negate their danger' (Evans, 2018: n.p.). It is, therefore, crucial that O9A activity continues to be monitored, reported, publicised and challenged. In their analysis of the O9A, Gartenstein-Ross and Chace-Donahue (2023: 1) argue that the 'O9A's philosophy and practice have meaningful overlaps with violent extremism but clearly identifiable acts of violent extremism are less easy to discern at the movement level'. As a fragmented, disparate phenomenon ('organisation' and 'movement' remain dissatisfactory terms for encapsulating the O9A), favouring loosely formed, leaderless 'nexions' over organised groups and leadership roles, the O9A champions individual agency so it is important not to lose sight of the specific acts of violent extremism conducted by individuals who claim an association with the O9A or who hold O9A materials in their possession. Examples of such incidents from the 1990s to the present together make a strong case for the proscription of the O9A as a terrorist threat.

The example of the O9A explored in this chapter demonstrates that racist Heathenry should not only be examined as a discrete historical phenomenon, as explored in the first part of this book, and in its main contemporary manifestations, as the 'three thorns' analysed in Chapter 6. Rather, as argued here, it should also be recognised as a phenomenon which permeates into wider culture beyond Heathenry itself. In the next chapter we explore this issue further, by exploring examples of racist Heathenry in the far-right cultural scene, focussing in particular on music.

8

Nazisploitation: racist Heathenry in the far-right cultural scene

Introduction

In the previous two chapters we have examined specific examples of racist Heathenry and occultism in the UK today. Whilst under-explored both by scholars and policing/intelligence agencies, the enduring relationship between racist Heathenry and occultism and the far right extends into popular culture, from literature, film and music to television, gaming and fashion. In the following two chapters we broaden our focus beyond 'religion' to consider the intersections of racist Heathenry and far-right politics in the wider popular culture scene. When discussing the example of Woden's Folk, for example, we pointed to how a popular television series, *Robin of Sherwood* (1984–1986), combined with the historic literary figure of 'Hern the Hunter' alongside the representation of the Long Man of Wilmington chalk hill figure in Sussex as a sacred site, coalesce in the work of Wulf Ingessunu in a potent clarion call for white English people to rise up in a spiritual revolution. Popular literature has been cited as an influence in specific instances of far-right terrorism too; for example, William Pierce's *The Turner Diaries* (1978), a futuristic novel outlining an apocalyptic race war, on Bob Matthews of The Order, the Oklahoma bomber Timothy McVeigh and the nail bomber David Copeland (Jackson, 2015: 86).

The far right's appropriation of the ancient past in the form of archaeological monuments and its representation of the past in the present in the form of re-enactment groups, are of particular note. Hoppadietz and Reichenbach (2019: 208–209), have examined how the aforementioned Guido von List, the founder of Ariosophy, as early as 1900 had himself planned for an archaeological park replete with costumed guides near the site of the Roman town of Carnuntum (Austria), all with a view 'to depict an esoteric Aryan cosmology and Germanic religion of his own design'. They also point to the role of Peter Seymour, a leading figure in the historical re-enactment society called the British Thorguard Vikings (founded 1971), who espoused 'racial values' and an 'ideology of strength' (Hoppadietz and Reichenbach,

2019: 219) and went on to inspire Ariosophic-inspired Viking re-enactment groups elsewhere including across Germany (Hoppadietz and Reichenbach, 2019: 219). Whilst we have found no evidence for the latter, Hoppadietz and Reichenbach also conclude that today in Central and Eastern Europe particularly, archaeological sites are being co-opted by the far right and historical re-enactment organisations are being influenced by 'neo-fascists and far-right groups' (Hoppadietz and Reichenbach, 2019: 211). And in the UK, we have pointed to the appropriation of the White Horse Stone in Kent as a sacred site for the Odinic Rite, the use of a disused church building as a temple by the Odinist Fellowship, and how Woden's Folk, in addition to the Long Man of Wilmington, have held rituals at Wayland's Smithy long barrow and Avebury stone circles. Some other communities in the UK are not only re-engaging and/or re-enacting the past but also attempting to revive it as a far-right idyll. The groups *Sovereign Mercia*, *Independent Mercia,* and *Independent Northumbria*, all identify as Pagan and:

> seek to return Britain to a devolved state of Anglo-Saxon Heptarchy by promoting exclusionary far-right ideologies, using familiar 'folkish' terminology to promote a Pre-Christian Anglo-Saxon community structure, legal system, and local authority with the same anti-Norman narrative as the far more militant White Nationalist group English Resistance, who utilise the anti-Norman narrative to convey their opposition to European influence and imposed Christianity, which it blames for multiculturalism, immigration, and miscegenation, using such emotive terms as 'white genocide' and describing the killing of the indigenous Pagan Brits as 'The English Holocaust' at the hands of 'William the Bastard'. (Pardy, 2023a: 19)

Certain politicised phrases, ideas and symbols from the far right have also entered the political mainstream, and this metapolitical instantiation of far-right thinking is only increasing. During his first administration, US President Donald Trump referenced the 'Great Replacement Theory' in relation to a false news story about the ANC killing white farmers in South Africa. A similar slippage occurred when Suella Braverman, the former UK's Home Secretary, cited 'cultural Marxism' and political correctness as an impediment to free speech and a threat to civilisation (Walker, 2019: n.p.). More recently still, an aide to Republican Presidential hopeful and Florida governor Ron DeSantis was fired for having displayed a Sonnenrad 'sun-wheel' image in a pro-DeSantis video (Pengelly, 2023: n.p.). The monitoring group Tech Against Terrorism, launched by the United Nations in 2016 to survey the online sphere against terror threats, identified in particular the need to monitor gaming platforms for this type of activity given their lack of content moderation and potential for radicalisation (Tech Against Terrorism, 2023).

In this chapter, therefore, we set out to explore several key instances of how the trappings of racist Heathenry have permeated popular culture, before going on to focus on the role of music and how these particular examples can all be theorised in terms of a metapolitical far-right agenda.

Metapolitics

It is useful to offer a reminder at this juncture, that metapolitics recognises the way in which the far right aims to sway the tide of popular political opinion by using such cultural forms as religion, music, literature, art and fashion. This radical switch from favouring political action, that is using party politics and the democratic system, to instead attempting to influence people through everyday forms of culture they engage with, is part of a calculated attempt to undermine liberal democracy so as to come to dominate the social–cultural sphere and, therefore eventually, control the political space as well (see e.g. Bale, 2020; Liyanage, 2020). Take the example of the writings of the New Right's/Nouvelle Droite's Groupement de Recherche et d'Études pour la Civilisation Européenne (GRECE) – a think-tank which explores how 'ideas play a fundamental role on collective consciousness' (de Benoist and Champetier, 2000: n.p.) – which seeks to deliberately undermine dominant western liberal and democratic orthodoxy with a view to replacing it with one sympathetic to the far right (Liyanage, 2020: n.p.). De Benoist's Nouvelle Droite has been described consequently by scholars as elitist, anti-egalitarian, quasi-fascist and pagan-inspired, with Baron (2014: 1, 27, 32) suggesting that it evolved as an intellectual force specifically to counter the then leftist dominance of 'the cultural terrain'. He says that it holds '"popes…and priests" of the West as being responsible for opening the doors to uncontrolled immigration…above their own: European ethnic groups' (2014: 22). Like Evola, de Benoist too looks to paganism/Paganism as one fertile source upon which to build a common and strong foundation for a renewed European civilisation.

Some British-based racist Heathen movements and individuals too have used their fora to prepare the social and cultural groundwork for a cultural shift to the far right. As the founder of Woden's Folk exclaimed after having witnessed the failure of so many ultranationalist political projects:

> We have seen how the past mistakes (particularly within British nationalism) were never learned, and have stuck to a *Religious Movement* rather than involving ourselves in the power-struggles of politics. The strongest movements in the world today are religious…so we must recognise the power inherent in a Religious Movement. (Inglinga, 2018a: n.p.; emphasis in original)

In a further example, Stead Steadman, a former organiser with the (nearly) defunct London Forum, a far-right discussion environment, now focuses his attention on running Heathen-style *blot* rituals in Rotherhithe, Southeast London. As Patrik Hermansson opined after infiltrating the group for a year: 'you have to see this as a cultural movement. Their goal is to change the culture, and that means making their ideas mainstream' (Illing, 2017: n.p.). According to Paul Wainwright in an exposé by *Searchlight*, a UK-based anti-fascist monitoring group: 'Steadman is an extremely well-connected player on the far right', and his *blots* are a method by which he provides additional platforms for 'white ethno-nationalist causes' (Wainwright, 2021: 16, 18). And, considering the far-right occult milieu too, David Myatt, a leading protagonist in the O9A, stated that instead of taking power through the ballot box or revolution, the movement should instead 'undermine the government by taking away the support it has from our people by seeking to convert our people to our cause' (Stirling, 2021: n.p.). In a similar vein, 'Beast Xeno', a contributor to an O9A website, promoted in a blog post (4 March 2022) the need to develop an 'acquisition of minds', a phrase often used by far-right tacticians as short-hand for a culture war.

When the racist Heathen organisation, the Odinist Fellowship (OF), then, celebrates the visits to its Newark Odinist Temple from local Church of England schoolchildren (see Chapter 6) as part of regularly organised trips, with one commentator stating, 'I think we have planted some seeds in their little minds and – who knows? – in years to come some of them may well become Odinists' (Newark Odinist Temple, n.d.b), alarm bells should be ringing with the Office for Standards in Education (Ofsted), local parish churches and with anti-racist Heathen organisations. This is especially so given that members of Patriotic Alternative, a British far-right and white supremacist movement renowned, according to Britain's *The Times* newspaper, for trying to recruit youngsters (Knowles *et al.*, 2020: n.p.), has been associated with the OF (Hope not Hate 2024: 106). It is worth repeating here, therefore, Pardy's caution that a key purpose of the temple is to 'actively recruit and radicalise those who attend' (Pardy, 2023a: 75). These examples reinforce the concerns of several NGOs, including Hope not Hate, Tech Against Terrorism, Searchlight and the Southern Poverty Law Center, about the need to monitor the radicalising tendencies of religious extremism including racist Heathenry.

Whilst racist Heathens are a minority within a minority religion, according to Griffin (2003: 49) the danger to the current democratic order is now that the sheer number of these diverse and highly vocal far-right groupuscules and their metapolitical strategies, 'could help ensure that the centre of gravity of western democracies stays firmly on the right'. Bale (2020: 30) has made a similar point about the significance of small far-right groups:

Since small size is in turn all too often equated with insignificance, scholars have tended to ignore the study of political groupuscules, which they view as unpopular fringe elements within the overall constellation of a given nation's political forces, and to focus their attention instead on larger and higher-profile organizations such as electoral parties.

Continuing this argument, Bale (2020: 25–26) goes on to argue that these groupuscules 'can become important incubators of, and transmission belts for, unconventional political ideas that eventually spread beyond their own boundaries'. Given the importance of monitoring such far-right metapolitics, especially when they use 'historical themes, imagery and language' to promote a particular brand of a new racist 'political discourse' (Woodbridge, 2015: 27–29), we devote the rest of this chapter to consider how the far right co-opts the trappings of heathenry/Heathenry in its metapolitics.

Nazisploitation

The fascination with occult Nazism in various strands of popular culture offers a good starting point for considering the metapolitics of racist Heathenry. Paralleling the growth of Pagan and Heathen movements themselves, the early 1970s also saw the rise of the 'Nazi Mysteries' genre and numerous literary bestsellers involving tales of post-war Nazi survival, black magic and demonic possession (Goodrick-Clarke, 2002: 108). Occult and Nazi-related groups, such as the Thule Society, thus appear in the pages of Umberto Eco's bestseller *Foucault's Pendulum* (1988). Occult Nazi themes are central in Norman Mailer's last novel, *The Castle in the Forest* (2007), which tells the tale of a daemon that grooms a young Adolf Hitler. The award-winning British Israeli science fiction author Lavie Tidhar in his short story *My Struggle* (2017), draws particular attention to this Nazi obsession with the occult and paganism. The tale revolves around an alternative history of Adolf Hitler who, having been defeated by the Communists in early 1930s Germany, ends up fleeing to London to begin a new career as a private detective nicknamed 'Wolf'. Wolf is subsequently hired by his former Nazi comrade Heinrich Himmler, also in exile in the UK, to procure 'The Holy Lance', which the Nazis believe will assist them in achieving world domination. At the end of their meeting Wolf, after pointing out that Himmler does not believe in Christ and is a Pagan, exclaims: 'Lord! Spare me from my former Nazi comrades and their eternal obsession with the occult!' (Tidhar, 2017: n.p.).

It is perhaps unsurprising too that some of the more sinister elements of J. K. Rowling's Harry Potter books (1997–2007) and films (2001–2011) have also taken their inspiration from occult Nazism and racist Heathenry. The lightning bolt scar on the forehead of Harry Potter, for instance, is in the form of a 'sun' (sowilo/sigel) rune, previously used by the SS and a popular symbol for racist Heathens and far-right occultists. Far-right themes are also evident in the story's central plotline surrounding a struggle between purebloods and 'muggles' (people lacking magical ability and not born into a wizarding family). Like the Ariosophists, Lord Voldemort's thuggish, black robed (as opposed to black shirted) Death Eaters were envisioned by Rowling as an 'elite force' intent on preserving their pureblood wizarding supremacy (Harry Potter Wiki, n.d.). Racialised thinking therefore has had an impact on children's (popular with adults too) as well as adult literature.

The occult-Nazi genre was perhaps most famously picked up by Hollywood in the Indiana Jones series of films, namely *Raiders of the Lost Ark* (1981), *The Last Crusade* (1989) and to some extent, with the search for the Lance of Longinus, in *The Dial of Destiny* (2023). All three films portray various Nazi agents trying to procure assorted fantastical objects with occult powers to enable Germany to win world domination. Guillermo del Toro's *Hellboy* (2004) is yet another film with a Nazi occult story, this time of Nazis summoning an inter-dimensional creature to assist them with their war effort. This 'long history of Nazi and neo-Nazi involvement with the occult and paganism' (Nanda, 2004: n.p.) has, in fact, become so pronounced in film that it has given rise to a specific subgenre known as 'Nazisploitation', described 'as utilizing Nazi themes…for titillation, but also [for] exploring transgressive themes' (Lee, 2018: 39). Nazisploitation is also now international in scale. In Japan, Hiromu Arakawa's best-selling manga series *Fullmetal Alchemist* (2001–2010) is replete with Nazi symbols and characters, all operating in a fantastical world of alchemic magic.

Videogaming arguably now has equal and if not more cultural weight than film, and has taken up the Nazisploitation theme with enthusiasm, with popular games such as *Spear of Destiny* (1992), *Return to Castle Wolfenstein* (2002), *Wolfenstein RPG* (2008), *Wolfenstein: The New Order* (2014) and *Wolfenstein: The Old Blood* (2015), being based on supernatural Nazi-based narratives involving occult objects and the paranormal. Whilst opposition to Nazism in gaming has resulted in it 'being scrubbed from most games released on home consoles over the past few decades' (Scimeca, 2014: n.p.), occult Nazi-themed games, such as *Nine Witches: Family Disruption* (2017), continue be released to popular acclaim.

We have set out these examples of Nazisploitation literature, film and gaming above to demonstrate a general popular interest in these themes and genres. Ironically, however, this popular interest stands in stark contrast with the fact that real-life racist Heathen/occult groups have been, with a few notable exceptions, understudied in the UK. They also demonstrate that, although frequently dismissed as merely frivolous 'trash', these and other pop culture spaces 'can offer up an understanding of society and culture beyond their context' (Lee, 2018: 40). According to Jackson (2018: 3, 23), unlike the majority of film and literary sources which are intended either for entertainment purposes and/or critiques of the far right, other more sinister elements of popular culture 'need further consideration' since this 'cultural turn' has in fact helped to kindle and sustain a reinvigorated and growing far-right milieu. The power of this metapolitical cultural strategy to nourish such ideologies and inspire violent repercussions was an important lesson learned from the investigations which followed the Christchurch mosque murders, namely that they can 'draw conspiracy-curious people towards... harder conspiratorial views' which can in turn 'translate into real-world hate and violence' (Spoonley and Morris, 2022: 310–312). Indeed, the 15 March terrorist himself admitted to becoming radicalised by watching YouTube (Daubs, 2022: 330). Having drawn attention to metapolitics, the specific genre of Nazisploitation and how a variety of popular culture fora can be used to disseminate consciously the 'ideas, values and beliefs' of a far-right racist Heathen counter-cultural struggle with its ambition to turn the cultural tide and to incite a far-right political struggle (Copsey and Richardson, 2015: 1), we now turn to consider specific instances of far-right cultural productions, namely fashion and online media, before considering music.

Fashion and online media

The far right has always expressed itself in powerful visual terms by using distinctive clothing designs, from the black uniforms of Mussolini's Blackshirts, the paramilitary wing of the National Fascist Party, to the white T-shirt, braces, jeans and DM boots of the skinheads. According to Colborne (2019: n.p.), '[t]he last decade has seen a number of far-right fashion brands make a name for themselves among Europe's far-right extremists'. The clothing company *Thor Steinar: Viking Brand*, for example, based in Dubai, has been banned in Germany (Knowles, 2019: 37) because of the right-wing imagery and text that its streetwear and outdoor gear brandishes. The brand is still operating online, with clothing bearing frequent references to Norse mythology, such as 'Wuotan Collection', combined with militarist terms like 'Valhalla Corp' and hyper-masculine slogans, such as 'Born to Fight'. There are also Nazi-like references such as 'Stormtropp' and 'Bergführer', while one hoodie named 'Drødning Division' includes a face covering as part of the design so that the wearer can become anonymous. A women's T-shirt available on their website bears a valknut symbol, often associated with the god Odin and appropriated by the far right, along with runes (inaccurately) spelling the company's name. A T-shirt has the militarist slogan 'Division Thor Steinar' juxtaposed with a double skull motif recalling the Nazi SS-Ehrenring and red blotches to suggest blood stains. Another of *Thor Steinar*'s T-shirts includes an image of a Viking with the slogan 'Voice of the blood', whilst a sweatshirt called 'Varg' was, according to Turner-Graham (2015: 130) apparently modelled on Varg Vikernes, the extreme-right black metal musician (discussed in more detail in the next chapter).

It is not difficult to see how this sort of clothing would appeal to the far right and racist Odinists in particular. In 2002 a Thor Steiner shop opened in North Finchley, London (Bentley and Paul, 2014), although it closed shortly after. With the demise of National Action after it was banned by the Home Office in 2016, one of the organisation's founding members, Ben Raymond, opened his own online clothing business called 'Blackguard', with clothing replete with Sonnenrad/Black Sun symbols and references to the likes of Savitri Devi (Dearden, 2020). Raymond has since been imprisoned on the basis that he was deliberately 'grooming' youngsters to support a race war and was described by the judge in his trial as being 'the group's [i.e. National Action's] propaganda chief' (BBC News, 2021). The examples of the Thor Steinar and Blackguard clothing brands show how fashion, drawing on ancient heathen, racist Heathen and neo-Nazi themes, can be implicated in the metapolitical agenda of the far right.

Arguably the forum with the greatest potential for far-right metapolitical impact is the internet. We will explore in Part III of this study how anti-racist Heathens are using the internet and social media to challenge racist Heathenry. Here, however, we want to point to the power of such internet platforms as YouTube by which far-right messaging is permitted to proliferate without the moderation of national watchdog agencies, such as Ofcom, the UK's communications regulator. Tom Rowsell's 'Survive the Jive' YouTube channel is a good place to start. With 219,000 subscribers at the time of Hope not Hate's *State of Hate report 2024*, it is highly popular, with Rowsell described by Hope not Hate as 'the far right's go-to expert on "Indo-European" history and Paganism, producing a regular stream of video, podcast and social media content that is often interspersed with racist tropes and far right talking points' (HnH, 2024: 107). Rowsell foregrounds his academic credentials (an MA in Medieval History from UCL) as well as professional experience as a journalist (he holds a BA in Media and Communications), but he is also a member of the racist Heathen Odinist Fellowship organisation (HnH, 2024: 107). Rowsell has attended fascist events in Europe, such as the Identitarian Ideas conference in Stockholm (in 2017), 'which was organised and addressed by leading white nationalists from across Europe and the US' (HnH, 2024: 107). He was also a speaker at the Generation Identity UK conference (July 2019), a Traditional Britain Group event (December 2021) (HnH, 2024: 107). Protagonists on the far right are increasingly looking to contemporary Paganism as a scene in which to spread their racist messaging, as we pointed out with the example of the Wryd Isle Collective (in Chapter 7). It is notable, then, that Rowsell was a leading figure at the 'Pagan Futures Conference' (London, 25 June 2022) where he spoke alongside other influential far-right figures, among them Dan Capp who performed as his solo 'Dark Folk' act 'Wolcensmen'. Capp is 'closely affiliated with Woden's Folk' (HnH, 2024: 107) and hosts the 'Fyrgen' website (https://fyrgen.com/) with 'podcasts and commentary from a Heathen perspective'; the former including such notable racist Heathen content as 'Folkish Religion' and 'Grand Humanism with Stephen McNallen' (i.e. the former leader of the racist Heathen AFA in the US). Capp is also a guitarist in the black metal band Winterfylleth (whose racist Heathenry is discussed in detail in Chapter 10).

Rowsell's 'Survive the Jive' YouTube channel purports to host historical documentaries, but such keywords in this content as 'spirituality', 'nature', 'ancestors', 'strength' and 'pride', are all terms typically co-opted into far-right metapolitics (as shown previously, for example, on the websites of the three racist Heathen groups in the UK). Rowsell's videos include Ariosophic-inspired themes such as the 'Real Hyperboreans' (11 August 2017) which has been viewed over 212,000 times and purports to give a more scientific defence for the existence of an ancient and 'robust' Northern Eurasian civilisation. Although couched in scientific terms, the film suggests that the bloodline of these 'Aryan' peoples disappeared due to 'race mixing', with a reference to the racist Italian philosopher Julius Evola thrown in for good measure. Such lost world theories, formerly found on the fringe and challenged by documentaries involving established academics, have found fertile ground online and are gradually gaining traction in the contemporary popular imagination, just as Atlantean Studies, which in its time had helped to influence the thinking of Theosophy and Ariosophy, came to prominence in the mid-to-late nineteenth century.

Another of Rowsell's videos is entitled 'The Knights Templars' (24 September 2015), which ends with a critique of international bankers that includes, alongside the narrative, a Nazi-era image of a Jew. What is more, the emblem of the production company at the end of the film, 'Lucio Films', is a crossed L and F, thereby resembling a swastika. The anti-Semitic nature of this Ariosophic-inspired narrative is found most overtly, perhaps, in an episode entitled 'Hebrew Anglo-Saxons? Medieval Conversion Tactics' (12 March 2018) which has nearly 74,000 views. Here Rowsell makes the contradictory argument that Jews used 'propaganda and psychology' to trick the heathen Anglo-Saxons into converting to Christianity as it made this form of Judaism more palatable to them. Other episodes on his platform include readings from fascist apologist Ezra Pound and a documentary on Evola.

Rather than just appearing on fringe internet sites, pseudo-archaeology can now also be seen on such popular subscription streaming services as Netflix. For example, the eight-episode mini-series *Ancient Apocalypse* (2022) has been highly popular. According to *British Archaeology* magazine, this production is 'probably the most watched recent archaeological broadcast' with as many as nine million viewers (*British Archaeology*, 2023: 66). Written and narrated by the alternative archaeologist Graham Hancock (b.1950), the production promotes the theory that there had once existed an ancient globe-spanning and highly advanced civilisation which collapsed at the end of the last Ice Age and whose material achievements endure in the form of several ancient sites across the world today. With visually stunning locations and high production values, the series offers an attractive, entertaining and apparently authoritative experience, all of which lends credence to its thesis. But the thesis itself lacks scientific foundation, relies on generalisation and grand statements, and draws upon theories which are all too likely to pander to far-right sensibilities.

For example, Hancock repeatedly states that mainstream archaeologists 'hate' him (episode 1) and that the discipline refuses to reconsider established findings in the face of the new evidence (episode 4). Yet, when discussing Mexican temples (in episode 2) and Göbekli Tepe in Turkey (in episode 5), Hancock admits that archaeologists recognise that these sites are older than previously thought; this suggests that the discipline is not as conservative as he pretends. Hancock has also advanced his theories not in academic and peer-reviewed publication outlets but instead on the likes of The Joe Rogan Experience, a podcast which has been critiqued by some for its far-right guests and conspiracy theorists, including Gavin McInnes (founder of the Proud Boys) and Alex Jones (founder of the fake news website InfoWars). It is partly for the latter reason, and Hancock resurrecting late nineteenth-century Atlantean ideas, that some more mainstream media outlets have labelled *Ancient Apocalypse* 'the most dangerous show on Netflix' (Heritage, 2022). As Fagan and Feder (2006: 720) warned, these sorts of 'alternative archaeologies' 'are not necessarily innocuous expressions by perfectly nice people…Mixed into the panoply of "alternatives" are a host of reconstructions that are anti-reason and anti-science, or, worse, hyper-nationalistic, racist and hateful'.

Online media platforms (such as YouTube), subscription streaming services (including Netflix) and social media channels (e.g. Facebook) have 'significant influence on the face of extremist Heathenry' (Pardy, 2019). Overall, says Jackson (2022: 131), 'the online space has become central to extreme right activism in a post-digital age'. For instance, Odinia International, a 'folkish Odinist' organisation based in Hawai'i (with 1,400 followers on Facebook by March 2024) celebrates 'putting blood before nationality', is overtly opposed to Judaism and interracial marriage, and has a UK subsidiary. For racist Heathens, the internet can therefore be identified 'as offering the best opportunity' for turning their political agenda 'global' (Macklin, 2005: 315). The extreme-right forum Iron March (IM), which went offline in 2017, had as many as 1600 users; and it was from this online group that the O9A-influenced AWD was formed. The AWD's call to arms came from Brandon Clint Russell who used the hackneyed racist Heathen pseudonym 'Odin' to announce the formation of the AWD on 12 October 2015 (SPLC, n.d.f). The AWD also utilised an anonymous freeware digital service for gamers, known as Discord, to host its chats, videos and images. According to Lawrence *et al.* (2020: 40), '[t]he internet, and particularly the encrypted platforms', especially 'the so-called Terrorgram network on the messaging app Telegram', were being utilised as secure locales for spreading much racist O9A propaganda. Consequently, whereas before it was much harder to come across extremist groups, or even know of their existence, let alone join them, 'Then came the internet' (Lowles, 2020: 10). This makes the work of anti-racists including amongst the Heathen community even more important, to counter the tsunami of racist and far-right agendas being promulgated.

Of course, in another manifestation of far-right metapolitics, racist Heathen discourse is also perpetuated in traditional face-to-face fora. We have already cited the example of Tom Rowsell who, outside of his popular 'Survive the Jive' YouTube channel, has been a prominent figure at such far-right events as the Generation Identity UK conference (2019), a Traditional Britain Group event (2021) and the Pagan Futures conference (2022) (HnH, 2024: 107). Troy Southgate, the aforementioned editor of Black Front Press (and publisher of books by Woden's Folk's Wulf Ingessunu, discussed in Chapter 6) and performing musician with the neofolk band H.E.R.R. (on which, more below), co-founded and led a now-defunct London-based 'meta-political lecture and discussion group…to discuss a range of "esoteric" ideas…that are traditionally…associated with extreme right-wing politics' (Macklin, 2015: 177). Influenced by the French Nouvelle Droite and called the London New Right, it utilised a Sonnenrad-/Black Sun-inspired design as its logo, proclaimed itself as elitist, polytheistic and rejecting egalitarianism, claimed a membership of around 150, and has hosted a number of talks on Heathen subjects, such as Wodenism, runes and the Black Sun (e.g. Macklin, 2015). According to Macklin (2015: 183), race was a prominent theme during these discussions. Intriguingly, Macklin (2015: 178) suggests that given its occult, racist, anti-Semitic and esoteric interests, an 'accurate comparison' to the London New Right actually 'might be the Thule society', the aforementioned early twentieth-century German social-political association which emerged partly out of Ariosophy and in turn was influential on the German Workers' Party (DAP) (see Chapter 3). Jackson (2022: 90), when discussing Southgate, proposes that he advocates 'forms of entryism, or the strategy of joining other political organisations and influencing their political direction'. Southgate, then, with his broadly spread associations in publishing, music and think-tanks, offers a good example of how the far right uses a wide range of established and new media in metapolitical attempts to influence wider culture.

The far-right music scene

While a variety of cultural fora have been implicated in the far-right cultural scene, music holds particular metapolitical resonance (e.g. François and Godwin, 2008; Ashby and Schofield, 2015). The subgenres of Heavy Metal rock music known as black metal (BM) and its offshoot National Socialist black metal (NSBM), with their combination of 'Nordic cosmology, magic and occultism' with a distinctive music style have had specific saliency as 'an attractive front for fascist and Nazi propaganda among the young (Goodrick-Clarke, 2002: 213; cf. Kahn-Harris, 2007; Shekhovtsov, 2009; Hill and Spracklen, 2010; Granholm, 2011; Hale, 2015: 113–114; Saunders, 2020). In this section we discuss examples of far-right metapolitics in neofolk, also known as 'Apocalyptic Folk', which emerged in the 1980s in part as 'an off-shoot of the goth and post-punk genres', but with a distinctive use of traditional folk and early music and instruments alongside electronic and industrial influences. While it has been described as revelling in 'taboo-breaking and flirtations with extremism' (Spracklen, 2015: 161), as with other musical genres neofolk cannot be generalised as entirely far-right. But in addressing such themes as 'paganism, occultism, traditionalism, philosophy, war, apocalypse, and nihilism' (Genius, 2023), which as we have shown do lend themselves to being especially attractive to the far right, some neofolk bands have shown a tendency to far-right cultural discourse and its perpetuation.

Death in June (DIJ), for example, is one of the most established, leading UK neofolk bands, and has been described as steeped in 'Germanic and Celtic paganism, *völkisch* mysticism and antimodernist imagery including National Socialism' (Hall, 2017: 60; also Keenan, 2016). The band's longstanding frontman, Douglas Pearce, disputes the latter associations (Hall, 2017: 60–62), a long-established tactic of the far right to say one thing while doing another. Critics of DIJ have certainly recognised this latter tactic:

Death in June (DIJ) is not a typical white power nazi band – they do not shave their heads, sing about lynching Blacks or rant about Jewish conspiracies. Nonetheless, DIJ's unabashed support for fascist ideology and aesthetics is just as strong. Their use of fascist symbolism goes far beyond shock tactics, and ultimately the artistic and philosophical message they put forward serves to create an interest and acceptance that fascist cultural activists can exploit. This is particularly dangerous at a time when the white power music business generates millions in sales each year and fascists increasingly seek to gain a foothold in new subcultures, particularly the goth, neofolk, experimental and industrial scenes. Douglas Pearce, the singer/songwriter and central person in DIJ, has always been careful to conceal his true political beliefs and avoid controversy, but a close examination of DIJ's interests and activities reveals where his loyalties lie. (Midwest Unrest, 2006: n.p.)

Just as music bands identifying as 'Satanic' view their music as providing 'a crucial role in providing new blood and vitality' to their movement (van Luijk, 2016: 382), it is likely that the far right see the potential appeal of the contemporary music scene in a similar fashion. The fact that DIJ has a popular reach of over five million views on their 'Death in June – Topic' YouTube channel (Death in June, n.d.) suggests the medium is certainly successful in getting the message across.

The following context offers some insight into how DIJ draw on far-right tropes in their music. The band takes its name from the Night of the Long Knives when Hitler arranged the murder of his rivals in the *Sturmabteilung* (Assault Division) who were critical of his policies. Nazi imagery, including the Death Head (worn by the SS), is a consistent theme on their album covers, as are such Germanic runes as Algiz and Odal, often favoured in far-right imagery following their appropriation by Nazis and neo-Nazis into blood and soil ideology. Pearce has also performed with Sonnenrad/Black Sun and Death's Head imagery as part of the set design (Figure 8.1). Given the above, as well as the band's many references to the Holocaust and Nazism, as exemplified in songs such as 'Lullaby to a Ghetto' or 'Kapò', it is not surprising that the Southern Poverty Law Center classifies their work as 'Hate Music' and 'white power music' (SPLC, n.d.g).

Other notable British-based neofolk groups with far-right associations include the bands Fire + Ice and Sol Invictus (translated as 'Unconquered Sun' after a third-century CE Roman pagan cult), the former headed by Ian Read, the latter Tony Wakeford in collaboration with Read. Just as the membership of far-right organisations and groupuscules often bleeds across different groups and organisations, so the neofolk scene often involves musicians from different ensembles working and performing in various iterations. Read has participated in a number of DIJ recordings, for instance, and his links to racist Heathenry are made evident by his work

Figure 8.1 DIJ performing with Black Sun and Death's Head imagery (Public domain).

in Edred Thorsson's Rune Gild, in his capacity as the editor of its journal, *Rûna*. Read attained the status of Rune Master in the Rune Gild, garnering this accolade in recognition of his work on the Fire+Ice album *Rûna*. Sol Invictus stands out in particular for its far-right politics and links with racist Heathenry. The band's founder, Tony Wakeford, is a former member of the National Front, has claimed inspiration from a number of extremist artists and writers, notably Julius Evola and Ezra Pound, and has also been associated with the racist Heathen organisation, the Odinic Rite (Backes, 2012: 413; Ansuz, 2019a) (see Chapter 6). Wakeford seems to have formed Sol Invictus primarily to avoid the criticism surrounding his earlier band, Above the Ruins, which was lambasted for its far-right sympathies (Ansuz, 2019a). It is also notable that the radiate crown or sunburst logo of Sol Invictus, while drawing on ancient Roman pagan imagery, also resembles the Sonnenrad/Black Sun.

The Odinic Rite associated with Wakeford is not the only one of the 'three thorns' of British racist Heathenry to be involved with far-right musical ensembles. The aforementioned Troy Southgate (see Chapter 5), in addition to working with Woden's Folk, plays and sings with a Dutch English group named after a seemingly palingenetically inspired vision of a new right world: Heilig Europe Romeins Rijk (Holy Europe of a Rome Reborn), or H.E.R.R. Southgate's history of involvement with far-right organisations challenges the denials from neofolk musicians and their fans who protest that their fascist Heathen trappings are no more than a countercultural aesthetic used for their shock value. Whilst these neofolk bands might not promote violence directly and, like the racist Heathen organisations they have been associated with, feign at being apolitical, elements of their musical output and the associations of their leading musicians with far-right groupuscules outside of music, evidence their far-right sympathies (Shekhovtsov, 2009: 443). Titles of some songs, such as H.E.R.R.'s 'The Fall of Constantinople' (2005), also play – literally – to fears over Muslim immigrants in Europe.

Conclusion

Macklin (2005: 303) has argued that if scholars of the far right in the UK look beyond a mere traditional narrow political lens, they will perchance see that a study of the far right in the UK, given its now very apparent wider cultural influence, deserves far more than a mere 'epilogue' or 'footnote' in the history books. In this chapter we have explored this wider far-right cultural milieu beyond racist Heathen religion and how its co-option of heathenry/Heathenry can be usefully identified as a metapolitical strategy. Across a wide range of media, including literature, film, fashion, gaming, the internet and music, the far right attempts to influence people through everyday forms of culture they engage with in their attempts to promote racism and ultimately undermine liberal democracy so as to thereby dominate the political sphere (see e.g. Bale, 2020; Liyanage, 2020). However unsuccessful this ultimate strategy may be, the Nazisploitation of cultural forms has been diversly used to disseminate the 'ideas, values and beliefs' of a far-right racist Heathen counter-cultural struggle (Copsey and Richardson, 2015: 1). Whilst others have commented upon the way in which Christian Nationalists are trying to infiltrate and influence mainstream Christian groups 'in order to pull Christians to the far right' (Liyanage, 2020: n.p.), and Hindutva politics has come to dominate Bollywood film production in India (Leidig, 2020), there is an urgent need now to monitor a similar development within Heathenry.

We closed this chapter with the example of the far-right music scene, particularly neofolk, which can be seen to promote racist Heathenry 'far more effectively than any number of meetings and marches could' (Macklin, 2005: 314). In order to develop our examination of the particular role of music in far-right and specifically racist Heathen metapolitics, in the next chapter we present a sustained case study of black metal, focussing on the Manchester-based band Winterfylleth who have achieved commercial success with several successful albums and by headlining a number of popular Heavy Metal festivals, such as Bloodstock UK. Winterfylleth are especially pertinent to this study because they promote a specific 'English Pagan' ultranationalist, hyper-masculine identity whilst paradoxically attempting to distance themselves from the far right. We are interested in the complexities of this contradiction, and how this enables Winterfylleth to maintain mainstream BM status and fandom, and so promote their racist Heathen message, despite their more extreme discourse.

9

Winterfylleth: from 'National Pride' in 'English Heritage' to '14W' and 'WPWW'

Introduction

Plato warned about the interconnectivity of politics and music (Askew, 2003: 609), and not surprisingly music is also a major flashpoint in the politics of the twenty-first century. In India, Hindutva Pop, a genre of pop music that promotes a Hindu nationalist agenda and which is often heard playing on loudspeakers during attacks on Muslims or accompanying speeches by BJP politicians, is attracting large audiences, with some garnering over sixty-five million YouTube viewings (Zafar and Pandit, 2022: n.p.). The music videos of female singer-songwriter Laxmi Dubey, for example, are replete with images of Hindu deities, bare-breasted and muscle-toned Indian men and the colour saffron (an overt signifier of a Hindu nationalist agenda). Meanwhile, in the US in the summer of 2023, national press stories were dominated by singer-songwriter Oliver Anthony's 'Rich Men North of Richmond' and whether or not the song, with lyrics railing against taxes, the obese and 'welfare cheats', and lauded by Joe Rogan among others, was seen to represent a new right-wing anthem (e.g. Chilton, 2023: n.p.). And in the UK, the band Forefather, who have been described as being 'anti-Christian' (The Metal Archives, n.d.c), explicitly celebrate their 'unique Anglo-Saxon roots' (Forefather, 2021), referring nationalistically to their music as 'Anglo-Saxon Metal' rather than black metal.

Having highlighted in the previous chapter how such fora as literature, film, fashion, the internet – and music – can be used in far-right metapolitical attempts to influence and disrupt the democratic system, in this chapter we present a case study of racism in the black metal scene focussing on the 'English Pagan' BM band Winterfylleth, who promote an English nationalist radical right identity whilst paradoxically attempting to distance themselves from the extreme right. We are interested in the complexities of this contradiction, and how this enables Winterfylleth, whose YouTube views number in the hundreds of thousands, to maintain mainstream BM status and fandom despite their more extreme discourse. We discuss various evidence implicating the band in the racist BM scene, contrary to the band's own assertions, and demonstrate how groups such as Winterfylleth thereby use metapolitics to perpetuate far-right ideologies amongst a broader fan-base than that attained by self-identifying far-right BM bands and in an arena well beyond mainstream party politics. We argue, therefore, that such manifestations of far-right racism co-opting Heathenry warrant ongoing monitoring and analysis.

Black metal

In addition to neofolk, the subgenre of black metal has been especially associated with a strong emphasis on pre-Christian pagan/heathen aesthetics combined with far-right politics (Burley, 2019: n.p.). BM has been described as 'uniquely heretical' (Peel, 2023: 167) as well as 'a form of extreme metal typified by evil sounds and elitist ideologies' with a number of bands drawing on 'nationalist and fascist images and themes' (Spracklen, 2015: 161; see also de Boise, 2012; Dyck, 2016). Its sound is generally characterised by shrieking and/or growling vocals, disjointed guitar riffs, a frenetic pace with an emphasis upon atmosphere, often deliberately created through distortion, a heavy use of delay and reverb, as well as a raw/'lo-fi' quality to the recording. Many BM performers adopt pseudonyms, sometimes for dramatic effect, other times as a form of liberation or expression, but also to conceal their identities, facilitating a wider BM culture of secrecy and obfuscation (Peel, 2023: 73). BM clothing typically involves wearing black, leather, and medieval or pseudo-medieval costume, as well as elaborate make-up, 'corpse paint' or 'battle paint' (*Encyclopaedia Metallum*: n.p.), further enabling the camouflaging of identity. Medieval weaponry, alongside Satanic and Pagan imagery, often conflating the two, additionally appear with relative frequency on BM websites, CD covers, clothing and fan/musician tattoos. Other common musical and visual leitmotifs include coldness (frost, hail, snow, ice), war, death, fantasy, the apocalyptic and the mythological, especially Norse mythology. Although such motifs might be viewed as deliberately traditional and/or transgressive simply to attract devotees to the music and its visual aesthetic, it is clear that such elements of BM can also function 'as a springboard from which violent actions could logically emerge', as in the case of the Norwegian church burnings in the 1990s, with the specific intent of 'reclaiming…a pagan heritage' (Phillipov, 2011: 152). It is important to state, however, that the genre 'is not a unified, monolithic culture' (Olsen, 2008: 4).

BM, like neofolk, cannot be generalised as being far-right and indeed has a radical left-wing contingent (e.g. Peel, 2023), but its critique of modern society and rejection of Heavy Metal's commercialisation (Alessio and Wallis, 2021) has proven particularly attractive to the far right (e.g. Olson, 2011; Phillipov, 2011; Buesnel, 2020). BM followers state that the music is primarily mystical, celebrating a romantic and idealised view of the past which is heavy on ritual and critical of secularism (Olson, 2011). Aron Weaver, of the US BM and Heathen-inspired band Wolves in the Throne Room, describes it 'as an artistic movement that is critiquing modernity on a fundamental level, saying that the modern world view is missing something' (Bubblegum, 2009: n.p.). It is often considered to have begun with the British band Venom, with their infamous second album *Black Metal*. While BM has frequently drawn on Satanic, Pagan and Heathen imagery since its inception, primarily out of a deliberate desire to break taboos and to acquire media attention, the music has become more ideologically oriented with the rise of a 'second wave' of racist Heathenry. This shift was exemplified by the Norwegian band Burzum, a music project by the aforementioned Kristian 'Varg' Vikernes. Burzum is known for its extreme ideological orientation as Vikernes openly embraced esoteric Nazism and in the 1990s promoted Odinism, or as he put it, 'National Heathenry' (Peel, 2023: 2). The case of Vikernes also demonstrates the real-world consequences that these ideologies can have, as he was convicted of the arson of three churches in 1994, as well as the murder of fellow BM musician and convicted church arsonist Euronymous of the BM band Mayhem (Peel, 2023: 129). Goodrick-Clarke (2002: 209) states that BM's 'fascination with the occult, evil, Nazism and Hitler' were also a possible motivation behind the 1999 massacre, on Hitler's birthday, of twelve students and a teacher at Columbine High School in Colorado. More recently, it was reported that Holden Matthew, the twenty-one-year-old charged with burning down three historically black churches in Louisiana, was influenced by BM and that he held racist Heathen beliefs (Kaur, 2019: n.p.). Some of BM's aesthetics even appear to have influenced the violent imagery of the neo-Nazi Atomwaffen Division whose James 'Rape' Denton, 'was spotted Sieg-heiling at a gig for the band Horna' (Kelly, 2021: n.p.). BM has since become so influential that one commentator defined it as 'Norway's greatest cultural export' (Grow, n.d.).

The proclivity to far-right thinking within BM has led to a unique subgenre, National Socialist black metal (NSBM), which has aimed to distinguish its politics and religiosity much more overtly than BM (Olson, 2011: 135). NSBM explicitly rejects Judaism, Christianity and Islam, and was very much influenced in its development by the actions of Varg Vikernes. According to Hoppadietz and Reichenbach (2019: 223), amongst NSBM musicians and their fans 'the Nazi era is viewed nostalgically as an occultist, esoteric phenomenon, and elements of Nordic mythology and a blood-and-soil ideology are used to produce the construct of "Aryan supremacy"'.

NSBM is also violent, exemplified by German NSBM band Absurd, and their killing of a fifteen-year-old boy which they also then referenced on their 1995 album cover Thuringian Pagan Madness. According to Olson (2008), NSBM fuses classical fascist ideological elements with racist and ethnic Paganism. Critics argue that NSBM is deliberately utilised 'as a vehicle to spread hate and radicalize nominally apolitical metal fans' (Kelly, 2021: n.p.). Whilst NSBM bands have a geographical focus in, for example, Scandinavia and Ukraine, the subgenre has become global. When the keywords 'National Socialism' are searched for in the online Metal Archives there are an astounding 1052 results of active bands worldwide. Although BM and neofolk are generally described as reflecting a minority counterculture, DIJ's track 'Fall Apart' (2010) has had well over a million YouTube views. By comparison, Varg Vikernes' band Burzum has had some twelve million YouTube views for its track 'Dunkelheit'. Accompanying fan comments from the latter also include violent anti-Christian statements, such as: 'Varg + he lives in france + black metal + notre dame', and 'Feeling cute might go burn down a church'.

While some BM bands are explicitly racist, others use the genre's ability to shock and entertain to promote their musical careers rather than any particular far-right agenda. The British 1980s–1990s Thrash Metal band Sabbat, for instance, 'introduced a markedly more folkloric English paganism into their lyrical themes and promo materials'; they did so, though, as teenagers on a whim and merely as a result of 'a book one of the band members' mums [sic] owned about witches' (Magee, 2023). There was no religious or political agenda. They also, nonetheless, played up their Pagan and Satanic notoriety for promotional reasons, often making anonymous complaints about themselves to local newspapers in order to deliberately generate publicity (Magee, 2023). But as one commentator has said 'for some musicians and fans, this artistic dalliance [with racist Paganism] was more than a frivolous matter' (van Luijk, 2016: 381). In some cases, the far-right politics are revealed when one scratches beneath the surface. The band 'Stuka Squadron' state that they are anti-Nazi, with 'no affiliation or beliefs with the white supremacy movement' (The Metal Archives, n.d.b). However, one of their founders, the bass player for the band, Graham Cushway, who has a PhD in History, performs 'wearing SS insignia'. Meanwhile, the fictional biography for Cushway's stage name, Lord Pryce, mentions that he was a member of the Thule Society (Lawrence, 2019). There are multiple further references in the band's music to Odinism and Ariosophy too, including to a racial war in the track 'One Eyed God King' (2011).

Other BM bands, such as Winterfylleth, are deliberately politically ambiguous in their lyrics, expressing their more controversial beliefs offstage, enabling them to continue to play at different venues and in turn to further proselytise their ideological agendas without censorship. It is this kind of borderline content which, according to Wegener (2023: n.p.), presents one of the biggest problems for terror or hate monitoring groups in terms of prevention activities. What makes understanding the motivations of some of these bands doubly difficult is that some musicians also use far-right imagery merely for shock value and commercial success. As Cronos of Venom stated when asked if he was a Satanist: 'We are entertainers first and foremost – if I wanted to be a murderer or a Satanist, I'd do that full time instead of playing songs for a living' (Kitts, 2018). Other artists, by contrast, might seem to utilise far-right imagery merely for commercial or aesthetic reasons, but in reality this enables them to garner further support from and for the far right. It is, consequently, difficult to quantify the impact of racist Heathen BM on the fan base and to demonstrate how, and indeed if, band followers develop 'a distinction between the sound and the ideologies' (Spracklen, 2015: 165).

Several neofolk and BM bands have subsequently similarly started to become explicitly anti-fascist in the face of the growing BM and NSBM genres. Some of them even adopt novel satirical resistance to the appropriation of their music. One such artist, the UK and London-based Gaylord, released an album titled *The Black Metal Scene Needs to be Destroyed* (2018). This album contains songs entitled 'Odin Doesn't Listen to NSBM You Inbred Alt-Right Shitheels' and 'Neo-Nazi Metalheads Will be Hanged and Their Broken Corpses Openly Mocked' (Kelly, 2018). There is no doubting here, as evidenced in the latter song, the anti-fascist politics in their lyrics either:

Nazi shithead black metal
Idiotic nationalistic garbage
The rifffs aren't even good...
Their rare Burzum vinyls
Set on fire and burned
Watch them cry in shame
Odin was not a capitalist

The Metal Archives, n.d.a

Another anti-NSBM band is the US-based Neckbeard Deathcamp with their 2018 album entitled 'White Nationalism is for Basement Dwelling Losers'. In a further interesting example, King ov Hell (n.d.) who identifies as Satanist and plays in the band Gorgoroth, states that 'I am totally against every form of flock ideology. Nazism is an ideology of the flock'. The Scandinavian neofolk band Heilung ('Healing'), on the other hand, recently issued a statement on the alleged harassment of a Black woman at one of their performances in New York: 'Apparently some people attended our ritual with the idea that Heilung is only for white people…This is not the case. Heilung is for ALL people, regardless of the color of the skin. And we are sorry that this happened at our show. We do not tolerate hate speech and racism' (BrooklynVegan, 2020: n.p.). In welcoming 'ALL people', however, the statement can be read as sidestepping an outright dismissal of their far-right fanbase. And it is notable that imagery used in their performances includes sun-wheels (for example made into brass talismans, attached to antlers in shamanic-like headgear) and swastikas (worn in clothing), and while these are unlike blatant Nazi/neo-Nazi Sonnenrad and swastika insignia, with an aesthetic drawing instead upon early medieval sun-wheels and swastikas, such imagery would be recognised by and identified with by racist Heathens in their fan base. Like Heathenry itself, black metal, like neofolk (see previous chapter) cannot be generalised as racist, but there are prominent racist Heathen elements within it. In order to develop our discussion of racist Heathenry in black metal specifically, we next offer a sustained case study of the UK band Winterfylleth and their discourse around a nationalist, white, hyper-masculine identity.

Winterfylleth

Winterfylleth formed in 2006 and derive their name from the Old English word for the month of October (as recorded by Bede; see Bosworth, 2014: n.p.). The band has released a total of seven albums (plus a live album, *Siege of Mercia: Live at Bloodstock* [2017] and an anthology), all of which have followed the band's distinctive BM sound apart from their sixth album, *The Hallowing of Heirdom* (2018), in which the band adopted a largely neofolk acoustic tone. While Winterfylleth is not well-known in the mainstream music scene the band is popular in both the English and international Heavy Metal scenes. Winterfylleth had 22,000 monthly listeners on Spotify and 234,112 views on their Vevo YouTube channel (as of April 2023). The band has also begun to achieve widespread mainstream critical success, with their albums being added to end-of-year lists on leading Heavy Metal webzines/magazines such as *Terrorizer*, *Kerrang!* and *Metal Hammer*. On their official website, and during interviews, Winterfylleth band members openly identify their musical output as nationalistic, describing it as 'English Heritage'-themed (Spracklen, *et al.*, 2014). When asked what this identity meant in an interview, Chris Naughton, the band's lead vocalist and guitarist said that instead of copying Scandinavian black metal the band wanted to 'put a uniquely, hopefully, English twist' [on their music] and 'talk about, well, stories of England and the British Isles and stuff that matters to us' (Rich Reviewz, 2013: n.p.). Having noted in previous chapters how the far right is increasingly drawing upon the British folklore and folk horror revival of the last few years (e.g. Chapter 7 regarding the Wyrd Isle Collective), it is worth adding to this that in the case of Winterfylleth the band have recorded versions of the well-known English folk tune John Barleycorn, as well as the Abbots Bromley Horn Dance.

Winterfylleth's nationalist approach to the ancient past is explicit in the band's lyrics and videos. Two songs which highlight this (and evidence the band's diverse music styles within and beyond BM), are 'Misdeeds of Faith', from the album *The Reckoning Dawn* (2020), and 'Latch to a Grave', from the acoustic album *The Hallowing of Heirdom* (2018). These two songs are especially relevant for analysis here because, excluding live performances, they are two of the most viewed songs on Winterfylleth's *Vevo YouTube* channel, with 30,000 and 34,000 views respectively. Furthermore, they have accompanying music videos which help to boost their songs' popularity and, by implication, their underlying political thinking. The lyrics in 'Misdeeds of Faith' recount the martial story of Mercian Anglo-Saxon warriors going into battle: 'forward went they, with weapons drawn...strong were they with hostile craft, men hell-prone, with wounding rage, with steadfast faith and soulful mind' (Genius, n.d.a: n.p.). Here we see a theme of heroic violence, presumably pitched between warring Anglo-Saxon factions.

'Latch to a Grave', by contrast, whilst also echoing the same theme of militarist Anglo-Saxon culture, is in the style of a lament for a lost heroic Anglo-Saxon past. The song begins, 'I am a Lord's attendant, A soldier's loyal kin, To my master dear, Companion to my king', whilst the video illustrates the story surrounding the death in battle and funeral of an Anglo-Saxon warrior noble (Genius, n.d.b: n.p.), and inheritance of the leadership role by a young kinsman. The warriors are dressed in the attire of early Anglo-Saxon heathen warriors and nobles, and the video is interspersed with footage of Winterfylleth performing the song in a medieval-themed hall. The underlying message is that the young, heroic male protagonist must take on the leadership role of his heathen Anglo-Saxon people after the death of the old guard. Given their nationalist position, Winterfylleth, in turn, arguably represent the contemporary inheritors of this tradition, taking up the banner for 'Anglo-Saxon' English (i.e. white) people today. We will develop our argument that the band's 'nationalist' approach veils a deeper ultranationalist and racist agenda, below. It is worth noting at this point that, given the production quality of both the videos and music of the two songs introduced above, Winterfylleth often appear as highly liked 'Pagan' artists on sites such as Rate Your Music (a massive community/fan database with well over three million reviews), as well as amongst individual fan lists (for example 'Pagan Black Metal Rarities', n.d.), or that they are reviewed positively as a 'pagan black metal band' on sites such as Angry Metal Guy. The band therefore have a broad reach to spread their message.

In an interview with the Heavy Metal magazine *Iron Fist*, Naughton said:

> In everything we do we are aiming to educate people about social issues and raise awareness of the link history can play in interpreting the modern world. Even if our songs are not always directly related to it, then [sic] underlying spirit that runs through Winterfylleth is that of change and of awareness. If our music makes you become more interested in history or in social issues, then it has done its job. (Brown, 2012: n.p.)

Other band members align their views with Naughton's nationalism. In an interview with the underground art blog *Lurker*, Winterfylleth's drummer, Simon Lucas, said that the band was founded 'with the intention of honoring England's proud ancestral heritage and rich national culture', adding that the band members 'are very proud and outspoken nationalists' (Richard, 2010: n.p.). Lucas has also stated that 'as a group of socially and culturally aware people…we seek to re-kindle…a sense of proud ancestral heritage in our land, our people, our folklore, our stories and our natural landscape. These are important things for a nation' (Richard, 2010: n.p.). But Lucas' reference to 'our people' and 'our nation' can be read as another way of saying 'white English people', as made more explicit in his concluding statement that, 'If we are not to take care of our own, surely we are forsaking our very existence?!' (Richard, 2010: n.p.). This sort of attention to 'our own' and their 'very existence' recalls not only the Odinic Rite's exclusivist maxim, 'Faith, Folk, Family', described as 'things to which we are linked by blood' (Odinic Rite, n.d.b), as well as the clarion call of Woden's Folk, 'Proud of our Land – Proud of our Folk – Proud of our Blood!' (Hall, 2019: n.p.), but also the 'Fourteen Words' (or 14W) slogan of white supremacists, coined by David Lane (co-founder of the racist Heathen organisation Wotansvolk), that 'we must secure the existence of our people and a future for white children', expressed today in terms of the 'Great Replacement' conspiracy theory. The nationalism expressed by Winterfylleth's Lucas and Naughton, then, has a deeper racist meaning than might appear on the surface of their public statements, as we shall go on to demonstrate.

Questioning the message

Despite the strong emphasis on a nationalist, white, hyper-masculine identity, as expressed in Winterfylleth's music and the public statements of band members, they do attempt to draw a line between their nationalist approach and the racist agenda of other BM bands. Naughton has said that 'nationalism is the devotion to the interests or culture of one's nation, the honoring of its unique sense of cultural and ancestral identity. It does not ever mean to hate another race of people or their culture' (Richard, 2010: n.p.). Naughton admits that their 'musical influence…unashamedly borrows from Burzum' and other BM bands on the extreme right, but also states that they do '*not necessarily*' [our italics] believe the message behind those bands (quoted in Brown, 2012: n.p.), an obtuse refusal rather than an outright rejection. Several other factors also contradict Winterfylleth's non-racist claims, including their use of a Nazi/neo-Nazi Black Sun symbol on one album cover (since removed) designed by Romanian artist Alexandru Moga, and the band's name itself which could reference a date of special importance to the far right, the month of October 1922, the birthdate of Fascism, when Benito Mussolini's Blackshirts marched on Rome.

Winterfylleth's far-right politics can be identified too in the messaging of band members online between the release of their first and second albums, in particular from comments on the private MySpace page of Chris Westby, the band's bassist (Mantie and Smith, 2017: 286). Here, Westby uses two acronyms used by white supremacists to attempt to veil their racism, the aforementioned '14W' ('we must secure the existence of our people and a future for white children'), and added to this, 'WPWW' ('white pride world-wide'). Westby's comments reinforce the real political intent behind Lucas' nationalist message that we (i.e. white English people) must 'take care of our own' otherwise 'we are forsaking our very existence'. Given these explicit white supremacist associations, Westby's words generated a massive outcry from anti-fascist Heavy Metal fans who used them as evidence to define the band as 'nazi scum', 'racist' (Urban 75, n.d.: n.p.) and part of the NSBM scene (Reddit, n.d.: n.p.). Westby then justified his use of the acronyms on his MySpace page. Regarding 'WPWW' he stated:

> I STRONGLY believe in this [phrase], as I believe that EVERYONE of every colour, creed and culture should be proud of their race and what it has achieved. I realise this slogan to some ill-informed people may read 'White Power' or 'Race Hate', and maybe even those who actually put the slogan together have more extreme 'unsavoury' opinions, I don't know. What I do know, and what I take from this phrase is honest. Everyone should be proud. I am not inciting racial hatred, I am displaying my pride. I am totally aware of what some White Nationalists believe and that they use phrases like this for more 'extreme purposes' but at least my interpretation of it is personal and means no harm. 'Black Pride' e.t.c. is accepted, and fair enough, so it should be, but why is White pride not? In a world where the White man is now a minority, especially in his homeland I feel it is totally acceptable and harmless

to display my pride. If people want to assume that I am inciting hatred, then that is their own silly, ignorant misinterpretation. (Urban 75, n.d.: n.p.)

He also explained his use of '14W' by stating:

This phrase was made by someone with more extreme views than myself. However, just as the same with 'WPWW' I feel the 14 words, in my personal interpretation are about pride for one's race, and the continuation of its bloodline. Of course I realise that this phrase is linked with neo-Nazism and other extreme views, views that I do not agree with. What I take from 14 words, again is personal to me. Every race should be proud and want to preserve it's [sic] pure bloodline, if you feel this incites hatred, again, your [sic] sorely mistaken, or at least in my opinion and usage of the 14 words. (Urban 75, n.d.: n.p.)

Westby concluded by saying that WPWW and 14W were, consequently, '2 phrases that I use and will continue to use' (Urban 75, n.d.: n.p.). An obtuse appeal to individual freedom of belief, however, does nothing to veil Westby's white supremacism and the potential impact of his views on the band's fanbase. Critics pointed to Westby's casual use of phrases he admits were coined by neo-Nazi and white supremacist groups, not forgetting that his mention of 'pure bloodline(s)' derives from Ariosophist ideology. Furthermore, his comment above that 'White man is now a minority, especially in his homeland', alludes to the far-right 'Great Replacement' conspiracy theory, which claims that white European populations are being culturally, racially and demographically replaced by immigrants from primarily Muslim-majority countries.

A side music project by Westby and Richard Brass, Winterfylleth's lead guitarist (also backing vocals), also generated significant debate because of its far-right elements. The project, titled R1st4nce, was described by Westby on his MySpace page as 'a noise art project' which 'features sound samples of speeches by Hitler and also uses modified samples of Third Reich marching bands' (Urban 75, n.d.: n.p.). Critics took this incorporation of Nazi sounds into R1st4nce's music to be yet another instance of Winterfylleth's far-right sympathies. Westby again attempted to justify himself by saying: 'We used these [sounds] because it links to the genre [of black metal] and its extreme nature and sound, and because we know the offense and controversy it would cause. That does not mean we endorse or follow such unsavoury views, politics, and thoughts' (Urban 75, n.d.: n.p.). However, the broader context of Westby's messaging, and that of other members of Winterfylleth, make it clear that the neo-Nazi aesthetics of R1st4nce were not simply to attract attention but part of a long-standing far-right narrative.

With all this controversy Winterfylleth has faced ever-increasing public scrutiny. They were, according to Spracklen (2017: 286), subsequently dropped from the line-up for a festival in Manchester. Both Westby and Brass then left the band in 2009 (Mantie and Smith, 2017: 286), but it is not clear whether this was voluntary or because they were ousted. With the absence of these two band members who had attracted negative attention, Winterfylleth tried to improve its reputation and distance itself from accusations of harbouring far-right sympathies. Once the issue had become public, however, it was hard to quell. Fans continued to question the political agenda of the remaining band members. On one online chat forum a user wrote: 'the whole band's racist...they all share these beliefs but Chris was the only one fucking stupid enough to think they could openly say it' (Urban 75, n.d.: n.p.). While Westby and Brass drew the most negative attention for their far-right sympathies, other band members have made their own far-right politics known as well. In an interview with the black metal blog *Ravishing Griminess*, Naughton advises his readers:

> Always strive to be informed about issues affecting your country or your culture and make sure that if you don't like something that is happening that you do something about it...[G]et people back in touch with who and what they are. A country without a culture or an identity is like an accident waiting to happen. Bottom line, people need to feel needed and if their culture, or family – because of a cultural confusion – cannot provide them with a sense of 'self' or 'community' then this is where problems will, and do, start to arise. Don't dwell in apathy...Hail Heritage! (Kelly, 2008: n.p.)

Naughton's comments about the importance of 'culture' and 'country', when placed in the context of other messaging from Winterfylleth, reifies the Nazi ideology of *Volksgemeinschaft* which proposed that all social ills could be cured by uniting people through their national identity. Further, his concern over 'cultural confusion' is a reference to what the far right identify as the problem of multiculturalism. His 'Hail Heritage!' sign-off, moreover, recalls the Nazi salute 'Hail Hitler', and perhaps more than coincidentally, the two share the same initials H.H., which are often used as a salutary acronym of the far right. While the remaining Winterfylleth band members have tried and failed to distance themselves from the far right following the departure of Westby and Brass, their drummer Simon Lucas has been photographed making a Nazi salute while wearing a false Hitler moustache (Urban 75, n.d.: n.p.). The online user who posted the image wrote: 'Winterfylleth are 100% nazi scum. Wodensthrone are no better. Here's the current drummer from Winterfylleth proving how he's definitely not a nazi' (Urban 75, n.d.: n.p.). Another user, 'karmapotrait', in reference to Winterfylleth's song 'The Threnody of Triumph', implied that they were even NSBM (Reddit, n.d.: n.p.). Another Winterfylleth band member, guitarist Dan Capp, as we pointed to previously (Chapters 6 and 8), is 'closely affiliated with the racist Heathen group Woden's Folk' (HnH, 2024: 107), hosts far-right podcasts on the 'Fyrgen' website (https://fyrgen.com/) and has a 'Dark Folk' solo project 'Wolcensmen' which performed at the 'Pagan Futures Conference' (London, 25 June 2022); other speakers included the far-right Heathen Thomas Rowsell of the Survive the Jive podcast. So, while Winterfylleth certainly express a strong nationalism in their lyrics and certain public statements, and have made attempts to distance themselves from the far right, taken in the wider context of their messaging in interviews and other fora, it is quite clear the band do nonetheless express a far-right agenda, thinly veiled behind their 'National Pride' in 'English Heritage'.

Collaborations with other far-right bands

The collaboration between members of Winterfylleth and other far-right musicians further demonstrates their far-right political views, as well of those of several other UK-based BM bands. Winterfylleth and the Sunderland-based band Wodensthrone (formed in 2005 and active until 2016), and cited by the critical fan comment above, are considered musical 'brothers-in-arms' because of their common BM musical style, focus on Anglo-Saxon heritage, and regular collaborations, including recordings and touring together. One anti-fascist Heavy Metal fan has commented online that 'Winterfylleth and Wodensthrone are two [BM bands] from the UK that are the dodgiest' (Urban 75, n.d.: n.p.). One critic describes Wodensthrone as flirting with 'Germanic paganism…runes and sunwheels used by openly neo-Nazi bands and organizations' (Spracklen, 2017: 289). The band members of Wodensthrone use aliases derived from Old English, making it hard to identify their actual identities. However, one user on an online chat board (Urban 75, n.d.: n.p.), whose view is supported by *Encyclopedia Metallum* (n.d.: n.p.), an online index of black metal bands, claims that Wildeþrýð, Wodensthrone's front man, was none other than Richard Brass, the former Winterfylleth band member who left the band following his use of Nazi material. While Winterfylleth appeared to distance themselves from Brass after he left the band, his involvement with Wodensthrone indicated that a close relationship continued. Wodensthrone's 'anti-Christian, pagan or heathen' bias was also evident in the way that band member Chris Walsh deliberately chose the pseudonym Raedwald, the historical Anglo-Saxon leader who was cited by Bede for his Pagan stubbornness (Spracklen, 2017: 288).

It is also notable that Winterfylleth and Wodensthrone both signed to the same record label, Candlelight Records, which also has far-right associations. One anti-fascist BM fan states that Candlelight has 'a reputation for being willing to sign up openly neo-Nazi groups' (Urban 75, n.d.: n.p.). They promote, for example, the band Zyklon which uses a sun-wheel symbol in its imagery. Another BM band with far-right sympathies signed to Candlelight Records and with close links to Winterfylleth, is the Norwegian group Enslaved. Winterfylleth's lead singer Naughton describes Enslaved as 'one of my biggest influences' (Blabbermouth, 2009: n.p.). The two bands share a close working relationship as they too regularly tour together. Enslaved's band members have been accused of being Nazis and members of the NSBM scene, claims that they have never chosen to deny (Metalious, n.d.: n.p.), unlike Winterfylleth which has embraced a nationalist identity while attempting to distance itself from the far right. It is also notable that Enslaved recorded a song with the band Emperor, yet another Norwegian BM group signed to Candlelight Records, in a collaboration just months after Emperor's drummer, who publicly goes by the name Faust, murdered a gay man in a hate crime (Metalious, n.d.: n.p.). Faust was convicted for the murder two years later (Moynihan and Soderlind, 1998: 111) and sentenced to fourteen years in prison (Bowar, n.d.). Enslaved's drummer then filled in for Emperor (Metalious, n.d.: n.p.). While some BM bands, such as Winterfylleth, attempt to distance themselves from the far right in public media, other musicians they are associated with are for more vocal in their far-right allegiances, and the close ties between them demonstrate that a wider nexus of far-right sympathies implicates Winterfylleth among them.

A final strand of evidence linking Winterfylleth to the far right is that the band also has a record of attracting fans who are members of neo-Nazi groups. One user wrote in an online forum that they recognised the band's far-right ties because Winterfylleth was 'developing a following from the Blood and Honour scene', a neo-Nazi political splinter group originating in the UK (Urban 75, n.d.: n.p.). This source also identifies supporters from the British Freedom Fighters 'headed by a longstanding neo-Nazi Wigan Mike, and they all kept turning up at metal nights at Manchester where Winterfylleth were playing' (Urban 75, n.d.: n.p.). Arguably, a band is defined to a significant extent by its fans, so if their music and live performances are attracting neo-Nazis then these fans must be drawn to the scene because they recognise those sympathetic to their values and music made for them. Added to this, if a band attracts neo-Nazis and does not do something about it, then they are expressly part of the problem. The link between Winterfylleth and a neo-Nazi fanbase, along with the other evidence presented above, including their nationalist music and video output, the white supremacist public statements of band members, and their musical collaborations and other associations within the BM and NSBM scene, does further evidence the links between Winterfylleth and the far right.

Conclusion

Whilst the bandmembers from Winterfylleth have tried to publicly detach themselves from the far right in some respects, promoting instead a right-of-centre 'national pride' in 'English Heritage', a variety of evidence, including public statements, musical collaborations and other far-right associations within the BM and wider far-right cultural scene, all indicate that their politics are firmly entwined with the far right and that their message is deeply implicated in white supremacism. As Spracklen (2015: 287) observes: 'While it is true to say that the band are not part of the NSBM movement and they are not neo-Nazi, they do use the same discourses and symbols of neo-Nazis'. Their disavowals, therefore, enable the band to continue to play in public spaces and so perpetuate their far-right agenda. Winterfylleth are part of a recent trend within black metal music of focussing their thinking around specifically English blood and soil themes. The aforementioned band, Forefather, for instance, not only describe their music as the distinct subgenre 'Anglo-Saxon Metal' rather than BM, but their music, with such songs as 'When our England Died' (2016), are very much in sync with the 'national pride' in 'English Heritage' promoted by Winterfylleth. There is then, a concerning element of BM music in the UK which articulates an explicitly 'English' or 'Anglo-Saxon' racist Heathen identity, which can have a metapolitical influence.

As a result, explicitly anti-racist Heathen musicians are kicking back. Responding to the appropriation of Heathenry in BM, for example, Heathens United Against Racism (HUAR) posted on their Facebook page on 4 April 2019: 'Showing some love for Wardruna for taking a stand against racists'. The Norwegian neofolk and Heathen band Wardruna, who contributed to the soundtrack of the History Channel series *Vikings* and so attracted a large audience to their music, have increasingly made prominent anti-racist statements. In a blog (Ansuz, 2019b) promoting 'antifascist neofolk bands from around the world', the band's lead, Einar Selvik states: 'It is a very positive effect, that increased interest does not allow the subculture on the extreme right wing to use our history in peace. We have somehow taken our own story back'. And in the UK, too, anti-racist Heathen musicians are taking a stand. The duo Runesine (one of whom, Wallis, is a co-author of this book) performed their 'Futhorc: New Sonic Rites for the Old English Futhorc' at the Acid Horse 2023 festival in Wiltshire. While the runes have been co-opted by the far right since List, the pamphlet they made available at the event included a translation of the Old English rune poem with a prominent anti-racist

Figure 9.1 'Runes and their meanings' anti-racist Heathen meme image (Public domain).

Figure 9.2 Digital release of Runesine's track *Futhorc: New Sonic Rites for the Old English Futhorc* with hashtag #heathensagainsthate displayed (Runesine).

meme image (Figure 9.1), and the cover image for their digital download of the track displays a prominent bindrune hashtag, #heathensagainsthate (Figure 9.2). The anti-racist Heathen organisation Heathens Against Hate, as well as HUAR and other anti-racist Heathens, are mobilising to counter the narratives of hate from racist Heathens. In Part III of this book, we balance our sustained treatment of racist Heathenry in Part II with close analysis of precisely how anti-racist Heathens are fighting back against the racists. This book itself, then, we hope, forms part of this fightback.

Part III

Heathens against hate

hvars þú bǫl kannt,
kveðú þat bǫlvi at
ok gefat þínum fjándum frið

Hávámal, 127 (Evans 1986: 65)

If evil thou knowest,
As evil proclaim it,
And make no friendship with foes.

trans. Adams Bellows, 1936: 60

10

Declaration 127 and anti-racist Heathen activism

Introduction

On Friday 8 September 2023, James Saunders, an American 'folk builder' (i.e. recruiter) for the Asatru Folk Assembly posted on X/Twitter that the AFA would hold its first Winter nights ritual at Stonehenge on 28 October 2023 at 7 p.m. Winter nights is an important Heathen festival celebrating the start of winter and is based primarily on the thirteenth-century record of Snorri Sturluson's *Heimskringla* (e.g. 1964). The possibility that the AFA, one of the world's largest racist Heathen organisations, actively seeking to expand beyond the US into the UK Pagan scene, would be permitted to use Stonehenge, the jewel in the crown of England's prehistoric heritage and one of the most contested 'sacred sites' (e.g. Wallis, 2015a) among today's Pagans (and other interest groups), caused a social media storm. Over the weekend following the AFA's announcement, Andy Pardy, the Chair of the Police Pagan Association, worked with other members of the UK Pagan community, including the Pagan Federation (PF), to draft a petition; this was released on the PPA website dated Monday 11 September, and posted on Change.org (the world's largest petition platform), on Tuesday 12 September (Pardy, 2023b: n.p.). Part of the statement reads:

> We cannot allow the AFA to desecrate a symbol of our cultural heritage and a site of spiritual significance to Pagans across the UK with their imported brand of racist, homophobic, misogynistic and anti-Semitic Paganism that shares nothing with the inclusive contemporary iteration of British Paganism, and which is fundamentally incompatible with the wonderfully diverse multicultural communities of the UK.
>
> The latest iteration of the PREVENT Duty Guidance rightfully identifies extreme right-wing ideology as a resurgent and significant threat to national security, however the AFA differs from the definition provided, in that they are an organised hierarchical group with territorial ambitions.

> Permitting the AFA to openly promote themselves by way of a public event at Stonehenge would assist them in establishing a foothold in the UK and providing the foundation they need to perpetuate their divisive and extremist narratives that will only contribute to the already increasing risk posed by extreme right-wing terrorism in the UK.
>
> We would like assurances from the agencies and statutory bodies responsible for protecting the safety and integrity of Stonehenge that they will assess this event and consider their duties under PREVENT and work in partnership to address this issue to prevent a symbol of national heritage being co-opted as a symbol of extremist far-right hate and division. (PPA, 2023)

The petition gained over 6,000 signatures and was endorsed by over fifty Pagan organisations, including such progressive Heathen groups as Asatru UK, The Confederation of UK Heathen Kindreds and Heathens of Mercia. By the following day, 13 September, the AFA had cancelled their planned event at Stonehenge. Sarah Kerr, the President of the Pagan Federation, published the following statement on the PF website:

> The many Pagan and Heathen organisations who worked in unity in this matter, and the thousands of Pagans, Heathens and others who signed the petition and made their opinions very clear, would like to thank the AFA for providing an opportunity for the Pagan and Heathen faith communities of the UK to show how well they work together in solidarity against an organisation which threatens the reputation of our religion and continues to dishonour us by promoting racism, misogyny, homophobia, and antisemitism under the guise of Asatru.
>
> In addition, we will state here, that any further attempts to establish a significant presence in the UK will be met with a similar display of solidarity, in which the many inclusive Pagan and Heathen organisations and the thousands who responded herein, will once again unite and stand up against you in order to protect the Pagan faiths of our country from your hateful interpretation of Heathenry, an interpretation that shares nothing with the true faith which you claim to practice, and which is fundamentally incompatible with the wonderfully diverse multicultural communities of the UK. (Kerr, 2023)

While it is not clear whether the petition itself made a direct impact on the AFA's decision-making, this direct action does offer a measure of the anti-racist sentiment among UK Heathens and the wider Pagan community. The AFA's failed attempt to co-opt Stonehenge to promote their racist agenda and gain traction within Heathenry in the UK, and the strength of the anti-racist Heathen and Pagan resolve to stop the AFA, whether by petition or other means, lends support to the argument made earlier in this book (Chapter 1), that it is no longer feasible to identify some Heathens ambiguously as 'non-racist' (Gardell, 2003: 153, 611) or 'a-racist' (von Schnurbein, 2017: 7), because Heathenry has become polarised along racist versus anti-racist lines. As Weber (2019: n.p.) proposes:

> universalists have collectively become fed up with their religious beliefs being used to justify bigotry and violence. These Heathens, despite being comprised primarily of White members, see the old Norse gods as deities who might call out to anyone, and they identify their community not through shared Whiteness but shared commitment to Heathen cosmology. Increasingly, they see it as their duty to not only distance themselves from White supremacist movements but to vocally denounce and organize against White supremacist Odinists.

The marked success of a Heathen and Pagan protest movement in preventing the appropriation of Stonehenge by a contemporary far-right Heathen organisation for its own racist agenda offers hope and marks an example to emulate for other anti-racists. The purpose of the next two chapters of this book is to explore additional ways by which anti-racist Heathens are rallying against the racist minority.

Declaring inclusivity

Over the last decade or so, in response to the increasingly public racist agenda of such organisations as the Asatru Folk Assembly and Odinic Rite, Heathen individuals, hearths/kindreds and larger organisations have themselves responded by taking an increasingly explicit anti-racist position. This builds on various historical precedents. For example, following the 'moral panic' surrounding the 'violent outbreaks of the Norwegian black metal scene, with the infamous church arsons and "Satanic" murders (which of course were not qualitatively different from other murders) as central points of reference', the Norwegian Heathen groups Bifrost and Foreningen Forn Sed adopted 'an explicitly anti-racist position' (Asprem, 2008: 44). In some cases, declaring inclusivity is a simple matter of how membership of an organisation operates. UKHeathenry, for example, started out in the year 2000 as an email list (on Yahoo) for like-minded progressive Heathens in the UK. There were clear conditions for membership from the start, and in 2013 they established a closed Facebook group, now with over a thousand followers (as of March 2025):

> This list is set up to facilitate networking and contact, relevant announcements, and discussion within UK Heathenry (including Elder Troth, Asatru, Norse, Germanic or Saxon Paganism, Northern Traditions, etc.) It is open to

all who are drawn to the Aesir and Vanir, the Disir, and/or the Land Spirits, and who want to network with other Heathens.

Restrictions on membership:
you live in the UK or close-by areas of Europe;
you respect the right of other list-members to be Heathen, regardless of sexuality, gender, or ethnicity or 'race'.

The inclusivity of the group is made clear in the statement that it is 'open to all' and 'regardless of sexuality, gender, or ethnicity or "race"'. The scare quotes around 'race' are particularly notable as an explicit action from the moderators to draw attention to this term as contested and discursive rather than self-evident or a fact. The exclusivity of the group is limited to those living 'in the UK or close-by areas of Europe'; membership is limited, therefore, by one's geographical location, but *not* ethnicity or similar criteria, as would be required in a racist Heathen group.

In another example of how progressive Heathens are taking an increasingly explicit anti-racist position, Asatru UK (AUK), whose closed Facebook group which started out in 2013 (3,800 followers as of March 2025) states, at the very start of their 'About' section: 'Our aim is to create an inclusive heathen community of those who follow the old northern European beliefs' (AUK, 2023: n.p.). The organisation has now expanded to organising face-to-face moots across the UK. Their universalist approach is reiterated by the fact that they devote a separate web page to 'Inclusivity', easily navigated to from the drop-down menu and populated by the Asatru-EU Network statement to which they are one of the signatories (Figure 10.1).

So while AUK are open to all, it is clear from their inclusivity statement that like UKHeathenry they are not open to racists. And in a final example, The Confederation of UK Heathen Kindreds, formed in 2017, state on Facebook that theirs is '[a] page for Inclusive Kindreds and Hearths in the U.K. to advertise their events and bring the Heathen community together'. In addition to these UK examples of inclusivity, it is worth remarking on the *Ásatrúarfélagið* in Iceland. While in its formative years this organisation tended towards traditionally conservative values (e.g. anti-abortion) and was criticised for some far-right affiliations (e.g. the Odinic Rite), under the leadership of Hilma Örn Hilmarsson (since 2003) the organisation has pursued an increasingly liberal political agenda, including campaigning on environmental issues and for the separation of church and state (e.g. Strmiska, 2000); it was also the first religious organisation in Iceland to endorse same-sex marriage (e.g. von Schnurbein, 2017: 69–70, 247). The following statement appeared on their website in 2014:

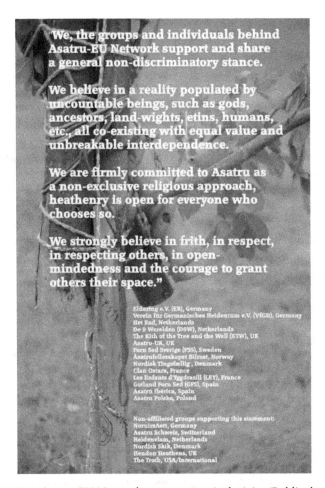

Figure 10.1 Asatru-EU Network statement on inclusivity (Public domain).

We strongly oppose any attempt by individuals to use their association with the *Ásatrúarfélagið* of Iceland to promote attitudes, ideologies and practices rejected by the leadership of the *Ásatrúarfélagið*. We particularly reject the use of Ásatrú as a justification for supremacy ideology, militarism and animal sacrifice. (https://asatru.is/statement/)

In addition to these examples of Heathen organisations which make clear, public, inclusivity statements (we deal with individual actions in the next chapter), organised protest groups across the spectrum of Paganism have formed and re-formed over recent years, including Heathens & Pagans Against Racism, Antifascist Pagan Action, Pagans Against Fascism, The Svinfylking – Heathens Fighting Hate, Anti-Racist Celts and Heathens

Unite (ÁRCHÚ), and Celtics Against Oppression, Racism, and Neo-Nazism (CAORANN). Heathens United Against Racism (HUAR), for example, was formed in 2012 and in May 2016 co-ordinated the Light the Beacons event when 'Heathens lit candles and bonfires at over 200 locations across four continents to demonstrate solidarity with inclusive Heathenry' (Weber, 2019: n.p.). The tragic Christchurch terrorist incident a few years later, on 15 March, 2019, led to another HUAR statement. The terrorist responsible, a white Australian living in New Zealand who had been radicalised by websites and face-to-face contacts with far-right groups in Europe, had bought into the Great Replacement theory. Indeed, that theory became the very title of his manifesto that went online as the shootings were taking place. HUAR, on its Facebook page on 27 March 2019, consequently decided to speak up about the attack given the prominent racist Heathen themes/ideas that appeared in this manifesto, evident by the *Sonnenrad* on its cover, its overt admiration for the openly Odinist Breivik and reference to the infamous fourteen words. HUAR responded:

> We oppose and condemn these acts of extreme violence and murder in the name of hate…[T]hese acts of terrorism are examples of what happens when white supremacy is globally normalized…[W]e wish to make it clear that as Heathens, we denounce the use of our path to promote or support such cruel acts against Muslims, or any other group targeted by terrorists and hate groups. There is nothing in our lore to suggest a path dedicated to white supremacy, ethnic cleansing, or hatred towards Muslims, is in any way an honorable path. (HUAR, 2019)

Another comment from one specific member on the same date reads:

> So that's it. I am no longer trying to find common ground, to reach out and educate those with folkish leanings against their will. I am a proud inclusionary Heathen, and I will not recommend or participate in groups that tolerate those who are not. If you have no local inclusive groups, start one – and make it clear what you'll be standing up for. Wear your hammer, or sickle, or boar, or whatever Heathen symbol you choose; and then represent inclusiveness in your daily life. We may not be able to do much on a large scale, but this kind of local movement will make a difference. (HUAR, 2019)

The example of HUAR accords with Nikitins' (2020: 114–115) argument that 'Pagan communities are beginning to push back against bigotry in their midst, and are trying to learn how to prevent encroachment on their communal spaces by white supremacists as well as further corruption of their sacred symbols'. We next discuss specific instances where Heathens have rallied against racism, beginning with 'Declaration 127', which began in the

US in response to the AFA's increasingly explicit white supremacist agenda, and had a widespread impact on Heathenry internationally.

Heathens Against Hate

On 6 May 2013, 'Heathens Against Hate' (HAH) made its first informal blog post (Schreiwer, 2013: n.p.), authored by the prominent Troth 'Steer' (i.e. elected president of the US-based inclusive Heathen organisation, The Troth) and manager of the online network Huginn's Heathen Hof, Robert L. Schreiwer (Figure 10.2). This comprised a statement regarding the murder of Colorado Department of Corrections chief Tom Clements on 19 March by prime suspect Evan Ebel, a white supremacist who self-identified as Asatru and who was eventually killed during a high-speed police chase two days later. Condemning far-right Heathenry, Schreiwer also stated: 'This is the first post on this new Heathens Against Hate blog, and it is most appropriate that it comes at a time when the public is being led by the media to a skewed understanding of what Heathenry is and who Heathens are' (Schreiwer, 2013: n.p.). Over the next five years, the HAH blog regularly reported on incidents of racist Heathen activity and how anti-racist Heathens were taking a stand against this abuse of Heathenry. For instance, following claims that the accused gunman in the Overland Park (Kansas) killings of three people was an Odinist, HAH blogged:

Figure 10.2 Heathens Against Hate logo (Public domain).

> We abhor the appropriation of any Heathen identity for racist and bigoted agendas. We reject the abuse of our religion as a justification for hateful and abominable actions. We condemn the violence and hatred that are at the root of this story. Let us all hail the victims and remember their names:
>
> Terri LaManno
> William Lewis Corporon
> Reat Griffin Underwood
>
> Our thoughts and prayers go out to the families and friends of the victims of this unconscionable act. (15 April 2014) (HAH, 2014: n.p.)

The website is also an educational platform for revising people's attitudes about Heathenry. For example, addressing how ancient heathen images have been co-opted by the far right, HAH states: 'Germanic symbols that carry importance in Heathenry have long been appropriated by extremists. They must be judged in context' (HAH, n.d.a). The swastika and Black Sun are singled out as two that cannot now and never should be used by progressive Heathens because of their negative historic associations with Ariosophy, Nazism and neo-Nazism. Other ancient heathen images, however, inclusive Heathens today 'work to reclaim'. Regarding the Othala or Odal rune, for example, they say: 'In white supremacist circles, misinformation propagates the rune to mean "bloodline" and "(white) heritage". In 2016, the National Socialist Movement (NSM) removed the Swastika from their banners, replacing it instead with the Othala rune' (HAH, n.d.a). In this way, HAH are addressing how ancient heathen imagery has been used for hate and are attempting to reclaim the imagery for positive, anti-racist ends.

Over time, the importance of HAH in the fight against racism is indicated by the way it was taken under The Troth's organisational umbrella as its anti-racist campaign wing. The HAH blog went idle in 2018 and a new HAH website (HAH, n.d.b) took shape, continuing the work started in the blog. Then, in 2020, in a further indication of its importance beyond the work of The Troth, HAH regained its sovereignty with 'a very specific mission which transcends association with any one particular organization':

> Our mission is to bring the Heathen community together to educate both each other and non-Heathens on the differences between commonly-held beliefs and practices and its extremism.
>
> We promote inclusivity and dialogue that is in league with better communication between individuals, Heathen kindred, and between Heathen and non-Heathen organizations.

Heathens Against Hate stand by the statement that: 'We Are Our Deeds'.

Thereby advancing inclusive Heathenry through our actions and hard work. (HAH, 2020: n.p.)

Declaration 127

The power of the original HAH blog as a productive force in anti-racist Heathenry came to the fore in 2016. Following McNallen's incendiary Facebook post (10 January 2016), 'Where are the Freikorps when we need them?', and his subsequent 'retirement' from the AFA (announced 1 May 2016; see Chapter 4), the new Alsherjargothi (leader), Matthew Flavel, stated on the organisation's Facebook page: 'The AFA celebrates our feminine ladies, our masculine gentlemen and, above all, our beautiful white children. The children of the folk are our shining future and the legacy of all those men and women of our people back to the beginning' (quote in: *The Wild Hunt*, 2016b: n.p.). The emboldened racist agenda of the AFA caused a renewed outcry against the organisation among progressive Heathens. HAH, by now a highly influential blog, responded by calling on all Heathens to 'state their complete denunciation of, and disassociation from, the Asatru Folk Assembly', and announced 'Declaration 127' in August 2016 (*The Wild Hunt*, 2016c: n.p.). The '127' of the title refers to stanza 127 of *Hávámal* (Sayings of the High One, i.e. Odin) in the Poetic Edda, with which we opened Part III of this book: 'When you see misdeeds, speak out against them, and give your enemies no peace' (Awaken the North, 2016). The declaration, paradoxically also fourteen words, is thus a symbolic riposte to Lane's infamous 'Fourteen Words' or '14W' slogan. Declaration 127 went viral on social media, and by 5 September 2016 was ratified by forty-six Heathen and related Pagan organisations worldwide (while the original website has ceased, Declaration 127 can be found at e.g. Heathen's Heart, 2020). By the end of 2023 this number of signatories stood at 136, a clear indication of support from many Heathen organisations worldwide. This was, as John T. Mainer, Redesman (the role of 'wise-person' or 'advisor') of The Troth, stated:

> the first time the entire Heathen community came together and spoke with one voice to state for the whole world to hear, that the modern heathen community is an inclusive heathen community. From Canada to Venezuela, Austria to Australia, and every corner of the US; whatever doctrinal differences we like to argue about, *we are united in the understanding that heathenry is inclusive by nature*. (Mainer, 2017: n.p., original emphasis)

But Declaration 127 did meet some criticism from within the Heathen community, among those who proposed that it should not be an end in itself. One commentator stated:

> What Heathenry needs is individuals going out of their way to contradict the hatred spread by the AFA. We shouldn't cloister whilst guffawing about bigotry. If you really care about countering the AFA get on there and counter them. Pitch articles about heathenry. Open a YouTube channel. Challenge them by not allowing them to define our faith. (Obline, 2016: n.p.)

More needed to be done than simply making a statement and signing up to it; so, 2017 became a landmark year in this regard, as we next discuss.

A year of anti-racist Heathen activism

The year 2017 was pivotal in the politics of the far right. Donald Trump was inaugurated as the forty-fifth President of the United States on 20 January. In May, Hungary's right-wing government under Viktor Orbán hosted the Christian-right World Congress of Families organisation, identified as a hate group by the Southern Poverty Law Center (SPLC, n.d.h). The same month, despite losing the presidential race to Emmanuel Macron, Marine Le Pen's far-right Front National party made historic gains among the French electorate. Following the Westminster Bridge terrorist attack on 22 March and the bombing of Manchester Arena on 22 May, the newly formed Football Lads Alliance marched in London in June expressing anti-Muslim and anti-EU sentiment; their second protest in October attracted 50,000 supporters and was addressed by former leader of the English Defence League, Stephen Yaxley-Lennon (aka Tommy Robinson) (Mulhall, n.d.; also Allchorn and Feldman, 2019). In August, the white supremacist James Alex Fields marched with a Black Sun flag at the Unite the Right Rally in Charlottesville and later killed Heather Heyer and injured thirty-five people by ramming his car into the crowd. In Gothenburg, Sweden, the neo-Nazi Nordic Resistance Movement (NMR) held a demonstration on 30 September, waving green and white flags bearing a Tyr rune. And in December 2017, Austria's conservative People's Party (OVP) formed a coalition with the right-wing, anti-immigration Freedom Party of Austria (FPO). These examples give a sense of how the far right became increasingly prominent and emboldened in 2017.

While Declaration 127 in 2016 had been an important step forward for progressive Heathens, it was clear that a declaration and the signing of it did not go far enough. The problem was much bigger than the AFA alone, and active participation in anti-racism was needed. As 'The Urban Druid' (2019: n.p.) stated: 'It is hard to speak out. It is often easier to turn away, but doing so for the sake of peace is not action. It lets the problem fester. Inclusivity must become an active way of being'. The ongoing gains and public attention gained by the far right in the year following Declaration 127 initiated such active participation. At far-right rallies in Europe and the US, for instance, Heathens turned out to protest. Members of the re-enactment group Vikings Against Racism (VAR), for example, were among the counter-protestors at the NMR demonstration in Gothenburg. The counter-protestors outnumbered the NMR and the demonstration was ended by police (Edwards, C., 2017: n.p.). VAR have also shown their support for LGBTIQA+ rights by marching at Stockholm Pride, and Heathens and Pagans in other European cities similarly perform regularly at Pride marches, such as in London. In Germany, the organisation Nornirs Ætt 'researches the way Heathen ideas as filtered through Nazism manifest themselves in contemporary far-right groups, which it exposes online through its Odin's Eye project' (Samuel, 2017: n.p.). Responding to the various right-wing events in the US in 2017, the prominent American Heathen Diana Paxson, stated:

> Before the last election, we in the U.S. could claim some liberal moral superiority. This is no longer the case…Ever since January I've been attending whatever rallies and marches I could and displaying heathen symbols…We have to be out there with placards and slogans and banners. Every time they [racists] come out with their message, we need to get out there with ours. (quoted in Samuel, 2017: n.p.; see also Paxson, 2020)

Paxson founded in turn the Alliance for Inclusive Heathenry, and with other anti-racist Heathens, protested at the 'Patriots Day Free Speech Rally' held at Berkeley on 15 April 2017, when Stephen McNallen was in attendance. One participant, Mardollsdottir, recalled: 'I acted as a medic during the protest, helping people who had been maced or hit with pepper spray or otherwise harmed during the confrontation' (Greene, 2017: n.p.). A Pagan journalist at the event writing for *The Wild Hunt*, commented: 'It was heartening to see Diana Paxson and other members of the Heathen community put themselves in harm's way in the fight against racism and bigotry' (Greene, 2017: n.p.). Many Heathens thus adopt the motto 'we are our deeds' (see e.g. Declaration of Deeds, n.d.). Anti-racist Heathens have, then, reflecting Beowulf's (l.289) advocacy of *worda ond worca* ('what's said and what's done' [Heaney, 2000: 210]), turned words into deeds, taking direct action at far-right demonstrations. Another way in which action has been taken to combat anti-racism is through education, as we next discuss.

Heathen education

Published literature written by Heathens for Heathens is extensive and diverse (as raised in Chapter 1). Certain elements within this corpus, such as that by authors Stephen McNallen, Wulf Ingessenu and other racist Heathens we have discussed in the previous chapters, base their understanding of Heathenry around such issues as ethnicity and race. The vast majority of the literature, though, reflecting Heathenry itself, is diverse and inclusive. But there is a tension across the racist/anti-racist spectrum, blurring the two into a grey area, when authors across the spectrum use problematic historical sources, such as those derived from Ariosophy, in their interpretations of the ancient sources. What has become known as 'runic yoga', for example, involving physical postures in the shape of runes, is often promoted across the spectrum of racist and progressive Heathen literature (e.g. Thorsson, 1984). But this practice ultimately derives from folkish Ariosophical sources, such as Peryt Shou (aka Albert Schultz and Jörg Schultz; see e.g. Shou, 2017). While to promote or practise runic yoga is not to promote or practise racism, the fact that the origin of such ideas lies in folkish Ariosophy does highlight the problem of Heathenry's sources being caught up within racist agendas. Some practitioner authors are upfront about this problem and treat it with some criticality (e.g. Fries, 2002 [1993]: 193–195). Other authors endeavour to avoid the twentieth-century sources altogether, basing their thinking and practice primarily on reconstructions from the ancient sources (e.g. Brown, 2022), which do themselves offer a rich source of evidence. But it is problematic to assert, consequently, that inclusive Heathens are thereby reclaiming 'their' religion. The use of the heathen past by racists is abhorrent; but it must be recognised that any interpretation of the ancient sources, whether academic or practitioner, racist or anti-racist, is just that, an interpretation, partial and subjective, as are all perceptions of the past (see discussion in Wallis, 2003: 140–141).

Heathen literature, like Heathenry itself, is, then, highly varied and in some instances highly problematic. While once the main route into Heathenry, up until the 1990s, was by published print literature, since the turn of the millennium sources and networks are also available on the internet, which of course presents its own problems (see e.g. Cowan, 2005; Campbell, 2012; Evolvi, 2020). For the seeker new to Heathenry, just a few clicks can lead to white supremacist material, even if, as in the case of the Odinic Rite, for instance, unlike Woden's Folk, their racism is not necessarily immediately obvious. Recognising the problem of how the available literature, both print and online, can promote hate, especially for those new to Heathenry, there have been considerable efforts on the part of anti-racist Heathens to take a more actively inclusive publication and education approach. A good example is the Ritona (n.d.) website, publishing articles, books and courses which promote a progressive Pagan agenda.

Following a conference in 2017, 'Frith Forge' (discussed in further detail in the next section, 'Frith Forge'), at which Heathens from across North America and Europe met to discuss the future for progressive Heathenry and the countering of racist Heathenry, a positive direction was found in developing a website resource, to 'provide guidance for those new to the religion – especially young people – to help them recognize warning signs of racist or otherwise extremist Heathenry'. Reporting on this development for *The Wild Hunt*, Siegfried (2017: n.p.) proposed that 'such a resource is much needed and can do a lot of good'. The latest iteration of The Troth's website (The Troth, 2024a), also offers a good example of inclusivist Heathen education in action. With the title 'The Troth: Education and Service for Inclusive Heathenry', this resource makes education and inclusivity central to their mission. The website is highly accessible and navigable with, for example, 'Heathenry Essentials' virtual events for beginners. It also facilitates critical engagement from the start: the 'resources' tab has a drop-down menu leading to, for example, 'beliefs' with a 'framework for analysis of Reconstructionist Beliefs', outlining the importance of 'induction, deduction and synthesis'. The approach to ancestors is important for eliding any need for ethnic or racial consideration:

> Ancestor spirits are spirits of our beloved dead and more: Heathens will sometimes see these spirits as specific people, sometimes as a non-specific 'ancestor' who represents the entire ancestral line, or sometimes as a patron of a particular vocation or profession. These need not be people who you're biologically related to. Some people have adopted families and don't know anything about their biological family, and that's perfectly fine too. Who you worship as an 'ancestor' has more to do with how you feel about them than whatever your biological relationship to them might or might not have been.

A second example of how progressive Heathens are pursuing an anti-racist educational agenda, is their work in prisons. Prisons have proven to be fertile ground for recruiting racist Heathens, usually identifying as Odinists (e.g. Lane's co-founding of Wotansvolk from prison; see Chapter 4); so, concerted efforts to counter extremism in penal spaces are especially important. There have been Pagan chaplains in the UK since the late 1990s. The Pagan Federation in the UK has a Pagan Prison Ministry; and the role of Pagan chaplain is now a salaried profession (PF, 2022). To qualify as a Pagan chaplain candidates must demonstrate their inclusive credentials, and the role can require them to work with prisoners of other faiths and none. In the US, The Troth runs a prison in-reach programme. As one such facilitator states: '[f]or many administrators and chaplains, Heathenry is an enigma, and most of their direct contact is tainted by white supremacism' (In-reach Heathen Prison Services, 2014). The in-reach programme 'provides the facility Chaplains and Administrative staff with positive and, as accurate as possible, information concerning our religion' (The Troth, 2024b). In another instance of prison in-reach, the Gullveig Press (2020) publishes resources for Pagans in prison across the US. In this way, progressive Heathen organisations can offer prisoners interested in Heathenry and those already identifying as Heathen positive guidance, ideally well before they are attracted to racist Heathenry in the first place. For those already involved in racist Heathenry it also offers a way out. Overall, these recent educational efforts do present a positive way forward for inclusive Heathens to reclaim Heathenry from the racists. As Ulrike Pohl, a member of Germany's Eldaring organisation states: '[i]f we can offer a sense of community and a sound theology, I think it'll be easier to explain to people why the blood-and-soil idea makes no sense historically or spiritually…The best way to get people to come over to the bright side is to simply be cool' (quoted in Samuel, 2017: n.p.).

Calling out racism online as done by Heathens Against Hate, visibly protesting at far-right demonstrations, and facilitating education in print, online and in prisons, are all important steps for progressive Heathenry. Individuals performing their Heathen identity on a daily basis also take part in this strategy by, for example, posting anti-racist messaging on social media (see the next chapter). Wearing Heathen symbols in public, such as Mjöllnir, Thor's hammer, can also help; for when someone asks about the pendant or questions its association with the far right, a response can be offered that while Heathenry has been hijacked by white supremacists the majority of Heathens are inclusive (see e.g. Nikitins, 2020: 123). But a question remains: how is the 'inclusive' in inclusive Heathenry actually constituted?

Frith Forge

In a concerted effort to develop the widespread support for Declaration 127 into positive action, progressive Heathens organised an international conference entitled Frith Forge, which was held in Germany in October 2017. There were thirty-one attendees representing fourteen Heathen organisations from twelve nations across Europe and North America. As Mainer of The Troth put it:

> To build inclusive heathenry into a whole and healthy culture, where each of the many groups who banded together under Declaration 127 can share and

work together requires work in building bridges of understanding, in building an understanding of the many different ways we have individually found to express inclusive heathenry. (Mainer, 2017: n.p.)

One issue addressed was how 'ancestors' are venerated in Heathenry, and how it is but a 'small step' from inclusive celebration to 'a racist ideology of Blut und Boden' (Siegfried, 2017: n.p.). This issue highlights a larger, ongoing problem for Heathens, namely that: Heathenry has a long history of association with the far right; that it tends to attract white people of European heritage; and, until recently, many organisations and individuals, particularly in the US, have been content to take a neutral stance on those groups and individuals who are racist. As Siegfried's (2017) review of the conference for *The Wild Hunt* suggested, the mood of the conference indicated a seed change in recent years, with many participants stating that only by taking an overt anti-racist stance would racists be deterred and those new to Heathenry steered towards inclusivity. But 'inclusivity' can take varied meanings. Siegfried (2017: n.p.) observes that for the European Heathens present, inclusivity is 'about speaking out against resurgent and racist nationalism, keeping hateful individuals out of their organizations, and actively challenging those who hold and promote racism'; while for US Heathens, inclusivity relates to diversity, by 'actively welcoming Heathens from diverse racial, ethnic, and cultural backgrounds, celebrating together in ritual, and building communities that reflect that diversity of the United States' (Siegfried, 2017: n.p.). Frith Forge was thus an important step forward for building a community against racist thinking and for critical self-reflection, and it has now become a regular fixture hosted internationally; it was planned for Canada but delivered online in 2020 due to the pandemic, with Costa Rica the chosen venue in 2024. Frith Forge even has its own YouTube channel, with discussion panels and assorted talks available to stream.

Negotiating equality, diversity and inclusion

But how diversity and inclusivity in Heathenry are constituted remains an enduring issue, even if there are regional and cultural differences. It is certainly an issue which intersects with such concerns in wider society over the last decade, particularly in light of the Black Lives Matter movement, again differently configured in various locales internationally. Siegfried (2017: n.p.) proposes, the:

> emphasis on inclusivity, coupled with a total lack of diversity, was really the glaring flaw of Frith Forge. In the 21st century, it's no longer enough to have a

room full of white people earnestly discuss the need for inclusiveness. We are far past that point. We need to have diverse voices in the discussion. We need to have diverse voices *leading* the discussion.

This point addressing equality, diversity and inclusion was already made some years earlier by Crystal Blanton (2011) in her edited volume *Shades of Faith: Minority Voices in Paganism*. The American authors who contributed to this book largely accord around the idea that while 'race' has been an issue among some Pagans they encounter, who assume people of non-European heritage should be practising religions associated with their own 'ancestral' traditions, such as (West African) Ifẹ̀ or (Egyptian) Kemitism, they have also encountered more inclusive Pagans who are open to their interest in and 'call' to such 'European' traditions as Heathenry, no matter their 'ethnicity', 'race' or skin colour. In the subsequent volume, *Bringing Race to the Table: Exploring Racism in the Pagan Community*, also lead edited by Blanton *et al.* (2015), a clearer case is made for Heathens and other Pagans to be 'allies to people of colour': 'becoming an ally is a journey that examines racism as it shows up in the life of the ally and the people around the ally, as well as what the ally will actually do to respond to racism' (Blanton *et al.*, 2015: 9). For Cecily Joy Willowe (2015: 76), a Black Wiccan, 'the individual Pagan and Pagan communities need to ask themselves what they can give back in return to communities of colour. The obvious offering that White Pagans can give is using their power and privilege to challenge racism and support people of colour in and outside of the pagan world'. Moreover, 'Pagans of Colour need front row seats at the table' and this requires White Pagans 'knowing when to take a backseat' (Willowe, 2015: 77). Perhaps more than in any other Pagan pathway, today's inclusive Heathens must arguably embrace equality, diversity and inclusion in their religion if they are truly to become 'allies'.

Conclusion

In order to challenge racism in its midst, it is important for Heathenry to identify as progressive and anti-racist. In this chapter we have shown how Heathens have taken action by placing restrictions on membership of their various organisations which exclude racists and by making anti-racist statements, including Declaration 127, in response to acts of hate. They have also protested at far-right demonstrations facilitated prison in-reach programmes, organised conferences and networking events on diversity and inclusion, and provided online and print educational materials about anti-racist Heathenry. Most recently in the UK, they have taken up leadership positions within and provided intelligence assistance to, the police and security forces (e.g. PPA). An important recent development in this regard is their cooperation, with other members of the Pagan and occult community, with SO15, the police unit attached to the UK's Counter Terrorism Command. Alongside colleagues from the Church of Rational Satanism (established in 2009), for example, as well as Wiccan and Druid groups, Heathens have also begun working regularly with British police to create an Esoteric Research Group investigating potential occult-related criminality, including monitoring some of the more fringe and dangerous elements found within such movements. Having now explored some of the ways in which anti-racist Heathens are kicking back against the racists, we next explore how social media platforms in particular are providing an ideal space for anti-racist campaigning, with a case study of 'visual–virtual Heathen politicking' on Instagram.

11

Visual–virtual Heathen politicking: anti-racist Heathenry on Instagram

Introduction

Following the attack on the Capitol building in Washington, DC, on 6 January 2021, a flurry of posts on Instagram with the hashtag #heathensagainsthate showed a snapshot from media reports of the so-called 'QAnon Shaman' (introduced in this book's Preface), juxtaposed with text captions espousing anti-racist messaging. One Instagrammer responded on the day of the attack with an image of the QAnon Shaman bearing tattoos including a Thor's hammer and valknut, by using the hashtag #heathensagainsthate accompanied by the caption: 'Wow, just unbelievable the audacity of these people. Not only has this piece of trash misappropriated Norse symbols he also has the nerve to wear indigenous head dress. Know the face of our enemy Heathens, give them no shelter [sic] name them traitors and oathbreakers'. Another user reused the hashtag and image to post on 7 January: 'So, "Ivar the Dickless" here is not representative of the pagan community despite his pagan tattoos. The events on [sic] our democracy yesterday was [sic] the second most heartbreaking thing I have ever seen on the news'. The anger and anguish voiced by Heathens and other Pagans in response to the Capitol insurrection was echoed on other social media platforms. On Facebook on 7 January, the Pagan Federation posted:

> The Confederation of UK Heathen Kindreds, Asatru UK and The Pagan Federation condemn the acts of violence that took place in Washington DC last night and in particular the misappropriation of our sacred symbols by some of the most visible individuals responsible. We join with faith leaders from around the globe in a prayer for peace to settle over the United States and that proper democratic process is not overruled by violence and intimidation. We support the right to peaceful protest and all those who seek to voice disagreements peacefully; we condemn the use of violence and the hate filled rhetoric that fuels it.

In subsequent days, many Instagrammers (also known as Instas) reused the QAnon Shaman meme image, #heathensagainsthate and similar hashtags, alongside anti-racist text captions, to challenge the appropriation of Norse imagery by the far right and their violent actions on that fateful January day. Having considered in the previous chapter examples of how anti-racist Heathens are fighting back against the extremist minority, with 'Declaration 127', protests at far-right rallies, participation in education, conferences and inter-faith forums and work with police and the intelligence agencies, in this chapter we examine their use of social media to counter racist Heathenry and its affiliates, focussing on Instagram, a platform with extensive reach for messaging like-minded Instagrammers and a wider audience. Given that '[w]hite-supremacist groups use social media as a tool to distribute their message, where they can incubate their hate online and allow it to spread' (Hatzipanagos, 2018: n.p.), it is imperative that anti-racist Heathen campaigners employ the same tools to counter this hate.

Bennett and Segerberg (2012) argue that social media has been dynamic and pervasive in its impact on the political landscape, shaping contemporary political movements by allowing them to evolve and respond rapidly to changing circumstances. According to the far-right-monitoring organisation Tech Against Terrorism Europe (2024: n.p.):

> On average, every minute Facebook users share 694,000 stories, X (formerly Twitter) users post 360,000 posts, Snapchat users send 2.7 million snaps and YouTube users upload over 500 hours of new content. The volume of data generated is growing exponentially and is currently estimated at 120 zettabytes every day. A vast amount of terrorist content is posted across the online ecosystem.

It is timely, then, to consider 'visual–virtual Heathen politicking' and the wider context of the politics of social media in general, as well as its representation of religion particularly (ff. Castells, 2015; Miller *et al.*, 2016; Granholm *et al.*, 2018; Downing, 2019). In July 2022, Ofcom, the UK's communications regulator, reported that 'For the first time, Instagram is the most popular news source among younger people – used by 29% of teens in 2022' (Sillito, 2022: n.p.). The platform is not only popular, but increasingly for young people it serves as a source of information including news, making it a powerful medium for spreading an anti-racist message. The 2020s is also arguably the decade of smartphone-mediated religion (Fewkes, 2019) which, according to the scholar of material and digital culture, Miller (2022: 371), is 'coming to epitomise twenty-first-century religion'.

In their article, 'Viking tattoos of Instagram', Bennett and Wilkins (2020: 1301) consider such use of social media in '[a] cultural moment when self-perception and social relations have become increasingly embedded in social media'. While it is viewed by some as a frivolous and potentially damaging digital aside to the 'meat' of real, embodied, human life, social media is nonetheless not simply an extension of identity but can be central to people's identity-formation. The 'cultural moment' Bennett and Wilkins identify increasingly concerns matters of race and intersectionality, with the emergence of the Black Lives Matter movement and increasing prominence of a decolonising agenda, over the decade-plus of Instagram's existence. Social media is fast-moving, as is the research conducted upon it (e.g. Grieve, 1995; Cowan, 2005; Prandner and Seymer, 2020; Duguay and Gold-Apel, 2023), and images and discussions change, can be deleted and move on. For instance, while Reels (short films) increasingly dominate Instagram feeds (much lamented by Instagram stalwarts who valued its focus on still image-making), our focus here is on still images which do not require much effort or time to access and can convey messages instantaneously and directly. This research, subsequently, captures just one slice of anti-racist Heathen activity on Instagram, but in so doing does demonstrate how important such social media campaigning is as part of inclusive Heathenry's anti-racist critique. We focus on the striking and effective juxtaposition of image and text to intervene and fight back against racism and other forms of discrimination.

Instagram

Designed as a photo-sharing social media platform, Instagram (also known as 'Insta' and 'IG') was released in August 2010. By the mid-2010s it had a global reach, and as of April 2024 there were two billion users every month, with 363 million in India (the leading country) and 170 million in the US (Statista, 2024). It is also the favourite social media platform of Gen Z (16 to 24-year-olds) with the biggest share of the platform's audience among 18 to 34-year-olds (McLachlan, 2022: n.p.). Instagram is, therefore, highly and increasingly popular, particularly with a younger, international audience. As Miller *et al.* (2016: 156) argue, 'the vast majority of all photography today now is social media photography [and] our relationship to visual images has reached a level of ubiquity that is historically unprecedented'. Social media images are ubiquitous, and along with digital platforms such as Instagram which host and disseminate them, they offer a powerful means by which individuals curate and articulate identities, as well as enabling the formation of digitally mediated relationships and communities (Serafinelli, 2018: 82). The use of Instagram by inclusive Heathens can therefore be seen as an important part of fighting back against racism and building relationships and communities around anti-racist activism.

Instagram 'is designed expressly for the purpose of circulating visual images' (Bennet and Wilkins, 2020: 1304), making it distinct from other social media platforms. For Manovich, the 'coherence and logical simplicity of Instagram… combines many activities together in a single structure – taking photos, editing and distributing them, viewing photos posted by people you follow, discovering other photos, commenting, etc' (Manovich, 2017: 18). Images can be shared instantly and are indexed and made searchable via hashtags. Using a combination of striking imagery with a variety of relevant hashtags, with the additional facility of adding a text 'caption' of up to 2,200 characters, users aim to gain likes on their posts, attract a following, and in turn like other posts and follow hashtags. This enables them to garner accolades, sell products or further spread their message. Instagram thus comprises 'a tool for curating the self' (Bennett and Wilkins, 2020: 1311). Hashtags 'illuminate the key terms by which Instagram users interpret their pictures and…the key terms by which they hope to have their pictures interpreted by others' (Bennet and Wilkins, 2020: 1304). In this way, as Downing discusses in her article on 'Hashtag Heathens', 'when an Instagram user posts images with specific hashtags anyone subscribing to such hashtags can be alerted to those images in their own feed' (Downing, 2019: 187). Instagrammers typically have public rather than private accounts in order to engage as widely as possible, to 'encourage public views of such accounts leading to increasing followers and likes', and often 'in the pursuit of popularity' (Downing, 2019: 187).

Instagram is not just about sharing images to gain popularity, however; it also offers a powerful means by which to spread an idea or message. The platform offers a 'unique milieu for individuals to broadcast their ideas and feelings to an audience in terms of instantaneous effect through imagery' (Downing, 2019: 188). There is also a strong element of community to the use of Instagram. Hashtagging can be theorised as a folk taxonomy or 'folksonomy', 'indicating the collective social organisation and description of information at the metadata level' (Highfield and Leaver, 2015: n.p.). But rather than involving a predetermined indexical structure, Instagram's folksonomy is 'created by users emergently and collectively' (Bennet and Wilkins, 2020: 1304). Hashtags are not always an indication of users' intentional aligning of their own images with other users, but they can 'lead to the formation of publics or communities' (Highfield and Leaver, 2015: n.p.). As such, 'hashtags can allow certain types of communities to emerge and form, including ad hoc publics, forming and responding very quickly in relation to a particular event or topical issue' (Highfield and Lever, 2015: n.p.). A good example of this is the anti-racist Heathen responses to the QAnon Shaman, cited above. Furthermore, 'These publics or communities may not persist for long periods but can be extremely efficient and significant' (Highfield and Lever, 2015: n.p.).

While Instagram has been seen as primarily a form of 'self-expression' (Lee *et al.*, 2015: 555) or 'self-presentation', 'expressing…identity through verbal and non-verbal messages' (Smith and Sanderson, 2015: 343), and there has been substantial discussion of the platform in terms of visuality (Manovich, 2017; Serafinelli, 2018; Hochman and Schwartz, 2021), there has been little discussion of Instagram *politics*. As Highfield and Leaver point out in their study of Instagram: 'The image has great social and political power, too – especially the digital image, which can drive political acts and protests in a safer arena than publicly in person' (Highfield and Leaver, 2016: 49). The forty-two million followers of Leonardo di Caprio's Instagram feed which campaigns for environmental sustainability are a case in point (Fomby, 2020: n.p.). Like other users, therefore, anti-racist Heathens similarly recognise that their posts have a currency which enables them 'to gain affirmation and influence amongst Heathens and the sympathetic users of Instagram' (Downing, 2019: 191), but in this case focussed around anti-racist campaigning as opposed to environmental action (although inclusive Heathens, especially those identifying as 'animist' are often environmentalists, a topic beyond the remit of this discussion). Since Instagram posts achieve 'an average reach of around 6,500 users' (Statista, 2024), efficient and significant anti-racist Heathen communities have emerged based around certain hashtags and posts which juxtapose image and text in rapidly consumable packages which have the potential to become memes, spreading the message of anti-racist Heathenry widely and persuasively. As with other memes, these anti-racist Heathen image/text posts are, as Miller *et al.* (2016: xvi) put it for the use of Instagram more broadly, 'particularly significant as a kind of moral police of the internet. By using them people are able to express their values and disparage those of others in less direct and more acceptable ways than before'.

Miller *et al.*'s (2016) theorising of 'social scalability' is salient at this juncture. Social scalability reflects 'how social media has colonised the space of group sociality between the private and the public…[and]…created scales, including the size of the group and the degree of privacy' (Miller *et al.*, 2016: x). The popular encrypted messaging service WhatsApp, for instance, is one of the least socially scalable platforms because it is a closed social group typically restricted to a small group of people. In contrast, Instagram, where individuals 'welcome strangers who can appreciate their images' (Miller *et al.*, 2016: 5), is the most public platform and therefore the most 'socially scalable' in that posts potentially capture the largest group of people (Miller *et al.*, 2016: 5). It thus enables users, such as anti-racist Heathens, to maximise the impact of their post and the products or messages they represent. X (formerly Twitter), another online and scalable networking service, whilst also utilising hashtags and now allowing images and videos, remains tweet (text/character) focussed, and is, therefore, not considered for discussion here. It is also centred on a much older adult demographic and has a much smaller user base (Miller, 2009). Additionally, it is in decline in recent years as other platforms, such as Instagram, and especially now TikTok (again beyond the remit of this study), have gained considerable traction.

Previous studies of Instagram (building on the pioneering work of boyd and Ellison, 2007), have focussed on the posting of photographs (e.g. Manovich, 2017), particularly the phenomenon of cute pets, kids and meals (e.g. Frier, 2020). But as other authors we have pointed to make clear, Instagram works harder than this, enabling other forms of visual communication and messaging, including artwork, memes, collages, inspirational quotes and political statements (e.g. Highfield and Leaver, 2016: 512; Omena, 2017). While boundaries between social media are permeable, with users occupying and posting the same or similar messages across several platforms, Instagram is particularly relevant with regard to visual–virtual Heathen politicking because it is an increasingly popular platform, with high social scalability, and one which enables a distinctive juxtaposition of image (often artwork) *and* text (such as a campaign slogan). It is the medium that offers, therefore, the best of both worlds, or to paraphrase the writing of Marshall McLuhan (e.g. 1964), with Instagram the 'medium is the message'.

Imagetext, image-text and imageXtext

We draw upon the influential thinking of W. J. T. Mitchell on image and text in our approach to anti-racist visual–virtual Heathen politicking on Instagram (first outlined in the Introduction to this book, but it is worth recapping here). In summary, Mitchell (1994, 2003, 2005, 2015) proposes that moving on from the typographical suturing of 'image/text':

1) 'imagetext' usefully 'designates composite, synthetic works which combine image and text' (Mitchell, 1994: 89);
2) 'image-text', with its hyphen, designates '*relations* of the visual and verbal' (Mitchell, 1994: 89, original emphasis);
3) 'imageXtext', with its 'X', cites 'the X factor' and 'the appearance of something neither text nor image' (Mitchell, 2015: 39, 43).

Instagram posts, comprising an image juxtaposed with text in the hashtag(s) and/or with text in the caption, and/or with text in the image, plus its scrolling function, mean that imagetext, image-text and potentially imageXtext framings are consumed very rapidly; they offer, consequently, a highly relevant and immediate social media platform for analysis in Mitchell's terms because Instagrammers convey their messages in ways beyond the mere image/text. The visual frame itself is typically complemented by using text in the hashtag and/or caption to make a relational image-text juxtaposition, with the first words of the caption (up to 2,200 characters) or the hashtags (in a potentially long list if the character limit in the caption has not been used up with phrasing) being visible in the Instagram feed. Scrollers consume, therefore, not only the framed image but also the complementary opening text/hashtags. Users can then also expand the caption to view the full text/hashtags, extending the relational interplay between framed image and complementary text, or image-text.

When Heathen Instagrammers use runic script, which embodies glyph/image, noun/word and object/referent, and where different runes are combined together into a single image, a so-called 'bind rune' made for magical anti-racist purposes, these posts not only reiterate how image and text are political and inseparable but also offer examples of imageXtext in action. If Mitchell (Mitchell, 1994: 369) recognises the potential of social media for 'soft facism', then Taussig proposes that 'fascism' (Taussig, 2020: 42) and other political catastrophes have a magic that one needs to 'mimetically match' with a 'counter-sorcery' (Taussig, 2020: 16) so as to challenge the far right at its core. We argue that the bind runes used by anti-racist Heathens on social media are 'neither text nor image' but comprise imageXtexts, embodying something eXtra and/or eXtraordinary, with the counter-sorcerous aim to attack racist Heathenry head-on.

Mitchell also proposes that new technologies 'are altering the conditions under which human vision articulates itself' (Mitchell, 1994: 24), with the boundary between public/private increasingly permeated in ways which facilitate both the virality of misinformation and opportunities for critical resistance (Mitchell, 1994: 369; 2015: 158–159, 209). New media, and social media in particular, especially on the dark web, enables covert communication, networking and recruitment among racist Heathen individuals and organisations. Note, for example, how Stephen McNallen, former leader of the racist Heathen organisation in North America, the AFA (see Chapter 4), posted 'An exercise in applied memetics' on his Wotan Network's Facebook page; he called for members 'to create memes, advertisements and propaganda material' to promote the Defend Europe group which aimed to block refugee boats and so prevent the 'Islamization of Europe' (see Smith and Burley, 2017: n.p.). While social media facilitates such expressions of 'soft facism' it is also a double-edged sword as it simultaneously enables critical engagement with the public domain (Mitchell, 1994: 369). Mitchell goes on to state that although 'we probably cannot change the world, we can continue to describe it critically and interpret it accurately. In a time of global misrepresentation, disinformation and systemic mendacity, this may be the moral equivalent of intervention' (Mitchell, 1994: 425). While it takes time for racist messaging to be removed by the providers of social media platforms (an ongoing concern for users and critics alike), such platforms as Instagram, with 'community guidelines' which (in principle) 'do not allow attacks or abuse based on race, ethnicity, national origin, sex, gender, gender identity, sexual orientation, religion, disability or disease' (Instagram 2018), do meanwhile enable anti-racist Heathens to intervene, critique and fight back against racism and other forms of discrimination, whether in the online or analogue world.

Heathen anti-racist hashtagging

We analyse here five hashtags by which Instagrammers organise, search for and follow anti-racist content: #heathensagainsthate, #heathensagainstracism, #heathensunitedagainstracism, #declaration127 and #paganantifa. The first two are arguably the pithiest of the five and have the most associated posts; the first three will be recognised by readers as the monikers of specific anti-racist Heathen organisations, and the fourth as the title of a major anti-racist Heathen campaign statement; while the fifth refers to the broader Pagan campaigning of anti-fascism. While the sheer number of posts offers a reflection of how many Heathen Instagrammers are tagging their images in alignment with an anti-racist stance, it would be misleading to associate certain posts with a single hashtag. Typically, each post is indexed by multiple hashtags, including one or more of those focussed on here. So overall, these five hashtags offer a good range of examples of how anti-racist Heathens are using hashtags, juxtaposed with imagery and other text, to contest against racist Heathenry. These five hashtags demonstrate how Instagrammers not only identify themselves with anti-racist Heathenry but also do so with an explicit, affirmative aim to counter racism within Heathenry, ultimately using social media as a powerful form of critical resistance. Regarding the ethics (e.g. Highfield and Leaver, 2015; 2016: 56–58) of this sort of 'observational research' (Moreno *et al.*, 2013) on social media: all of the images examined have been posted publicly; none of them can be identified to a particular user; they have been reused by other users many times; and there has been no interaction between the researchers and subjects in the process of this research.

#heathensagainsthate

The hashtag #heathensagainsthate is associated with thousands of posts (5,000+, 3 March 2025). In addition to being a bite-size, alliterated and memorable hashtag, it derives from the epigrammatic slogan of the campaign group Heathens Against Hate, which (as discussed in Chapter 10), began as an anti-racist blog, became affiliated with The Troth and now operates as an autonomous agency. Figure 10.2 shows a post with the logo of Heathens Against Hate which comprises a white wild boar with interlace accompanied by the title of the organisation written in block capitals and repeated in runes, all white, upon a red background. The boar image is in the style of various early medieval art objects, such as the boar-crest on the seventh-century CE Benty Grange helmet (Derbyshire) and Knocknagael Pictish symbol stone (Inverness). In the image the boar has been combined with Viking art style interlace. The use of the boar, interlace and runes immediately marks the image out visually as having a 'Heathen' aesthetic. The use of capitals in the English text is notable because in social media the use of capitals tends to indicate one is shouting. The runes, in addition, reiterate the Heathen aesthetic and for those who can read them (many Heathens are so rune-literate) repeat the message. Users posting using this hashtag, together with this composite, synthetic 'imagetext', then, may show either or both their affiliation with an idea in principle and an organisation in practice, and their expression of it in an affirmative, 'shouty' or loud tone.

Figure 11.1, by contrast, incorporates three images and substantial text in black on white with the header 'Heathens Against White Supremacy'; this is followed by the subtitle 'Commonly Appropriated and Misused Symbols', accompanied by three images of a 'Valknut', 'Mjöllnir' and the 'Othala/Odal' rune respectively, with brief contextual statements about each. The combination of image and text in capitals identifies and shouts out at racist Heathens and their misappropriation of Norse symbols by setting out contextual information clarifying what is and what is not known about these symbols; in doing so, it corrects white supremacist rhetoric and enables other Instagram users to recognise how and when Heathen symbols are being misused. The website address at the bottom of the image, www.houseofgrimnir.com, is now inactive, but it is associated with the active inclusivist group Grimnir's Crossroad Kindred (GCK) in Bloomington, Indiana, whose goal, stated on their website, 'is to inform and educate the general population about Asatru, to combat the negative reputation given to Heathens by those who use the various faiths within the category to discriminate and spread hate, and to foster an environment of unity and inclusiveness within the greater Heathen community' (GCK 2023).

A comparable image shows black text and image on a white background, entitled 'Runes and their meanings', again in capitals but using a clearer sans serif font (see Figure 9.1, Chapter 9). Beneath each rune of the rune row, in place of the actual historic name for each rune is the affirmative, increasingly expletive text: 'these do not belong to white supremacists', 'fuck white

Figure 11.1 Instagram post hashtagged #heathensagainsthate about Heathen symbols (Public domain).

supremacists', 'white supremacists can fuck right off', 'leave these symbols alone you nazi fuck', 'stop dragging everyone down with your appropriation of these symbols' and finally, in shouting capitals, 'THESE DO NOT BELONG TO YOU NAZI'. In this example of a composite, synthetic, 'imagetext' post, anti-racist Heathens translate the runic glyphs ironically to challenge the appropriation and interpretation of them by the far right, historically (especially in the work of List; see Chapter 3) and into the present.

Figures 9.1 and 11.1 show a heavy use of text to carry their messages; but most Instagrammers prefer simpler imagery, reserving text primarily for the caption and the hashtags. The simplicity of the imagery Instagrammers use is important across the platform because it is these striking posts which can be made sense of in a few moments while scrolling through one's feed. They capture attention, both visually and algorithmically, as well as attract likes and enable users to gain followers. And in terms of communication, their

Figure 11.2 Instagram post hashtagged #heathensagainsthate with a gold hammer of Thor upon the LGBTIQA+ rainbow flag (Public domain).

simplicity assists in spreading the message. In essence, 'simple images do well on Instagram. That's why there are so many popular accounts devoted entirely to minimalist photographs' (Shutterstock, 2017: n.p.). A simple post with the hashtag #heathensagainsthate shows a gold hammer of Thor upon the rainbow flag reflecting the diversity of the LGBTIQA+ community and the spectrum of human sexuality and gender (Figure 11.2). This simple but arresting image combines a well-known Heathen symbol with the rainbow of LGBTIQA+ pride, to insist that progressive Heathens welcome all. An accompanying hashtag from one Instagrammer also includes #inclusiveheathenry to maximise the impact of the imagetext package.

#heathensagainstracism

#heathensagainstracism has 1,000+ posts (3 March 2025). One of these has a green fern-leaf background, reflecting the way in which Heathens (and other Pagans) make relationships with and show respect for nature, with the statement 'HEATHENS AGAINST RACISM' in capitalised English language in the centre, with certain of these letters also composed into 'bind runes' (Figure 11.3). The contemporary practice of making bind runes

Figure 11.3 Instagram post hashtagged #heathensagainstracism with bind runes (Public domain).

draws upon archaeological sources including a small number of Viking Age runestones in Scandinavia, and a late medieval magical practice in Iceland. These sources are interpreted by today's Heathens as combining runes together into a visually arresting glyph which is made for magical purposes (e.g. Fries, 2002 [1993]: 255–268; drawing on e.g. Spare, 1913). Bind runes can be made simply and quickly for immediate effect, for instance in the air using one's finger or a preferred magical tool, or in ink on a slip of paper which can be hidden in a particular place to perform its magic in secret. Or bind runes can be made over a sustained period using longer-lasting media and displayed publicly, such as in a flag or banner displayed at a street protest. When posted on Instagram, the use of bind runes can be interpreted as having particular saliency because they hold 'power' whenever a user views them, and they can continue to hold this potency for the time that they persist in an Instagram feed. In Figure 11.3, the specific bind runes within the circle of the entire rune row (in this case the Germanic futhark), itself held by some Heathens as a magical formula or charm of making (e.g. Johnson and Wallis, 2022: 275), offer a highly salient example of 'imageXtext', embodying something eXtra and/or eXtraordinary, with the post encompassing an intended magical formula in and of itself in order to counter racist thinking.

A second image in the #heathensagainstracism feed comprises the text 'BLACK LIVES MATTER', the rallying call of the eponymous BLM movement; this is juxtaposed with runic script on a hammer which translates as Mjöllnir and is held within a fist of many skin colours (Figure 11.4). The text in the caption accompanying the image pithily states: 'Odin is the All-Father not the Some-Father', a phrase often repeated by anti-racist Heathens on social media in a reclaiming of the god from those Odinists who interpret the god in racist terms. The hashtags here also include the related forms, #heathensagainsthate, #heathensagainstracism, #heathensagainstfacism and #heathensagainstwhitesupremacy.

The following three hashtags have many fewer posts, in the hundreds rather than the thousands, indicating that posts tagged in this way reach a smaller audience. But it remains important to examine #declaration127, #heathensunitedagainstracism and #paganantifa for reasons which will become clear shortly.

#declaration127

The hashtag #declaration127 has 400+ posts (3 March 2025) and is significant because of its reference to the aforementioned anti-racist declaration made by Heathens in 2016 and revised and relaunched as Declaration 127 2.0 (The Troth, 2022: n.p.). So, users of the hashtag #declaration127 are explicitly identifying their posts as aligning with this declaration in particular and with inclusivist Heathenry more broadly. Figure 11.5 shows the motif of the Declaration 127 movement, specifically the tree of life or world tree of Norse mythology termed Yggdrasill, with the text 'DECLARATION 127' nestled in the space between roots, trunk and branches, in stark black on a pale background. An 'F' rune at the top of the trunk cites the *frith* (ON) 'peace', which progressive Heathens seek, surrounded by nine dots, nine being a sacred number of the north, for example representing the nine worlds of Yggdrasill (see also the discussion in Chapter 9). The roots of the tree entwine to form the shape of Thor's hammer, Mjöllnir. Finally, an arc of text in Old Norse stretches from the tips of the branches to those of the roots, stating the final two lines of *Hávámal* 127 at the core of Declaration 127 (cited above and in the epigram to Part III of this book). The imagery aligns key traits of Heathenry – the world tree, the nine worlds of Norse cosmology, the principle of *frith* (peace), Thor's hammer and *Hávámal* – with

Figure 11.4 Instagram post hashtagged #heathensagainstracism promoting Black Lives Matter (Public domain).

Figure 11.5 Instagram post hashtagged #declaration127 with the logo of Declaration 127 (Public domain).

inclusive Heathenry, and in contrast to the appropriation of them by racist Heathens. In the caption for this specific post of the image on Instagram, the text reads:

> The AFA's views do not represent our communities. I hereby declare that I do not condone hatred or discrimination carried out in the name of our religion, and will no longer associate with those who do. There is no room for hatred in not only the heathen community but hatred has no room in anyone's community! I stand with declaration 127!

This Instagrammer thereby protests against racist Heathenry by sharing the logo of Declaration 127 as well as juxtaposing this with affirmative text which calls for action against racism within Heathenry. What is more, this user only associates the single hashtag #declaration127 with the post, focussing attention on this key force of progressive, anti-racist Heathenry. Each re-sharing of the image, using the same or diverse hashtags, reinforces and spreads the message. Downing (2019: 208) remarks on how female Heathens particularly use Instagram as a platform for facilitating 'agency and authority within the religion', as well as 'participating in and producing the religious brand' and so 'strengthening their sense of self, of community, and of Heathenry itself'. Similarly, the visual–virtual Heathen politicking in this specific imagetext Instagram post can be read as an agentive, activist act, in tune with the way inclusivist Heathens read the teaching of *Hávámal* 127 and the specific call from universalist Heathen organisations to push back against the white supremacy of the AFA.

A second image associated with the hashtag #declaration127 (Figure 11.6) uses the LGBTIQA+ rainbow as a background, with the main text in black capitals: 'NORSE PAGANS AGAINST RACISM'. The so-called valknut of three interlocking triangles, understood by Heathens today as a symbol

Figure 11.6 Instagram post hashtagged #declaration127 using the valknut against racism (Public domain).

associated with Odin, with its nine points citing the nine worlds of the Yggdrasill world tree, dominates the centre of the flag. Within the triangles is the grey capitalised text, 'THE VALKNUT IS FOR HOPE NOT HATE'. This combination of text and image reclaims the valknut, often used as a symbol by racist Odinists, for progressive Heathenry. In combination with the rainbow, it also reclaims the god Odin into thinking which does not discriminate based on sexuality and gender. There was an ambivalent attitude to homosexuality in Viking Age society, perhaps encapsulated by the god Odin himself, a god of warriors and battle on the one hand, but at the same time a practitioner of *seidr* (sorcery/'women's magic', taught to him by the goddess Freyja) and so labelled with the insult *ergi*, 'unmanly' (used in some instances to mean 'passive male homosexuality') by the god Loki (e.g. Blain, 2002: 123). The contradiction of a warrior god being simultaneously 'gay' (in today's nomenclature) is, therefore, claimed in a positive way by Heathens posting this imagetext of inclusivist Heathen pride combining the rainbow and affirmative phrasing. With the addition of the valknut, a magical symbol associated with Odin, the post can be interpreted as having imageXtext potential, in challenge to the homophobia of far-right and racist Heathenry.

#heathensunitedagainstracism

The hashtag #heathensunitedagainstracism has fewer than one hundred posts (3 March 2025), despite once being the eponymous title of the activist wing of The Troth, the largest Heathen organisation in the US (and worldwide), although now it is a sovereign organisation. Two posts with this hashtag are particularly notable. The first comprises a simple black-and-white image of Adolf Hitler performing a Nazi salute, his head and arm being smashed, like glass, by the hammer of Thor (Figure 11.7). Rather than destroying a *jötunn* (ON 'giant'), the chief enemy of the gods in Norse mythology and against whom Thor often fights using his hammer and wins, the hammer and text in this composite and synthetic imagetext, destroys the architect of Nazi rhetoric and positively reclaims its use of 'Gothic' font.

The second post with the hashtag #heathensunitedagainstracism comprises a textile patch upon tartan clothing with an image of Thor's hammer emblazoned with rainbow-coloured interlace surrounded by the pink text 'NO NAZIS IN VALHALLA' (Figure 11.8). The image reclaims the Norse mythological hall of fallen warriors away from its use by militarist far-right and racist Heathens to within a progressive Heathenry. As such, it stands in vivid contrast to the final words of the racist Heathen-influenced

Figure 11.7 Instagram post hashtagged #heathensunitedagainstracism with Thor's hammer smashing Hitler (Public domain).

Christchurch murderer's 2019 manifesto and his acclamation to 'see you in Valhalla'. The Instagram caption states: 'Odin did not hang himself so Nazis could use the runes for hate, the gods do not smile upon these scum who tarnish our symbols, and their ancestors hide their faces in shame. A rainbow this [sic] faith, this hammer smashes fascists'. The inclusivist imagetext in the Instagram post insists that for progressive Heathens all are welcome in the Norse hall of the slain, *Valhǫll*, apart from racists and bigots, reiterated by the rainbow colours of LGBTIQA+ pride. The use of a textile patch and tartan cloth immediately evokes a DIY-style punk aesthetic (e.g. Larsen, 2013; Prinz, 2014). Like punk, the imagery is visually simple (Larsen, 2013), and worn upon personal clothing it spreads a message when socially interacting, and in an Instagram context, like punk, the forum is relatively democratic (Ensminger, 2011: 3). This imagetext post makes a public statement on Instagram and also cites the original public display of the patch on clothing, thereby occupying a dual function in kicking back against racist Heathenry in both the digital and analogue worlds.

Figure 11.8 Instagram post hashtagged #heathensunitedagainstracism stating NO NAZIS IN VALHALLA (Public domain).

#paganantifa

The final hashtag we explore here is #paganantifa. Anti-fascist movements have a historical origin in 1930s Europe in response to the rise of National Socialism and fascism more broadly (e.g. Balhorn, 2017). However, in the US they gained momentum in the anti-skinhead protests of the 1980s and more recently in response to the rise of the alternative right (alt-right) in the 2000s and 2010s (Bray, 2017; Bogel-Burroughs and Garcia, 2020). Two of the fewer than one hundred #paganantifa posts (3 March 2025) are especially notable. The first consists of a black field superimposed with grey, block capital sans serif text, dominating the picture plane, stating 'THIS HAMMER SMASHES FASCISTS' (Figure 11.9). As well as making a clear Heathen-inflected statement against fascism, given the origins of anti-fascist movements in leftist politics this slogan may also offer a play on the hammer and sickle of Soviet communism which expressed the unity of the working people. At the top of the slogan is Thor's hammer with beak-head and interlace, like that from the Viking Age found at Skåne, Sweden (see e.g. Andersson, 2002: 31). The message is simple: that progressive Heathenry defeats racist Heathenry and that Thor's hammer and racist thinking are incompatible. In its simple use of imagetext (in contrast to, for example, Figure 11.1), the post is comparable to a political campaign or advertising

Visual–virtual Heathen politicking 229

Figure 11.9 Instagram post hashtagged #paganantifa with Thor's hammer against facism (Public domain).

poster, or even a T-shirt slogan; it grabs viewers' attention and communicates its message quickly. Instagrammers scrolling through their feed would not need to dwell on this post for long to understand it, and, if likeminded, appreciate it and further disseminate it by liking and/or reposting it. In one sense Instagram posts are also like posters and T-shirt slogans in being highly ephemeral (Ensminger, 2011: 10), as viewers scroll through their feed moving from one post to the next in a matter of seconds. But despite this ephemerality, Instagram posts do have an inbuilt digital longevity, via hashtag indexing, unless deleted by the account holder of the post. They also have digital longevity via repeated sharing; hence the posts we highlight here recur across other account holders and hashtags, becoming memes which anti-racist Heathens can use to their advantage, spreading their inclusivist message across a global-reaching social media platform.

A second #paganantifa post has a white Nazi Sonnenrad/Black Sun symbol covered with a 'no entry' sign paint-like daubing in red, the text stating 'ECLIPSE THE FUCKING SUN', with an Anarchist 'A-in-circle' motif emblazoned top left and a number of runes filling the rest of the space (Figure 11.10). These runes, readable to those with some elementary knowledge, comprise: the arrow-shaped 'Tyr' rune, referring to the god of the same name, repeated three times and pointing at the cancelled Black Sun to maximise the magical imageXtext impact, with, bottom left, runes

Figure 11.10 Instagram post hashtagged #paganantifa with a Black Sun cancelled (Public domain).

reading 'KILL NAZIS'. In contrast to the clean and clear image and message of the previous post (Figure 11.9), which draws on minimalist graphic design principles, this one has an anti-art DIY punk-like aesthetic. While striking, this image would require more than a few seconds attention from Instagrammers to decode the message in full. But with its shouty text to challenge racist Heathenry and its cancelling of Nazi imagery, and with its use of runes to magical effect, it does possess potent imageXtext saliency.

Conclusion: anti-racist Heathenry on Instagram

The anti-racist Heathen use of Instagram is interesting in five main respects. First, Instagram is highly public and has the most reach of all social media platforms to maximise on messaging impact; so, it is a top choice for making protest statements. Second, it shows a highly creative use of text and image. In particular, it forms simple, composite and synthetic framings, in Mitchell's terms 'imagetexts'; these are consumed very rapidly, conveying and maximising the impact of messaging by means beyond the ruptured 'image/text', including the juxtaposing of image-text relations and magical forms of 'imageXtext', such as bind runes and rune-codes for 'those in the know'. Third, the posts have clear political messages divorced of references to individuals, when the majority of other posts on Instagram are apolitical, individualised and, using selfies and filters, focussed on self-presentation with the view to invite accolade. This 'visual–virtual Heathen politicking' on Instagram thus, fourthly, enables anti-racist Heathens to counter racist Heathenry, to reclaim images and ideas from ancient sources which have been appropriated by the far right, and to reposition them in positive and affirmative terms in tune with progressive Heathenry. Finally, it is interesting to reflect on the diversity of visual representation used in spreading similar messaging, from the multi-colourful, nature-inspired and diversity affirming, to a harsher, DIY punk activism. Not only is the latter of aesthetic and academic interest but it may result also in a wider appeal given its variety of styles.

Racist Heathens have utilised social media and memes to successfully perpetuate their negative ideology. In this chapter, by contrast, we have analysed how progressive Heathens are campaigning to spread an anti-racist message via the highly popular social media platform of Instagram. Studies of Instagram have tended to focus on the primary role of the photograph and the act of photo-sharing (e.g. Manovich, 2016), alongside the folksonomy of hashtagging (Highfield and Leaver, 2015), as a means by which individuals curate and articulate identities and form digitally mediated relationships and communities (e.g. Serafinelli, 2018: 82). In her analysis of how Heathen women use Instagram in altruistic 'virtual priestessing', Downing (2019: 186) identifies an 'affirmative nonpolitical epistemology'. But posts with the hashtags #heathensagainsthate, #heathensagainstracism, #heathensunitedagainstracism, #declaration127 and #paganantifa demonstrate that Instagram is not only a social (and as Downing [2019] demonstrates, religious) platform, but also a *political* one (ff. e.g. Highfield and Leaver, 2016; Omena, 2017); in other words, it is both religious politics and political religion (as discussed in Chapter 2). We have drawn upon Mitchell's thinking on image and text to analyse, consequently, how anti-racist Heathens articulate a visual–virtual Heathen politicking using the social media platform with high social scalability, using striking and effective Instagram posts to intervene, critique and fight back against racism and other forms of discrimination.

Conclusion: inferences, implications and future directions

Introduction

In this book we have examined racist and anti-racist Heathenry and occultism today, with a particular focus on the case of Britain given the latter's significant role in the history of these groups. While the subject might seem fringe and eccentric, we have argued that the study of it is necessary and important. With regard to racist Heathenry, it is worth reiterating Evans' (2018: n.p.) point that:

> one of the more frustrating elements about covering the fascist right is that much of what they say sounds ridiculous and makes them appear less than serious. This is why it is important to remember that these groups have a body count and represent a real threat. Their absurdity does not negate their danger.

Or, as Voltaire is said to have pithily opined: '[t]hose who can make you believe absurdities, can make you commit atrocities' (see Olson, 2020: n.p.). Given the long history of Ariosophy and its different permutations leading up to the various racist Heathen iterations we see today, the fact that its fingerprints can be identified in many major far-right global terrorist incidents of the last few decades and not forgetting its potential role in leading to the Holocaust, it is certainly timely to have analysed this shadowy ideology, its history, legacy and critical responses to it.

In our analysis of this apposite topic, we began the book by exploring the spectrum of Heathen thinking and practice, emphasising that while Heathenry has been associated with far-right politics, this is but a small exclusivist element within a majority inclusivist contemporary Pagan pathway. We next traced the historical origins of racist Heathenry to the nineteenth century with the emergence of nationalism, nationalist Romanticism, race theory and Social Darwinism. This racialised thinking was expressed in especially spiritual terms in Blavatsky's Theosophy and List's Ariosophy which in the early twentieth century then fed into the far-right politics of

National Socialism and Fascism. Occult or esoteric Nazism took a particular interest in the ancient heathen past as 'ancestral' for the German people or 'folk', promoting the idea of an ideal Aryan race. The Nazis incorporated runes and other ancient Germanic imagery into their iconography, and also appropriated from Germanic archaeology, mythology and other literature, as part of their racist agenda. We do not suggest that Hitler was a 'Heathen' or that Ariosophy is the most important element in the rise of German Nazism, but only that it should be considered an integral part of studies examining the early history of this ideology. Despite the defeat of Nazism on the battlefield in the Second World War, the far right persisted after that conflict and forms of racist Heathenry continued to thrive. This continuous but under-explored tributary should also be considered when examining the historical and theoretical implications of the German variant of fascism and its ongoing effects.

From Christensen's the Odinist Fellowship and the Wotanism perpetuated by the Lanes' with McVan, to McNallen's Asatru Folk Assembly, the US has been a focus for scholarly analysis. The case of racist Heathenry in the UK has been neglected, however, and we have sought to redress this imbalance by exploring how Mills, Leese and Jordan, among others, developed distinctive British articulations of racist Heathenry which in turn influenced not only events and individuals here but also in the US. The White Defence League, British National Party and National Action stand out as specific examples of far-right movements in the UK which have drawn upon the trappings of ancient Heathenry as well as National Socialism in their expressions of racist agendas. Set against this historical context, we have discussed in detail the 'three thorns' of contemporary racist Heathenry in the UK: the Odinic Rite, the Odinist Fellowship and Woden's Folk. Given the intersecting historical trajectories of Paganism and esotericism over the last hundred years or so, we have also explored the example of the Order of the Nine Angles which draws upon a range of eclectic sources, including racist Heathenry, in its own peculiar and pernicious far-right esoterrorist ambitions. Our analysis of these groups and their membership has pointed to such enduring, politically charged and highly problematic themes within them as racial ancestry, traditionalism, tribal indigeneity, nativist claims to land and separatism.

Whilst the racist Heathen and occult organisations in the UK are small, they have obtained an international reach, particularly with the growth of social media and instant messaging. The British academic Roger Griffin terms such minor far-right organisations 'groupuscules' (2003: 30); that is, small entities within a wider, amorphous, leaderless and centreless cellular network of far-right political ideology and which are generally intent on pursuing a palingenetic overthrow of the liberal-democratic order. Two of these four movements, Woden's Folk and the O9A, certainly fit this description when it comes to promoting an overt militarist or violent political agenda; the other two, the Odinic Rite and the Odinist Fellowship, are not explicitly racist but do still make appeals to 'the folk', indigeneity and native ancestry. What is more, they are using their public platforms, such as the OF's Odinist Temple, in order to gain influence. These organisations also have indirect influence on the wider far-right scene; for example the 'QAnon Shaman' followed the OR on Facebook, and several convicted British terrorists have had O9A materials in their possession.

The enduring relationship between racist Heathenry and esotericism and the far right extends into popular culture, and so we have also explored attempts to achieve influence outside of mainstream politics and the democratic process by changing the popular discourse on a particular subject; that is, the involvement of, for example, literature, film, music, television, gaming, fashion and the internet, in metapolitics. We focussed particularly on the genres of neofolk and black metal, demonstrating the power of music to promote far-right messaging and even acts of violence. Whilst some subgenres, such as National Socialist black metal, are explicitly far-right in their politics, with such convicted terrorists as Kristian 'Varg' Vikernes' promoting racist Odinism, or as he put it, 'National Heathenry', other neofolk and BM musicians often distance themselves from the far right in public but make racist statements in their music and other fora. This tactic enables them to maintain their status and fandom and still promote their racist messaging. In other instances, the trappings of Heathenry are used for their aesthetics and shock value, and in some cases also utilise Christian imagery, in, as Pardy (2023a: 76) puts it, 'a seemingly counterintuitive pairing [that] is more about the conveyance of an ideology than about genuine religiosity'.

Heathenry is a diverse contemporary Pagan path and, as we have shown, racism is a minority ideology within it. Inclusive Heathens take an interest in ancestors and land too, but in contrasting ways to the racist groups. Ancestors are conceived in a much broader and looser sense, without recourse to notions of race, ethnicity or blood linkages. For these Heathens, anyone who takes an interest in Heathenry can legitimately practise it. While the three thorns of UK racist Heathenry that we have discussed approach their spiritual interests in the land in terms of nationhood, ethnicity, indigeneity and/or race, inclusive Heathens, like most other Pagans, build their spiritual connections to the land though relationships with and respect for nature in the place that they live without recourse to racist tropes. In broad terms, the traditionalist, conservative and far-right politics of the racist Odinist groups can be contrasted with the more liberal politics of inclusive Heathens, even if the political leanings of Heathenry broadly cast can be 'conservative with a small c'. In the face of increasingly emboldened racist Heathen factions, inclusive Heathens are finding ways to take a stand against the racist appropriation of their religion, and this provided the focus for Part III of this book. We discussed how progressive Heathens have taken action by restricting membership of their organisations to exclude or dissuade racists, by making vocal anti-racist statements and especially Declaration 127, as well as protesting at far-right demonstrations. They have also facilitated prison in-reach programmes, organised conferences and networking events on diversity and inclusion, and provided online and print educational materials about anti-racist Heathenry. Most recently in the UK, they have taken up leadership positions within and provided intelligence assistance to, the police and security forces. We would like to close this study by paying particular attention to the next steps for anti-racist Heathen activism, but before doing so, offer some final thoughts on the importance of examining and monitoring racist Heathen groupuscular thought and action, and the significance of the history of racist Heathenry and its transnational appeal.

Size

All of the racist Heathen associations studied here share a small membership, varying between 40 and 200 members (Woden's Folk) to perhaps as many as 2,000 (O9A). Whilst numbers of followers remain modest there remains, however, *multum in parvo*. Consequently, we argue that size should not be an indicator of significance; and so, we have demonstrated in this study that such groups can still wield considerable influence, both directly or indirectly, as well as nationally and transnationally. We consequently make the case that these groups present a very real and present danger. To paraphrase one source linked with the intelligence community who requested anonymity, and who commented on the genuine danger which certain extremist groups presented: 'these guys are so scary that even the fucking regular Nazis are frightened of them'. So many of the most extreme far-right activities of the past few decades, ranging from Columbine to Christchurch and Bologna to Breivik, have all had some kind of affiliation with, or been influenced by, varying forms of racist Heathenry. This fact alone suggests that historic Ariosophy and its ideological racist Heathen variants since, require far more serious attention from both academics and the security services. As Jackson (2022: 3) argues in relation to the danger that small 'fringe' far-right groups present overall, they can still have 'a real impact'.

This radical influence can be made manifest in numerous ways. In particular, it can turn disaffected loners into violent lone wolves. As Cunningham *et al.* (2023: 324) concluded with their post-Christchurch analysis: 'what is already clear is that extreme convictions and ideologies are a pre-condition of extreme violence'. Indeed, in addition to the Christchurch terrorist, Anders Breivik, David Copeland and Thomas Mair are all indicative of this propensity. The same holds true for the various members of the Sonnenkrieg Division which was banned in the UK as a terrorist organisation in 2020 because of its 'attempts to draw vulnerable people down a path towards extremism and violence' (Counter Terrorism Policing, 2020: n.p.). Atomwaffen, a US-based and extremely violent neo-Nazi terror organisation which traces its roots to The Order and is described as being 'steeped' in 'esoteric religions', and which became heavily influenced by the O9A, is another case in point (SPLC, n.d.i). Even before the advent of social media, however, it was always the case that such extreme propaganda could have a dire effect. Jackson (2018), for example, noted that attacks in the UK on Jewish synagogues as early as the mid-1960s by members of the National Socialist Movement were the direct result of Colin Jordan's racist publicity. The advent of the internet has since only served to extend the ease, speed, reach and impact of dissemination; the medium now really is the message *in extremis*. Some members of these groups have also sought, nonetheless, other more insidious channels to propagate their ideology. The O9A, for instance, with its 'insight' activists, 'seek to infiltrate and covertly influence the attitudes and actions of larger, more conventional political parties and other relatively mainstream socio-cultural bodies' (Bale, 2020: 26). The violent results of such a subversive technique have been pointed out in our preface and addressed in the chapter focussing on the O9A.

Given their violent extremism and varied techniques for communicating their racist Heathen beliefs, there is a danger, therefore, that even small organisations can morph into larger and more consequential movements. This highlights another reason for our study: the threat of popular contagion. Hitler, for example, was aware of this particular potentiality for expansion during the early years of the NSDAP when he stated: 'We may be small but a man once stood up in Galilee and now his doctrine dominates the world' (quoted in Piper, 2007: 50). Griffin (2003: 31), too, suggested that the development from small to significant occurred with the transition of Anton Drexler's small *volkisch Deutsche Arbeiterpartei* (DAP) into the Nazi Party. Likewise, Macklin (2020: 15) proposes, in relation to a specific British example, that it was the coagulation of numerous extreme-right groupuscules in the UK in the mid-twentieth century, who all drew upon racist Heathenry to varying degrees, that led eventually to the establishment of the much larger National Front in 1966.

History

In addition to articulating the significance of small fringe extremist groups and the dangers they can present, another reason to examine the history of these UK-based racist Heathen groupuscules and their individual members is that they helped to keep the flames of far-right hate alive in periods of 'a hostile post-fascist interregnum' (Macklin, 2020: 15). This in fact is the crux of our argument in Part I of the book that discusses early and mid-twentieth-century racist Heathenry focussing on the UK. Racist Heathenry was a driving force behind Leese, Jordan and Myatt. Its tentacles were also apparent to some extent in the later behaviour of Nick Griffin. Variants of Ariosophic thinking were additionally at play in the thoughts and actions of other earlier inter-war racist Pagan or Heathen groups. We take our cue, subsequently, from Pugh's (2006: 3) history of inter-war extreme-right activity in Britain. After studying now three generations of such movements here, we concur that 'fascism enjoyed a longer history in Britain than is usually recognised and that it was far from being simply an import from abroad'.

This common and long-standing ideological history does not as yet appear to have been fully explored and/or recognised. While there has been relatively substantial discussion of racist Heathen and Pagan groups in the US (e.g. Gardell, 2003; Goodrick-Clarke, 2002; Snook, 2015) and Europe (e.g. papers in Rountree, 2015a, 2017; von Schnurbein, 2015; Aitamurto and Downing, 2025), there has been little examination of cases in the UK specifically, nor of their current links to right-wing populist politics, aside from Doyle White's (2017) recent and important article on what we have described as the 'three thorns'. By taking simultaneously both a deeper and a broader view of the development of racist Heathenry from the late nineteenth century through to the present, and by expanding our study to cover a wider range of groups and the mediums they use to promulgate their ideology, including their extensions into and associations with racist Heathenry internationally, we have additionally underlined just how long-standing and simultaneously broad this racist Heathen and occult influence on the far right has been. We have, consequently, traced the Ariosophic influence particularly over a hundred-year span from early twentieth-century Austria, through to Nazi Germany, and then the US and more widely in Europe. Throughout this narrative, British variants and voices have played a leading role. By tracing this transnational history we have demonstrated how the ideology and culture of one extreme-right groupuscule, namely the early followers of Ariosophy, has successfully adapted and evolved to ensure that 'extreme variants of revolutionary nationalism...survive in the "post-fascist" age' (Griffin, 2003: 27). Consequently, we conclude that racist Heathenry provides an important and necessary case study for Griffin's theoretical approach to groupuscular thinking.

Transnationalism and Fascism

Although this work has focussed particularly on the UK, given the origins of racist Heathenry in Europe and its subsequent influence globally, inevitably at times it has ranged into international territory. This can be evidenced in particular by the ways in which racist Heathenry has influenced popular culture, inter alia, music, fashion and various internet fora. As Jackson (2022: 6) contends, the far right has been very 'successful in terms of creating a diverse counterculture, one fostered by a bewildering array of groups that draw followers from a range of age groups and classes'. Indeed, the international proliferation of extremist black metal could be seen to represent a form of the O9A's so-called 'aeonic Magick' which is designed to nexionically influence society as a whole. Attempts to counter this magic are made, in turn, by anti-racist Heathens in their ritual-like music, as well as by those Heathens making and sending magical bind runes into digital space via social media.

In his analysis of 'How the British Far-Right Appropriate and Misrepresent Pagan Iconography', Pardy (2023a: 75–76) makes the important point that the use of 'these symbols is not simply a mimicry of the Nazi regime – although it is undoubtedly a contributory factor – but of a desire to perpetuate a Brito-centric narrative that seeks to tie fascist thought to an idealised and often wilfully reinterpreted version of Britain's history, utilising the indigenous faith of Paganism as a means to do so'. For example, the White Stag Athletic Club (WSAC), an avowedly anti-democratic and violent fascist fitness club, recruits members online via Telegram and uses a runic-inspired logo. And O9A affiliates have promoted various esoteric bodybuilding regimes, such as the Folk Horror Fitness Club, and Centurion Method used by National Action, via Instagram. Indeed, racist Heathen imagery and themes have been identified in the social media accounts of at least twenty-seven of forty far-right groups operating in the UK (Pardy 2023a: 77). These visual trappings and themes of racist Heathenry have spread transnationally, especially as memes on the internet, and are increasingly evident in the general mainstream as far-right politics have become normalised. In Australia, for instance, the celebrity chef Pete Evans included a Sonnenrad Black-Sun symbol on his social media account (BBC News, 2020b). Therefore, whilst we have concentrated on the UK, Ariosophy and its virulent racist Heathen offshoots are significant for their transnational impact on the history of, and contemporary iterations of, the international far right.

Whilst we have used the term 'far right' throughout this study, taking one of the best-known definitions of fascism, that of Roger Griffin's 'palingenetic ultranationalism', Ariosophic-inspired movements would also qualify as fascistic themselves. According to Griffin (2018: 27), whose work focuses upon 'how the fascists themselves saw the ultimate goals of their movement', an Ariosophic emphasis upon a Hyperborean myth of decline and renewal when combined with the concept of 'an Aryan super-race' suggests, therefore, a fascist-like foundation myth for these groups. Their worldview is, for example, based on a mythic core of blood and genetics which is anti-liberal, anti-rational, violent, militarist and racist. Whilst this book does not claim to be a study of theories of fascism and whilst it certainly does not imply that there was an intentional strategy on behalf of Hitler to develop an Ariosophic-inspired Third Reich, given the cross-over between racist Heathenry and fascism, perhaps this study should have been called instead *Faith, folk and fascism*?

The future of faith, folk and the far right

Clearly, given all of the above, it would be a mistake to dismiss how racist Heathen organisations use the past as fringe and eccentric. Romanticised notions of the ancient past as mystical and unchanging abound in the mainstream media and popular culture. As one archaeologist responded to news reports about the rituals conducted by Woden's Folk at Wayland's Smithy long barrow, despite the nuanced interpretations of academics 'a conservative, nostalgic narrative of a lost rural England' plays into the hands of racist extremists (Last, 2019; also Williams, 2019). As such, it is important to draw attention to and challenge such pernicious appropriations of the past as those of Woden's Folk and their racist Heathen conspirators. But it is also important for academics to engage with inclusive Heathens and other Pagans interested in diverse pasts as potential allies (ff. Wallis, 2003); and, as Last and Williams emphasise, to celebrate the past as belonging to everyone.

As racist Heathenry continues to grow, in tune with the growth in influence of populist politics and the far right as a whole, it is important to monitor such organisations and examine how they co-opt ancient heathen religion to support their agendas. According to Jackson (2022: 76), '[s]uch esoteric themes can confer a sense of deeper meaning that appeal to some drawn to extreme right spaces, helping some within this culture consider their activism as part of a wider cosmic order'. As this sort of far-right thinking that finds validation in religion proliferates exponentially through various internet algorithms, Daubs (2022: 335) presciently concludes that the term 'lone wolf' can perhaps no longer even be considered a suitable descriptor of the extreme terrorist actions of these individuals given the extent of the communities and channels of hate proselytising such ideas. We agree. Our aim in this work, therefore, has been to engage critically with contemporary racist Heathen and occult groups in the UK who espouse varied forms of far-right thinking with a view to challenging their pernicious rhetoric and culture.

The sources for this study, given the extreme nature of the actors, have of necessity been restricted primarily to the publicly available and accessible materials available, most of which are online. We have also benefited from several intelligence sources. Nevertheless, we acknowledge that there are gaps in the study and there is certainly potential for further research. We have not, for example, accessed those materials hidden behind firewalls and encrypted messaging services which would have deepened the reach of our analysis. It is also difficult to measure the impact of anti-racist Heathen activity online, especially as the main social media providers have increasingly restricted public access to their data and withdrawn from using such platforms as CrowdTangle to evaluate how content is being shared. It would be unethical to engage in covert ethnography with racist Heathens, but our study would have benefitted from interview data to enrich the picture of anti-racist Heathenry and occultism. Our work has also mainly tackled male protagonists but we do of course recognise that some women have played influential roles in the history and development of racist Heathenry on these shores, and of course anti-racist Heathenry too. Gleaning such information on the roles of women within racist Heathen organisations is difficult, however, because there is even less information available on them than there is for their male counterparts.

Jackson's biography of Colin Jordan, for instance, merely hints that there were some women present at their summer camps in the 1960s given that there was a single tent provided for them, but offers no further details (Jackson, 2018: 102). But certainly, many of these women were agentive, with notable individuals, such as Savitri Devi, taking leadership positions, while others could capture national media attention, as was the case with Françoise Dior. A more recent example is offered by Alice Cutter, National Action's 'Miss Hitler', also known as the 'Buchenwald Princess', who was reported to have joked about gassing Jews and using the head of a Jew as a football. Cutter, who with her ex-partner Mark Jones was convicted and jailed in 2020 for membership of a proscribed terrorist group, is thought to have held a position of influence in National Action (*The Economic Times*, 2022: n.p.). It is also worth reiterating that women – exclusively white women, that is – are viewed by racist Heathens as essential for the preservation of Aryan offspring, albeit restricting their agency to the roles of childbearer, child-carer and homemaker, according with the contemporary meme of the 'tradwife'. But the application of this sort of racist and sexist thinking to interpreting the ancient heathen past in Britain, however, is as we have explored, a damaging construct, '[i]gnoring historical, archaeological and genetic evidence, [to] fabricate 'Anglo-Saxons as the epitome of Aryan greatness and purity' (Pardy, 2023a: 77).

With the growth in the influence of the far right it is important to monitor racist Heathenries and to engage critically with their co-option of ancient heathen religion to support their racist and often sexist, homophobic and generally discriminatory militant agendas. This is especially the case given that, as we have shown, a recent revival of interest in Paganism, herb witchery, folklore and folk horror, has seen the far right co-option of these themes in order to garner metapolitical influence in the wider Pagan/folklore scene. It is intriguing to note, therefore, that at the time of writing, the UK-based anti-fascist organisation Hope not Hate has, for the first time, published a separate section on racist Heathen groups in the 2024 State of Hate report (HnH, 2024: 106–107).

The number of self-identifying Pagans and Heathens in the UK is increasing according to data in the UK's 2021 National Census which, whilst not comprehensive or complete, offers an insight into this development, given that 74,000 stated 'Pagan' and 4,722 'Heathen'. It should be noted too that some Heathens may also have preferred to list another tradition they feel affiliated with, such as 'Shamanism', which saw a tenfold increase since the 2011 census, up from 650 to 8,000 (ONS, 2022: n.p.). Given this exponential rise in numbers and the potential for Paganism as a recruitment ground for the far right and as a growing scene in which to gain metapolitical influence, it remains essential that racist Heathenry is scrutinised, both by the security services and academics but also by the very members of these communities themselves. The need to counter the racist message is all the more urgent too for Heathen and Pagan communities in the UK to avoid the negative publicity and its violent consequences that impacted Muslim communities in Britain in the wake of the so-called 'War on Terror'; the impact of this continues to reverberate since the Israel–Hamas war (following the Hamas-led attack on Israelis on 7 October 2023), with anti-war demonstrations dubbed 'hate marches' by the then Home Secretary Suella Braverman and hate crimes against both Muslims and Jews on the rise.

Anti-racist Heathen activism now

Having discussed racist Heathenry at length and balanced this in Part III of the book with sustained discussion of the anti-racist stand being taken by inclusive Heathens, it is important to conclude by considering the progress and future of anti-racist Heathen activism. The vast majority of today's Heathens are from a cross-section of society, from teachers and factory workers to farmers, police officers and academics, and their politics are similarly broad. As such, our discussion has attempted to offer a more even-handed evaluation and a fuller picture which challenges the view that Heathenry is a far-right religion. To be sure, Ariosophy in particular, with its conspiratorial and imaginative lost world narrative, when combined with its secretive yet influential history, is quintessentially an extremist fantasy. Yet it offered a compelling worldview to its believers, with a concept of Aryan supremacy which influenced National Socialism and the mass violence of the Holocaust. This thinking also went on to influence more recent iterations of racist Heathenry which have had violent consequences. As Miller-Idriss (2019) warns, it is especially essential to challenge extremist fantasies which inspire violence. Weber (2019: n.p.) argues that anti-racist advocates now need to 'continue their sustained and vocal pushback on the increasing prominence and validity given to these types of groups'. Furthermore, Heathens need 'a combined strategy…that blends internal theological work, public political activity, and education geared at non-heathens' (Samuel, 2017: n.p.).

Addressing how Heathens are taking up this challenge, we have explored how Declaration 127 made a clear statement against the Asatru Folk Assembly and other racist Heathens that was ratified by many progressive Heathen groups internationally. Since then, the ongoing series of Frith Forge conferences has aimed to find ways to discuss racism within Heathenry and counter this racism especially through education. The formation of such organisations as Heathens Against Hate and Heathens United Against Racism has made a visible presence at far-right demonstrations and enabled online anti-racist messaging. Weber (2018: n.p.) thinks that 'partnering with anti-racist Heathen groups like HUAR does make it possible that White supremacist Odinism can be countered'. Additionally, large national organisations, such as The Pagan Federation, have worked in collaboration with Heathen activists against the far right, including the successful campaign to cancel the appropriation of Stonehenge for a Winter nights ceremony by the AFA. Along with the PF, international organisations like The Troth are involved in prison in-reach programmes in order to educate and counter racist Odinist activity in secure environments.

But, in addition, Heathens do need to continue to critically evaluate the ways in which they draw upon the past, too. Pardy makes the key point that,

> By reframing the physiolatrous basis of Paganism through an eco-fascist lens, the British far-right utilise Paganism as a platform on which they can fight against modernity, blurring environmental concerns with right-wing ethnonationalist traditionalism to reframe territorial separatism and a nativist concept

of a 'homeland' requiring protection from those not connected to it by blood, using Pagan imagery as a means to convey an exclusive myth of common ancestry. (Pardy, 2023a: 76)

Such dear-held concepts as 'tradition', 'ancestors', 'land' and, indeed, relationships with 'gods' and other beings, are not self-evident but in a process of construction and negotiation, and so must be critically engaged with. As Hale states:

> For Pagans and esotericists, the ideals of the New Right can potentially resonate with an attraction to an imagined past of simplicity, folk aesthetics, tradition and premodern social orders. As Pagans continue to define their place in the modern world, however, an increasing desire for legitimacy through tradition based authenticity, may prove to be even more challenging. Perhaps increased internal conversations within both Pagan and esoteric communities around the way in which legitimacy and authenticity is constructed will produce a more critical paradigm which is less reliant on tradition and transmission as being ultimately authoritative. This will at least provide a more broadly analytical framework for assessing the assertions and platforms of the New Right when they are encountered. (Hale, 2015: 121)

Inclusive Heathens cannot and should not have to rally against racist Heathenry alone, but in collaboration with other anti-racist groups, including other Pagans as well as non-Pagan anti-racist NGOs, such as Hope not Hate (Figure 12.1). To this end, it is notable that Heathens are now working in leadership positions within, and providing intelligence assistance to, police and security forces, such as the Pagan Police Association. The work of the Esoteric Research Group and SO15, the police unit attached to the UK's Counter Terrorism Command, is testament to this. This alliance of Pagans and occultists working alongside the forces of law and order against occult neo-Nazi and other racist religious groups who, inter alia, claim a lineage from lost Atlanteans and are intent on world domination, might have all the hallmarks of Nazisploitation fantasy literature or cinema, but it is a very real and necessary part of today's fightback against racist Heathenry and occultism in the UK.

Taking all of these positive developments into account, it is important to continue to identify and call out racist Heathenry and those using the veneer of 'indigeneity' and/or 'ethnicity' to cloak their racism. As we raised in our Introduction, it is problematic for privileged 'white' Europeans in northwestern Europe to appeal to these concepts when the Sámi, like other recognised Indigenous peoples worldwide, are continuing to negotiate their own self-determination and survivance (see Vizenor, 2008). It is thus no longer correct or useful to identify some Heathens as 'a-racist' or 'non-racist'; there

Figure 12.1 Witches Against White Supremacy counter-protestors at the Boston Free Speech rally, 19 August 2017 (Photograph by GorillaWarfare – Own work, CC BY 4.0).

are now only racists and anti-racists. We have approached Heathenry as racist or anti-racist not to reify the increasing polarisation of society nor to impose categories of identity (religion, gender, ethnicity, race) onto individuals or communities. As Siegfried remarks, '[m]irroring today's political world, a harder turn to the right is opposed by more aggressive calls for diversity, especially by younger [Heathen] practitioners' (Siegfried, 2021: 51). Our distinction between racists and anti-racists, then, accords with a progressive trend in Heathenry. This distinction has enabled us to address how racist Heathens define themselves and differentiate themselves from others primarily based on the pernicious category of 'race', while anti-racists by contrast welcome all those called to Heathenry no matter the colour of their skin.

A distinction between racists and anti-racists thereby enables us to point to race as a construct of hate, to identify those individuals and organisations who are racist and to highlight how anti-racists are kicking back. Those Heathens identifying as ethnicist (as somehow a value-free self-designation), a-racist or non-racist cannot afford to remain neutral or on the sidelines anymore. For example, while The Troth's mission statement proclaims inclusivity, their membership policy also permits membership of folkish organisations, so as Siegfried (2021: 51) argues, '[t]he reality that The Troth welcomes AFA members to join without renouncing membership in the folkish organisation casts a shadow over the many public statements Troth leadership has made against the AFA'. All Heathens should take a stand and be involved in the production and promotion of an inclusive, universalist, progressive – and anti-racist – Heathenry for the twenty-first century, and one which will not tolerate racism but with 'hope not hate' eradicate once and for all the far-right elements in its midst. We hope that this book helps to contribute to this vision.

A closing *galdr*/prayer

Given the considerations of this book, and the historic ways in which the far right has used and abused religious praxis of all kinds for its own political agenda, we end this study by calling for greater collaboration on this issue by all religious groups within the UK and internationally, both 'fringe' and mainstream, polytheistic and monotheistic, big and small. We hope the fact that a Heathen and a Catholic collaborated on this project offers a small step in this direction. Racism is anathema to all of our gods/God(s).

References

Adams Bellows, H. (1936) *The Poetic Edda*. Princeton, NJ: Princeton University Press. Available: https://sacred-texts.com/neu/poe/poe.pdf (accessed 13 October 2023).

Ahmad, A. (2000) *Lineages of the Present: Ideology and Politics in Contemporary South Asia*. London: Verso Books.

Ahmed, M. A. F. and A. A. Hoti (2023) 'Re-tribalization in the 21st century, part 2', *Anthropology Today*, 39:6 (2023), 6–10.

Aitamurto, K. (2015) 'More Russian than orthodox Christianity: Russian paganism as nationalist politics', in L. M. Herrington, A. Mckay and J. Haynes (eds) *Nations under God: The Geopolitics of Faith in the Twenty-First Century*, 126–132. Bristol: E-International Religions.

Aitamurto, K. and S. Simpson (eds) (2013) *Modern Pagan and Native Faith Movements in Central and Eastern Europe*. Durham: Acumen.

Aitamurto, K. and R. Downing (eds) (2025) *Germanic and Slavic Paganisms: Security Threats and Resliency*. London: Bloomsbury.

Aldsidu (n.d.) *Homepage*. Available: www.aldsidu.com/about (accessed 20 November 2023).

Alessio, D. (2000) 'Gender, spiritualism and reform in late 19th century New Zealand: Lotti Wilmot's *New Zealand Beds*', *British Review of New Zealand Studies*, 12 (2000), 55–86.

Alessio, D. (2008) *The Great Romance: A Rediscovered Utopian Adventure*. Lincoln, NE: University of Nebraska Press.

Alessio, D. (2016) 'Easter Island and the lost continent of Mu', in I. Conrich (ed.) *Easter Island: Cultural and Historical Perspectives*, 51–64. Berlin: Frank and Timme.

Alessio, D. and R. J. Wallis (2019) *Gods of Blood and Soil – Return: The Appropriation of Norse Religion by the New Right*, Century of Radical Right Extremism: New Approaches Conference, Centre for Analysis of the Radical Right and Richmond the American International University Inaugural Conference, 15–17 May 2019.

Alessio, D. and R. J. Wallis (2020) 'Racist occultism in the UK: Behind the order of Nine Angles (O9A)', Centre for the Analysis of the Radical Right, 23 July 2020. Available: www.opendemocracy.net/en/countering-radical-right/racist-occultism-uk-behind-order-nine-angles-o9a/ (accessed 3 July 2023).

Alessio, D. and R. J. Wallis (2021) 'The musical is political: Black metal and the Extreme Right', 10 August 2021. Available: www.fairobserver.com/region/europe/dominic-alessio-robert-wallis-black-metal-extreme-right-music-scene-news-41994/ (accessed 3 July 2023).

Allchorn, W. (2021a) *From Street-Based Activism to Terrorism and Political Violence: UK Radical Right Narratives and Counter-Narratives at a Time of Transition*. Granada: CARR/Hedayah/EU.

Allchorn, W. (2021b) *Tackling Hate in the Homeland: US Radical Right Narratives and Counter-Narratives at a Time of Renewed Threat*. Granada: CARR/Hedayah/EU.

Allchorn, W. and M. Feldman (2019) *The (Democratic) Football Lads Alliance: A Far Right Antechamber?* London: Faith Matters. Available: www.faith-matters.org/wp-content/uploads/2019/04/dfla.pdf (accessed 20 October 2023).

Alvesson, M. and K. Sköldberg (2000) *Reflexive Methodology: New Vistas for Qualitative Research*. London: Sage.

Amster, M. H. (2015) 'It's not easy being apolitical: Reconstruction and eclecticism in Danish Asatro', in K. Rountree (ed.) *Contemporary Pagan and Native Faith Movements in Europe*, 43–63. Oxford: Berghahn.

Andersson, K., A. Knape, J. P. Lamm, M. Rasch and G. Tegnér (2002) *The Gold Room: Historiska Museet*. Stockholm: Statens Historiska Museum / Trosa Tryckeri.

Ansuz (2019a) 'From subculture to hegemony: Transversal strategies of the new right in neofolk and Martial Industrial', *A Blaze Ansuz: Antifascist Neofolk*, 23 April 2019. Available: https://antifascistneofolk.com/tag/sol-invictus/ (accessed 7 March 2024).

Ansuz (2019b) 'Wardruna is taking back nordic Pagan culture and music from the Far-Right', *A Blaze Ansuz: Antifascist Neofolk*, 4 April 2019. Available: https://antifascistneofolk.com/2019/04/04/wardruna-is-taking-back-nordic-pagan-culture-and-music-from-the-far-right/ (accessed 6 July 2021).

Anti-Defamation League (ADL) (2017) 'Christian identity'. Available: www.adl.org/resources/backgrounder/christian-identity (accessed 6 July 2021).

Anti-Defamation League (ADL) (n.d.a) 'Burning cross'. Available: www.adl.org/resources/hate-symbol/burning-cross (accessed 9 November 2023).

Anti-Defamation League (ADL) (n.d.b) 'Celtic cross'. Available: www.adl.org/resources/hate-symbol/celtic-cross (accessed 9 November 2023).

Archambault, E. and Y. Veilleux-Lepage (2019) 'The soldiers of Odin in Canada: The failure of a transnational ideology', in T. Bjørgo and M. Mareš (eds) *Vigilantism Against Migrants and Minorities*, 272–285. London: Routledge.

archive.today (n.d.) Webpage capture. Available: https://archive.ph (accessed 1 November 2023).

Arngart, O. (1981) 'The Durham proverbs', *Speculum*, 56:2 (1981), 288–300.

Asatru Folk Assembly (2024) 'Declaration of purpose'. Available: www.runestone.org/declaration-of-purpose/ (accessed 4 March 2024).

Asbjørn J. A. (1999) '"Skeggøld, skálmöld; vindøld, vergøld": Alexander Rud Mills and the Ásatrú faith in the new age', *Australian Religion Studies Review*, 12:1 (1999), 77–83.
Asbrandir (n.d.) 'What it means to be folkish'. Available: https://odinic-rite.org/main/what-it-means-to-be-folkish/ (accessed 20 November 2023).
Ashby, S. and J. Schofield (2015) 'Hold the Heathen hammer high: Representation, re-enactment and the construction of "Pagan" heritage', *International Journal of Heritage Studies*, 21:5 (2015), 493–511.
Askew, K. M. (2003) 'As Plato Duly warned: Music, politics, and social change in coastal East Africa', *Anthropological Quarterly*, 76:4 (2003), 609–637.
Asprem, E. (2008) 'Heathens up north: Politics, polemics, and contemporary Norse Paganism in Norway', *Pomegranate*, 10:1 (2008), 41–69.
Aswynn, F. (1990) *Leaves of Yggdrasil: A Synthesis of Runes, Gods, Magic, Feminine Mysteries and Folklore*. Woodbury, MN: Llewellyn.
AUK (Asatru UK) (2023) 'About Asatru UK'. Available: www.asatruuk.org/about (accessed 29 February 2024).
Audun (2009) *The Dreccian Way*. Privately published by O9A.
Avsnitt (n.d.) 'The Odinist fellowship and their Pagan Temple – Interview with Ralph Harrison', *Survive the Jive Podcast*. Available: https://poddtoppen.se/podcast/1468883050/survive-the-jive-podcast/the-odinist-fellowship-and-their-pagan-temple-interview-with-ralph-harrison (accessed 27 February 2024).
Awaken the North (2016) 'Declaration 127'. Available: https://awakethenorth.wixsite.com/awakenthenorth/declaration-127 (accessed 29 February 2024).
Azani, E., L. Koblenz-Stenzler, L. Atiyas-Lvovsky, D. Ganor, A. Ben-Am and D. Meshulam (2020) 'Norse Paganism, Odinism and Wotanism', in E. Azani, L. Koblenz-Stenzler, L. Atiyas-Lvovsky, D. Ganor, A. Ben-Am and D. Meshulam (eds) *The Far Right – Ideology, Modus Operandi and Development Trends*, 31–33. International Institute for Counterterrorism. Available: www.ict.org.il/images/The%20Far%20Right%20%E2%80%93%20Ideology.pdf (accessed 4 April 2024).
Bach, S. (2007) *Leni: The Life and Work of Leni Riefenstahl*. London: Little, Brown.
Backes, U. (2012) *The Extreme Right in Europe: Current Trends and Perspectives*. Göttingen: Vandenhoeck and Ruprecht.
Badiou, A. (2005) *Metapolitics*. London: Verso.
Baker, J., S. Perry and A. Whitehead (2020) 'Keep America Christian (and White): Christian nationalism, fear of ethnoracial outsiders, and intention to vote for Donald Trump on the 2020 presidential election', *Sociology of Religion: A Quarterly Review*, 81:3 (2020), 272–293.
Bale, J. M. (2020) '"National Revolutionary" groupuscules and the resurgence of "left-wing" fascism: The case of France's Nouvelle Résistance', *Patterns of Prejudice*, 36:3 (2020), 24–49.
Balhorn, L. (2017) 'The lost history of Antifa', *Jacobin*, 5 August 2017. Available: https://jacobin.com/2017/05/antifascist-movements-hitler-nazis-kpd-spd-germany-cold-war (accessed 4 April 2024).

Bar-on, T. (2014) 'The French New Right: Neither right, nor left?', *Journal for the Study of Radicalism*, 8:1 (2014), 1–44.

Bates, B. (1983) *The Way of Wyrd*. London: Arrow.

Bates, B. (1996) *The Wisdom of the Wyrd: Teachings for Today from Our Ancient Past*. London: Rider.

Bayly, C. A. (2010) 'India, the Bhagavad Gita and the world', *Modern Intellectual History* 7:2 (2010), 275–295.

BBC News (2019) 'Teenage neo-Nazis jailed over terror offences', *BBC News*, 18 June 2019. Available: https://www.bbc.co.uk/news/uk-48672929 (accessed 27 January 2025).

BBC News (2020a) 'Durham neo-Nazi teenager detained for terror attack plan', *BBC News*, 7 January 2020. Available: www.bbc.co.uk/news/uk-england-tyne-51022706 (accessed 9 November 2023).

BBC News (2020b) 'Pete Evans: Australian celebrity chef's books pulled over neo-Nazi symbol', *BBC News*, 17 November 2020. Available: www.bbc.co.uk/news/world-australia-54972101 (accessed 11 March 2024).

BBC News (2021) 'National action: Ben Raymond guilty of terror charges', *BBC News*, 30 November 2021. Available: www.bbc.co.uk/news/uk-england-wiltshire-59475899 (accessed 6 April 2024).

Benn, M. (2014a) 'Woden's folk'. Available: https://rationalwiki.org/wiki/Woden%27s_Folk (accessed 1 November 2023).

Benn, M. (2014b) 'Wulf Ingessunu and Woden's Folk: How a 1980s TV series inspired a racist cult', *Britain is Radical*, 13 June 2014. Available: http://radicalbritain.blogspot.com/2014/06/wulf-ingesunnu-and-wodens-folk-how.html (accessed 1 November 2023).

Bennet, L. and K. Wilkins (2020) 'Viking tattoos of Instagram: Runes and contemporary identities', *Convergence: The International Journal of Research into New Media Technologies*, 26:5–6 (2020), 1301–1314.

Bennett, W. L. and A. Segerberg (2012) 'The logic of connective action: Digital media and the personalization of contentious politics', *Information, Communication and Society*, 15:5 (2012), 739–768.

De Benoist, A. and C. Champetier (2000) 'MANIFESTO of the French New Right in the year 2000'. Available: www.4pt.su/en/content/manifesto-french-new-right (accessed 23 April 2023).

Bentley, P. and J. Paul (2014) 'German clothing brand favoured by neo-Nazis sparks anger', *Daily Mail*, 16 April 2014. Available: www.dailymail.co.uk/news/article-2605814/German-clothing-brand-favoured-neo-Nazis-sparks-anger-opening-shop-yards-office-UKs-Chief-Rabbi.html (accessed 18 March 2019).

Berger, H. (2020) 'Preface', in N. S. Emore and J. M. Leader (eds) *Paganism and Its Discontents: Enduring Problems of Racialized Identity*, viii–xiii. Cambridge: Cambridge Scholars.

Blabbermouth.net (2009) 'Winterfylleth signs with Candlelight Records'. Available: https://blabbermouth.net/news/winterfylleth-signs-with-candlelight-records (accessed 17 March 2024).

Black, M. and E. Kurlander (eds) (2015) *Revisiting the 'Nazi Occult': Histories, Realities, Legacies*. Rochester, NY: Camden House.

Blain, J. (2002) *Nine Worlds of Seid-Magic: Ecstasy and Shamanism in North European Paganism*. London: Routledge.

Blain, J., D. Ezzy and G. Harvey (eds) (2004) *Researching Paganisms: Religious Experiences and Academic Methodologies*. Walnut Creek, CA: AltaMira.

Blain, J. and R. J. Wallis (2000) 'Seidr and gender', *Idunna: A Journal of Northern Tradition* (Spring 2000), 30–38.

Blain, J. and R. J. Wallis (2002) 'A living landscape? Pagans and archaeological discourse', *3rd Stone: Archaeology, Folklore and Myth – The Magazine for the New Antiquarian*, 43 (Summer 2002), 20–27.

Blain, J. and R. J. Wallis (2006) 'Ritual reflections, practitioner meanings: "performance" disputed', *Journal of Ritual Studies* 20:1 (2009), 21–36.

Blain, J. and R. J. Wallis (2007) *Sacred Sites, Contested Rites/Rights: Contemporary Pagan Engagements with Archaeological Monuments*. Brighton: Sussex Academic Press.

Blain, J. and R. J. Wallis (2009a) 'Beyond sacred: Recent Pagan engagements with archaeological monuments – Current findings of the Sacred Sites Project', *Pomegranate: The International Journal of Pagan Studies*, 11:1 (2009), 97–123.

Blain, J. and R. J. Wallis (2009b) 'Heathenry and its development', in J. Lewis and M. Pizza (eds) *Handbook of Contemporary Paganism*, 413–431. Handbook of Contemporary Religion. Leiden and Boston, MA: Brill Academic Publishers.

Blain, J. and R. J. Wallis (2015) 'The "ergi" seidman: Contestations of gender, shamanism and sexuality in northern religion, past and present', in J. H. Prior and C. M. Cusack (eds) *Religion, Sexuality and Spirituality: Critical Concepts in Religious Studies: Volume II: Gender – Roles, Bodies, Identities*, 395–411. London: Routledge.

Blanton, C. (ed.) (2011) *Shades of Faith: Minority Voices in Paganism*. Stafford: Megalithica.

Blanton, C. (2015) 'Understanding the definition of racism and its power in our community', in C. Blanton, T. Ellwood and B. Williams (eds) *Bringing Race to the Table: Exploring Racism in the Pagan Community*, 12–19. Stafford: Megalithica.

Blanton, C., T. Ellwood and B. Williams (eds) (2015) *Bringing Race to the Table: Exploring Racism in the Pagan Community*. Stafford: Megalithica.

Blavatsky, H. P. (1888) *The Secret Doctrine*. Available: www.holybooks.com/secret-doctrine-blavatsky/ (accessed 29 March 2024).

Blee, K. M. and K. A. Creasap (2010) 'Conservative and right-wing movements', *Annual Review of Sociology*, 36 (2010), 269–286.

Bogel-Burroughs, N. and S. E. Garcia (2020) 'What is Antifa, the movement Trump wants to declare a terror group?', *New York Times*, 28 September 2020. Available: www.nytimes.com/article/what-antifa-trump.html (accessed 4 April 2024).

de Boise, S. (2012) 'Music and online far-right extremism', *Global Network on Extremism and Technology*, 28 October 2021. Available: https://gnet-research.org/2021/10/28/music-and-online-far-right-extremism/ (accessed 17 March 2024).

Bosworth, J. (2014) 'Winter-fylleþ', in T. Northcote Toller, C. Sean and O. Tichy (eds) *An Anglo-Saxon Dictionary Online*, Faculty of Arts, Charles University. Available: https://bosworthtoller.com/35945 (accessed 20 October 2023).

Bowar, C. (n.d.) 'Faust interview: Conversation with the legendary black metal drummer'. Available: https://web.archive.org/web/20060629000801/http://heavymetal.about.com/od/interviews/a/faust.htm (accessed 20 October 2023).

boyd, d. and Ellison, N. B. (2007) 'Social network sites: Definition, history and scholarship', *Journal of Computer-Mediated Communication*, 13:1 (2007), 210–230.

Brackman, H. (2020) 'From the Kaisar to Hitler', 27 May 2020. Available: https://www.algemeiner.com/2020/05/27/from-the-kaiser-to-hitler/ (accessed 28 January 2025)

Bray, M. (2017) *Antifa: The Anti-Fascist Handbook*. London: Melville House Publishing.

Breenan, G. (2019) 'After the BNP: What the Nazis did next', *Searchlight* (Winter 2019), 24–29.

Brighton Antifascists (n.d.) *Guide to Far Right Symbols*. Available: https://brightonantifascists.com/2015/02/02/guide-to-far-right-symbols/ (accessed 31 October 2023).

British Archaeology (2023) 'Spoilheap: Netflix and the beguiling awe of fabricated history', *British Archaeology*, March/April 2023: 66.

BrooklynVegan (2020) 'Heilung react to incident at show: "We do not tolerate hate speech and racism"', *BrooklynVegan*, 31 January. Available: www.brooklynvegan.com/heilung-react-to-show-incident-we-do-not-tolerate-hate-speech-and-racism/ (accessed 21 February 2021).

Brown, L. (2012) 'Winterfylleth Interview: There's a lot to be learned by going out into the country', *Iron Fist*, 7 September 2012. Available: www.ironfistzine.com/2012/09/07/winterfylleth-interview-theres-a-lot-to-be-learned-by-going-out-into-the-country/ (accessed 20 October 2023).

Brown, P. D. (2022) *Thirteen Moons: Reflections on the Heathen Lunar Year*. North Augusta, SC: Gilded Books.

Bubblegum, B. (2009) 'An interview with Wolves in the Throne Room's Aron Weaver', *BrooklynVegan*, 6 May 2009. Available: https://www.brooklynvegan.com/an-interview-w-13/ (accessed 22 May 2009).

Buesnel, R. (2020) 'National socialist black metal: A case study in the longevity of far-right ideologies in heavy metal subcultures', *Patterns of Prejudice*, 54:3 (2020), 393–408, https://doi.org/10.1080/0031322X.2020.1800987

Burley, S. (2019) 'Tradition and resistance: Reclaiming neofolk for Antifascism', *Protean Magazine*, 1 December 2019. Available: https://proteanmag.com/2019/12/01/tradition-and-resistance-reclaiming-neofolk-for-antifascism/ (accessed 4 April 2024).

Butler, C. and M. Bell (2022) 'Further excavations at the Long Man, Wilmington', *Sussex Past Newsletter*. Available: www.cbasltd.co.uk/_files/ugd/472ea5_2f9e36a7ecf048868d7bfa35389b5548.pdf (accessed 25 March 2024).

Calico, J. F. (2018) *Being Viking: Heathenism in Contemporary America*. Sheffield: Equinox.

Calico, J. F. (2020) 'Performing "American Völkisch"', in N. S. Emore and J. M. Leader (eds) *Paganism and its Discontents: Enduring Problems of Racialized Identity*, 22–46. Cambridge: Cambridge Scholars.

Callison, W. and Q. Slobodian (2021) 'Coronapolitics from the Reichstag to the Capitol', *Boston Review*, 12 January 2021. Available: www.bostonreview.net/articles/quinn-slobodian-toxic-politics-coronakspeticism/ (accessed 24 February 2024).

Campbell, H. A. (ed.) (2012) *Digital Religion: Understanding Religious Practice in New Media Worlds*. New York, NY: Routledge.

Campion, D. E. (2018) *'The Culling Texts': Mythology, Authority, and Human Sacrifice in the Order of the Nine Angles*. Available: https://www.semanticscholar.org/paper/"The-Culling-Texts":-Mythology,-Authority,-and-in-Campion/eb9eec8886ebf0578d99ffef27ebb9172b9267f1 (accessed 3 January 2024).

Candlelight Records. Available: https://spinefarm.merchnow.com/collections/candlelight-records-1?page=2 (accessed 20 October 2023).

Carver, M., A. Sanmark and S. Semple (eds) (2010) *Signals of Belief in Early England: Anglo-Saxon Paganism Revisited*. Oxford: Oxbow.

Castells, M. (2015) *Networks of Outrage and Hope: Social Movements in the Internet Age*. Cambridge: Polity.

Castleden, R. (2012) *The Wilmington Giant: The Quest for a Lost Myth*. Winnipeg: Turnstone Press.

Chandler, D. and J. Reid (2019) *Becoming Indigenous Governing Imaginaries in the Anthropocene*. Lanham, MD: Rowman & Littlefield.

Chilton, L. (2023) 'Do Republican anthems have to be quite so terrible as Rich Men North of Richmond?', *Independent*, 22 August 2023. Available: www.independent.co.uk/arts-entertainment/music/features/rich-men-north-of-richmond-lyrics-controversy-b2397249.html (accessed 8 March 2024).

Christos Beest (2008) *Sinister Tarot*. O9A: Skull Press. Available: https://archive.org/details/SinisterTarotByChristosBeest/page/n1/mode/2up (accessed 2 February 2024).

Churchward, J. (1974 [1931]) *The Lost Continent of Mu*. Aylesbury: First Future.

Cobain, I. (2016) 'Jo Cox murder suspect collected far-right books, court hears', *Guardian*, 21 November 2016. Available: www.theguardian.com/uk-news/2016/nov/21/jo-cox-suspect-collected-far-right-books-court-hears (accessed 14 March 2024).

Cobain, I., N. Parveen and M. Taylor (2016) 'The slow burning hatred that led Thomas Mair to murder Jo Cox', *Guardian*, 23 November 2016. Available: www.theguardian.com/uk-news/2016/nov/23/thomas-mair-slow-burning-hatred-led-to-jo-cox-murder (accessed 20 October 2023).

Cobain, I. and M. Taylor (2016) 'Far-right terrorist Thomas Mair jailed for life for Jo Cox murder', *Guardian*, 23 November 2016. Available: www.theguardian.com/uk-news/2016/nov/23/thomas-mair-found-guilty-of-jo-cox-murder (accessed 14 March 2024).

Cohen, M. (2004) *Methods of Enquiry: Theoretical and Conceptual Issues in Educational Research*. Lecture for the Doctor in Education (EdD) International Programme, Institute of Education, University of London, London.

Colborne, M. (2019) 'The Far Right's secret weapon: Fascist fashion', *New Republic*, 26 February 2019. Available: https://newrepublic.com/article/153161/far-rights-secret-weapon-fascist-fashion (accessed 7 March 2024).

Coles, S. (2011) 'The importance of preserving heritage, tradition and race'. Available: https://odinic-rite.org/main/the-importance-of-preserving-heritage-tradition-and-race/ (accessed 28 October 2023).

Collier, M. and P. Pedley (2000) *Germany 1919–45*. Oxford: Heinemann.

Connolly, K. (2016) 'Cologne inquiry into "coordinated" New Year's Eve sex attacks', *Guardian*, 5 January 2016. Available: www.theguardian.com/world/2016/jan/05/germany-crisis-cologne-new-years-eve-sex-attacks (accessed 3 November 2023).

Copsey, N. and J. E. Richardson (2015) *Cultures of Post-War British Fascism*. London: Routledge.

Counter Terrorism Policing (2020) 'Neo-Nazi group Sonnenkrieg Division proscribed'. Available: www.counterterrorism.police.uk/neo-nazi-group-sonnenkrieg-division-proscribed-counter-terrorism-police/ (accessed 11 March 2024).

Cowan, D. (2005) *Cyberhenge: Modern Pagans on the Internet*. London: Routledge.

Cragle, J. M. (2017) 'Contemporary Germanic/Norse Paganism and recent survey data', *Pomegranate*, 9:1 (2017), 77–116.

Crenshaw, K. (1989) 'Demarginalizing the intersection of race and sex: A Black feminist critique of antidiscrimination doctrine, feminist theory and antiracist politics', *University of Chicago Legal Forum*, 1 (1989), 139–167.

CTEC (Center on Terrorism, Extremism and Counterterrorism) Staff (2021) 'Christian identity's new role on the extreme right'. Available: https://www.middlebury.edu/institute/academics/centers-initiatives/ctec/ctec-publications/christian-identitys-new-role-extreme-right (accessed 1 April 2024).

CTEC (Center on Terrorism, Extremism and Counterterrorism) Staff (2023) 'Dangerous organizations and bad actors: National action', 23 August 2023. Available: www.middlebury.edu/institute/academics/centers-initiatives/ctec/ctec-publications/dangerous-organizations-and-bad-actors-5 (accessed 1 April 2024).

Cunningham, M., M. La Rooij and P. Spoonley (2022) 'Introduction: Exploring radical intolerance and extremism in New Zealand', in M. Cunningham, M. La Rooij and P. Spoonley (eds) *Histories of Hate, The Radical Right in Aotearoa New Zealand*, 9–41. Dunedin: Dunedin University Press.

Dack, J. (2015) 'Cultural regeneration: Mosley and the Union Movement', in N. Copsey and J. E. Richardson (eds) *Cultures of Post-War British Fascism*, 8–26. London: Routledge.

Darkness Converges (n.d.) 'Our objective'. Available: https://darknessconverges.wordpress.com/wsa352-the-white-star-acception/our-objective/ (accessed 5 March 2024).

Daubs, M. (2022) 'Internationalising white extremism: Far-right networks in New Zealand and Beyond', in M. Cunningham, M. La Rooij and P. Spoonley (eds) *Histories of Hate, The Radical Right in Aotearoa New Zealand*, 325–341. Dunedin: Otago University Press.

Davies, N. (1999) *The Isles: A History*. London: Macmillan.

Davies, P. and D. Lynch (2002) *Fascism and the Far Right*. London: Routledge.

Davy, B. J. (2006) *Introduction to Pagan Studies*. Walnut Creek, CA: AltaMira.

Davy, B. J. (2023) 'Inclusive Heathens practice ancestor veneration, but not pride in ancestry'. *Nova Religio*, 26:3 (2023), 30–51.

Dearden, L. (2020), 'Terrorist group founder now running online neo-Nazi T-shirt business'. *Independent*, 15 November 2020. Available: www.independent.co.uk/news/uk/home-news/national-action-neo-nazi-terrorist-group-founder-ben-raymond-blackguard-b1723241.html (accessed 7 March 2024).

Death in June (n.d.) 'Death in June – Topic', *YouTube*. Available: www.youtube.com/channel/UC8RSQh7MWhS1TOnhH8nnTzA/about (accessed 15 May 2023).

Declaration of Deeds (n.d.) 'Declaration of deeds'. Available: https://declarationofdeeds.com (accessed 29 February 2024).

Delzell, C. F. (ed.) (1971) *Mediterranean Fascism, 1919–1945*. Toronto: Harper & Row.

Derby, M. (2022) 'Devils are in Demand: Arthur Desmond's "Might Is Right" and its present-day influence on the Far Right', in Matthew Cunningham, Marinus La Rooj and Paul Spoonley (eds) *Histories of Hate, The Radical Right in Aotearoa New Zealand*, 97–112. Dunedin: Dunedin University Press.

diZerega, G. (2020) 'Strange bedfellows: NeoPaganism, the *Volk*, and the Contemporary NeoPagan right', in N. S. Emore and J. M. Leader (eds) *Paganism and Its Discontents: Enduring Problems of Racialized Identity*, 85–112. Cambridge: Cambridge Scholars.

Dodd, V. (2020) 'Met officer arrested on suspicion of belonging to banned rightwing group', *Guardian*, 5 March 2020. Available: www.theguardian.com/uk-news/2020/mar/05/met-police-officer-arrested-suspected-of-belonging-to-group-linked-to-terrorism?CMP=Share_iOSApp_Other (accessed April 13, 2020).

Downing, R. (2019) 'Hashtag Heathens: Contemporary Germanic Pagan feminine visuals on Instagram', *Pomegranate*, 21:2 (2019), 186–209.

Doyle White, E. (2016) 'Old stones, new rites: Contemporary Pagan interactions with the Medway megaliths', *Material Religion*, 12:3 (2016), 346–372.

Doyle White, E. (2017) 'Northern gods for northern folk: Racial identity and right-wing ideology among Britain's folkish Heathens', *Journal of Religion in Europe*, 10:3 (2017), 241–273.

Dubow, S. (1998) 'Placing "race" in South African history', in W. Lamont (ed.) *Historical Controversies and Historians*, 65–78. London: University College London.

Duguay, S. and H. Gold-Apel (2023) 'Stumbling blocks and alternative paths: Reconsidering the walkthrough method for analyzing apps', *Social Media + Society*, 9:1 https://doi.org/10.1177/20563051231158

Dyck, K. (2016) *Reichsrock: The International Web of White-Power and Neo-Nazi Hate Music*. New Brunswick, NJ: Rutgers University Press.

Eatwell, R. (2003) 'Reflections on fascism and religion', *Totalitarianism Movements and Political Religions*, 4:3 (December 2003), 145–166.

ECER (European Congress of Ethnic Religions) (1998) '2nd Declaration (25th October 1998)'. Available: https://ecer-org.eu/about/declaration/ (accessed 6 November 2023).

ECER (European Congress of Ethnic Religions) (2023) 'Congress news: The European Congress of ethnic religions 2023 in Latvia'. Available: https://ecer-org.eu/category/the-oaks/congress/ (accessed 6 November 2023).

The Economic Times (2022) '"Miss Hitler" beauty queen Alice Cutter jailed for partaking in neo-Nazi group National Action, to be freed early', 12 October 2022. Available: https://rb.gy/v9gxii (accessed 1 April 2024).

Edwards, C. (2017a) 'We can't let racists re-define Viking culture', *The Local*, 6 October 2017. Available: https://www.thelocal.se/20171006/we-cant-let-racists-re-define-viking-culture-far-right-runes-swedish (accessed 3 May 2019).

Edwards, K. (2017b) 'How the English Far Right co-opted Christianity – And why its "crusade" shouldn't be ignored', *The Conversation*, 23 August 2017. Available: https://theconversation.com/how-the-english-far-right-co-opted-christianity-and-why-its-crusade-shouldnt-be-ignored-82842 (accessed 24 January 2024).

Emore, N. S. and J. M. Leader (2020a) 'Introduction', in N. S. Emore and J. M. Leader (eds) *Paganism and Its Discontents: Enduring Problems of Racialized Identity*, xiv–xv. Cambridge: Cambridge Scholars.

Emore, N. S. and J. M. Leader (eds) (2020b) *Paganism and Its Discontents: Enduring Problems of Racialized Identity*. Cambridge: Cambridge Scholars.

Encyclopedia Metallum: The Metal Archives (2023) 'Wodensthrone'. Available: https://www.metal-archives.com/bands/Wodensthrone/83954 (accessed 20 October 2023).

Ensminger, D. A. (2011) *Visual Vitriol: The Street Art and Subcultures of the Punk and Hardcore Generation*. Jackson, MS: University Press of Mississippi.

Eowyn (2008) 'Men and women in Odinism and the OR'. Available: https://odinic-rite.org/main/men-and-women-in-odinism-and-the-or/ (accessed 10 March 2024).

Eowyn (2010) 'Attracting women to the rite: Some considerations'. Available: https://odinic-rite.org/main/attracting-women-to-the-rite-some-considerations/ (accessed 10 March 2024).

Evans, D. A. H. (1986) *Hávámal* (Viking Society for Northern Research, University College London). Exeter: Short Run Press.

Evans, R. (2005) *The Third Reich in Power*. London: Allen Lane.

Evans, R. (2007) 'Nazism, Christianity and political religion: A debate', *Journal of Contemporary History*, 42:1 (2007), 5–7.

Evans, R. (2018) 'From memes to infowars: How 75 fascist activists were "red-pilled"'. Available: www.bellingcat.com/news/americas/2018/10/11/memes-infowars-75-fascist-activists-red-pilled/ (accessed 13 February 2024).

Evola, J. (1928) *Pagan Imperialism*. Available: https://dn790008.ca.archive.org/0/items/pagan-imperialism-julius-evola/Pagan%20Imperialism%20-%20Julius%20Evola.pdf (accessed 20 April 2024).

Evola, J. (1934) 'The mystery of the prehistorical Arctic'. Available: https://arktos.com/2023/06/27/the-mystery-of-the-prehistorical-arctic-thule/ (accessed 20 April 2024).

Evolvi, G. (2020) 'Materiality, authority, and digital religion, the case of a neo-Pagan forum', *Entangled Religions*, 11:3 (2020).

Ezzy, D. (2014) *Sex, Death and Witchcraft: A Contemporary Pagan Festival*. London: Blooomsbury.

Fagan, G. G. and K. L. Feder (2006) 'Crusading against straw men: An alternative view of alternative archaeologies: Response to Holtorf (2005)', *World Archaeology*, 38:4 (December 2006), 718–729.

Faiola, A. (2016) 'Soldiers of Odin: The far-right groups in Finland "protecting women" from asylum seekers', *Independent*, 1 February 2016. Available: www.independent.co.uk/news/world/europe/soldiers-of-odin-the-farright-groups-in-finland-protecting-women-from-asylum-seekers-a6846341.html (accessed 3 November 2023).

Fairclough, N, P. Graham, J. Lemke and R. Wodak (2004) 'Introduction', *Critical Discourse Studies*, 1:1 (2004), 1–7.

Farley, H. (2021) 'Danyal Hussein: A teenage murderer with far-right links'. *BBC News*, 6 July 2021. Available: www.bbc.com/news/uk-england-london-57722035 (accessed 22 March 2024).

FBI Records (1989) 'Christian identity movement'. Available: https://vault.fbi.gov/Christian%20Identity%20Movement%20/Christian%20Identity%20Movement%20Part%201%20of%201/view.

Feinstein, Y. and B. Bonikowski (2019) 'National narratives and anti-immigrant narratives: Exceptionalism and collective victimhood in contemporary Israel', *Journal of Ethnic and Migration Studies*, 47:3 (2019), 741–761, https://doi.org/10.1080/1369183X.2019.1620596

Feldman, M. (2021) 'The Holocaust in the NDH: Genocide between political religion and religious politics', in M. Feldman (ed.) *Politics, Intellectuals and Faith: Essays*, 174–195. Stuttgart: Ibidem.

Fewkes, J. H. (2019) *Anthropological Perspectives on the Religious Uses of Mobile Apps*. London: Palgrave Macmillan.

Findell, M. (2013) 'From Hávamál to racial hygiene: Guido List's *Das Geheimnis der Runen*, "The Secrets of the Runes" (1908)', in C. Lee and N. McClelland (eds) *Germania Remembered, 1500–2009: Commemorating and Inventing a Germanic Past*, 251–271. Binghamton, NY: State University of New York.

Fischer-Galati, S. (2006) 'Codreanu, Romanian national traditions and charisma', *Totalitarian Movements and Political Religions*, 7:2 (2006), 245–250.

Flowers, S. E. (1990) *Fire and Ice: Magical Teachings of Germany's Greatest Secret Occult Order*. Woodbury, MN: Llewellyn.

Flowers, S. E. (1997) *Lords of the Left-Hand Path. A History of Spiritual Dissent*. Smithville, TX: Rûna-Raven Press.

Flowers, S. E. (2022) *The Occult in National Socialism: The Symbolic, Scientific, and Magical Influences on the Third Reich*. Rochester, VT: Inner Traditions/Bear.

Fomby, D. (2020) 'How Instagram Influencers help bring attention to environmental issues', *vapur*, 22 April 2020. Available: www.vapur.us/about/blog/how-instagram-influencers-help-bring-attention-to-environmental-issues.html (accessed 22 March 2024).

Fonneland, T. (2017) *Contemporary Shamanisms in Norway: Religion, Entrepreneurship, and Politics*. Oxford: Oxford University Press.

Forefather. Available: http://www.forefather.net/band.html (accessed 16 May 2021).

Fortune, D. (1962) *Aspects of Occultism*. London: Aquarian Press.

Foucault, M. (1972) *The Archaeology of Knowledge*. London: Tavistock.

François, S. and A. Godwin (2008) 'The Euro-Pagan scene: Between Paganism and radical right', *Journal for the Study of Radicalism*, 1:2 (2008), 35–54, https://doi.org/10.1353/jsr.2008.0006

Frier, S. (2020) *No Filter: The Inside Story of Instagram*. New York, NY: Simon & Schuster.

Fries, J. (2002 [1993]) *Helrunar: A Manual of Rune Magick*. Oxford: Mandrake Press.

Gallagher, A.-M. (1999) 'Weaving a tangled web? Pagan ethics and issues of history, "race" and ethnicity in Pagan identity', *Pomegranate*, 10 (Autumn 1999), 19–29.

Gallagher, A.-M. (2009) 'Weaving a Tangled Web? Pagan ethics and issues of history, "race" and ethnicity in Pagan identity', in J. R. Lewis and M. Pizza (eds) *Handbook of Contemporary Paganism*, 577–590. Leiden: Brill Academic Publishers.

Gardell, M. (2003) *Gods of the Blood. Pagan Revival and White Separatism*. London: Duke University Press.

Gardell, M. (2009) 'Wolf age Pagans', in J. Lewis and M. Pizza (eds) *Handbook of Contemporary Paganism*, 611–626. Leiden: Brill Academic Publishers.

Garrity, C. (2014) 'Alternative histories: Observing theosophical "truths" in Hindu nationalism', SIT Digital Collections. Available: https://digitalcollections.sit.edu/cgi/viewcontent.cgi?article=2835&context=isp_collection.

Gartenstein-Ross, D. and E. Chace-Donahue (2023) 'The order of Nine Angles: Cosmology, practice & movement', *Studies in Conflict and Terrorism*. Available: www.tandfonline.com/doi/abs/10.1080/1057610X.2023.2186737?journalCode=uter20 (accessed 24 December 2023).

GCK (Grimnir's Crossroad Kindred) (2023) 'About Grimnir's Crossroad Kindred'. Available: www.facebook.com/GrimnirsCrossroadKindred/about_details (accessed 3 July 2023).

Geise, S. and C. Baden (2014) 'Putting the image back into the frame: modeling the linkage between visual communication and frame-processing theory', *Communication Theory*, 25:1 (2014), 46–69.

Genius, 'About neofolk'. Available: https://genius.com/tags/neofolk (accessed 15 May 2023).

Genius (n.d.a) 'Latch to a grave'. Available: https://genius.com/Winterfylleth-latch-to-a-grave-lyrics (accessed 20 October 2023).

Genius (n.d.b) 'Misdeeds of faith'. Available: https://genius.com/Winterfylleth-misdeeds-of-faith-lyrics (accessed 20 October 2023).

Gentile, E. (2005) 'Fascism, totalitarianism and political religion: Definitions and critical reflections on criticism of an interpretation', in R. Griffin (ed.) *Fascism, Totalitarianism and Political Religion*, 32–81. London: Routledge.

Gerrard, K. (2009) *Odin's Gateway: A Practical Guide to the Wisdom of the Runes through Galdr, Sigils and Casting*. London: Avalonia.

Gershoni, I. (2012) 'Why the Muslims must fight against Nazi Germany: Muḥammad Najātī Ṣidqī's plea', *International Journal for the Study of Modern Islam*, 52:3–4 (2012), 471–498.

Gibson, S. (2021) 'Special branch inquiry led to student's terror-related arrest', *LeicestershireLive*, 12 August 2021. Available: www.leicestermercury.co.uk/news/leicester-news/special-branch-inquiry-led-students-5780488 (accessed 13 February 2023).

Givetash, L. (2020) 'U.S. soldier's alleged connection to satanic Nazi extremist group renews calls to ban it', *NBC News*, 25 June 2020. Available: www.nbcnews.com/news/world/u-s-soldier-s-alleged-connection-satanic-nazi-extremist-group-n1231851 (accessed 31 December 2023).

Goodrick-Clarke, N. (1985) *The Occult Roots of Nazism. The Ariosophists of Austria and Germany, 1890–1935*. Wellingborough: Aquarian Press.

Goodrick-Clarke, N. (2000) *Hitler's Priestess: Savitri Devi, the Hindu-Aryan Myth, and Neo-Nazism*. New York: New York University Press.

Goodrick-Clarke, N. (2002) *Black Sun: Aryan Cults, Esoteric Nazism and the Politics of Identity*. New York, NY, NY: New York University Press.

Goodwin, M. J. (2016) *New British Fascism: Rise of the British National Party*. London: Routledge.

Gov.UK (2022) Population of England and Wales. Available: https://rb.gy/3v8d7e (accessed 29 October 2023).

Granholm, K. (2004) *Embracing the Dark: The Magic Order of Dragon Rouge – Its Practice in Dark Magic and Meaning Making*. Åbo: Åbo Akademi University Press.

Granholm, K. (2010) 'The Rune-Gild: Heathenism, traditionalism, and the left-hand path', *International Journal for the Study of New Religions*, 1:1 (2010), 95–115.

Granholm, K. (2011) '"Sons of northern darkness": Heathen influences in black metal and meofolk music'. *Numen*, 58 (2011), 514–544.

Granholm, K. (2016) 'Embracing others than Satan: The multiple princes of darkness in the left-hand path milieu', in J. A. Petersen (ed.) *Contemporary Religious Satanism: A Critical Anthology*, 85–102. London: Routledge.

Granholm, K., M. Moberg and S. Sjö (eds) (2018) *Religion, Media and Social Change*. London: Routledge.

Grant, K. (1975) *Cults of the Shadow*. London: Frederick Muller.

Greaves (2017) 'I'm a founder of the Satanic Temple. Don't blame Satan for white supremacy', *Washington Post*, 23 August 2017. Available: www.washingtonpost.com/news/posteverything/wp/2017/08/23/im-a-founder-of-the-satanic-temple-dont-blame-satan-for-white-supremacy/ (accessed 18 February 2024).

Gregorius, F. (2015) 'Modern Heathenism in Sweden: A case study in the creation of a traditional religion', in K. Rountree (ed.) *Contemporary Pagan and Native Faith Movements in Europe*, 64–85. Oxford: Berghahn.

Green, N. (2015) 'The global occult: An introduction', *History of Religions*, 54:5 (May 2015), 383–393.

Greene, H. (2017) 'Berkeley rally draws Pagan and Heathen attendees', *The Wild Hunt: Modern Pagan News and Commentary*, 19 April 2017. Available: https://wildhunt.org/2017/04/berkeley-rally-draws-pagan-and-heathen-attendees.html (accessed 20 March 2021)

Greenwood, C. and E. Sinmaz (2016) 'Did neo-Nazi murder Jo over fear he'd lose council house he grew up in? Terrorist thought property could end up being occupied by an immigrant family – And the MP wouldn't help him', *Mail Online*, 24 November 2016. Available: www.dailymail.co.uk/news/article-3966766/Did-Neo-Nazi-murder-Jo-fear-d-lose-council-house-grew-Terrorist-thought-property-end-occupied-immigrant-family-MP-wouldn-t-help-him.html (accessed 7 April 2022).

Gretzinger, J., D. Sayer and P. Justeau (2023) 'The Anglo-Saxon migration and the formation of the early English gene pool', *Nature*, 610 (2022), 112–119. Available: www.nature.com/articles/s41586-022-05247-2 (accessed 29 October 2023).

Grieve, G. P. (1995) 'Imagining a virtual religious community: Neo-Pagans and the internet', *Chicago Anthropology Exchange*, 7 (1995), 98–132.

Griffin, R. (2003) 'From slime mould to rhizome: An introduction to the groupuscular right', *Patterns of Prejudice*, 27:1 (2003), 27–50.

Griffin, R. (ed.) (2005) *Fascism, Totalitarianism and Political Religion*. London: Routledge.

Griffin, R. (2017) 'Interregnum or endgame? The radical right in the "post-fascist" era', in C. Mudde (ed.) *The Populist Radical Right*, 15–27. London: Routledge.

Griffin, R. (2018) *Fascism: An Introduction to Comparative Fascist Studies*. Cambridge: Polity.

Griffiths, B. (1996) *Aspects of Anglo-Saxon Magic*. Norfolk: Anglo-Saxon Books.

Grow, K. (n.d.) 'Gorgoroth', *Revolver*. Available: https://web.archive.org/web/20080515141650/http:/www.revolvermag.com/content/gorgoroth (accessed 20 October 2020).

Grundy, S. (2020) 'Reconstruction and racism in modern Heathenry', in N. S. Emore and J. M. Leader (eds) *Paganism and Its Discontents: Enduring Problems of Racialized Identity*, 135–148. Cambridge: Cambridge Scholars.

Guerilla Survivalism (2023) 'Edel Project – Sussex update', 8 September 2023. Available: https://guerillasurvivalism.blogspot.com (accessed 6 April 2024).

Gullveig Press (2020) 'Resource Center for Pagans in prison'. Available: https://gullveigpress.wordpress.com/2020/08/02/resource-center-for-pagans-in-prison/ (accessed 20 October 2023).

Gunnell, T. (2005) 'The background and nature of the annual and occasional rituals of the Ásatrúarfélag in Iceland', *Ritual Year*, 10 (2015), 28–40.

Hale, A. (2011) 'John Michell, radical traditionalism, and the emerging politics of the Pagan New Right', *Pomegranate*, 13:1 (2011), 77–97.

Hale, A. (2015) 'Marketing "Rad Trad": The growing co-influence between Paganism and the New Right', in T. Ellwood, C. Blanton and B. Williams (eds) *Bringing Race to the Table: Exploring Racism in the Pagan Community*, 103–122. London: Immanion Press.

Hall, D. (2019) 'Dark religion. Inside the sinister world of "Far Right" Woden's Folk Cult', *Sun*, 20 August 2019. Available: www.thesun.co.uk/news/9722484/secret-world-odin-wodens-folk/ (accessed February 2020).

Hall, M. M. (2017) 'Death in June and the Apoliteic specter of neofolk in Germany', *German Politics and Society*, 35:123 (summer 2017), 60–79.

Halsall, M. (1981) *The Old English Rune Poem: A Critical Edition*. Toronto: Toronto University Press.

Hammer, O. (2004) *Claiming Knowledge: Strategies of Epistemology from Theosophy to the New Age*. Leiden: Brill Academic Publishers.

Harner, M. (1980) *The Way of the Shaman*. New York, NY: Harper & Row.

Harrison, F. V. (1997) *Decolonizing Anthropology: Moving Further Toward an Anthropology for Liberationan*. Arlington, VA: American Anthropological Association.

Harry Potter Wiki (n.d.) 'Death Eaters'. Available: https://harrypotter.fandom.com/wiki/Death_Eaters (accessed 7 March 2024).

Harvey, G. (1995) 'Satanism in Britain today', *Journal of Contemporary Religion*, 10:3 (1995), 283–296.

Harvey, G. (2011) *Contemporary Paganism: Listening People, Speaking Earth* (2nd ed.). New York, NY: New York University Press.

Harvey, G. (2016) 'Satanism: Performing alterity and othering', in J. A. Petersen (ed.) *Contemporary Religious Satanism: A Critical Anthology*, 27–40. London: Routledge.

Harvey, G. (ed.) (2020) *Indigenizing Movements in Europe*. Sheffield: Equinox.

Harvey, G. and C. Hardman (eds) (1995) *Paganism Today: Wiccans, Druids, the Goddess and Ancient Earth Traditions for the Twenty-First Century*, 242–251. London: Thorsons.

Hatewatch Staff (2018) 'Atomwaffen and the SIEGE parallax: How one neo-Nazi's life's work is fueling a younger generation', Southern Poverty Law Center, 22 February 2018. Available: www.splcenter.org/hatewatch/2018/02/22/atomwaffen-and-siege-parallax-how-one-neo-nazi's-life's-work-fueling-younger-generation (accessed 23 March 2020)

Hatzipanagos, R. (2018) 'How online hate turns into real-life violence', *Washington Post*, 30 November 2018. Available: www.washingtonpost.com/nation/2018/11/30/how-online-hate-speech-is-fueling-real-life-violence/ (accessed 22 March 2024)

Heaney, S. (trans.) (2000), *Beowulf*. New York, NY: Farrar, Straus and Company.

Heathens Against Hate (HAH) (2014) 'Benefit for the victims of the Kansas city shooting'. *Heathens Against Hate Blog*, 22 May 2023. Available: http://heathensagainsthate.blogspot.com/2014/ (accessed 21 October 2023).

Heathens Against Hate (HAH) (2020) 'Sovereignty statement', 13 October 2020. Available: www.heathensagainst.org/post/hah-sovereignty-statement (accessed 21 October 2023).

Heathens Against Hate (HAH) (n.d.a) 'Heathen iconography'. Available: https://www.heathensagainst.org/heathen-iconography (accessed 22 October 2023).

Heathens Against Hate (HAH) (n.d.b) 'Homepage of Heathens Against Hate'. Available: https://www.heathensagainst.org (accessed 3 July 2023).

Heathen's Heart (2020) *Declaration 127*. Available: https://heathensheart.com/disclaimer/declaration-127/ (accessed 20 April 2024).

Hegner, V. (2015) 'Hot, strange, Völkisch, Cosmopolitan: Native faith and Neopagan witchcraft in Berlin's changing urban context', in K. Rountree (ed.) *Contemporary Pagan and Native Faith Movements in Europe*, 175–195. Oxford: Berghahn.

Henderson, A. (2020) 'Introduction', in A. Henderson (ed.) *Politics, Intellectuals, and Faith: Essays by Matthew Feldman*, 6–20. Stuttgart: Ibidem.

Henry, C. (2022) 'The Swords of Wayland: From family television to fascist mythos'. Available: www.radicalrightanalysis.com/2022/01/20/the-swords-of-wayland-from-family-television-to-fascist-mythos/ (accessed 30 October 2023).

Heritage, S. (2022) 'Ancient Apocalypse is the most dangerous show on Netflix'. *Guardian*, November 23, 2022. Available: www.theguardian.com/tv-and-radio/2022/nov/23/ancient-apocalypse-is-the-most-dangerous-show-on-netflix (accessed 27 April 2023).

Highfield, T. and T. Leaver (2015) 'A methodology for mapping Instagram hashtags', *First Monday*, 20:1 (2015), https://doi.org/10.5210/fm.v20i1.5563

Highfield, T. and T. Leaver (2016) 'Instagrammatics and digital methods: Studying visual social media, from selfies and GIFs to memes and emoji', *Communication Research and Practice*, 2:1 (2016), 47–62.

Hill, R. and K. Spracklen (eds) (2010) *Heavy Fundamentalisms: Music, Metal and Politics*. Oxford: Inter-Disciplinary Press.

Hochman, N. and R. Schwartz (2021) 'Visualizing Instagram: Tracing cultural visual rhythms', *Proceedings of the International AAAI Conference on Web and Social Media*, 6:4 (2021), 6–9. Available: https://ojs.aaai.org/index.php/ICWSM/article/view/14361 (accessed 7 August 2022).

Hope not Hate (HnH) (2019a) 'Order of Nine Angles'. Available: https://hopenothate.org.uk/2019/02/16/state-of-hate-2019-order-of-nine-angles/ (accessed 13 February 2024).

Hope not Hate (HnH) (2019b) *State of Hate 2019: People VS the Elite*. Available: https://hopenothate.org.uk/2019/02/17/state-hate-2019/ (accessed 20 April 2024).

Hope not Hate (HnH) (2020a) 'Order of Nine Angles: An incubator of terrorism'. Available: https://hopenothate.org.uk/chapter/order-of-nine-angles-an-incubator-of-terrorism/ (accessed 13 February 2024).

Hope not Hate (HnH) (2020b) *State of Hate 2020: Far Right Terror Goes Global*. Available: https://hopenothate.org.uk/wp-content/uploads/2020/02/state-of-hate-2020-final.pdf (accessed 30 December 2023).

Hope not Hate (HnH) (2021) *State of Hate 2021: Backlash, Conspiracies and Confrontation*. Available: https://hopenothate.org.uk/wp-content/uploads/2021/02/state-of-hate-2021-v21Oct.pdf (accessed 30 December 2023).

Hope not Hate (HnH) (2024) *State of Hate 2024: Pessimism, Decline and the Rise of the Radical Right*. Available: https://hopenothate.org.uk/wp-content/uploads/2024/03/state-of-hate-2024-v15.pdf (accessed 20 April 2024).

Hoppadietz, R. and K. Reichenbach (2019) 'Nationalist appropriations of open-air museums and prehistory re-enactment in Germany and Poland: Past and current trends of the politicisation of archaeological heritage', in R. Kusek and J. Purchla (eds) *Heritage and Society*, 207–232. Krakow: International Cultural Centre.

Horrell, T. N. (2013) 'Heathenry as a postcolonial movement', *Journal of Religion, Identity, and Politics*, 1:1 (2013), 1–14.

Howard, M. (1985) *The Wisdom of the Runes*. London: Rider.

HUAR (Heathens United Against Racism), 'Facebook post, 15 March 2019'. Available: www.facebook.com/HeathensUnited/posts/1872416769554644?comment_tracking=%7B%22tn%22%3A%22O%22%7D (accessed 29 February 2024).

Hutton, R. (1991) *The Pagan Religions of the Ancient British Isles: Their Nature and Legacy*. Oxford: Blackwell.

Hutton, R. (1996) 'Introduction: Who possesses the past?', in P. Carr-Gomm (ed.) *The Druid Renaissance: The Voice of Druidry Today*, 17–34. London: Thorsons.

Hutton, R. (2013) *Pagan Britain*. New Haven, CT: Yale University Press.

Illing, S. (2017) 'A grad student spent 12 months undercover in Europe's alt-right movement', *Vox*, 29 November 2017. Available: www.vox.com/policy-and-politics/2017/10/11/16424576/europe-alt-right-nationalism-racism-trump-brexit (accessed 20 October 2023).

Inglinga (2014) 'The hooded man prophecy'. Available: http://inglinga.blogspot.com/2014/05/the-hooded-man-prophecy.html (accessed 6 April 2024).

Inglinga (2015a) 'At-al-land and the Hale-Bopp Comet'. Available: http://inglinga.blogspot.com/2015/11/at-al-land-and-hale-bopp-comet.html (accessed 6 April 2024).

Inglinga (2015b) 'Woden's Folk "year to come"'. Available: http://inglinga.blogspot.com/2015/12/wodens-folk-year-to-come.html (accessed 31 October 2023).

Inglinga (2018) 'Religion in today's world', 12 November 2018. Available: http://inglinga.blogspot.com/2018/11/religion-in-todays-world.html (accessed 4 June 2019).

In-reach Heathen Prison Services (2014) Available: http://in-reach-heathen.blogspot.com/search?updated-max=2014-12-12T18:04:00-08:00&max-results=7 (accessed 20 October 2023).

Instagram (2018) 'Instagram community guidelines FAQs'. Available: https://about.instagram.com/blog/announcements/instagram-community-guidelines-faqs (accessed 3 July 2023).

International Business Times (2013) 'Is Varg Vikernes a terrorist? A brief history of the Burzum frontman's neo-Nazi, Pagan views', 16 July 2013. Available: www

.ibtimes.com/varg-vikernes-terrorist-brief-history-burzum-frontmans-neo-nazi-pagan-views-1348789 (accessed 20 October 2023).

Introvigne, M. (2016) *Satanism: A Social History*. Leiden: Brill Academic Publishers.

IPSO (Independent Press Standards Organisation) (2020) 'Resolution statement – 06622-20 Moult v Sunday Mail', 3 July 2020. Available: https://www.ipso.co.uk/rulings-and-resolution-statements/ruling/?id=06622-20 (accessed 22 April 2024).

ISD (Institute for Strategic Dialogue) (n.d.) 'The Order of the Nine Angles'. Available: www.isdglobal.org/explainers/the-order-of-nine-angles-explainer/ (accessed 24 December 2023).

ISSEME (International Society for the Study of Early Medieval England) (2019) 'Statement on the term "Anglo-Saxon"'. Available: https://isseme.org/2019/11/21/statement-on-the-term-anglo-saxon/ (accessed 19 August 2022).

Ivakhiv, A. (2005) 'Nature and ethnicity in East European Paganism: An environmental ethic of the religious right?', *The Pomegranate*, 7:2 (2005), 194–225.

Ivakhiv, A. (2009) 'Nature and ethnicity in East European Paganism: An environmental ethic of the religious right?', in B. Davy (ed.) *Paganism: Critical Concepts in Religious Studies, Volume 2: Ecology*, 213–242. London: Routledge.

Jackson, P. (2014) 'Failed agendas and white nationalism', *Searchlight* (Autumn 2014), 6–11.

Jackson, P. (2015) 'British Neo-Nazi fiction: Colin Jordan's *Merrie England – 2000* and *The Uprising*', in N. Copsey and J. E. Richardson (eds) *Cultures of Post-War British Fascism*, 86–107. London: Routledge.

Jackson, P. (2016) 'Behind the Lone Wolf', *Searchlight* (Autumn 2016), 18–21.

Jackson, P. (2018) *Colin Jordan and Britain's Neo-Nazi Movement. Hitler's Echo*. London: Bloomsbury.

Jackson, P. (2022) *Pride in Prejudice: Understanding Britain's Extreme Right*. Manchester: Manchester University Press.

Jenkins, R. (2000) 'Disenchantment, enchantment and re-enchantment: Max Weber at the millennium', *Max Weber Studies*, 1 (2000), 11–32.

Johnson, N. J. and R. J. Wallis (2022) *Galdrbok: Practical Heathen Runecraft, Shamanism and Magic*. Winchester and London: The Wykeham Press.

Jones, P. and N. Pennick (1995) *A History of Pagan Europe*. London: Routledge

Jordan, C. (n.d.) *Britain Reborn: The Will and Purpose of the National Socialist Movement*. Wiener Holocaust Library Collections, OSP 71.

Kahn-Harris, K. (2007) *Extreme Metal – Music and Culture on the Edge*. Oxford: Berg.

Kallis, A. (ed.) (2003) *The Fascism Reader*. London: Routledge.

Kapiris, M. (2019) 'Analysing anti-O9A prejudice and propaganda', 20 June 2019. Available: www.o9a.org/2019/06/analysing-anti-o9a-prejudice-and-propaganda (accessed 25 March 2020).

Kaplan, J. (1996) 'The reconstruction of the Ásatrú and Odinist traditions', in J. R. Lewis (ed.) *Magical Religion and Modern Witchcraft*, 193–236. Albany, NY: State University of New York.

Kaplan, J. (1997) *Radical Religion in America: Millenarian Movements from the Far Right to the Children of Noah*. Syracuse, NY: Syracuse University Press.

Kaplan, J. (1999) 'Savitri Devi and the national socialist religion of nature', *Pomegranate*, 7 (Winter 1999), 4–12.

Kaplan, J. (ed.) (2000) 'Order of Nine Angles', in J. Kaplan (ed.) *Encyclopedia of White Power: A Sourcebook on the Radical Racist Right*, 235–238. Lanham, MD: AltaMira Press.

Kaplan, J. (2001) 'The post-war paths of occult national socialism: From Rockwell and Madole to Manson', *Patterns of Prejudice* (December 2001), 41–67.

Katz, D. S. (2007) *The Occult Tradition. From the Renaissance to the Present Day*. London: Pimlico.

Kaur, H. (2019) 'Authorities say black metal may have influenced the Louisiana church fires suspect. Here's what to know', *CNN*, 12 April 2019. Available: https://edition.cnn.com/2019/04/11/entertainment/black-metal-church-burning-explainer/index.html (accessed 27 February 2020).

Kelly, K. (2008) 'Voices of blood: Winterfylleth', *Ravishing Grimness*, 12 November 2008. Available: https://ravishinggrimness.blogspot.com/2008/11/voices-of-blood-winterfylleth.html (accessed 20 October 2023).

Kelly, K. (2018) 'Unmasking Gaylord, black metal's latest anti-fascist enigma', *Vice*, 21 August 2018. Available: www.vice.com/en/article/vbjnqx/gaylord-anti-fascist-black-metal-interview (accessed 20 October 2023).

Kelly, K. (2021) 'What covering heavy metal taught me about spotting Nazis', *Columbia Journalism Review*, 12 January 2012. Available: www.cjr.org/first_person/heavy-metal-capitol-spotting-nazis.php (accessed 20 October 2023).

Keenan, D. (2016) *England's Hidden Reverse: A Secret History of the Esoteric Underground*. London: Strange Attractor Press.

Kerr, S. (2023) 'An update regarding the proposed Asatru Folk Assembly Winter Nights event at Stonehenge', 13 September 2023. Available: www.paganfed.org/an-update-regarding-the-proposed-asatru-folk-assembly-winter-nights-event-at-stonehenge/ (accessed 18 October, 2023).

Kershaw, I. (1998) *Hitler 1889–1936: Hubris*. London: Penguin Books.

Kershaw, I. (2001) *Hitler 1936–1945: Nemesis*. New York, NY: W. W. Norton.

Khan, M. (2019) 'Racism stole Heathenry's past and threatens our future'. Available: www.patheos.com/blogs/heathenatheart/2019/03/racism-stole-past/ (accessed 5 November 2023).

King ov Hell (n.d.) 'King ov Hell'. Available: www.maelstrom.nu.

Kitts, J. (2008) 'Venom's Cronos: The Guitar World interview', 18 November 2008. Available: www.guitarworld.com/features/venoms-cronos-guitar-world-interview (accessed 15 March 2020).

Kitts, M. (2022) 'Contextualizing the Proud Boys: Violence, misogyny, and religious nationalism', in *Oxford Research Encyclopedia of Religion*. Available: https://oxfordre.com/religion/display/10.1093/acrefore/9780199340378.001.0001/acrefore-9780199340378-e-1066?p=emailAS4wDI3q1j0Pw&d=/10.1093/acrefore/9780199340378.001.0001/acrefore-9780199340378-e-1066 (accessed 1 May 2024).

Klein, L. (2004) *The Resurrection of Perun: Toward the Reconstruction of East Slavic Paganism*. Saint Petersburg: Eurasia.

Knowles, T. (2019) 'Facebook let advertisers seek out Nazi sympathisers', *The Times*, 23 February 2019, 37.

Knowles, T., F. Hamilton and J. Simpson (2020) 'Far Right recruiting children on YouTube', *The Times*, 6 October 2020. Available: www.thetimes.co.uk/article/far-right-recruiting-children-on-youtube-0xknjffws (accessed 21 March 2024).

Koch, A. (2022) 'The ONA network and the transnationalization of neo-Nazi-Satanism', *Studies in Conflict and Terrorism*. Available: www.tandfonline.com/doi/full/10.1080/1057610X.2021.2024944?src=recsys (accessed 24 December 2023).

Koehne, S. (2014) 'Were the national socialists a *Völkisch* party? Paganism, Christianity, and the Nazi Christmas', *Central European History*, 47 (2014), 760–790.

Kraft, S., T. Fonneland and J. Lewis (eds) (2015) *Nordic Neoshamanisms*. London: Palgrave Macmillan.

Krasskova, G. (2013) *Transgressing Faith: Race, Gender, and the Problem of 'Ergi' in Modern Heathenry*. New York, NY: Sanngetall Press.

Krasskova, G. (2020) *Modern Guide to Heathenry: Lore, Celebrations & Mysteries of the Northern Traditions*. York Beach: Red Wheel / Weiser.

Krüger, O. (ed.) (2005) 'Discovering the invisible internet: Methodological aspects of searching religion on the internet', *Heidelberg Journal of Religions on the Internet*, 1:1 (2005) *Special Issue on Theory and Methodology*, https://doi.org/10.11588/heidok.00005828

Kurlander, E. (2012) 'Hitler's monsters: The occult roots of Nazism and the emergence of the Nazi "supernatural imaginary"', *German History*, 30:4 (2012), 528–549.

Kurlander, E. (2015) 'The Nazi magicians' controversy: Enlightenment, "border science", and occultism in the Third Reich', *Central European History*, 48:4 (2015), 498–522, https://doi.org/10.1017/S0008938915000898

Kurlander, E. (2017) *Hitler's Monsters: A Supernatural History of the Third Reich*. New Haven, CT: Yale University Press.

Kveldulfr Gundarsson (1990) *Teutonic Magic: The Magical and Spiritual Practices of the Germanic Peoples*. Woodbury, MN: Llewellyn.

Kveldulfr Gundarsson (2020) 'Ancestry and heritage in the Germanic tradition'. Available: https://hrafnar.org/articles/kveldulf/ancestors/ (accessed 23 March 2024).

Lamoureux, M. (2020) '"Random" murder of Muslim man linked to "neo-Nazi death cult": Report', *Vice*, 19 September 2020. Available: www.vice.com/en/article/k7qvny/random-murder-of-muslim-man-linked-to-neo-nazi-death-cult-report (accessed 7 February 2024).

Larrington, C. (1993) *A Store of Common Sense: Gnomic Theme and Style in Old Icelandic and Old English Wisdom Poetry*. Oxford: Clarendon Press.

Larrington, C. (trans.) (2014 [1996]), *The Poetic Edda*. Oxford: Oxford University Press.

Larsen, A. (2013) 'Fast, cheap and out of control: The graphic symbol in hardcore punk', *Punk & Post Punk*, 2, 91–106, https://doi.org/10.1386/punk.2.1.91_1

References

Last, J. (2019) 'Et in Avebury ego'. Available: https://prehistorian.postach.io/post/et-in-avebury-ego (accessed 28 February 2024).

Lawrence, D. (2019) 'Exposed: Brexit party candidate's Nazi-inspired band', *Hope not Hate*, 8 November 2019. Available: https://hopenothate.org.uk/chapter/exposed-brexit-party-candidates-nazi-inspired-band/ (accessed 20 April 2024).

Lawrence, D., P. Hermansson and N. Lowles (2020) 'Order of Nine Angles: An incubator of terrorism', in D. Lawrence, P. Hermansson and N. Lowles (eds) *State of Hate 2020*, 36–41. London: Hope not Hate.

Layton-Scott, D. (2019) Personal communication, 11 June 2019.

Lee, E., J. A. Lee, J. H. Moon and Y. Sung (2015) 'Pictures speak louder than words: Motivations for using Instagram', *Cyberpsychology, Behavior, and Social Networking*, 18:9 (2015), 552–556.

Lee, J. (2018) *Nazism and Neo-Nazism in Film and Media*. Amsterdam University Press, https://doi.org/10.2307/j.ctv56fgmk

Leese, A. (n.d.) 'Fascism is a renovated state of mind', Wiener Holocaust Library Collections.

Leese, A. (c. mid-1930s) 'The plan of the Jews', Wiener Holocaust Library Collections 16899c.

Leese, A. (c. 1930s) 'St. George our Guide', lyrics by Henry Hedges. Wiener Holocaust Library Collections.

Leese, A. (1947) *Racial Inequality in Europe*. London: The Carmac Press. Wiener Holocaust Library Collections, SP 01355.

Leese, A. (1949) 'Our Jewish aristocracy. A revelation', Hollywood, CA: Sons of Liberty. Wiener Holocaust Library Collections, 105637.

Leese, A. (1951?) 'Out of step. Events in the two lives of an anti-Jewish camel doctor', Wiener Holocaust Library Collections, X3a.

Leidig, E. (2020) 'Hindutva as a variant of right-wing extremism', *Patterns of Prejudice*, 54:3 (2020), 215–237, https://doi.org/10.1080/0031322X.2020.1759861

Lewis, J. R. (2016) 'Infernal legitimacy', in J. A. Petersen (ed.) *Contemporary Religious Satanism: A Critical Anthology*, 41–58. London: Routledge.

Lewis, J. and M. Pizza (eds) (2009) *Handbook of Contemporary Paganism*. Leiden: Brill Academic Publishers.

Liddell, C. (2012) 'Interview: John Bean, Veteran British Nationalist', British Democrats, November 2012. Available: http://www.britishdemocrats/uk/interview-john-bean-veteran-british-nationalist/ (accessed 1 April 2021).

Lindquist, G. (1997) 'Shamanic performance on the urban scene: Neo-Shamanism in contemporary Sweden', Stockholm Studies in Social Anthropology 39 (1997). Stockholm: University of Stockholm.

Linsell, T. (1992) *Anglo-Saxon Runes*. Middlesex: Anglo-Saxon Books.

Liyanage, C. (2020) 'The metapolitics of the Far Right', Centre for Analysis of the Radical Right, 7 February 2020. Available: www.radicalrightanalysis.com/2020/02/07/the-metapolitics-of-the-far-right/ (accessed 23 April 2023).

Lo Mascolo, G. and K. Stoeckl (2023) 'The European Christian right: An overview', in G. Lo Mascolo (ed.) *The Christian Right in Europe. Movements, Networks, and Denominations*, 11–42. Bielefeld: Verlag.

Longerich, P. (2012) *Heinrich Himmler*. Oxford: Oxford University Press.

Lowles, N. (2019–2020) 'In search of hope', *Hope not Hate* (Winter 2019–2020), 8–10.

Lowles, N. (2021) 'Government misses opportunity to proscribe Order of Nine Angles'. Available: https://hopenothate.org.uk/2021/04/19/atomwaffen-order-nine-angles/ (accessed 30 December 2023).

van Luijk, R. (2016) *Children of Lucifer: The Origins of Modern Religious Satanism*. Oxford: Oxford University Press.

Mackley, J. (2020) Personal communication (21 June 2019).

Macklin, G. (2005) 'Co-opting the counter-culture', *Patterns of Prejudice*, 39:3 (2005), 301–326.

Macklin, G. (2015) 'The "Cultic Milieu" of Britain's "New Right": Meta-political "Fascism" in contemporary Britain', in N. Copsey and J. E. Richardson (eds) *Cultures of Post-War British Fascism*, 177–201. London: Routledge.

Macklin, G. (2018) '"Only bullets will stop us!" – The banning of national action in Britain', *Perspectives on Terrorism*, 12:6 (2018), 104–122.

Macklin, G. (2020) *Failed Führers: A History of Britain's Extreme Right*. London: Routledge.

Magee, T. (2023) 'Mass brawls and possessed guitar pedals: The high-speed hijinks of British thrash metal', *Guardian*, 24 April 2023. Available: www.theguardian.com/music/2023/apr/24/mass-brawls-and-possessed-guitar-pedals-the-high-speed-hijinks-of-british-thrash-metal?CMP=Share_iOSApp_Other (accessed 26 April 2023).

Mainer, J. T. (2017) 'Building inclusive Heathenry: The Troth', *The Troth News*, 12 September 2017. Available: https://thetroth.co.uk/index.php/news/inclusive-heathenry-build (accessed 19 October 2023).

Maingueneau, D. (2006) 'Is discourse analysis critical?', *Critical Discourse Studies*, 3:2 (2006), 229–230.

Maly, I. (2024) *Metapolitics, Algorithms and Violence: New Right Activisim and Terrorism in the Attention Economy*. Abingdon: Routledge.

Mamlëz, B., F. McAlinden and R. Katula (2021a) 'David Myatt – A new hope for Nazis', The Empire Never Ended, 5 March 2021. Available: https://podtail.com/en/podcast/the-empire-never-ended/1-david-myatt-a-new-hope-for-nazis/ (accessed 23 April 2024).

Mamlëz, B., F. McAlinden and R. Katula (2021b) 'David Myatt III – Rehash of the Jedi', The Empire Never Ended, 8 March 2021. Available: www.podparadise.com/Podcast/1559931189 (accessed 23 April 2024).

Manovich, L. (2017) *Instagram and Contemporary Image*. Available: http://manovich.net/index.php/projects/instagram-and-contemporary-image (accessed 3 August 2022).

Mantie, R. and G. D. Smith (2017) *The Oxford Handbook of Music Making and Leisure*. Oxford: Oxford University Press.

Marcus, G. (1998) *Ethnography through Thick and Thin*. Princeton, NJ: Princeton University Press.

Marzinzik, S. (2013) *Masterpieces: Early Medieval Art*. London: British Museum Press.

Matthews, C. (2009) *Modern Satanism. Anatomy of a Radical Subculture*. London: Praeger.

McLachlan, S. (2022) '35 Instagram stats that matter to marketers in 2022', *Hootsuite*, 18 January 2022. Available: https://blog.hootsuite.com/instagram-statistics/#General_Instagram_statistics (accessed 3 August 2022).

McLuhan, M. (1964) *Understanding Media: The Extensions of Man*. New York, NY: McGraw-Hill.

McGregor, R. (1997) *Imagined Destinies. Aboriginal Australians and the Doomed Race Theory, 1880–1939*. Melbourne: Melbourne University Press.

McLean, I. and A. McMillan (2003). *Oxford Concise Dictionary of Politics*. Oxford: Oxford University Press.

McNallen, S. (2006) *The Philosophy of Metagenetics: Folkism and Beyond*. Nevada City, CA: Asatru Folk Assembly.

McNallen, S. (1998) 'Wotan vs. Tezcatlipoca: The spiritual war for California and the southwest', *The Runestone: Celebrating the Indigenous Religion of European Americans*, 22 (Summer 1998), 3–6. Available: http://runestone.org/wp-content/uploads/The-Runestone-Summer-1998.pdf (accessed 6 November 2023).

Memmi, A (2000) *Racism*. Minneapolis, MN: University of Minnesota Press.

The Metal Archives (n.d.a) 'Gaylord: The black metal scene needs to be destroyed'. Available: www.metalarchives.com/albums/Gaylord/The_Black_Metal_Scene_Needs_to_Be_Destroyed/728885 (accessed 7 March 2023).

The Metal Archives (n.d.b) 'Stuka Squadron'. Available: www.metal-archives.com/bands/Stuka_Squadron/3540266533 (accessed 7 March 2024).

The Metal Archives (n.d.c) 'Forefather'. Available: www.metal-archives.com/bands/forefather/781 (accessed 7 March 2023).

The Metal Archives (n.d.d) 'Winterfylleth'. Available: https://www.metal-archives.com/bands/Winterfylleth/1%2007837 (accessed 18 October 2023).

Metalious (n.d.) 'Enslaved is racist'. Available: www.metalious.com/enslaved/eld/racist (accessed 20 October 2023).

Michael, G. (2023) 'The new media and the rise of exhortatory terrorism', *Strategic Studies Quarterly*, 7:1 (2023), 40–68.

Midwest Unrest (2006) 'Death in June: A Nazi band?', 19 November 2006. Available: https://libcom.org/article/death-june-nazi-band-midwest-unrest (accessed 21 March 2024).

Miller C. C. (2009) 'Who's driving Twitter's popularity? Not teens', *New York Times*, 25 August 2009. Available: www.nytimes.com/2009/08/26/technology/internet/26twitter.html (accessed 3 July 2023).

Miller, D. (2018) 'Beyond the iron gates: How Nazi-satanists infiltrated the UK underground', *Quietus*, 27 November 2018. Available: https://thequietus.com/articles/25716-ona-fascism-nazis-folk-horror-underground-occult (accessed 29 January 2024).

Miller, D. (2022) 'Review of J. H. Fewkes (2019) *Anthropological Perspectives on the Religious Uses of Mobile Apps*', *Journal of the Royal Anthropological Institute*, 28 (2022), 351–384.

Miller, D., E. Costa, N. Haynes, T. McDonad, R. Nicolescu, J. Sinanan, J. Spyer, S. Venkatraman and X. WangBottom of Form (2016) *How the World Changed Social Media*. London: University College London Press. Available: www.uclpress.co.uk/products/83038 (accessed 14 July 2022).

Miller-Idriss, C. (2019) 'Keynote: A century of radical right extremism: New approaches', Centre for Analysis of the Radical Right Inaugural Conference at Richmond American University London, 15–17 May 2019.

Minority Rights Group International (2007) World Directory of Minority and Indigenous Peoples – Iceland. Available: https://www.refworld.org/docid/4954ce0323.html (accessed 3 January 2024).

Mitchell, W. J. T. (1994) *Picture Theory: Essays on Verbal and Visual Representation*. Chicago, IL: The University of Chicago Press.

Mitchell, W. J. T. (2003) 'Word and image', in R. S. Nelson and R. Schiff (eds) *Critical Terms for Art History*. Chicago, IL: The University of Chicago Press. Available: http://libezproxy.open.ac.uk/login?url=https://search.credoreference.com/content/entry/uchicagoah/word_and_image/0?institutionId=292.

Mitchell, W. J. T. (2005) *What Do Pictures Want?: The Lives and Loves of Images*. Chicago, IL: The University of Chicago Press.

Mitchell, W. J. T. (2015) *Image Science: Iconology, Visual Culture and Media Aesthetics*. Chicago, IL: The University of Chicago Press.

Molas, B. (2021) 'Exposing the philosophy behind neo-Nazism', Centre for the Analysis of the Radical Right, 1 December 2021.

Monette, C. R. (2015) *Mysticism in the 21st Century*. Wilsonville, OR: Sirius Academic Press.

Moreno M. A., N. Goniu, P. S. Moreno and D. Diekema (2013) 'Ethics of social media research: Common concerns and practical considerations', *Cyberpsychology, Behavior and Social Networking*, 16:9 (2013), 708–713. Available: www.ncbi.nlm.nih.gov/pmc/articles/PMC3942703/.

Mount, R. (1965) 'The most outrageous woman in Britain', *News of the World*, 17 January 1965. Wiener Holocaust Library Collections, 1658/9/3/7.

Moynihan, M. and D. Soderlind (1998) *Lords of Chaos: The Bloody Rise of the Satanic Metal Underground*. Port Townsend, WA: Feral House.

Mudde, C. (2005) *Populist Radical Right Parties in Europe*. Cambridge: Cambridge University Press.

Mudde, C. (2016) 'The study of populist radical right parties: Towards a fourth wave. C-Rex Working Paper Series, No. 1', Center for Research on Extremism, The Extreme Right, Hate Crime and Political Violence, University of Oslo, Oslo.

Mudde, C. (2019) 'Keynote: A century of radical right extremism: New approaches', Centre for Analysis of the Radical Right Inaugural Conference at Richmond American University, London, 15–17 May 2019.

Mudde, C. and C. R. Kaltwasser (2012) 'Exclusionary vs. inclusionary populism: Comparing contemporary Europe and Latin America', *Government and Opposition*, 48:2 (2013), 147–174.

Mudde, C. and C. R. Kaltwasser (2017) *Populism: A Very Short Introduction*. Oxford: Oxford University Press.

Mulhall, J. (n.d.) 'Modernising and mainstreaming: The contemporary British Far Right'. Available: https://assets.publishing.service.gov.uk/media/5d8b882 740f0b6098d33fefa/Joe_Mulhall_-_Modernising_and_Mainstreaming_The _Contemporary_British_Far_Right.pdf (accessed 20 October 2023).

Myatt, D. (2003) 'The religion of National Socialism'. Available: https://archive.org /details/davidmyatt-ns-religion (accessed 28 January 2025).

Myatt, D. (2013) *Myngath: Some Recollections of a Wyrdful and Extremist Life*. Available: https://archive.org/details/Myngath-SomeRecollectionsOfAWyrdful AndExtremistLife (accessed 30 April 2024).

Myatt, D. (2016) *Selected National Socialist Writings of David Myatt*. Order of the Nine Angles.

Myers, F. (1988) 'Locating ethnographic practice: Romance, reality, and politics in the outback', *American Ethnologist*, 15:4 (1988), 609–624.

Nagl, M. (1974) 'SF, occult sciences, and Nazi myths', *Science Fiction Studies*, 1:3 (Spring 1974), 185–197.

Nameless Therein (2022) 'Sutor, ne ultra crepidam', 13 June 2022. Available: www .o9a.org (accessed 29 June 2022).

Nanda, M. (2004) 'EcoSpirituality, neo-Paganism and the Hindu right: The dangers of religious environmentalism', *Women and Environments International Magazine*, 64/65 (Fall/Winter 2004), 19–22. Available: https://www.yorku.ca/ weimag/BACKISSUES/images/WEI%20scan%202004-%2064-65.pdf (accessed 20 April 2024).

Newark Odinist Temple (n.d.a) Homepage. Available: www.odinisttemple.uk (accessed 29 October 2023).

Newark Odinist Temple (n.d.b) News. Available: www.odinisttemple.uk/news.php (accessed 29 October 2023).

Nicolson, S. (2017) 'Who are the Scottish Dawn neo-Nazi group', *BBC News*, 27 September 2017. Available: www.bbc.co.uk/news/uk-scotland-41440467 (accessed 24 April 2024).

Nikitins, T. J. (2020) 'Sacred symbols becoming battlegrounds', in N. S. Emore and J. M. Leader (eds) *Paganism and Its Discontents: Enduring Problems of Racialized Identity*, 113–125. Cambridge: Cambridge Scholars.

North of Annwn (2019) 'This is your reminder that Stephen Flowers and Edred Thorsson are the same person'. Available: https://north-of-annwn.tumblr.com/ post/189259675495/this-is-your-reminder-that-stephen-flowers-and (accessed 5 November 2023).

Oates, L. L. (2021) 'The Theosophical Society and transnational cultures of print', *Imperial and Global Forum*, 5 May 2021. Available: https://imperialglobalexeter .com/2021/05/05/the-theosophical-society-and-transnational-cultures-of-print/ #more-7784 (accessed 7 May 2021).

Obline, S. M. (2016) 'The problem with Declaration 127'. Available: https://medium.com/@RogerRiga/the-problem-with-declaration-127-da118323da4f (accessed 22 October 2023).

The Odinic Rite (n.d.a) 'About us: what our members say'. Available: https://odinic-rite.org/main/what-our-members-say/ (accessed 24 April 2024).

The Odinic Rite (n.d.b) 'Frequently asked questions: Does the Odinic Rite take a political viewpoint?' Available: https://odinic-rite.org/main/about/or-faq/#toggle-id-8 (accessed 28 October 2023).

The Odinic Rite (n.d.c) 'Frequently asked questions: What is the meaning of the OR logo?' Available: https://odinic-rite.org/main/about/or-faq/#toggle-id-8 (accessed 28 October 2023).

The Odinic Rite (n.d.d) 'The nine noble virtues and charge'. Available: https://odinic-rite.org/main/about/the-nine-noble-virtues-and-charges-of-the-odinic-rite/ (accessed 19 August 2022).

The Odinic Rite (n.d.e) 'Welcome to the Odinic Rite: Folkish Odinism in the Modern World'. Available: https://odinic-rite.org/main/ (accessed 28 October 2023).

The Odinist Fellowship (n.d.) 'All about Odinism'. Available: https://www.odinistfellowship.co.uk (accessed 29 October 2023).

O'Leary, S. D. (1996) 'Cyberspace as sacred space: Communicating religion on computer networks', *Journal of the American Academy of Religion*, 64:4 (1996), 781–808. Available: www.jstor.org/stable/1465622.

Olson, B. H. (2008) 'I am the black wizards: Multiplicity, mysticism and identity in black metal music and culture', MA thesis, Bowling Green State University, May 2008. Available: https://pdfcoffee.com/olson-benjamin-hedge-pdf-free.html (accessed 16 May 2021).

Olson, B. H. (2011) 'Voice of our blood: National socialist discourses in black metal', *Popular Music History*, 6.1/6.2 (2011), 135–149.

Olson, W. (2020) *The Origins of a Warning from Voltaire*. Available: https://www.cato.org/publications/commentary/origins-warning-from-voltaire (accessed 24 March 2024).

Omena, J. J., E. Rabello, A. G. Mintz, S. Ozkula, G. Sued, E. Elbeyi and A. Cicali (2017) *Visualising Hashtag Engagement: Imagery of Political Engagement on Instagram Summary of Key Findings*. Available: www.academia.edu/34546911/Visualising_Hashtag_Engagement_Imagery_of_Political_Engagement_on_Instagram (accessed 3 July 2023).

ONS (Office for National Statistics) (2022) Religion, England and Wales: Census 2021, released 29 November 2022. Available: www.ons.gov.uk/peoplepopulationandcommunity/culturalidentity/religion/bulletins/religionenglandandwales/census2021 (accessed 9 October 2023)

Order of the Nine Angles (O9A/ONA) (n.d.) *Introducing the Order of Nine Angles*. Order of the Nine Angles.

Order of the Nine Angles (O9A/ONA) (1986) *The Culling Texts – Order of Nine Angles the Theory and Practice of Sacrificial Human Culling*. Available: http://www.o9a.org/wp-content/uploads/o9a-culling-texts-v7a.pdf (accessed 20 April 2024).

References

Order of the Nine Angles (O9A/ONA) (2008) *Satanism: Epitome of Evil*. Order of the Nine Angles.

Order of the Nine Angles (O9A/ONA) (2012) 'Labyrinthos Mythologicus – FAQ'. Available: https://lapisphilosophicus.wordpress.com/about-2/O9A-faq/ (accessed 29 March 2020).

Order of the Nine Angles (O9A/ONA) (2019) 'The Nihilist O9A', 25 January 2019. Available: http://www.o9a.org/2019/01/ (accessed 25 March 2020).

Owen, S. (2019) 'Is Druidry Indigenous? The politics of Pagan indigeneity discourse', *International Journal for the Study of New Religions*, 9:2 (2019), 235–247.

Pagan Black Metal Rarities (n.d.) Available: https://rateyourmusic.com/list/ASpiritualMoon/pagan-black-metal-rarities/ (accessed 20 October 2023).

The Pagan Federation (PF) (2022) 'Becoming a Pagan Prison Chaplain'. Available: https://www.paganfed.org/becoming-a-pagan-prison-chaplain/ (accessed 20 October 2023).

The Pagan Federation (PF) (2023) 'Heathenry'. Available: https://paganfed.org/index.php/paganism/heathenry (accessed 2 November 2023).

Pardy, A. (2019) Personal correspondence, 18–20 June 2019.

Pardy, A. (2023a) 'How the British Far-Right appropriate and misrepresent Pagan iconography', MA Thesis, Richmond American University, London. Digital access available on request to the RAUL librarian.

Pardy, A. (2023b) *Stop the Asatru Folk Assembly Winter Nights event at Stonehenge*. Change.org petition. Available: https://www.change.org/p/stop-the-asatru-folk-assembly-winter-nights-event-at-stonehenge (accessed 18 October 2023).

Partridge, C. (2013) 'Esoterrorism and the wrecking of civilization: Genesis P-Orridge and the rise of industrial Paganism', in D. Weston and A. Bennett (eds) *Pop Pagans: Paganism and Popular Music*, 189–212. London: Routledge.

Passmore, K. (2002) *Fascism: A Very Short Introduction*. Oxford: Oxford University Press.

Paxson, D. (2005) *Taking Up the Runes: A Complete Guide to Using Runes in Spells, Rituals, Divination and Magic*. York Beach: Red Wheel / Weiser.

Paxson, D. (2006) *Essential Asatru: Walking the Path of Norse Paganism*. New York, NY: Citadel Press Books.

Paxson, D. (2017) *Odin: Ecstasy, Runes and Norse Magic*. Newburyport, MA: Weiser Books.

Paxson, D. (2020) 'Balancing on the rainbow bridge: The challenge of inclusive Heathenry', in N. S. Emore and J. M. Leader (eds) *Paganism and Its Discontents: Enduring Problems of Racialized Identity*, 65–84. Cambridge: Cambridge Scholars.

Paxson, D., R. Schreiwer and L. Wood (2015) 'Heathens in the hall: A report on Troth participation at the Parliament of World Religions', *Idunna*, 106 (Winter 2015), 22–28.

Payne, S. G. (1995) *A History of Fascism*. London: Hodder & Stoughton.

Pearce, R. (1997) *Fascism and Nazism*. London: Hodder & Stoughton.

Peel, B. (2023) *Tonight It's a World We Bury: Black Metal, Red Politics*. London: Repeater Books.

Pengelly, M. (2023), 'DeSantis aide fired after sharing video featuring symbol used by Nazis', *Guardian*, 26 July 2023. Available: www.theguardian.com/us-news/2023/jul/26/desantis-campaign-video-nazi-symbol-fired-aide?CMP=Share_iOSApp_Other (accessed 2 January 2023).

Pennick, N. (1992) *Rune Magic: The History and Practice of Ancient Runic Traditions*. London: Thorsons.

Pepper, D. (1996) *Modern Environmentalism. An Introduction*. London: Routledge.

Petric, N. and M. Borenović (2020) 'Native faith group Veles: A case study of Slovene contemporary Paganism', *Pomegranate*, 22:2 (2020), 174–195.

Phelps, R. H. (1963) '"Before Hitler came": Thule Society and Germanen order', *The Journal of Modern History*, 35:3 (September 1963), 245–261.

Phillipov, M. (2011) 'Extreme music for extreme people? Norwegian black metal and transcendent violence', *Popular Music History*, 6.1/6.2 (2011), 150–163.

Piper, E. (2007) 'Steigmann-Gall, the holy Reich', *Journal of Contemporary History*, 42:1 (2007), 47–57.

Possamai, A. and B. S. Turner (2012) 'Authority and liquid religion in cyber-space: The new territories of religious communication', *International Social Science Journal*, 63 (2012), 197–206.

Powell, T. E., H. G. Boomgaarden, K. De Swert and C. H. de Vreese (2015) 'A clearer picture: The contribution of visuals and text to framing effects', *Journal of Communication*, 65:6 (2015), 997–1017.

PPA (Pagan Police Association) (2023) 'A response to the proposed Asatru Folk Assembly Winter Nights event at Stonehenge'. Available: https://onedrive.live.com/view.aspx?resid=306D2D2CF2B010A7!4163&ithint=file%2cdocx&wdo=2&authkey=!ACzMLlhNMrJiWiY (accessed 18 October 2023).

Pollington, S. (2000) *Leechcraft: Early English Charms, Plantlore and Healing*. Hockwold cum Wilton: Anglo-Saxon Books.

Prandner, D. and A. Seymer (2020) 'Social media analysis', in P. Atkinson, S. Delamont, A. Cernat, J. W. Sakshaug and R. A. Williams (eds) *SAGE Research Methods Foundations*, n.p., https://doi.org/10.4135/9781526421036921823

Price, N. (2020) *The Children of Ash and Elm: A History of the Vikings*. London: Penguin Books.

Prinz, J. (2014) 'The aesthetics of punk rock', *Philosophy Compass*, 9:9 (2014), 583–593.

Pugh, M. (2006) *'Hurrah for the Blackshirts!' Fascists and Fascism in Britain Between the Wars*. London: Pimlico.

Railbeart (2020) 'Grey squirrel folk allegory'. Available: https://odinic-rite.org/main/grey-squirrel-folk-allegory/ (accessed 28 October 2023).

Rasmussen, R. H. (2021) *The Nordic Animist Year*. Nordic Animism.

Rate Your Music. Available: https://rateyourmusic.com/release/album/winterfylleth/the-ghost-of-heritage/ (accessed 18 October 2023).

RDM Crew, 'Fake news'. Available: www.o9a.org/2019/03/fake-news/ (accessed 25 March 2020).

Reddit, 'Winterfylleth – The Threnody of Triumph [Atmospheric Black]', r/metal. Available: www.reddit.com/r/Metal/comments/3c70h3/winterfylleth_the_threnody_o f_triumph_atmospheric/ (accessed 20 October 2023).

Reid Ross, A. and S. Burley (2016) 'With enemies at the gate: A discussion between Alexander Reid Ross and Shane Burley on Paganism and the resistance to Fascism', *It's Going Down*, 18 December 2016. Available: https://itsgoingdown.org/enemies-gate-discussion-alexander-reid-ross-shane-burley-paganism-resistance-fascism/ (accessed 11 April 2019).

Renton, D. (2020) *Fascism: History and Theory*. London: Pluto Press.

Rich Reviewz (2013) 'Winterfylleth Interview: "If you want to look at people wearing corpse paint, then don't come watch a Winterfylleth show"', *Eyesore Merch*, 25 March 2013. Available: https://blog.eyesoremerch.com/2013/03/25/winterfylleth-interview-if-you-want-to-look-at-people-wearing-corpse-paint-then-dont-come-watch-a-winterfylleth-show/ (accessed 20 October 2023).

Richard (2010) 'Winterfylleth: Defenders of the Realm', *Lurker*, 24 August 2010, Available: https://lurkersgrave.com/2010/08/24/winterfylleth-defenders-of-the-realm/.

Rinallo, D., P. Maclaran and L. Stevens (2016) 'A mixed blessing: Market-mediated religious authority in Neopaganism', *Journal of Macromarketing*, 36:4 (2016), 425–442, https://doi.org/10.1177/0276146716655780

Ritona (n.d.) Homepage: A beautiful resistance. Available: https://abeautifulresistance.org (accessed 21 October 2023).

Rosendahl, J. (2016) 'Anti-immigrant "Soldiers of Odin" raise concern in Finland', *Reuters*, 13 January 2016. Available: www.reuters.com/article/us-europe-migrants-finland-idUSKCN0UR20G20160113 (accessed 3 November 2023).

Rountree, K. (ed.) (2015a) *Contemporary Pagan and Native Faith Movements in Europe*. Oxford: Berghahn.

Rountree, K. (2015b) 'Introduction: Context is everything: Plurality and paradox in contemporary European paganisms', in K. Rountree (ed.) *Contemporary Pagan and Native Faith Movements in Europe: Colonialist and Nationalist Impulses*, 1–23. Oxford: Berghahn.

Rountree, K. (ed.) (2017) *Cosmopolitanism, Nationalism and Modern Paganism*. London: Palgrave Macmillan.

Rudgard, O. (2017) 'Pagans demand return of church buildings "stolen" 1,300 years ago', *Telegraph*, 27 August 2017. Available: https://rb.gy/uizbza (accessed 1 November 2023).

Runic John (2004) *The Book of Seidr: The Native English and Northern European Shamanic Tradition*. Chieveley: Capall Bann.

Runic John (2013) *Up and Down the Tree: Exploring the Nine Worlds of Yggdrasil*. Milverton and Taunton: Capall Bann.

Runic John (2023) Personal communication, 22 March 2024.

Salomonsen, J. (2015) 'Graced life after all? Terrorism and theology on July 22, 2011', *Dialog: A Journal of Theology*, 54:3 (2015), 249–259.

Samuel, S. (2017) 'What to do when racists try to hijack your religion', *Atlantic*, 2 November 2017. Available: https://www.theatlantic.com/international/archive/2017/11/asatru-heathenry-racism/543864/ (accessed 3 May 2019).

Sandford, D. and D. de Simone (2018) 'British neo-Nazis suggest Prince Harry should be shot', *BBC News*, 5 December 2018. Available: https://www.bbc.co.uk/news/uk-46460442 (accessed 14 March 2019).

Saunders, R. A. (2012) 'Pagan places: Towards a religiogeography of neopaganism', *Progress in Human Geography*, 37:6 (2012), 786–810.

Saunders, R. A. (2020) 'Völkisch vibes: Neofolk, place, politics, and pan-European nationalism', in T. Nieguth (ed.) *Nationalism and Popular Culture*, 36–58. London: Routledge, https://doi.org/10.4324/9780429321764-4

Sauvage, C. (ed.) (2013) *Hostia: Secret Teachings of the ONA*. CreateSpace Independent Publishing Platform: Order of Nine Angles.

Sayer, D. (2017) 'Why the idea that the English have a common Anglo-Saxon origin is a myth', *The Conversation*, 15 December 2017. Available: https://theconversation.com/why-the-idea-that-the-english-have-a-common-anglo-saxon-origin-is-a-myth-88272 (accessed 29 October 2023).

Scheer, C. M., S. V. Turner and J. G. Mansell (eds) (2019) *Enchanted Modernities: Theosophy, the Arts and the American West*. London: Fulgur.

von Schnurbein, S. (2015) 'Tales of reconstruction: Intertwining Germanic neo-Paganism and Old Norse scholarship', *Critical Research on Religion*, https://doi.org/10.1177/2050303214567671

von Schnurbein, S. (2017) *Norse Revival: Transformations of Germanic Neopaganism*. Chicago, IL: Haymarket Books.

Schreiwer, R. L. (2013) 'Response to media descriptions of Asatru in the Clements' murder', *Heathens Against Hate*, 6 May 2013. Available: http://heathensagainsthate.blogspot.com/2013/05/ (accessed 21 October 2023).

Scimeca, D. (2014) 'The controversial world of Nazi video games', *Salon*, 12 April 2014. Available: www.salon.com/2014/04/12/the_controversial_world_of_nazi_video_games/ (accessed 14 May 2023).

Scull, C. (2011) 'Social transactions, gift exchange and power in the archaeology of the fifth to seventh centuries', in D. Hamerow (ed.) *The Oxford Handbook of Anglo-Saxon Archaeology*, 848–864. Oxford: Oxford University Press.

Sedgwick, M. (2023) *Traditionalism: The Radical Project for Restoring Sacred Order*. London: Penguin.

Senholt, J. C. (2013) 'Secret identities in the sinister tradition: Political esotericism and the convergence of radical Islam, satanism and national socialism in the Order of Nine Angles', in J. A. Petersen (ed.) *The Devil's Party: Satanism in Modernity* (2012), 250–274. Oxford: Oxford University Press

Senholt, J. (2017) 'Order of Nine Angles'. Available: https://wrldrels.org/2017/04/25/order-of-nine-angles/ (accessed 25 March 2020).

Serafinelli, E. (2018) *Digital Life on Instagram (Digital Activism and Society: Politics, Economy and Culture In Network Communication)*. Bingley: Emerald, https://doi.org/10.1108/978-1-78756-495-420181009

Shaffer, L. S., E. A. Leach and H. A. Berger (2021) *Voices from the Pagan Census: A National Survey of Witches and Neo-Pagans in the United States*. Columbia, SC: University of South Carolina Press.

Shah, S., J. Cooper and S. Newcombe (2023) 'Occult beliefs and the Far Right: The case of the Order of Nine Angles', *Studies in Conflict & Terrorism*, 1:21 (2023), https://doi.org/10.1080/1057610X.2023.2195065?src=recsys

Shekhovtsov, A. (2009) '*Apoliteic* music: Neo-folk, martial industrial and "metaphysical fascism"', *Patterns of Prejudice*, 43:5 (2009), 431–457.

Shlapentokh, D. (2012) 'The anti-Semitism of history: The case of the Russian neo-Pagans', *European Review*, 20:2 (April 2012), 264–275.

Shnirelman, V. (2002) 'Christians! Go home: A revival of neo-Paganism between the Baltic Sea and Transcaucasia (An Overview)', *Journal of Contemporary Religion*, 17:2 (2002), 197–211.

Shou, P. (trans. S. Flowers) (2017) *The Edda as the Key to the Coming Age*. Columbia, MD: Lodestar.

Shutterstock (2017) '14 secrets to going viral on Instagram', 11 May 2017. Available: www.shutterstock.com/blog/14-secrets-going-viral-instagram (accessed 22 July 2022).

Sieg, G. (2013) 'Angular momentum: From traditional to progressive Satanism in the Order of Nine Angles', *International Journal for the Study of New Religions*, 4:2 (2013), 251–282.

Siegfried, K. (2013) 'Worldwide Heathen Census 2013: Results and analysis', *The Norse Mythology Blog*. Available: www.norsemyth.org/2014/01/worldwide-heathen-census-2013-results.html (accessed 12 April 2019).

Siegfried, K. (2017) 'Column: Report from Frith Forge', *The Wild Hunt: Pagan News and Perspectives*, 22 November 2017. Available: https://wildhunt.org/2017/11/column-report-from-frith-forge.html (accessed 20 October 2023).

Siegfried, K. (2021) 'Children of Heimdall: Ásatrú ideas of ancestry', in B. Singler and E. Barker (eds) *Radical Transformations in Minority Religions*, 39–54. London: Routledge.

Sillito, D. (2022) 'Teens shun traditional news channels for TikTok and Instagram, Ofcom says', *BBC News*, 21 July 2022. Available: www.bbc.co.uk/news/entertainment-arts-62238307 (accessed 21 July 2022).

de Simone, D. (2019) 'Durham teen neo-Nazi became "living dead"', *BBC News*, 22 November 2019. Available: www.bbc.co.uk/news/uk-england-tyne-50397477 (accessed 17 August 2022).

de Simone, D. (2020) 'UK Nazi Satanist group should be outlawed, campaigners urge', *BBC News*, 2 March 2020. Available: www.bbc.co.uk/news/uk-51682760 (accessed 17 August 2022).

de Simone, D. (2021) 'Ryan Fleming: Neo-Nazi paedophile jailed for messaging children', *BBC News*, 12 February 2021. Available: www.bbc.co.uk/news/uk-england-leeds-56044179 (accessed 1 April 2024).

de Simone, D. (2022) 'Darlington boy youngest to be committed of terror offence', *BBC News*, 19 January 2022. Available: www.bbc.co.uk/news/uk-england-tees-60056108 (accessed 22 March 2024).

Smith, L. R. and J. Sanderson (2015) 'I'm going to Instagram it! An analysis of athlete self-presentation on Instagram', *Journal of Broadcasting & Electronic Media*, 59:2 (2015), 342–358, https://doi.org/10.1080/08838151.2015.1029125

Smith, R. and S. Burley (2017) 'Asatru's Racist Missionary: Stephen McNallen, defend Europe and the weaponization of folkish Heathenry'. Available: https://abeautifulresistance.org/site/2017/09/14/asatrus-racist-missionary-stephen-mcnallen-defend-europe-and-the-weaponization-of-folkish-heathery (accessed 6 November 2023).

Snook, J. (2015) *American Heathens: The Politics of Identity in a Pagan Religious Movement*. Philadelphia, PA: Temple University Press.

Snook, J., T. Horrell and K. Horton (2017) 'Heathens in the United States: The return to "tribes" in the construction of a peoplehood', in K. Rountree (ed.) *Cosmopolitanism, Nationalism, and Modern Paganism*, 43–64. New York, NY: Palgrave MacMillan.

Snorri Sturluson (trans. A. Faulkes) (1998) *Edda*. London: J. M. Dent.

Snorri Sturluson (trans. L. M. Hollander) (1999) *Heimskringla: History of the Kings of Norway*. Austin, TX: American-Scandinavian Foundation and University of Texas Press.

Somerville, E. (2023) 'Hunt for "satanists" after bizarre ritual discovered in New Forest', *Telegraph*, 23 January 2023. Available: www.telegraph.co.uk/news/2023/01/23/police-hunt-new-forest-satanists-pig-heart-ritual/ (accessed 31 December 2023).

Southern Poverty Law Center (SPLC) (n.d.a) 'Aryan Brotherhood'. Available: www.splcenter.org/fighting-hate/extremist-files/group/aryan-brotherhood (accessed 24 March 2024).

Southern Poverty Law Center (SPLC) (n.d.b) 'Asatru Folk Assembly'. Available: www.splcenter.org/fighting-hate/extremist-files/group/asatru-folk-assembly (accessed 24 March 2024).

Southern Poverty Law Center (SPLC) (n.d.c) 'Atomwaffen and the Siege Parallax', 22 February 2018. Available: www.splcenter.org/hatewatch/2018/02/22/atomwaffen-and-siege-parallax-how-one-neo-nazi's-life's-work-fueling-younger-generation (accessed 25 March 2024).

Southern Poverty Law Center (SPLC) (n.d.d) 'Atomwaffen Division'. Available: www.splcenter.org/fighting-hate/extremist-files/group/atomwaffen-division (accessed 24 March 2024).

Southern Poverty Law Center (SPLC) (n.d.e) 'Augustus Sol Invictus'. Available: www.splcenter.org/fighting-hate/extremist-files/individual/augustus-sol-invictus (accessed 24 March 2024).

Southern Poverty Law Center (SPLC) (n.d.f) 'Extremist group info: World Congress of families'. Available: www.splcenter.org/fighting-hate/extremist-files/group/world-congress-families (accessed 24 March 2024).

Southern Poverty Law Center (SPLC) (n.d.g) 'Flags and other symbols used by far-right groups in Charlottesville'. Available: www.splcenter.org/hatewatch/2017/08/12/flags-and-other-symbols-used-far-right-groups-charlottesville (accessed 24 March 2024).

Southern Poverty Law Center (SPLC) (n.d.h) 'Neo-Volkisch'. Available: www.splcenter.org/fighting-hate/extremist-files/ideology/neo-volkisch (accessed 24 March 2024).

Southern Poverty Law Center (SPLC) (n.d.i) 'Statement regarding Soleilmoon recordings and death In June', 7 March 2017. Available: www.splcenter.org/hatewatch/2017/03/07/statement-regarding-soleilmoon-recordings-and-death-june (accessed 24 March 2024).

Spare, A. O. (1913) *The Book of Pleasure (Self-Love): The Psychology of Ecstasy*. London: Author.

Spoonley, P. and P. Morris (2022) 'Identitarianism and the Alt-Right. A new phase of far-right politics in Aotearoa New Zealand', in M. Cunningham, M. La Rooij and P. Spoonley (eds) *Histories of Hate, The Radical Right in Aotearoa New Zealand*, 305–324. Dunedin: Otago University Press.

Spotify, 'Winterfylleth'. Available: https://open.spotify.com/artist/0cKyWvYnOGpPV2NpulEYf5 (accessed 20 October 2023).

Spracklen, K. (2015) 'Nazi punks folk off: Leisure, nationalism, cultural identity and the consumption of metal and folk music', in N. Copsey and J. E. Richardson (eds) *Cultures of Post-War British Fascism*, 161–176. London: Routledge.

Spracklen, K. (2017) 'Developing a cultural theory of music making and leisure: Baudrillard, the *Simulcra* and music consumption', in R. Mantie and G. Dylan (eds) *The Oxford Handbook of Music Making and Leisure*, 281–296. Oxford: Oxford University Press.

Spracklen, K., C. Lucas and M. Deeks (2014) 'The construction of heavy metal identity through heritage narratives: A case study of extreme metal bands in the north of England', *Popular Music and Society*, 37:1 (2014), 48–64.

Stanley, E. G. (1964) *The Search for Anglo-Saxon Paganism*. Cambridge: Brewer.

Statista (2023) Instagram statistics and facts. Available: https://www.statista.com/statistics/1353274/average-reach-posts-instagram-by-number-of-followers/ (accessed 3 March 2025).

Statista (2024) 'Leading countries based on Instagram audience size as of January 2022 (in millions)'. Available: www.statista.com/statistics/578364/countries-with-most-instagram-users/ (accessed 3 March 2025).

Stevens, B. (2022) 'Metaprometheanism', 4 March 2022. Available: www.o9a.org/2022/03/metapromotheanism/ (accessed 29 June 2022).

Stiegmann-Gall, R. (2005) 'Nazism and the revival of political religion theory', in Roger Griffin (ed.) *Fascism, Totalitarianism and Political Religion*, 82–102. London: Routledge.

Stirling, R. (2018) 'The European Satanism of the O9A: An heretical presencing'. Available: http://www.o9a.org/wp-content/uploads/o9a-european-satanism-v4.pdf (accessed 25 April 2024).

Stirling, R. (2021) *The Peregrinations of David Myatt: National Socialist Ideologist, 2021*. Available: https://archive.org/details/myatt-peregrinations-ideologist (accessed 8 August 2023).

Stone, D. (2003) 'The English Mistery, the BUF, and the Dilemmas of British Fascism', *The Journal of Modern History*, 75:2 (June 2003), 336–358.

Storms, G. (1948) *Anglo-Saxon Magic*. The Hague: Martinus Nijhoff.
Stott, P. (2019) 'The White Wolves: The terrorist manifesto that wasn't', *Perspectives on Terrorism*, 13:4 (2019), 56–62.
Strmiska, M. (2000) 'Ásatrú in Iceland: The rebirth of Nordic Paganism?', *Nova Religio: The Journal of Alternative and Emergent Religions*, 4:1 (2000), 106–132.
Strmiska, M. (2005) 'Modern Paganism in world cultures: Comparative perspectives', in Michael Strmiska (ed.) *Modern Paganism in World Cultures: Comparative Perspectives (Religion in Contemporary Cultures)*, 1–54. Santa Barbara, CA: ABC-CLIO.
Strmiska, M. (2007) 'Putting the blood back into blot: The revival of animal sacrifice in modern Nordic Paganism', *Pomegranate*, 9:2 (2007), 154–89, http://dx.doi.org/10.1558/pome.v9.i2.3921
Strmiska, M. (2018) 'Pagan politics in the 21st century', *Pomegranate*, 20:1 (2000), 5–44.
Strmiska, M. (2020) 'Arguing with the ancestors: Making the case for a Paganism without racism – Keynote address', in N. S. Emore and J. M. Leader (eds) *Paganism and Its Discontents: Enduring Problems of Racialized Identity*, 1–21. Cambridge: Cambridge Scholars.
Taussig, M. (2020) *Mastery of Non-Mastery in the Age of Meltdown*. Chicago: Chicago University Press.
Tech Against Terrorism (2023) 'State of play: Trends in terrorist and violent extremist use of the internet 2022', 19 January 2023. Available: https://techagainstterrorism.org/news/2023/01/19/state-of-play-trends-in-terrorist-and-violent-extremist-use-of-the-internet-2022 (accessed 6 March 2024).
Tech Against Terrorism Europe (2024) 'Using artificial intelligence and machine learning to identify terrorist content online', 15 January 2024. Available: https://rb.gy/u7z8qa (accessed 29 February 2024).
Theosophical Society of England (2024) 'More about theosophy and the society'. Available: https://theosophicalsociety.org.uk/about-us (accessed 25 April 2024).
Thomas, D. E. (1971) 'Esoteric religion and racism in the thought of Houston Chamberlain', *The Journal of Popular Culture*, 5:3 (1971), 697–709.
Thomas, D. (2007) 'Corpus linguistics and ideology: A study of racist discourse in the Odinic Rite website'. Available: www.birmingham.ac.uk/Documents/college-artslaw/cels/essays/corpuslinguistics/DaxThomas2007a.pdf (accessed 30 October 2023).
Thorsson, E. (1984) *Futhark: A Handbook of Rune Magic*. York Beach, ME: Samuel Weiser.
Thorsson, E. (1987) *Runelore: A Handbook of Esoteric Runology*. York Beach, ME: Samuel Weiser.
Tidhar, L. (2017) 'My struggle', *Apex Magazine*, 101 (2017). Available: https://apex-magazine.com/short-fiction/my-struggle/ (accessed 25 April 2024).
Trigger, B. C. (2006) 'Review of H. Pringle (2006) The Master Plan: Himmler's Scholars and the Holocaust', *Bulletin of the History of Archaeology*, 16:2 (2006) 45–46. https://www.researchgate.net/publication/272714723_Heather_Pringle_2006_The_Master_Plan_Himmler's_Scholars_and_the_Holocaust_New_York_Hyperion (accessed 13 June 2019).

Trilling, D. (2013) 'Greece's people show the politicians how to fight Golden Dawn', *Guardian*, 6 May 2013. Available: www.theguardian.com/commentisfree/2013/may/06/golden-dawn-greece-fight (accessed 6 September 2018).

The Troth (n.d.) 'Frith Forge 2017'. Available: https://thetroth.org/event-recap/frith-forge-2017/ (accessed 23 February 2024).

The Troth (2022) 'The Troth Signs the Declaration of Deeds and Declaration 127 2.0'. Available: https://thetroth.org/news/declaration-deeds-127-troth-signs (accessed 3 July 2023).

The Troth (2024a) 'Our organisation'. Available: https://rb.gy/yzh7z7 (accessed 4 March 2024).

The Troth (2024b) 'Prison in-reach'. Available: https://thetroth.org/in-reach/ (accessed 29 February 2024).

The Troth (2024c) *The Troth* website. Available: www.thetroth.org (accessed 21 October 2023)

Turner-Graham, E. (2015) 'Subcultural style: Fashion and Britain's extreme right', in N. Copsey and J. E. Richardson (eds) *Cultures of Post-War British Fascism*, 128–141. London: Routledge.

T. W. S. Nexion (ed.) (2018) 'A modern mysterium: The enigma of Myatt and the O9A'. Available: https://dokumen.tips/documents/a-modern-mysterium-the-enigma-of-myatt-and-the-o9a-mystical-philosophy-centred-on.html?page=1 (accessed 3 January 2024).

Urban 75 (n.d.) 'Black metal that is not politically dodge'. Available: www.urban75.net/forums/threads /black-metal-that-is-not-politicallydodge.316565/page-3 (accessed 25 April 2024).

The Urban Druid (2019) 'Declaration 127, folkism, and inclusivity', 21 April 2019. Available: www.urban-druid.com/2019/04/21/declaration-127-folkism-and-inclusivity/ (accessed 29 Feburary 2024).

Vizenor, G. (2008) *Survivance: Narratives of Native Presence*. Lincoln, NE: Nebraska University Press.

Waggoner, B. (2020) 'Reclaiming the double helix: Countering racist Heathenry's co-option of human genetics', in N. S. Emore and J. M. Leader (eds) *Paganism and Its Discontents: Enduring Problems of Racialized Identity*, 47–64. Cambridge: Cambridge Scholars.

Waggoner, B. (2022) *Our Troth: Volume 3: Heathen Life*. Berkeley, CA: The Troth.

Wainwright, P. (2021) 'London Blót: New name, old doctrine', *Searchlight* (Summer 2021), 16–18.

Walker, P. (2019) 'Tory MP criticised for using antisemitic term "cultural Marxism"', *Guardian*, 26 March 2019. Available: www.theguardian.com/news/2019/mar/26/tory-mp-criticised-for-using-antisemitic-term-cultural-marxism (accessed 16 May 2021).

Wallis, R. J. (2003) *Shamans/Neo-Shamans: Ecstasies, Alternative Archaeologies, and Contemporary Pagans*. London: Routledge.

Wallis, R. J. (2010) '"In mighty revelation": The Nine Herbs charm, Mugwort lore and elf-persons – An animic approach to Anglo-Saxon magick', *Strange Attractor Journal*, 4 (2010), 207–240.

Wallis, R. J. (2012a) 'A Heathen in place: Working with mugwort as an ally', in G. McLellan and S. Cross (eds) *The Wanton Green: Contemporary Pagan Writings on Place*, 24–37. Oxford: Mandrake.

Wallis, R. J. (2012b) 'Pagans in place, from Stonehenge to Seahenge: "sacred" archaeological monuments and artefacts in Britain', in T. A. Heslop, E. Mellings and M. Thøfner (eds) *Art, Faith and Place in East Anglia: From Prehistory to the Present*, 273–286. Woodbridge: Boydell & Brewer.

Wallis, R. J. (2015a) 'Paganism, archaeology and folklore in twenty-first century Britain: The case study of "The Stonehenge Ancestors"', *Journal for the Academic Study of Religion* (Special issue: *Religion, Archaeology and Folklore*), 28:2 (2015), 129–157.

Wallis, R. J. (2015b) 'Wights, ancestors, hawks and other significant others: A heathen-archaeologist-falconer in place', in P. Davies and C. Matthews (eds) *This Ancient Heart: The Threefold Relationship Between Landscape, Ancestor and Self*, 63–75. Winchester: Moon Books.

Wallis, R. J. (2021) 'Hunters and shamans, sex and death: Relational ontologies and the materiality of the Lascaux "shaft-scene"', in M. Porr and O. Moro-Abadía (eds) *Ontologies of Rock Art: Images, Relational Approaches and Indigenous Knowledges*, 319–334. London: Routledge.

Wallis, R. J. (ed.) (2023a) *The Art and Archaeology of Human Engagements with Birds of Prey: From Prehistory to the Present*. London: Bloomsbury.

Wallis, R. J. (2023b) 'Relating to raptors: The "upper part of a hawk's head and beak" in a Chalcolithic/early Bronze Age "beaker" grave, Driffield, East Yorkshire', in R. J. Wallis (ed.) *The Art and Archaeology of Human Engagements with Birds of Prey: From Prehistory to the Present*, 119–135. London: Bloomsbury.

Wallis, R. J. (2024, in press) '"The hawk in hand": Falconry in early medieval England', in G. Owen-Crocker and M. Clegg-Hyer (eds) *Animalia: Animal and Human Interaction in Daily Living in the Early Medieval English World (The Material Culture of Daily Living, Vol. 5)*. Liverpool: Liverpool University Press.

Wallis, R. J. and D. Alessio (2022) *Faith, Folk and the Far Right: Visual Cultures of Anti-Racist Heathenry on Instagram*, Inform (Information on New Religious Movements) Seminar, 'New Media and New Religiosity: Possibilities and Pitfalls', Kings College London, London, 12 July.

Wallis, R. J. and J. Blain (2006) 'Re-presenting spirit: Heathenry, new-indigenes, and the imaged past', in I. A. Russell (ed.) *Image, Simulation and Meaning in Archaeology: Archaeology and the Industrialisation and Marketing of Heritage and Tourism*: 89–118. London and New York, NY: Springer.

Wallis, R. J. and J. Blain (2012) 'Negotiating archaeology/spirituality: Pagan engagements with the prehistoric past in Britain', in K. Rountree, C. Morris and A. Peatfield (eds) *Archaeology of Spiritualities (One World Archaeology Series)*, 47–68. London and New York, NY: Springer.

Wallis, R. J. and M. Carocci (eds) (2021/2022) 'Art, animism and shamanism', *Religions* (Special issue). Available: www.mdpi.com/journal/religions/special_issues/shamanism_animism (accessed 7 April 2024).

Watts, M. (2021) 'Calls to ban Nazi occultist group after Satanist murders of Bibaa Henry and Nicole Smallman', *Evening Standard*, 28 October 2021. Available: www.standard.co.uk/news/uk/danyal-hussein-nazi-occultist-group-order-of-nine-angles-wembley-deaths-sisters-b963111.html (accessed 19 November 2022).

Weber, M. (1946) *Essays in Sociology* (edited and translated by H. H. Gerth and C. Wright Mills). Oxford: Oxford University Press.

Weber, S. (2019) 'White supremacy's old gods: The Far Right and Neopaganism', *Political Research Associates: Challenging the Right, Advancing Social Justice*. Available: www.politicalresearch.org/2018/02/01/white-supremacys-old-gods-the-far-right-and-neopaganism/ (accessed 3 May 2019).

Webster, L. (2012) *Anglo-Saxon Art*. London: British Museum.

Wegener, F. (2023) 'Year in review: 2023. Trends in terrorism and violent extremist use of the internet and the online counterterrorism response'. Available: https://gifct.org/events/year-in-review-2023-trends-in-terrorist-and-violent-extremist-use-of-the-internet-and-the-online-counterterrorism-response/ (accessed 7 March 2024).

Wessinger, C. (2000) *How the Millennium Comes Violently: From Jonestown to Heaven's Gate*. New York, NY: Seven Bridges Press.

WikiPagan (n.d.) 'International Asatru-Odinist Alliance'. Available: https://pagan.fandom.com/wiki/International_Asatru-Odinist_Alliance (accessed 28 October 2023).

The Wild Hunt (TWH) (2016a) 'Pagan community notes: Denton CUUPS, convocation, Asatru Folk Assembly, and more', *The Wild Hunt: Pagan News and Perspectives*, 22 August 2016. Available: https://wildhunt.org/2016/08/pagan-community-notes-denton-cuups-convocation-asatru-folk-assembly-and-more.html (accessed 22 October 2023).

The Wild Hunt (TWH) (2016b) 'Pagan community notes: HUAR, Lily and Deirdre, Black Witch, and more!', *The Wild Hunt: Pagan News and Perspectives*, 25 January 2016. Available: https://wildhunt.org/2016/01/pagan-community-notes-huar-lily-and-deidre-black-witch-and-more.html (accessed 3 November 2023).

The Wild Hunt (TWH) (2016c) 'Pagan community notes: Solidarity statement, declaration 127, Fallon Smart and more!', *The Wild Hunt: Pagan News and Perspectives*, 5 September 2016. Available: https://wildhunt.org/2016/09/pagan-community-notes-solidarity-statement-declaration-127-fallon-smart-and-more.html (accessed 18 October 2023).

The Wild Hunt (TWH) (2018) 'Pagan community notes: The Troth, Baphomet in Arkansas, Solar Cross Temple and more', 20 August 2018. Available: https://wildhunt.org/2018/08/pagan-community-notes-the-troth-baphomet-in-arkansas-solar-cross-temple-and-more.html (accessed 5 November 2023).

The Wild Hunt (TWH) (2021) 'Heathens respond to "Q-Shaman" and Norse imagery in Capitol Riot', 7 January 2021. Available: https://wildhunt.org/2021/01/heathens-respond-to-q-shaman-and-norse-imagery-in-capitol-riot.html (accessed 18 October 2023).

Williams, G., P. Pentz and M. Wemhoff (eds) (2014) *Vikings: Life and Legend*. London: British Museum Press.

Williams, H. (2019) 'Archaeorants: Wayland's Smithy and neo-Nazis'. Available: https://howardwilliamsblog.wordpress.com/2019/08/13/waylands-smithy-and-neo-nazis/ (accessed 28 February 2024).

Williams, L. (2020) *Miracles of our Own Making: A History of Paganism*. London: Reaktion Books.

Williams, R. (2021) 'In a sorry state', *Searchlight* (Spring 2021), 10–12.

Willowe, C. J. (2015) 'Derailing the conversation: Cultural appropriation in online Pagan communities', in C. Blanton (ed.) *Shades of Faith: Minority Voices in Paganism*, 67–77. Stafford: Megalithica.

Winston, A. (2023) 'A 23-year-old was arrested for gun possession. It led the FBI to a global Satanic cult', *Guardian*, 28 September 2023. Available: www.theguardian.com/us-news/2023/sep/28/new-york-satanic-cult-764-fbi (accessed 29 December 2023).

Wodak, R. and M. Meyer (2001) *Methods in Critical Discourse Analysis*. London: Sage.

Woden's Folk (n.d.a) Community blogspot, 'A new force of resistance'. Available: http://wodenfolk-community.blogspot.com/p/a-new-force-of-resistance-we-oppose.html (accessed 4 June 2019).

Woden's Folk (n.d.b) Community blogspot, 'The English struggle'. Available: http://wodenfolk-community.blogspot.com/p/the-english-struggle-there-can-be-no.html (accessed 21 July 2024).

Woden's Folk (n.d.c) Community blogspot 'The Spiritual Centre'. Available: http://wodenfolk-community.blogspot.com/p/the-spiritual-centre-sacred-centre-or.html (accessed 4 June 2019).

Woden's Folk (n.d.d) 'Woden's folk books'. Available: https://wodensfolk.blogspot.com/p/blog-page.html) (accessed 31 October 2023).

Woden's Folk (n.d.e) 'Woden's folk magazines'. Available: http://wodenism.blogspot.com/p/wodenic-magazines.html (accessed 31 October 2023).

Woden's Folk (n.d.f) 'Woden folk religion'. Available: https://wodensfolk.blogspot.com/p/the-woden-folk-religion-woden-folk.html (accessed 7 April 2024).

Wolffram, H. (2009) *The Stepchildren of Science: Psychical Research and Parapsychology in Germany, c.1870–1939*. London: Editions Rodopi B.V.

Wolffram, H. (2010) 'The Nazi occult and *The Castle in the Forest*: Raw history and fictional transformation', in J. Whalen-Bridge (ed.) *Norman Mailer's Later Fictions*, 139–156. New York, NY: Palgrave Macmillan.

Womack, Y. L. (2013) *Afrofuturism. The World of Black Sci-Fi and Fantasy Culture*. Chicago, IL: Lawrence Hall Books.

Woodbridge, S. (2015) 'History and cultural heritage: The Far Right and the "Battle for Britain"', in N. Copsey and J. E. Richardson (eds) *Cultures of Post-War Fascism*, 27–48. London: Routledge.

Wulf2014 (n.d.) 'The decline of English nationalism'. Available: https://web.archive.org/web/20181126054215?https:/wulf2014.wordpress.com/ (accessed 20 October 2023).

Yorke, B. (1990) *Kings and Kingdoms of Early Anglo-Saxon England*. London: Routledge.

Yorkshire Post (October 7, 1963) Wiener Holocaust Library Collections, 1658/9/3/7/21.

Zafar, H. and D. Pandit (2022) 'Hindutva Pop is the new soundtrack to the anti-Muslim movement in India', *Time*, 20 December 2022. Available: https://time.com/6242156/hindutva-pop-music-anti-muslim-violence-india/ (accessed 7 March 2024).

Zoëga, G. T. (2004) *A Concise Dictionary of Old Icelandic*. Toronto: University of Toronto Press.

Index

Alliance for Inclusive Heathenry 203
Anglecyn Church of Odin 81, 103, 124
Anti-Defamation League 50
Antifascist Pagan Action 197
Anti-Racist Celts and Heathens Unite (ÁRCHÚ) 197
Ariosophy 10, 31, 54, 55–58, 60, 62–78, 135, 155, 200, 204
Aryan Brotherhood 82–83
Aryan Nation 50, 82
Aryan Strikeforce 107
Asatru
   Academy 94
   Alliance 82, 84, 117
   Folk Assembly (AFA) 8, 12, 33, 79, 81, 82, 84, 90, 92–94, 98, 106, 123, 193, 195
   religion 15, 24, 26, 27, 28, 30, 31, 33, 84, 131, 197, 199, 218
   UK 169, 194, 196, 210
Ásatrúarfélagið 25, 33, 85, 86, 196, 197
Aswynn, Freya aka Elizabeth Hooijschurr 84, 85
Atomwaffen Division (AWD) 97, 169, 177

Beamish, Henry Hamilton 99
Bean, John 45, 110
Besant, Annie 65
Bifrost 18, 195
Black Lives Matter (BLM) 207, 222
Black Order, The 146
Blavatsky, Helena 64–65, 66, 67, 76, 150, 155
Blood and Honour 107
blood and soil 85, 86–89, 90, 98, 100, 104, 105, 129, 171

Blunt, Herman Poole 66
Bologna 57, 236
Brass, Richard 184, 186
Breivik, Anders 51, 129, 198
Britain First 52
British Fascisti (BP) 99
British National Fascists (BNF) 101
British National Party (BNP) 2, 106, 107, 110, 111, 113
British Thorguard Vikings 159
British Union of Fascists 44, 104–105, 113
Brons, Andrew 106

Capitol, the 32, 210
Capp, Dan 167, 185
Celtics Against Oppression Racism and Neo-Nazism (CAORANN) 198
Chamberlain, Houston Stewart 63, 64, 68, 76, 98
Chesterton, A. K. 100
Chisholm, James 83
Christchurch 129, 165, 198, 227
Christensen, Else 81, 97, 104, 117, 124, 233
Christian Identity 49
Church of Satan 67, 83
Churchward, James 66, 135
Codreanu, Corneliu Zelea 46, 47, 54
Columbine 3, 177, 235
'Combat 18' 107, 131, 142
Confederation of UK Heathen Kindreds 194, 196
Copeland, David 138, 159, 236
Crowley, Aleister 143, 155

'Declaration 127' 198, 201–202, 208, 211, 225

Devi, Savitri aka Maximiani Julia Portas 51, 66, 106, 110, 155, 166
Dior, Françoise 51, 111–112

education, Heathen 204–206
Eldaring 206
English Defence League 107
English Mistery 100, 101, 104
Erikson, Leif 90
European Congress of Ethnic Religions (ECER) 86
Evola, Julius 57, 66, 106, 161, 167, 168, 172

fashion 165–170
Fields, James Alex 93, 202
Fiore, Roberto 106
Flavel, Matthew 93, 201
Foreningen Forn Sed 195
Fourteen Words (14W) 82, 175, 182, 183, 184, 201
Fraser, Craig aka Rafe Grimes 145–146
Freedom Party of Austria (FPO) 202
Frith Forge 33, 205, 206–207

Gardiner, Rolf 100
German Faith Community 72
Germanenorden (Germanic Order) 70, 71
Germanic Community of Faith 72
de Gobineau, Arthur 63
Golden Age 68–69
Golden Dawn Party 58
Greater Britain Movement (GBM) 106
Great Replacement, the 91, 101, 160, 182, 184, 198
Griffin, Nick 106–107, 134, 237
Günther, Hans E. K. 63

Hall, Patricia 93
Hancock, Graham 168
Harrison, Ralph aka Ingvar 122, 124
hashtagging 217–230
Hávamál 139, 222, 225
Heathen Temple 124
Heathens Against Hate 190, 191, 199–201, 206, 218
Heathens and Pagans Against Racism 197
Heathens Fighting Hate 197
Heathens of Mercia 194
Heathens Unite 198

Heathens United Against Racism (HUAR) 188, 198
Herne the Hunter 135
Hess, Rudolph 63, 71, 78
Hilmarsson, Hilmar Örn 196
Himmler, Heinrich 56, 70, 73, 74–77, 78, 108
Hindutva 19, 50, 51, 65, 173, 175
Hitler, Adolf 46, 56, 70, 71–74, 98, 155, 163, 226
Hope not Hate 8, 44, 114, 116, 126, 131, 139, 146, 162, 166, 226, 241, 243, 245

Imperial Fascist League 101, 102, 105
Instagram 212–215
International Ásatrú/Odinist Alliance (IAOA) 117
Joe Rogan Experience, The 168
Jordan, Colin 7, 51, 52, 55, 97, 108–113, 124, 142, 155
Joyce, William aka Lord Haw-Haw 99

Kennewick Man 90

Lane, David 82, 182
Lane, Katja 67, 82
Lanz, Adolf Josef aka Jörg Lanz von Liebenfels 60, 68–72, 82, 101, 102
LaVey, Anton 67, 83
Le Pen, Marine 202
Lebensborn, policy of 70
Leese, Arnold 97, 100–105, 106, 109, 113, 142, 233, 237
Lintorn-Orman, Rotha 99
von List, Guido 12, 60, 61, 63, 66, 67, 68, 69, 70, 71, 72, 76, 82, 83, 155, 159, 219
London New Right 134, 169–170
Long Man of Wilmington, the 132, 133, 159, 160
Lucas, Simon 182, 185
Ludovici, Anthony 98
Lymington, Lord, Earl of Portsmouth 100

McNallen, Stephen 79, 82, 83, 89–90, 91, 92, 106, 167, 201, 203, 204
McVan, Ron 82
McVeigh, Timothy 113, 159
Mair, Thomas 236
Manchester Arena 202

Matthew, Holden 177
metagenetics 12, 89–90
metapolitics 7, 160–163
Mills, Alexander Rud 80–81, 97, 104, 124,
Morthwork, Michael 146, 147
Moult, Richard 143, 144, 147, 151
Murray, Michael aka Valguard 81
music 170–173
   black metal (BM) 145, 170, 176–180, 234
   Burzum 177, 178
   Death in June 144, 170
   Fire + Ice 171, 172
   Gaylord 179
   H.E.R.R. 172–173
   National Socialist black metal (NSBM) 170, 177–178
   neofolk 85, 144, 145, 170, 171, 173, 179, 180, 188, 234
   Sol Invictus 144, 171, 172
   Stuka Squadron 178
   Venom 177, 179
   Winterfylleth 45, 167, 173–174, 175–176, 178, 180–182, 187
Mussolini, Benito 19, 46, 52, 59, 99, 155, 165, 183
Myatt, David aka Anton Long 51, 107, 124, 142, 147, 152, 155

National Action (NA) 107
National Front (NF) 105, 113
National Socialist Movement (NSM) 111, 113
Naughton, Chris 45, 180, 182, 183, 185, 187
'Nazisploitation' 163–165
New Right 31, 32, 53, 106
nexions 144, 146, 148, 157
Nordic Resistance Movement (NMR) 202, 203
Nordisk Tingsfæling (NTF) 85

Odinia International 169
Odinic Rite, the (OR) 4, 16, 27, 41, 97, 113, 116–122, 160, 172, 182, 195, 196, 204
Odinist Fellowship, the 16, 81, 104, 113, 116, 122–125, 131, 160, 162, 166, 233, 234
   temple 124, 125, 160, 162

Orbán, Viktor 202
Order, The 50, 82, 113, 159
Order of the Nine Angles, the (ONA or O9A) 3, 44, 51, 97, 107, 113, 138–158
Ordo Novi Templi (ONT) 70, 72

Pagan Federation 193, 205, 210
Pagans Against Fascism 197
Patriotic Alternative 162
Paxson, Diana 84, 203
People's Party (OVP) 202
Poetic Edda(s) 10, 54, 62, 67, 102, 201
Police Pagan Association 9, 30, 131, 193, 208
Pound, Ezra 168, 172

'QAnon Shaman' aka Jake Aleri/Angeli, Jacob Anthony Chansley 210

Ra, Sun 66
Rashtriya Swayamsevak Sangh 50–51
Read, Ian 84, 171
Redbeard, Ragnar aka Arthur Desmond 67
religious leaders and fascism 58–59
Riefenstahl, Leni 70
Rockwell, George Lincoln 98
Romanian Legion of the Archangel Michael aka Iron Guard 46–47
Rosenberg, Alfred 63
Rowsell, Thomas 146, 166–167, 169
rune(s) 54, 67–68, 72, 107, 108, 146, 164, 171, 189, 200, 202, 218, 221, 229
   see also bind rune
Rune-Gild 83, 85, 172
Runesine 188
Runic John 36, 38

Satanism 3, 149–152
Saunders, James 193
Schreiwer, Robert 199
Scottish Dawn 107
Sebottendorff, Rudolph von, aka Adam Alfred Rudolph Glauer 70, 71
Serrano, Miguel 58
Social Darwinism 62, 64, 155
Soldiers of Odin 79, 92
Sonnenkrieg Division (SKD) 3, 104–108, 114, 131, 138, 144, 236
Southern Poverty Law Center 8, 93, 162, 171, 202

Index

Southgate, Troy 134, 169, 170, 172
'Survive the Jive' 9, 146, 166, 167
Svinfylking, The 197
symbol
   Celtic 13
   Mjöllnir aka Thor's hammer 206, 210, 222, 226
   Sonnenrad/Black Sun 160, 166, 171, 172, 180, 183, 187, 198, 200, 202, 229
   sun wheel 18, 108, 109, 110, 111, 119
   swastika 18, 67, 70, 71, 72, 82, 101, 119, 127, 128, 146, 167, 180, 200
   triskel 119
   valknut 165, 210, 225, 226
   wolf 128
   Wolfsangel 127, 128, 129, 146
   Yggdrasill 153, 154, 222, 226
System Resistance Network 107

Tech Against Terrorism 162, 211
Tempel ov Blood 143, 199, 200
Temple of THEM 143
Terza Posizione (TP) 106, 107
Theosophy 63–65, 66, 68, 72, 76, 133, 135, 150, 155, 232
Thorsson, Edred aka Stephen Flowers 83
Thule Society 63, 71, 72, 73, 99, 155, 163, 170, 178
Troth, The 11, 12, 16, 24, 33, 34, 81, 83, 84, 85, 199, 200, 201, 205, 218, 226, 242, 245
Trump, Donald 201
Tyndall, John 45, 105–106

UK Independence Party (UKIP) 2
Ustaša 52

Vikernes, Kristian 'Varg' 3, 4, 177, 178
Viking Brotherhood, the 81
Vikings Against Racism (VAR) 203

Waddell, Lawrence Augustine 102
Wakeford, Tony 144, 171
Wardruna 188
Wayland's Smithy 131, 136, 160, 239
Westby, Chris 183, 184
Westminster Bridge 202
Wewelsburg Castle 74, 75
White, Arnold 98
White Defence League 109
White Horse Stone 131, 160
White Wolves 107
Wiligut, Karl Maria 74, 76, 78
Woden's Folk 4, 16, 17, 27, 41, 42, 107, 125–136, 153, 157, 159, 160, 161, 172, 182, 185, 204
Wodensthrone 186, 187
World Union of National Socialists (WUNS) 111
Wotan Network 92, 216
Wotansvolk 82, 98, 113, 205
Wulf Ingessunu, aka Geoffrey Dunn 125, 126, 132, 133, 134, 135, 159, 204
Wyrd Isle Collective 146, 167, 181

Yaxley-Lennon aka Tommy Robinson 202

Zadruga 58

EU authorised representative for GPSR:
Easy Access System Europe, Mustamäe tee 50,
10621 Tallinn, Estonia
gpsr.requests@easproject.com

www.ingramcontent.com/pod-product-compliance
Lightning Source LLC
LaVergne TN
LVHW052015230825
819359LV00004B/123